Shifting Priorities

Stanford University Press
Stanford, California

Chapter 1 reprinted from "Vermeer and the Balance of Destiny," in
Essays in Northern European Art Presented to Egbert Haverkamp-Begemann
(Doornspijk, Davaco, 1983), 216–221.

Chapter 2 reprinted from "Political Iconography in a Painting
by Jan Miense Molenaer," *Mercury* (fall 1986): 23–38.

Chapter 4 reprinted from "Jan Steen's Formulation of the Dissolute Household:
Sources and Meanings," in *Holländische Genremalerei im 17.Jahrhundert*
(Berlin, Gebr. Mann, 1987), 315–344.

Chapter 7 reprinted from "Early Netherlandish Bordeeltjes and the Construction
of Social 'Realities,'" in *The Public and Private in Dutch Culture of the Golden Age*,
edited by Arthur Wheelock and Adele Seeff (Newark: University of Delaware
Press, 2000), 141–163. The ideas were first presented in a talk titled "Genre Paintings
and the Bordello Narrative," given at the conference "The Public and Private in
Dutch Culture," sponsored by the Center for Renaissance and Baroque Studies
at the University of Maryland at College Park, April 1993.

Chapter 8 reprinted from "Domesticating the Peasant Father: The Confluent
Ideologies of Gender, Class, and Age in the Prints of Adriaen van Ostade,"
in *Images of Women in Seventeenth-Century Dutch Art: Domesticity and the
Representation of the Peasant*, edited by Patricia Phagan (Athens: Georgia
Museum of Art, University of Georgia, 1996), 41–70.

Chapter 9 reprinted from "Vermeer's Women: Changing Paradigms in Mid-Career,"
in *The Practice of Cultural Analysis: Exposing Interdisciplinary Interpretation*, edited by
Mieke Bal (Stanford, Calif.: Stanford University Press, 1999), 44–59.

Printed in the United States of America on acid-free, archival-quality paper

Library of Congress Cataloging-in-Publication Data

Salomon, Nanette.
   Shifting priorities : gender and genre in seventeenth-century Dutch painting /
Nanette Salomon.
      p. cm.
   Includes bibliographical references and index.
   ISBN 0-8047-4476-9 (alk. paper)—ISBN 0-8047-4477-7 (pbk. : alk. paper)
   1. Genre painting, Dutch—17th century.   2. Symbolism in art.
3. Gender identity in art.   I. Title.
ND1452.N43 S24   2004
754'.09492'09032—dc22   2003025165

Original Printing 2004
Last figure below indicates year of this printing:
13   12   11   10   09   08   07   06   05   04

Typeset by James P. Brommer in 11/15 Garamond

Cultural Memory
in
the
Present

Mieke Bal and Hent de Vries, Editors

Shifting Priorities

Gender and Genre in Seventeenth-Century Dutch Painting

Nanette Salomon

STANFORD UNIVERSITY PRESS

STANFORD, CALIFORNIA

2004

Contents

Figures

Following p. 105

Acknowledgments

This work owes a debt of gratitude to a great number of institutions and individuals. I hope they will find themselves duly acknowledged in the appropriate places. There are, however, some whose advice, assistance, and support go beyond specific instances to the very core of my work, and I am happy to have the chance to thank them once again here. I want to thank Helen Tartar for all of her attention and assistance in making this project a reality. I am especially grateful to the Research Foundation of the City University of New York and all of my colleagues at CUNY who sat on the Research Foundation's art history committee over the years for providing me with a steadfast source of support through a number of generous grants. I am happy to thank the acting provost and academic vice president of the College of Staten Island, David Podell, for his timely support that contributed assistance in the purchase of photographs and permission to reproduce them. The Watson Library and the Education Department of the Metropolitan Museum of Art have provided me a place where I could learn and grow as nowhere else. I am grateful for the opportunity to thank them here. In particular I would like to acknowledge Kenneth Soehner, the Arthur K. Watson Chief Librarian, and Kent Lydecker, associate director for education. I would also like to thank the staff of the Rijksbureau voor Kunsthistorische Documentatie in The Hague and especially my dear friend Marijke C. Kinkelder.

The sage counsel and caring guidance provided by Griselda Pollock, Mieke Bal, and Walter Liedtke have sustained me all these years and surely go far beyond anything simple thanks could ever sufficiently address. With great respect I dedicate this volume to them.

Shifting Priorities

Pro/visions, Re/visions, Tele/visions

It is always daunting to stop and assess where you are, where you have been, and how you got from point A to point B. It is especially daunting to lay that all out in a single place and exhibit it in a public forum. It is hoped that the rewards of doing so are greater than the pleasures of narcissistic indulgence but will also aid and abet an understanding of the terms and negotiations worked through the material to gain self-knowledge, and, through the self as index, knowledge of the world that made this self.

This volume re-presents essays on Dutch genre painting written between 1983 and 1998. Some have been published, in a variety of different venues; three were given as papers, and I have expanded and published them here for the first time. I have ordered the essays more or less chronologically—at which point they seemed to naturally fall into three sections.

I	II	III
Pro/visions	Re/visions	Tele/visions
Vermeer	Jan Steen	Bordeeltje
Jan Miense Molenaer	Jan Steen	Van Ostade
Ter Borch	Jan Steen	Vermeer

The essays gathered together here can be seen as both similar and different, having the character, like most cultural artifacts, of both a continuum and a progression. On the first count they are all concerned with the interpretation of seventeenth-century (and in one case sixteenth-century) Dutch genre painting, an artistic category whose fictive "realism"—a style that strives to be invisible as such—renders them particularly propitious for a particular kind of analysis of culture. The fiction of their "artlessness," like that of the realism of their antecedents in northern Renaissance painting, has, nonetheless, not saved them from hard-core iconographic interpretations, the primary interpretive device of conventional art history. This was, and is, effectively brought to bear through an extension of what Erwin Panofsky (in speaking of the fifteenth century) called "disguised symbolism" and what Eddy de Jongh (in speaking of the seventeenth century) called *schijnrealism*, or "apparent realism."[1] In this system so-called everyday objects are interpreted as having symbolic meanings that, taken together, contribute to the meaning of the painting as a whole.

There is something to be said for the kind of mind-set that looks to see an abstraction behind (or in) the real and that renders both as concrete and definable, and there certainly is evidence in the records of spoken sermons and printed emblem books that such a mind-set found ample outlet for expression in the early modern period under discussion. It is perhaps, to some degree, in this mind-set that the first three essays are most at home, although, even there, some sense of a progressive loosening of the grip of iconography is evident. Significantly, although that mind-set might have had a stake in these paintings, it was certainly not an exclusive or even necessarily a dominant one. And although it must be said that some element of iconography is present in all the essays, the significance of that apparatus within the larger inquiry into meaning is always relativized. It becomes, in fact, treated more and more as an option among options and finally as a social frame, rather than as a singular and decisive answer to the question of meaning.

Moreover, when iconographic "symbolism" is incurred, it is best understood when viewed as operating on a confined and regulated level of interpretation. Indeed, iconographic insights produce grist (provisions) for the analytic and social interpretive mill in and of themselves. For example, one might go further and ask why "Vanitas," arguably the most endemic iconographic concept in the seventeenth century, is so compelling for the Dutch? Why it is almost exclusively applied as a characteristic of women rather than men or just people in general? How is it to be thought of within the larger issues of visual representation in the form of costly oil paintings or within the issues of paintings as a form of social regulation? For me, iconographic mechanisms needed to be mastered so that they could be taken into account. For this reason the heading "Pro/visions" seems particularly apt for this first section. In the end the immersion in iconography was not only a useful preliminary move—it also provided me with the provisions I needed as nurture to move away from it.

All but one essay offer close readings of a particular image. In that sense they are all heavily invested in the assessment of the intelligible visual language of those paintings as the first and foremost evidence in the pursuit of visual understanding. This method entails something quite different from piecing together the iconographic puzzle of their parts or appreciating their abstract aesthetic forms, as in stylistic analysis. Rather, the essays all seek to respect the visual logic at work in the formation of these works through the integrated, inseparable, if not symbiotic, relationship between their form and their content. My endeavor remains the appreciation of a painting as a creative, organic articulation, a unity that is coherent in its own visual terms as communication.

Like—and unlike—the language of words, visual language connects with us through complex marking systems. The intricate distinctions and sociopolitical implications of these systems as the semiotics of art have been the lifelong work of Mieke Bal and Griselda Pollock, whose dazzling scholarship can, in some way, be the stimulus for the changes in this author, as in the field of art history itself.[2] Their projects underlie the shifting priorities in these essays. Just as some scholars work in new paradigms, others create them. For me, as for so many others, it was possible to shift my priorities only after these paradigms were pioneered in their writings. They provided the example and examples in both theory and practice of how and why a work of art could be analyzed as a work of culture, circulating in the realms of the social, political, and psychoanalytic, rather than as the hermetic enclosed expression of a socially isolated artistic "genius."

The terms of my shifting priorities can be traced in the greater acknowledgment that paintings operate and communicate, in a sense, within the spheres of ongoing social discourses—that they are part and parcel of the ways the "world" and its parts are organized (some would say hierarchically) and made sense of, ordered and regulated. Works of art as cultural works are freed up with this perspective to obtain significance through their participation in various operative systems of communication. In the end they are not fixed by these discourses but rather precisely because of their malleability can effectively move both synchronically and diachronically from discourse to discourse, alternatively and often incompletely relinquishing and holding meaning as they go. In that way they participate in normalizing relationships, desires, and the more general terms of social value.

The later essays in this volume also manifest an ever-greater degree of self-reflexivity on—and of—my part as author. To this end the readings of these paintings are more open on one level and more focused in their political, that is, feminist, project on another level. I have, and my writing has, become more and more sensitized to the vagaries of history writing and to the speciousness of traditional art-historical methodology. This is not to say that these positions were not part of my considerations from the very beginning, only that they have become self-assertively more so.

In so mapping this pilgrim's progress, or, to borrow a phrase from Mieke Bal, my "intellectual itinerary,"[3] from the practice of art history to the analysis of visual culture, these studies together produce a personal history; they mark who I was in the early 1980s and who I have become, with all the attendant stages along the way. Yet each essay has a place in its time as a mirror of the terms and limits that were possibilities at various stopping points along the way of those two crucial decades. After much consideration I have refrained from rewriting the earlier essays, in small and not so small ways, like softening the self-evident appeal to intentionality that pops up in them from time to time. And although (or precisely because) I might now cringe at some formulations, I have for the most part kept the wording as it was published to maintain the historical validity of the group. In that sense they track a progression whose implications are larger than the individual. They reflect the terrain of the ever-widening topography of the discipline of art-history writing.

Because writing history is always a social endeavor and as such is subject to constant negotiation, the history of the reception of these essays in the world of Dutch art history, for which, at least initially, they were written, is as telling as any analysis of my position or intention within them. Recounting, however briefly, the critique of these essays, particularly the early ones, is a valuable exercise in order to tease out their terms and throw into high relief exactly what is at stake in the contest for interpretation that has been going on for at least two decades in the humanities.

Self-consciousness is a luxury, but it is also a necessity, one that, at least in the history of these essays, could not be denied. That much was learned from my very first published endeavor, "Vermeer and the Balance of Destiny," and its initial and prolonged polemical reception. The criticism of this piece began and ended with my proposition that Johannes Vermeer had portrayed the woman with the balance in his painting of the same name, now in the National Gallery of Art in Washington, as pregnant.[4] Despite the general agreement that pregnancy as such was not out of Vermeer's purview in another painting, this assertion here was considered untenable; indeed, it was intolerable. The reaction in print, in symposia, in Dutch art history classrooms, and mostly at dinner parties lasted for years.[5] Although I had not set out to write a feminist piece, or even to examine the "image" of a woman, I had in fact done so. From this I came to know firsthand how all history writing is political and interventionist. I also came to realize how closely conventional readings and disciplinary borders are patrolled. Tellingly, the strongest published support for this essay came from interdisciplinary "interlopers" into the boundaries of Dutch art history.[6] Despite all, these early lessons did not immediately, overtly translate into an altered methodology for me.

If I had attempted to "make sense" of Vermeer's image as a whole rather than as a series of individuated iconographic parts, and if I had sought the logic in his visual language as a telling praxis, I had not particularly sought the role of my own eye in that telling. The essay on Jan Miense Molenaer's *The Musical Duet*, as a political statement, can be said to share the methodology of the first Vermeer article. As a work with many iconographic "pieces" it, too, makes sense in my reading as a complete image, a sense that is larger than the addition of its parts. Although the reaction to this piece was not nearly as vituperative nor as endemic, since after all it did not quite strike the nerve of calling a woman by "Vermeer" pregnant, it, too, was seen by some well-placed art historians as unacceptable.[7] Oddly, the critique of the piece, like that of the *Woman with the Balance*, broke into camps along national lines—the Americans and Germans for; the Dutch and English against—all of which is grist for the sociologists' mill.

The final essay in the first section was originally given as a talk in 1982. I have written and rewritten it several times since then. The analysis of the role of pendant or companion paintings as a determining factor of meaning in Ter Borch's genre imagery is a rich and complex endeavor and one that could easily sustain interesting treatment from almost any methodological point of view. I have here, however, tried to stick to the original sense of the paper as it was given, filling out only the kind of details that expand the argument I advanced at that time. For that reason I have not pursued the fascinating issue of the "double," embodied in these paintings by Ter Borch's sister Gesina. Nor have I developed the connotation of their sibling relationship and the role of identity and identification in these pendants. How did Ter Borch come to substitute his sister in the place traditionally held by the wife or lover of the artist, as is found, for example, in Rembrandt or Metsu? Those issues must remain for another time. What I have tried to show is how these images circulate in a series of visual conventions and how their dynamism is anchored by the physical context of pairing. Their visual logic leaps across frames to make sense of the images by including the frames into the fiction. In the consideration of several pairs of pendants, this study also touches on changes evident in the course of genre painting's history in the seventeenth century, a subject I have become increasingly interested in. The larger process of what might be called modernization or gentrification of seventeenth-century Dutch genre painting—as I put forth in my study of Jacob Duck[8]—was already manifest in this study.

The second section, "Re/visions," also contains three essays. In this case they all deal with the prodigious genre paintings of Jan Steen. This trilogy marks a decisive shift in paradigm toward a more self-reflexive model. The first essay, "Jan Steen's Formulation of the Dissolute Household: Sources and Meanings," written in 1984, shares its method with the studies in the first section. Once again, the interpretation is guided by close reading. In Steen's case this reading is guided by his own acute self-reflexivity, which is apparent in his practice of overt quotations (and self-quotation), as well as in his witty reiterations of earlier, sometimes by one hundred years, imagery. These are drawn from both paintings and popular prints and rewoven by him into an organic, new fabric that is, again, greater than and essentially different from the sum of its parts.

It is altogether appropriate that *my* revisions should have taken place in the study of Jan Steen, for no other artist rivals *his* practice of self-consciousness in, among other strategies, the remaking of his own art. This, too, is nowhere more apparent than in his series of paintings on the subject of the so-called dissolute household. "'There's No Place like Home': Jan Steen and Domestic Ideology" is, thus, both self-reflexive and about self-reflexivity. It considers the discourse of domesticity not as a given but as a cultural fabrication, one whose ideology and presentation are clearly related to its binary—itinerancy. The latter, as a foundational preoccupation of Dutch genre painting throughout the sixteenth and for the first half of the seventeenth century, has still not been adequately appreciated or even recognized. The negotiations and interrelations between these two concepts were particularly brilliantly put forth in the late sixteenth century by the noncanonical painter, Marten van Cleve, a phenomenon that surely did not escape Steen's perceptive artist's eye. Van Cleve's general marginalization in Dutch art history can be accounted for by a number of factors, including his "troublesome" participation in the two competing Netherlandish styles in the late sixteenth century, Romanism and Bruegelism. Even though art historians are happy to see Bruegel's influence on Jan Steen, as Master to Master, they have been less keen to see the effects of an uncanonical painter like Marten van Cleve on the seventeenth-century master.

Van Cleve's device of organizing the composition of his canvas by dividing it into two distinct parts down the center clearly has structural affinities with the idea of the pendant; each produces the visual cues of a relational opposition. It is worth noting that Steen opted for the more old-fashioned-looking manner of creating this effect, quoting Van Cleve, rather than choosing the more modern and "realist" solution of genre pendants favored by Ter Borch or, for that matter, a host of other seventeenth-century painters working after midcentury.

Although unpublished, this talk was quick to be noted and produced a response in print that has some bearing on the nature of the change that had taken place. Unlike my earlier article on Jan Steen, which, shockingly, was omitted from almost all the subsequent articles, books, and otherwise printed discussions on Steen's *Dissolute Household* despite their long and seemingly exhaustive scholarly bibliographies—and we can assume that omission is at least some form of critique in its own right—until the catalog of the Jan Steen exhibition in 1996,[9] this paper, to the contrary, found response almost immediately. The idea that Steen's paintings were, indeed, not primarily moralizing, that is, did not actively admonish the viewer to cleave to virtue over vice, was seen as out of step with the seventeenth-century mind.[10] This view is endemic in Dutch art history and therefore stands as the official position passed along to the art-consuming public.[11] To insist that paintings are moralizing is to equate them with Christian sermons. The assumption is that the Dutch required, or at least desired, a constant moral reminder in their art, more often than not constructed in the form of the most rudimentary notions of good and evil as prescribed in Christian literary texts. Yet these literary texts themselves have discursive orientations and are therefore not "proofs," not "context," but were circulated as cultural fabrications just as the visual images. Moreover, invoking these iconographic traditions without any consideration of how such pronouncements are shaped by modern reception cannot, in my view, advance and may in some instances positively impede our understanding of their history. Indeed, such scholarship merely identifies what has to be explained—as if they were explanations in and of themselves. In the end they produce an impression of the seventeenth-century Dutch as a people who were incredibly naive and simplistic, a move that allows the twentieth-century person to appear sophisticated and complex by comparison.

Another significant consequence of reiterating Christian moral discourse as meaning is the continual recycling and refixing of an adjudicator—who is primarily male—and an object being judged—who is primarily female. Much can be said of the role of women in Dutch paintings as the figuration of various essentialist paradigms. In fact, Jan Steen's paintings are precisely about throwing into question that kind of binary, just as they contest fixity itself. His comic strategies open up the play of images, known and unknown, and allow for positions of ever-greater flexibility to be taken before them. This is the case I make for his *Dissolute Household* paintings and the case for *The Morning Toilet*, in the Royal Collection of Buckingham Palace, the last piece of the middle section.

Like the other works in this volume, and particularly the others by Jan Steen, this painting is composed of many details that lend themselves to iconographic interpretation. The painting is also spatially complex as the primary scene is essentially viewed through a diaphragm arch. At the heart of the configuration is an "alluring" young woman seated on her bed and disrobing. In traditional accounts of this painting the skull and music book strategically placed on the liminal space of the threshold have allowed the traditional virtue/vice identification as meaning to spring into action. My essay, rather, sets into play the wide range of possibilities allowed by the image in its reworking and renovating various genre tropes to produce this image of a consummate modern woman. Here the woman as sign of urban modernity frames the physical cum sexual through the medium of painting. As with the other studies in this volume this essay also identifies the various visual networks that the painting both circulates within and expands on—and assesses them from a feminist perspective. The resonance of *The Morning Toilet* is enhanced through these sorts of identifications and recognitions but cannot be fixed by them. In the end the new "whole" fabricated by Jan Steen configures an image of accessibility and distance through the modulation of inner and outer, light and darkness, figure and field.

The final section, "Tele/visions," continues this feminist orientation, seeking out ever-more consciously through close reading the cultural terms of the feminine, both then and now. The common thread that runs through these essays concerns the illusionistic spaces that, more than any other single element, function to define the category of Dutch genre painting. My work here is predicated on the understanding of these spaces as meaningful on several levels. One is the identification of the pictorial, contemporarily defined interior space with Northern Netherlandish cultural production per se. The related next level is the identification of those spaces with the sexualized body of the women portrayed within them.

The first essay in this section deals with the production of the *bordeeltje*, or small bordello. It is distinguished as the only essay here that does not focus on a single image but rather on the phenomenon of the type as it was proliferated throughout the sixteenth century. The ideas of Michel Foucault were particularly useful for me in clarifying the position of these works in what he insightfully recognized as the ever-widening discourse on sex in the early modern period. Again, rather than seeing these paintings and prints as the consequences of a moralizing urge to restrict the discourses of sex, they may be seen as part of the mechanisms of its incitement.

Although I do not focus on a single image in this essay, I do look at the visual language that made this group of images readable as a type and thus enabled it to function as the nexus of various arenas of identity formation, including those of nationality, class, and gender. It seemed especially important to me to stress their fictitious nature and the work that they perform as cultural fabrications, given the predominant art-historical treatment of these foundational images, perhaps, even more than any other type of genre painting—although typical of the treatment of genre painting in general—as moralizing. Indeed, this treatment vacillates somewhat illogically between "interpreting" these paintings as reflections of real conditions and as moralizing injunctions against profligate behavior. The seventeenth-century term for this painting type, *bordeeltje*, is useful on several counts. It locates the artful (or artificial) conditions of its existence; and, perhaps of greater significance, it indicates that, rather than being character-identified as titles such as *Procuress* or *Courtesan* would indicate, the images were primarily space-identified. Griselda Pollock's now classic chapter on femininity and the spaces of modernity in her work on nineteenth-century Parisian painting was of great consequence for me.[12] It is here that I introduce the notion of an interiorized, contemporary space in Netherlandish painting that works as a double for the body of the women who inhabit it. It is an argument that is relevant, in varying degrees of emphasis, for all three essays of the last section. Among its salient features is the strategic position of the man framed by the liminal space of the doorway. It will be these "disappearing men," the elimination of the masculine factor, that sanitizes this pictorial space and renders it pure and "domestic."

The degree to which men become increasingly absent from domestic interiors in genre paintings is dependent upon a middle-class definition of their subject matter. The effect of class on this phenomenon is explored in the second piece, "Domesticating the Peasant Father: The Confluent Ideologies of Gender, Class, and Age in the Prints of Adriaen van Ostade." Here I consider three etchings by Adriaen van Ostade that include the peasant father in the domestic interior with the family and represent him respectfully in the role of the "voedster" (nourishing) father. This "experiment" took place briefly around midcentury and was abandoned for a more ideologically conventional treatment of masculinity and femininity in the home. As part of the negotiating factors that ameliorated Van Ostade's interventions is the issue of age, particularly the old age of the men in these prints. They seem to be more grandfathers than fathers, or perhaps they are old in the sense of being weathered by the sun and hard work. Ageism, and the terms of its stereotypes, is a subject that still requires a hyperattentive reading, for its contribution to the shaping of social life is enormous, and it has not yet entered the mainstream of cultural study.

This book ends, as it begins, with Vermeer. One of the main differences is that here my study is deliberately feminist in its methodology and, even more, in its politics. In this essay I trace the changing paradigms in the signification of "woman," Vermeer's primary artistic concern, from the early genre paintings, where she is a sign of the sexual, to the later works, where she is a sign of the civil. In the former, women participate in the kind of narratives of itinerancy that were endemic in Netherlandish genre painting of the sixteenth and early seventeenth centuries, the kind identified as such in the *bordeeltje* essay.

The change from one kind of sign to another is, of course, larger than Vermeer and can be distinguished as a project of Dutch visual culture that runs throughout the seventeenth century. In the end it can be seen as an index of the modernizing role played by Dutch culture. It is manifest, for example, in the change performed by the two sets of pendants by Ter Borch. It informs and frames the topsy-turvy joke in Jan Steen's *Dissolute Household* paintings, and it is the point around which the satire of his *Morning Toilet* revolves.

The essay also allows for the mutually inclusive validation of both contemporary and historical claims of relevance to be made in the analysis of visual culture—an issue that is at stake in all the essays. As such it explicitly examines both positions from their relative points of origin and requests a dialogue between them to be brought out into the open as part of the art-historical endeavor. In this sense the last essays are most aptly considered tele/visions, images seen from afar but brought close by means of careful, attentive reading and open, sympathetic identification. As the heirs of both early modern ideologies and their communicative structures, we can allow ourselves to see the past as of our making and to permit these paintings to channel communication between us then and us now.

I

Pro/visions

1

Vermeer and the Balance of Destiny

In his insightful article in the Festschrift honoring Pinder on his sixtieth birthday Herbert Rudolph recognized the importance of meaning in the work of Jan Vermeer.[1] There he examined the *Woman Holding a Balance* (fig. 1), now in the National Gallery in Washington, in light of the continuing tradition of didactic content in art that had been well established since the medieval period. For Rudolph the *clavis interpretandi* of the presence, as well as the nature of Vermeer's deeper message, was the painting within the painting, a depiction of the Last Judgment (fig. 2).[2] He concluded that the woman's activity, weighing pearls, should be read in contrast to the ultimate weighing of souls and proclaimed her to be a personification of base worldly concerns or, in a word, "Vanitas."[3] This idea was confirmed by the various objects found in the room, such as the mirror, the costly materials and trinkets on the table, and the string of pearls, all of which had had at least some previous associations with the theme of worldliness and vanity.[4] Although this interpretation, with minor variations, has been followed by the majority of writers on Vermeer since Rudolph, it fails to take into account another essential element of the picture: the woman's pregnant state.[5]

Of the several authors who acknowledge her condition, only Carstensen and Putscher attempt to integrate it into the fundamental subject of the picture. Their theory refers to the folk tradition of divining the sex of an unborn child through weighing pearls.[6] Aside from its disregard for the prominent *Last Judgment*, which has no real place in this context, this idea can now be refuted also on the basis of recent microscopic examination of the painting. Contrary to the prevalent belief, which dates back to 1696,[7] that the woman is weighing either gold or pearls, we now know that she is actually adjusting an empty balance, a fact to which we will return.[8] Nonetheless, the woman's pregnancy is an undeniable fact of the painting and cannot be dismissed as a misunderstanding of costume or fashion. As a subject it is not unique in Vermeer's work, being preceded by the *Woman in Blue Reading a Letter*, in the Rijksmuseum in Amsterdam. Naive interpretations of this subject have led writers to see the woman in these two paintings as Catharina Bolnes, Vermeer's wife and the mother of his fourteen children.[9] Although we now consider such immediate reflections of everyday life insufficient as the motivation for the creation of a seventeenth-century painting, it would be equally naive to believe that the compelling personal circumstance of his wife's frequent pregnancies would not lead Vermeer to deeper thoughts on the implication of birth and death, on the nature of human life itself.[10]

Vermeer's use of light to place a symbolic accent on the swelling abdomen of the expectant mother is a well-known and particularly meaningful technique in the northern European painting tradition.[11] This is evident in the unusual light of the room, which is mostly dim, with large masses of darkness dominating the lower left corner and to a certain extent the upper right. Bright light from the window on the left falls distinctly only on the face and body of the woman who stands facing it. It particularly strikes her stomach, which, like an annunciate Mary's, glows as if from an internal light source. The area is further highlighted by the introduction of an orange accent at the opening of her jacket, the single note of intense, warm color in the entire composition and different in color from the rest of her garment. How can one reconcile the various and seemingly diverse elements of Vermeer's painting—the unborn soul, the empty scales, and the *Last Judgment*? A significant clue lies in a literal interpretation of the artist's formal means.

Vermeer, like his contemporaries, often included an image within his painting in the form of a mirror, map, or framed picture. Recently the physical relationships between such fictive images and the protagonists of Dutch paintings have been analyzed for their potentially meaningful associations. So, for instance, E. de Jongh in his study of seventeenth-century Dutch "Vrouw Wereld" (Lady World) imagery points to the convention of the map in a painting literally crowning a woman's head as a means of imparting to her the attribute of worldliness.[12] The woman's position relative to the painting on the wall in Vermeer's Washington painting also has not been overlooked. She is often referred to as holding the position of St. Michael, whose role as the weigher of souls is supplanted by her own mundane weighing.[13] One could say, further, that her exact placement in the very center of the *Last Judgment* is emphatic when we realize that Vermeer has included the entire feigned painting, frame to frame, within the limits of the real one. She stands, therefore, specifically neither with the saved nor the damned but in the iconographically neutral area between them. Her precise position could not have been overlooked in a century and a country such as Vermeer's, which was torn in strife over the issue of predestination and free will. The crux of this issue revolved around determining the moment when a Christian soul obtained grace and salvation.

The religious question of the day resulted in a rift even among contemporary Protestants, who, ever since the Synod of Dordrecht in 1618, had fallen into defined factions for and against the doctrine of the elect. The followers of Gomarus believed in an individual's predetermined state of grace, whereas those of Arminius believed in the efficacy of good works.[14] Vermeer's position on this issue is now clear, since recently discovered archival evidence all but proves his conversion to Catholicism at the time of his marriage.[15] His opinion, therefore, on the state of grace of the unborn soul, such as the one that resides in the womb of the woman in this painting, would have been one of a proper Catholic—that is, that it was as yet undetermined.

The Catholic iconography suggested here for Vermeer's Washington painting is not without precedent in his oeuvre. De Jongh has uncovered the Jesuit sources for details in Vermeer's *Allegory of the Christian Faith*, which hangs in the Metropolitan Museum of Art in New York.[16] His findings are especially convincing in light of the archival evidence of Vermeer's family connections with the Jesuit community in Delft.[17] The very presence of so traditional a religious subject as the Last Judgment connects this painting with the *Allegory*, which includes a Crucifixion after Jacob Jordaens. We may easily imagine that the two were painted for patrons of similar taste and religious beliefs. Although Protestant theology did not, in general, eliminate the idea of a last reckoning, its portrayal by non-Catholic artists of the seventeenth century is rare.[18] Moreover, an attempt to identify the sixteenth-century author of the *Last Judgment* in the *Woman Holding a Balance* invariably leads to Catholic painters and, thereby, to a specifically Catholic formulation of the subject.[19]

An examination of the various other details in the painting in light of this interpretation proves equally fruitful. The pearls and the mirror are exceptionally flexible iconographic references in Dutch painting, being applicable to a host of positive and pejorative meanings. Often the pearl is used as a reference to the soul itself.[20] Furthermore, a rich font of pearl iconography derived from its Latin word, *margarita*, and in this context its association with St. Margaret is most revealing. Devotion to St. Margaret continued well into the seventeenth century, despite the general decline of saint cults in this period.[21] Her ongoing popularity can be attributed to her role of intercessor at childbirth as an assurance of a full and successfully completed term of pregnancy.[22] Her evocation here in the rosary-like string of pearls relates to the woman's rather advanced state of pregnancy. The mirror is equally telling in this regard. Among its many applications, a common association of the mirror was Truth, as was explained by Ripa.[23] The Socratic enjoinder "Know thyself" had a long and popular life in the folk hero Till Eulenspiegel, whose attributes, an owl and a looking glass, symbolized his uncompromisingly truthful yet humorous exposure of pretense and hypocrisy in the self-satisfied members of upstanding society. Roemer Visscher, in his thirtieth emblem of *Sinnepoppen*, which appeared in Amsterdam in 1614, says, "For in the mirror is nothing but an illusion; that which you desire to see in it you yourself must bring before you: The person you wish to play in this world you must form in yourself."[24] In this context it is significant that the mirror is as yet blank. All that this child will be, the role he or she will play in life, is still unknown, although it is on the verge of becoming clear.

Scales were also applied to a variety of iconographic ends in Holland in the seventeenth century. They were primarily, then as now, a symbol of justice, and for that purpose they belong to St. Michael at the time of the Last Judgment. The allusion of Vermeer's scales to those of St. Michael in the weighing of souls cannot be denied. The reference, however, is general rather than specific. One could conclude that no pearl rests on the trays of the balance, since at this point in time the outcome of the soul's fate is unascertainable. From a slightly different point of view the balance can be understood as the unblemished soul itself, which has as yet neither enacted good works nor committed sins. The balance is even.

However strong a reference the woman and her scales make to St. Michael, they also evoke another iconographic tradition, one that Vermeer was equally aware of. The word for scales in Dutch, *weegschaal*, is the same word used for the astrological sign of Libra, the sign of September and October. Astrology was an accepted discipline in the seventeenth century, and it had long been reconciled with the ideas of Christianity.[25] Vermeer's own acceptance of it is attested to by the painting the *Astrologer* (fig. 3), in the Louvre, Paris. There the serious and scientific nature of the man's work is conveyed through his dignified appearance and intense concentration. The figure is usually referred to in modern literature as an astronomer, but, as James Welu has rightly pointed out, the instruments on his table and around him are those used by both astrologers and astronomers.[26] Moreover, the title given to Vermeer's painting in eighteenth-century auction catalogs was *Astrologist*.[27] His specific activity and vocation may be clarified by relating the painting within the painting to the main figure. This painting within the painting has been identified as part of the *Finding of Moses*, which appears in its totality in Vermeer's *Woman Writing a Letter with Her Maid*, in the Beit Collection.[28] The story of Moses, among other references, announces the arrival of a baby, albeit in a less direct fashion than Vermeer's Washington picture.[29] The astrologer reaches for the celestial globe decorated with the zodiac signs in order to chart the baby's destiny. Vermeer's positioning of this globe, a real one made by Jodocus Hondius and published in 1600,[30] makes the sign of Libra in the lower right quarter particularly visible. The fashioning of the scales in both paintings by this artist must surely be a meaningful coincidence.

The mirror and pearls may now be seen as having another meaning in the painting, that of the attributes of Venus, the goddess who ruled Libra. Possibly also referred to in this painting are the images of the astrological signs as rulers of different parts of the body, wherein a woman (Virgo) holding a balance (Libra) governs the abdomen area.[31] The astrological references are ultimately subordinated to the Christian ones, with the figure of a glowing God crowning the woman's head.[32]

Ingeniously, with a single device, Vermeer brings forth the two established systems for determining human fate in the seventeenth century. Theology and science are reconciled in a unified program that is dominated by the primacy of free will. For if astrology had been accepted in Christian circles, it was with the understanding that the stars impel; they do not compel.[33]

The young woman who looks down at the scales with the trace of a smile on her lips provides the final determining factor of her child's destiny. In the end it is she who will bring the necessary guidance in a Catholic home that is blessed by faith and characterized by charitable good works.[34] One can imagine her thoughts to be along the lines of the Dutch proverb, "Het licht wel eer bij mij bemint, dat geef ick u mijn weerde kint."[35] The larger meaning of the painting, then, can be understood as the significance of the mother and the value of the home as the person and place to ensure the continued proper observance of the Christian faith.

The religion portrayed in *Woman Holding a Balance* is Catholic. The rarified patronage suggested for this painting may account for the confusion about its precise subject as early as 1696.[36] It is to be remembered that the Catholic presence in Delft was in constant danger, and the church house of the Jesuits, which recorded Vermeer and his family in its registry, held ceremonies only in secret.[37] In 1708 the entire Delft Jesuit station was banished from the city on the orders of the states of Holland.[38] This interpretation may also explain the unusual description of the painting in 1696, "Een Juffrouw, die goud weegt, in een kasje."[39] Dutch paintings were sometimes placed in small boxes to protect them, as a sign of their high value—an aspect of *Woman Holding a Balance* that is attested to by the high price it brought at the 1696 auction.[40] However, another reason for putting such an object in a box was to ensure its private viewing. Gerard Dou had provided just such a *kasje* for an ivory crucifix made, no doubt, as W. Martin conjectured, also for Catholic patrons.[41] Vermeer's painting, taken from the context of its intended audience and given a new meaning by its description in 1696, quickly became absorbed into the general culture.

Finally, within the context of its original conception the painting's archaistic reference to Netherlandish Renaissance painting takes on new significance. This aspect of Vermeer's art, which has always been intuitively noticed, is manifested both formally and iconographically. The use of light and color for their explicative and descriptive value has already been discussed. Vermeer's allusion to the annunciate Mary, humble and pure, is conveyed by her clothing, expression, and general demeanor, as well as by her location in the room facing the window. The spiritual quality of the setting in its abstraction and control of form and light convey the sense of a temporal moment frozen for eternity, as can be observed also in the art of Jan van Eyck. Even Vermeer's allusion to St. Michael and his scales must be seen as a reference to the art of the fifteenth century, for that motif had all but disappeared in the sixteenth century, with only a single notable example after 1500.[42]

These references are best understood as a self-conscious reassertion of the pietistic attitude that came to be associated with Flemish art of the past, the same art that was so brutally attacked by radical reformers in the sixteenth century. It is in perfect keeping with the personal and deeply religious nature of this work that it participates in the revival and survival of the great tradition of northern European Christian painting.

Political Iconography in a Painting
by Jan Miense Molenaer

The Musical Duet (A Young Man Playing a Theorbo and a Young Woman Playing a Cittern), by Jan Miense Molenaer, in the National Gallery in London (fig. 4), painted in the 1630s, presents a familiar and comforting image of a young couple making music in the context of a domestic interior. It evokes an atmosphere of security and well-being commonly found in Dutch genre painting of the seventeenth century and may be interpreted simply as a descriptive mirror of daily life.[1] Yet there are intrinsic and extrinsic determinants that suggest that the painting was both made and received in a more complex fashion. As external evidence the main subject, music making, must be viewed with the idea that it was among the most popular and versatile subjects in Dutch paintings and prints of the seventeenth century and that its implications are many and varied.[2] Often presented with didactic texts or in conjunction with other images, music could function as an illustration of the sense of hearing, the sanguine temperament, the element Earth, or the idea of "Vanitas," among others.[3] In some instances music also had a decidedly positive association: as a means to calm the spirit, as an aid in the service of love, or as an expression of harmony and accord.[4] I hope to demonstrate that it is in the positive sense that the music in Molenaer's work was intended. The idea of romantic harmony has already been put forward as the central meaning of this painting.[5] Before examining that specific suggestion, a brief discussion of the internal, formal devices employed by Molenaer that often imply deeper meaning is here in order.

The couple is seated in a shallow yet fully furnished and richly embellished room. The overabundance of details in this room serves to represent an opulent lifestyle and, as we shall see, presents a coherent program with a deeper iconographic purpose for the painting as a whole. In this context the most significant surrounding details are a portrait of a man on the rear wall, a dog, a servant bringing in a cooked chicken, a large feathered hat precariously perched on a cello leaning against the table, and two columns with elaborate capitals flanking the partially opened door.

The compositional arrangement, with its somewhat stilted outward orientation of the figures, can be found earlier in the work of Molenaer's Haarlem contemporary Willem Buytewech. It is in Buytewech's work that Würtenberger and Haverkamp-Begemann have convincingly interpreted this formal device as indicative of emblematic meaning.[6] In Molenaer this self-conscious tendency is even more pronounced, and with the unusual juxtaposition of a hat placed on a cello it even breaks with the general "realistic" tenor of the painting as a whole.

The painting within a painting, as a starting point for a specific interpretation of Molenaer's work, may be seen here, as it has been in other Dutch genre paintings, as the *clavis interpretandi* of the meaning.[7] This is especially evident here because of its important placement in the composition. Furthermore, it has long been recognized that this particular portrait within the painting is of Frederick Henry, stadholder of the United Provinces and the son and heir of William of Orange, the great hero of the Dutch revolt against Spain.[8] The portrait resembles the one painted by Michiel van Mierevelt, which is known today through an engraving by W. Delff of about 1632 (fig. 5).[9] The presence of the central Dutch political figure of the day certainly conjured up its own set of associations at this moment in history.

The relative amount of the stadholder's power, and by implication that of the House of Orange from which he traditionally came, was a central issue of internal controversy in the Dutch Republic throughout the seventeenth century.[10] The seven northern provinces of the Netherlands, which had united militarily to overthrow the yoke of Spanish oppression, were determined to maintain their power of self-government rather than surrender it to a strong centralized agency. These particularist interests, spearheaded by the States of Holland, came into constant conflict with those of the House of Orange, the single most powerful force in the coordinating central organization. By the 1650s the conflict between the supporters of the stadholder Frederick Henry's son, William II, and those of Holland deepened to the point where one could actually speak of two opposing political parties. On one side were the Orangists, who were proponents of a strong centralized government with a singular leader, an "Eminente Hoofd," and on the other were the Republicans or States party, who were in favor of a loosely knit confederation in which each of the provinces maintained a large degree of independence. Maurice, Frederick Henry's predecessor, had been the subject of much distrust and hostility. His ambitious campaigns and strong-handed dealings with dissent paved the way for the rift of the midcentury. Frederick Henry, on the other hand, was far more cautious and attempted to reconcile the various factions of the Dutch Republic, religious and political, to bring them into harmony, so to speak. It is in this context that this portrait within Molenaer's painting is best understood.

In the painting the portrait of Frederick Henry is positioned directly above a large hat resting on a cello. The strange conjunction of hat and cello, as well as their intrusive placement partially obscuring the maid's face, works to emphasize their importance within the program of the painting. Our attention is further drawn to them by the maid, who fixes her gaze on them. Although the hat, like so many items in Dutch paintings, had various associations and meanings, the most popular and long-standing was as a symbol of liberty.[11] Among the oldest references to it as such is the text in Appian's *Roman History* where one of Caesar's murderers "bore a cap on the end of a spear as a symbol of freedom."[12] The commentary below explains that the cap (pileus) was given to enfranchised slaves and ransomed captives as a sign of their liberty.[13] Appian may well have been the source for Cesare Ripa, who explains the Roman origins of the hat in his emblem of *Libertas*, where it is seen with other items.[14] From Roman times through the Renaissance the device became a standard one seen especially often on coins. First used on the medal of Marcus Junius Brutus, it was taken over by Lorenzo de Medici and subsequently became one of the most popular motifs on Netherlandish coins of the sixteenth and seventeenth centuries commemorating the Dutch revolt (fig. 6).[15] The explanatory texts of the two leading numismatists of Dutch coins, Pierre Bizot and Gerard van Loon, writing in 1688 and 1732, respectively, discuss the hat as a symbol of Dutch freedom in a variety of contexts.[16] The hat on Dutch coins could appear either on the end of a spear or lance, as it was described in Appian, or simply by itself. Among other variables, the hat also took on different shapes from coin to coin. In this context it is significant that the 1644 Dutch translation of Ripa with its new illustrations, definitively transformed the cap into a modern hat.[17]

Variations can also be seen in the numerous appearances of the liberty hat in Netherlandish prints, sculpture, and paintings of the seventeenth century. One constant, however, was its visual connection with the various members of the House of Orange. For example, in the illustration from Adrianus Valerius's *Nederlandtsche gedenck-clanck . . .* , printed in Haarlem in 1626, William the Silent takes a sword of justice from the Netherlandish Lion, which holds a lance with the hat on it.[18] Further examples can be found in the work of Crispin van de Passe and others.[19] Perhaps the most influential statement of this idea was made by Hendrick de Keyser in his impressive tomb of William of Orange, completed in 1623.[20] "Aurea Libertas" stands as one of four allegorical figures, one in each of the four corners of the monument. Placed in the privileged corner at the right of the seated national hero, she carries a large hat in one hand and a scepter in the other.[21]

In paintings the motif was common in overt allegories that celebrated not only William but all the subsequent heirs of the House of Orange to become stadholders. Jan Tengnagel's *Allegory of the Prosperity of the Republic under Maurice of Orange,* in the Gemeente Musea Delft, Stedelijk Museum Het Prinsenhof Collection (fig. 7), shows the enthroned personification of the Northern Netherlands presenting to Prince Maurice, William's eldest son, a lance with a conically shaped hat on it. This motif works with the others in Tengnagel's paintings, as it does in Molenaer's, to develop the theme of the well-being of the free Dutch people under the authority of an Orangist government.[22] The hat appears once again in Theodorus van Thulden's *Naming of the Young William II in the Survivance of the Stadholder, Captain and Admiralship,* painted for the Oranjezaal in Huis ten Bosch (fig. 8).[23] In Van Thulden's painting the hat on the lance sports a long white feather and is thus similar to the hat in Molenaer's painting.

These prints, sculpture, and paintings indicate that even if the association of the liberty hat with the House of Orange was not an exclusive one,[24] the hat was surely one of the symbolic devices that would by the 1630s have called to mind the heroic and valiant history of the Orange achievement.[25] The painting by Molenaer makes the association visually clear by placing the hat in such close proximity to the stadholder's portrait. Molenaer's painting thus communicates its political message by means that are at once realistic and emblematic. He was, however, not unique in effecting this symbiosis.[26] A similar phenomenon can be observed in Jan Steen's painting celebrating the birth of William III, *Prinsjesdag,* as it is traditionally called, in the Rijksmuseum in Amsterdam (fig. 9). Steen's work is also a positive Orangist image presented in both emblematic and realistic terms.[27] The keeper of a tavern, which is decorated with a portrait of William III on the back wall,[28] falls to his knees and proposes a toast. The text of his toast is given on a piece of paper on the floor in the middle of the composition: "Op de gesondheyt van het nassaus basie, in de eene hant het rapier, inde andere hant het glaesie" (To the health of the Nassau lord, in one hand a glass, and in the other a sword). Conspicuously in the center of the foreground, below and axially aligned with the portrait of William, Steen painted a hat with a stick resting against it. The allusion to the liberty hat is by now clear, and the visual conjunction of the stadholder's portrait with that hat must have been an expression of a well-understood political device by the late 1660s, when this painting was made.[29]

Whereas Steen positioned the portrait within the painting, the hat and stick and the written toast in the center of his composition, Molenaer gave that dominant place to the music-making couple. Exactly how they fit into the scheme of the painting must now be addressed. Music frequently represented the notion of harmony, and, as has been noted, Molenaer's painting has been interpreted as an illustration of the harmony of true love.[30] Stringed instruments were seen as particularly well-suited emblems for domestic concord.[31] Numerous examples of the romantic connotations of musical harmony exist in paintings and prints of the seventeenth century.[32] Several important examples occur in Molenaer's own work, notably the *Family Concert*, in the Frans Halsmuseum in Haarlem.[33] Nevertheless, given the specific circumstances of Molenaer's London painting, the primary meaning of his duet is more probably in the realm of political harmony.[34]

Political harmony was a frequently employed subject in all forms of cultural and artistic expression in the seventeenth century. It is the subject of many emblems, paintings, and prints of the period. For example, Alciati explained the lute in his *Emblemata*, originally published in 1531 and reprinted many times thereafter, as illustrating the concept of "Foedera Italorum."[35] Further, in Zincgreff's *Emblematum Ethico Politicorum Centuria*, published in Heidelberg in 1633, emblem 97 shows a lute with the inscription (in translation):

HARMONIZE THROUGH DIVERSITY

The lute is strung with coarse and fine strings
Of several sorts of sound,
And who shall strike it
To produce a proper harmony
Must know it well.
Good government requires skill with a diversity of people.[36]

In fact, the analogy between government and music abounds in Renaissance theory. Its earliest expression is in Plato's *Republic*,[37] which was as popular as ever in the seventeenth century. The comparison between musical harmony and political harmony is also central to the work of the sixteenth-century French jurist Jean Bodin. Bodin's influence is attested to by the numerous translations of his work into Latin, English, and Dutch from the late-sixteenth to the mid-seventeenth century.[38] In his *Republic* the king acts to unify the country, and here the author asserts that good government and music succeed only in the proper proportions of their parts. The king who embodies all power and peace is likened to the musical octave, which contains all the consonances.[39] Bodin emphasizes that the primary responsibility of the powerful monarch is to see to the needs of all the governed classes so that the land is brought into concord, just as all the chords and strings of music and musical instruments must be brought into tune with one another.[40] Bodin's concepts were clearly as relevant to the circumstances of the Northern Netherlands in the time of Frederick Henry as they were in France in the sixteenth century, when they were formulated.

These ideas, either stemming from Bodin or generated independently, were to be found in various other arenas in Europe in the sixteenth and seventeenth centuries. Shakespeare, for example, employs a similar analogy between music and government in *Henry V* when Exeter declares:

> For government, though high and low and lower
> Put into parts, doth keep in one consent.
> Congreeing in a full natural close like music.[41]

The degree to which music played a role in the self-definition of the "myth of Venice" in the sixteenth century has been well studied.[42] It permeated the theoretical notions of government, officially patronized painting programs, and even government building projects, as well as, of course, the real production of civic and religious music in Venice.[43] For the Venetians, music was perceived as the most "appropriate symbol of a government well tempered, harmonious, consonant, (and) balanced in the relationship of its parts."[44] In England Charles I was panegyrized in similar terms in the 1630s by E. Waller:

> Those antique minstrels sure were Charles-like Kings,
> Cities their lutes, and subjects hearts their strings;
> On which with so divine a hand they strook,
> Consent of motion from their breath they took.[45]

Thus the interpretation here proposed for the *Musical Duet* concurs with ideological formulations found elsewhere in Europe in this period. Although one cannot say it was employed exclusively for the cause of sovereignty or of a single ruling figure in whatever form, it does appear to have been applied more often in those cases, perhaps because of the nature of the metaphor or perhaps because of the influential writings of Bodin.

The musical harmony of the young couple can thus be seen as operating on several levels, all working to evoke the positive feeling of harmony under the rule of Frederick Henry. The fact that Molenaer chose to depict a male/female couple could also have had iconographic implications in the seventeenth century. Although usually represented as a young virgin,[46] the "Netherlands" had in several instances been personified as a man and woman. For example, Adriaen van de Venne had represented them thus in his *Allegory of the Truce of 1609*, now in the Louvre (fig. 10).[47] There, in the middle of the foreground, the northern and southern provinces are dressed as bride and groom, respectively (fig. 11).[48] Furthermore, a couple representing the Northern Netherlands alone can be found in at least one commemorative coin, minted in 1585, which Bizot describes as: "The Queen of England presents an abundance of flowers and roses to two people who represent the United Provinces, indicating that they make an alliance with her."[49] Nor is the romantic and domestic interpretation that is usually given to this painting incompatible with the political interpretation proposed here. As Natalie Zemon Davis has pointed out in discussing this period: "In the little world of the family, with its conspicuous tension between intimacy and power, the larger matters of political and social order could find ready symbolization."[50] Indeed, historically, major writers including Luther and Calvin had expressed the view that the family and its government could be seen as a microcosm of the state and its government.[51] The levels of meaning possible for this duet are thus further expanded.

From a methodological point of view the validity of this interpretation depends on the remaining details of the painting being explainable as, at the very least, not in conflict with the proposed political message. The two most imposing details are the maid, who enters the room with a chicken, and the two columns, with their ornate capitals flanking the door through which she enters. The maid's appearance is particularly noteworthy since domestic servants as such are scarce in Dutch paintings before 1650.[52] She reinforces the sense of a well-to-do home both by her presence and by the cooked chicken she carries.[53] Her dutiful behavior, unlike the idle or drunken behavior of servants in paintings by Nicolaes Maes and Jan Steen of a slightly later date, enhances the sense of propriety in the household of Molenaer's painting.[54] She may also remind one of a social class beneath that of her music-making employers. She glances at the cello, and although it would certainly have been a breach of social protocol to have her join them in concert, her participation is at least alluded to.

The columns can be related to the other political and Orangist components of the painting in several ways. They are traditional emblems of strength or "Constancie," both of which are applicable in this context. The column was included in the latter sense on a coin minted in 1630 that celebrates Frederick Henry, whose portrait is on the obverse.[55]

The columns in Molenaer's paintings are more likely an allusion to the legendary columns or Pillars of Hercules, which had provided Charles V with the central image of his famous impresa.[56] Well known throughout Europe in the sixteenth century, it was not only applied to the imperial rule of Charles but also eventually used in the ruler imagery of Elizabeth I,[57] Philip II,[58] and Henry IV.[59] In a political context the columns stood for the boundaries of the ancient world that had been surpassed by the discovery and conquest of the New World.[60] They, with or without the motto "Plus Ultra," came to be understood in two primary ways, either as an admonition for restraint and for limiting worldly ambitions or as a challenge to the adventurous to traverse worlds unknown.[61] Although the former explanation may at first seem preferable, given the Dutch predilection for the virtue of temperance, the evidence shows that it was the more modern spirit expressed in the latter that was associated with Frederick Henry. This is evident in the coin of 1631 (fig. 12), with a profile portrait of Frederick Henry on the obverse and on the reverse a lion moving one of two columns. The inscription reads "Herculas Ultra Extulit Colunas."[62] The columns in Molenaer's painting can thus be viewed as references to Frederick Henry's successful exploits in the New World and, more generally, to the benefits enjoyed by the Dutch as their result.

Other details of the painting that can be interpreted compatibly with this view of it are the dog and the foot warmer. The dog that sits by the side of his master and mistress is as well behaved as the servant. He is also the perennial symbol of fidelity and watchfulness and as such is equally appropriate in either a domestic or a political context.[63] The foot warmer is usually interpreted as either a symbolic reference to passion[64] or, as Roemer Visscher explained in his book *Sinnepoppen*, as emblematic of humility and simple practicality.[65] Another notion, one that has as yet not been noted and supports the newly proposed context of this painting, can be found in Henry Peacham's *Minerva Britanna* of 1612 in the emblem of *Melancholia*: "One foote on Cube is fixt upon the ground, The which him plodding Constancie affordes."[66] The foot warmer projects the same notion of security and "Constancie" as the cube in Peacham's emblem.

Together the larger signs of the political intention of Molenaer's painting would have been clear to many educated Dutchmen of the 1630s. The portrait of Frederick Henry, the liberty hat, the columns, and the harmonizing, music-making couple all point to the political concerns of the period and celebrate the harmony achieved by Frederick Henry. A proper, if somewhat cumbersome, title for the painting might well be *The Harmony and Well-Being of the Prosperous Dutch Republic Under the Leadership of the House of Orange.*

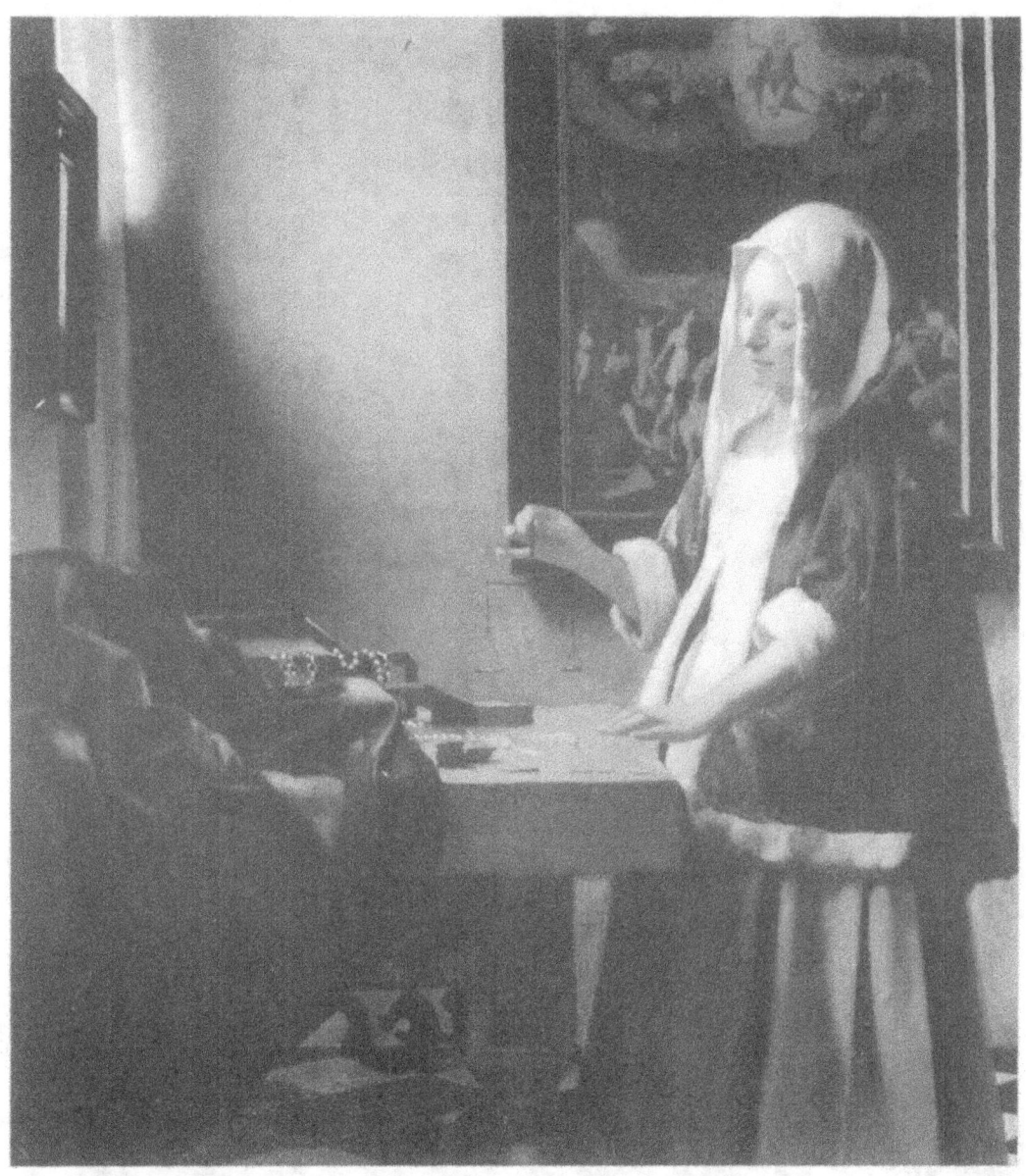

FIGURE I. Johannes Vermeer, *Woman Holding a Balance*. National Gallery of Art, Widener Collection, Washington, DC.

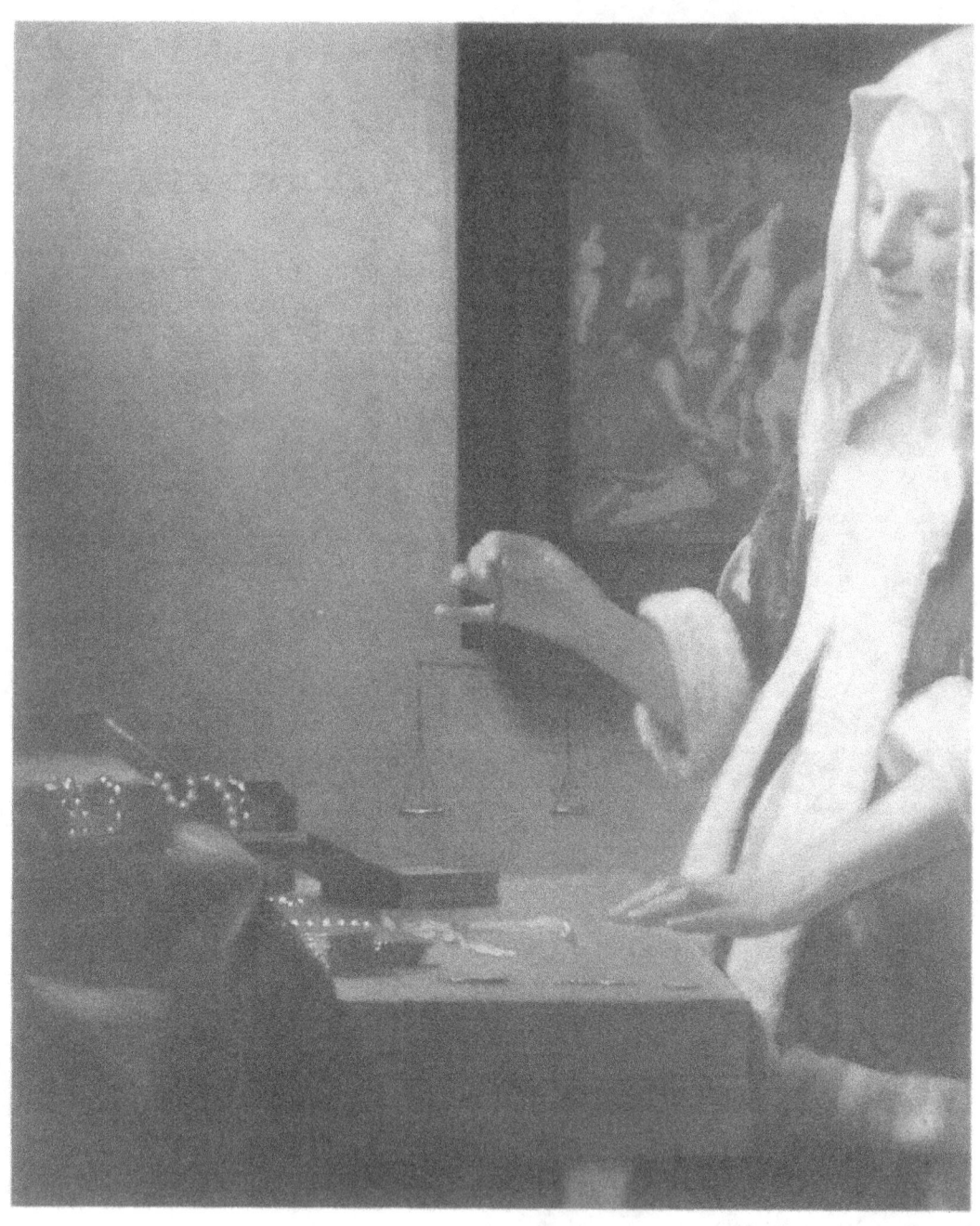

FIGURE 2. Detail of Vermeer's
Woman Holding a Balance.

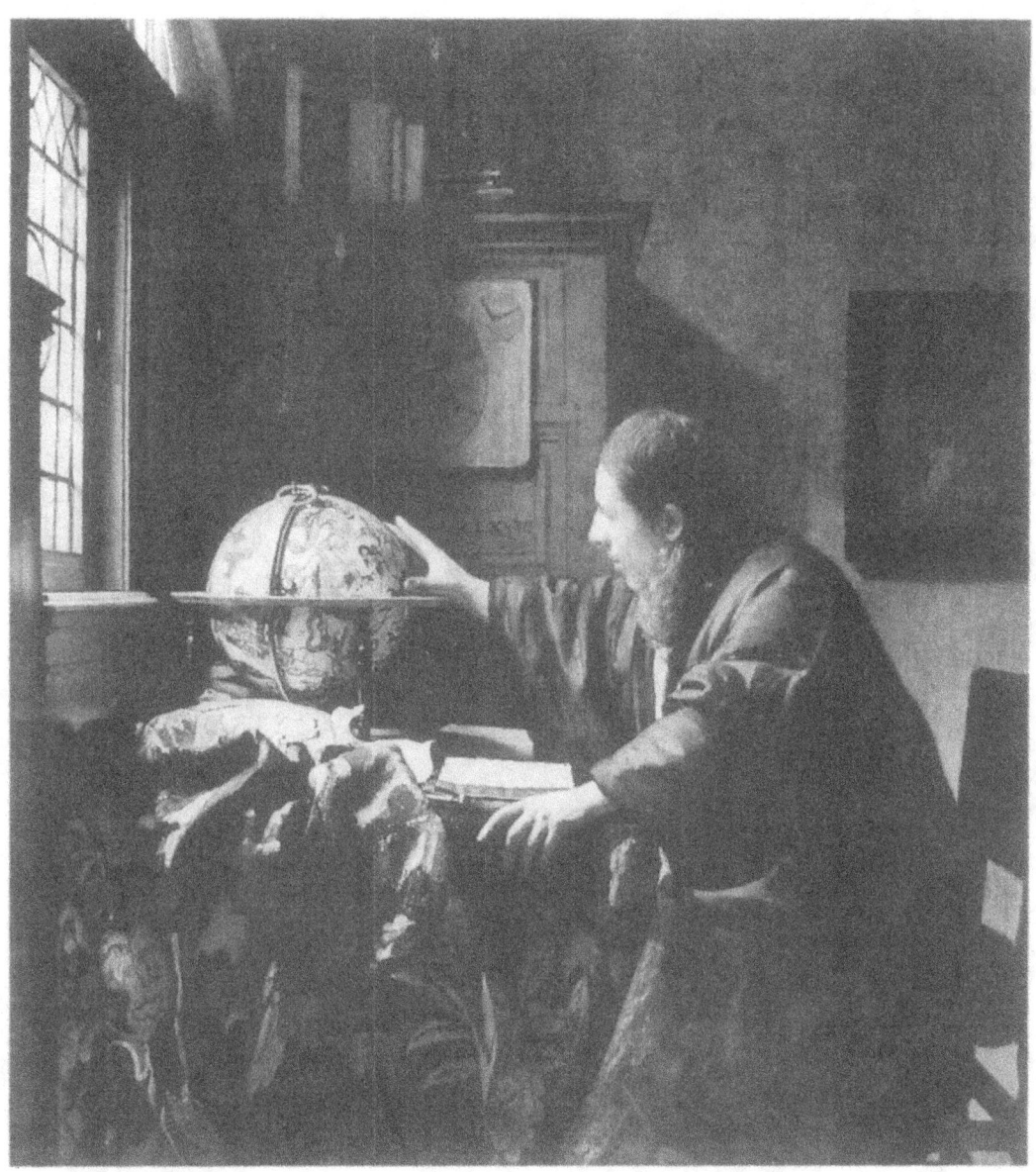

FIGURE 3. Johannes Vermeer, *Astrologer*
(or *Astronomer*). Louvre, Paris.

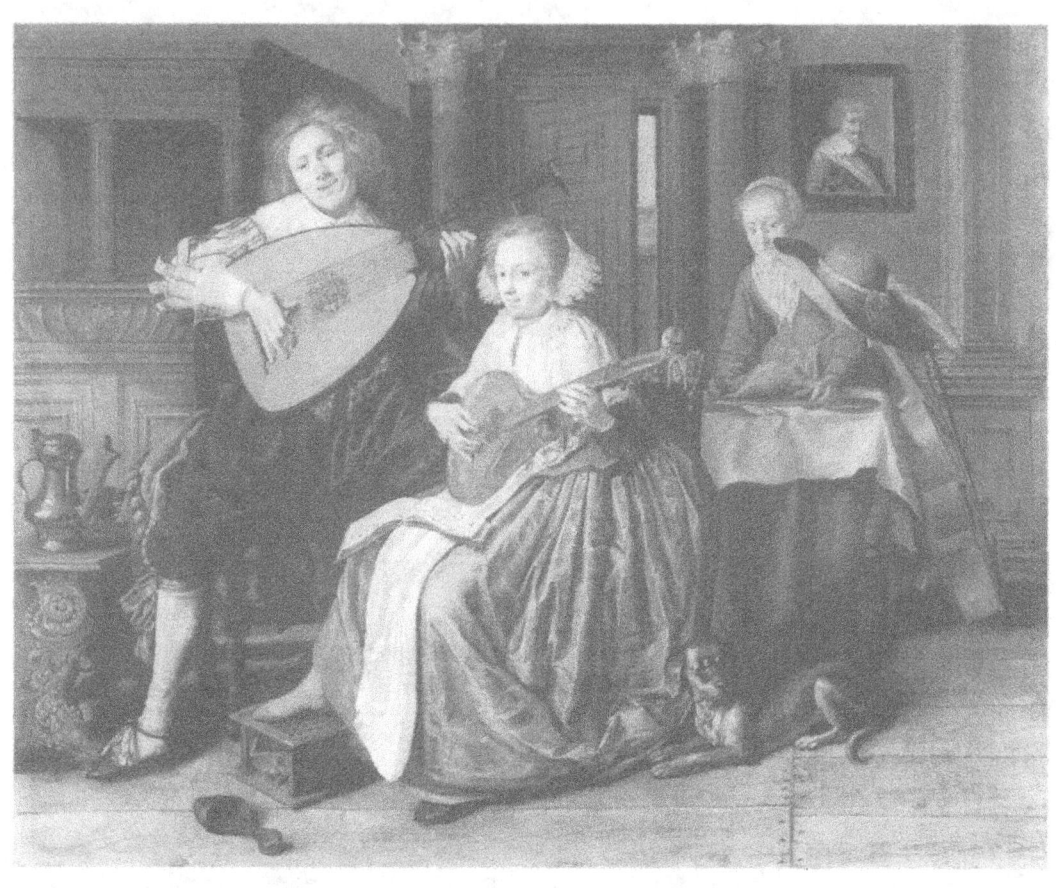

FIGURE 4. Jan Miense Molenaer,
The Musical Duet (A Young Man Playing a
Theorbo and a Young Woman Playing a Cittern).
Signed. National Gallery, London.

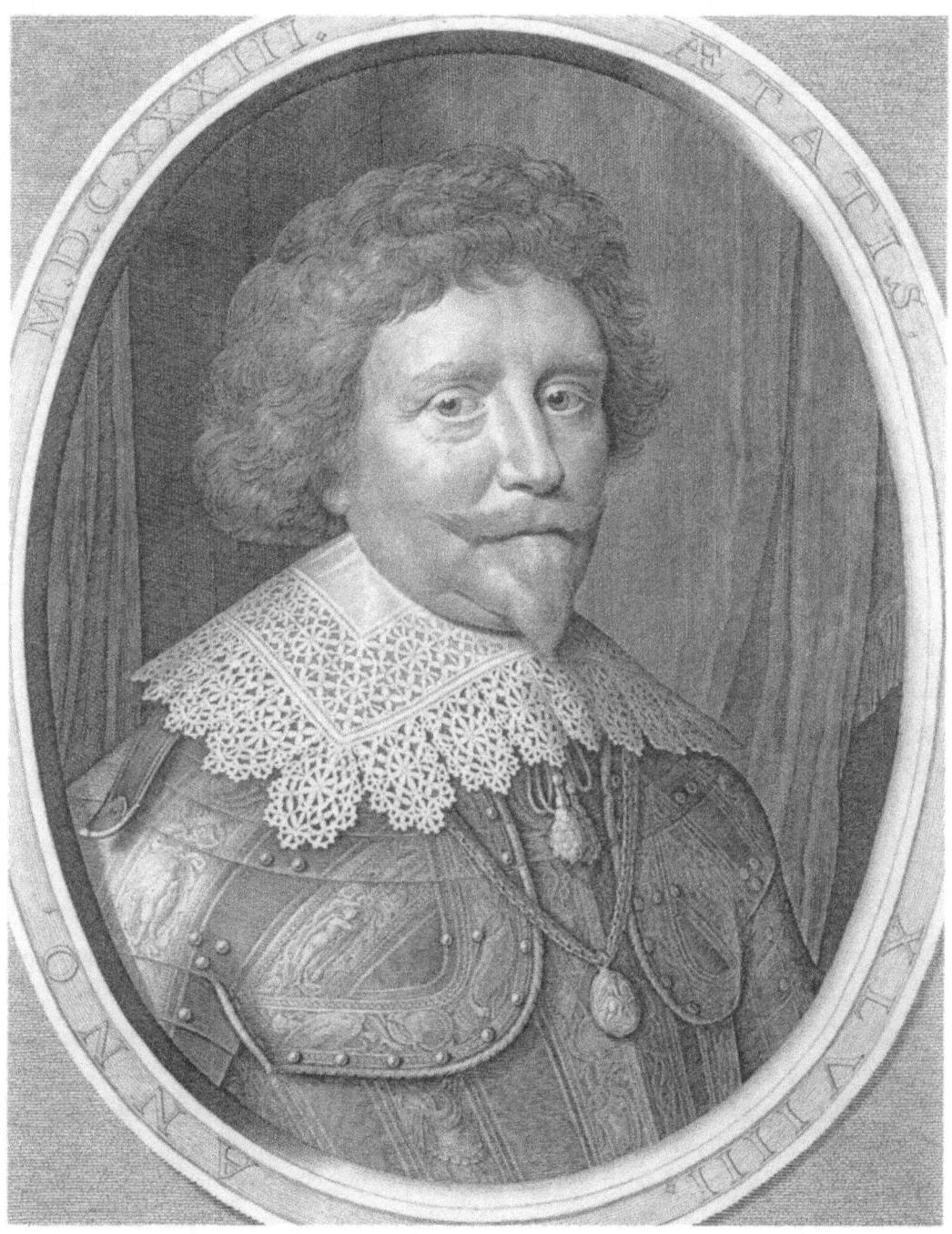

FIGURE 5. W. Delff after Michiel van Mierevelt,
Frederick Henry, Prince of Orange Nassau.
Rijksmuseum, Amsterdam.

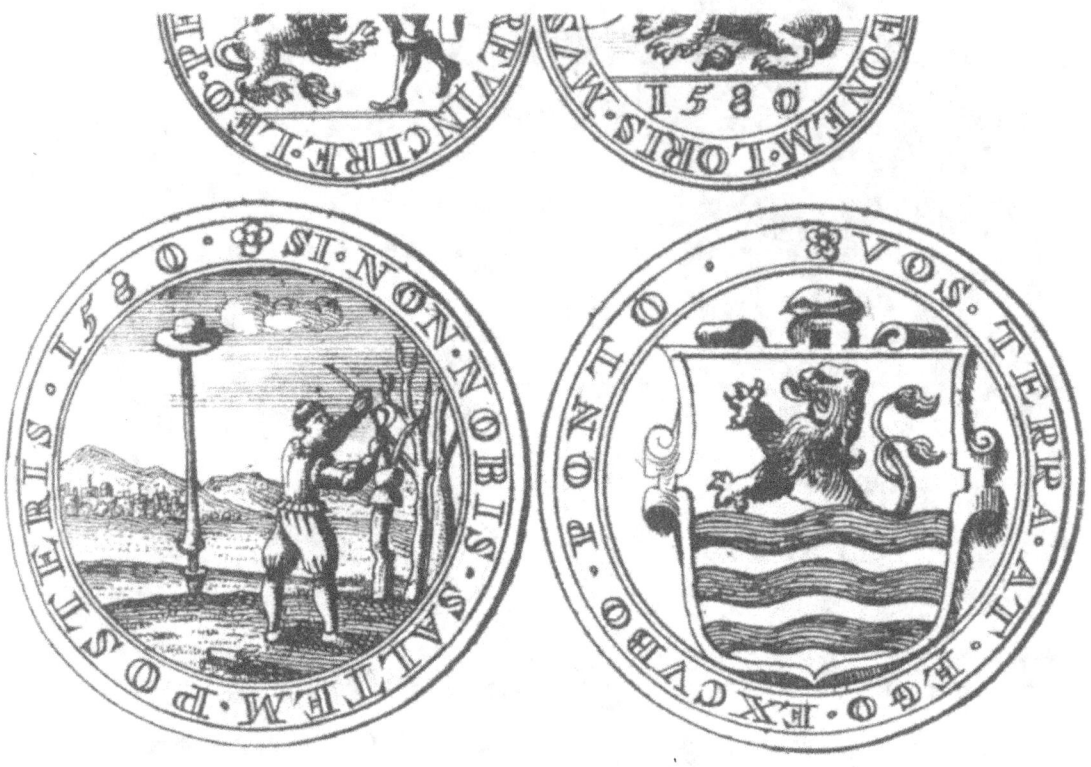

FIGURE 6. Anonymous, Netherlandish coin
of 1580 (taken from Bizot). Engraving.
Photograph by author.

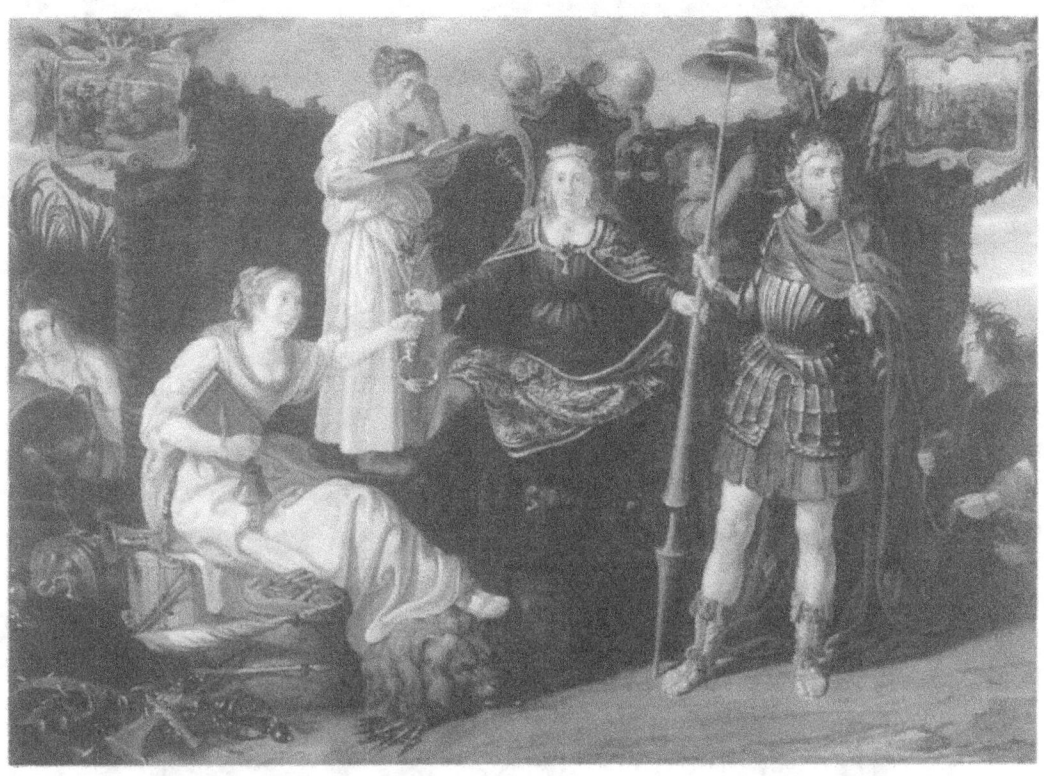

FIGURE 7. Jan Tengnagel, *Allegory of the Prosperity
of the Republic under Maurice of Orange.* Gemeente
Musea Delft, Delft, Collectie Stedelijk Museum
Het Prinsenhof, The Netherlands. Photograph
by Tom Haartsen.

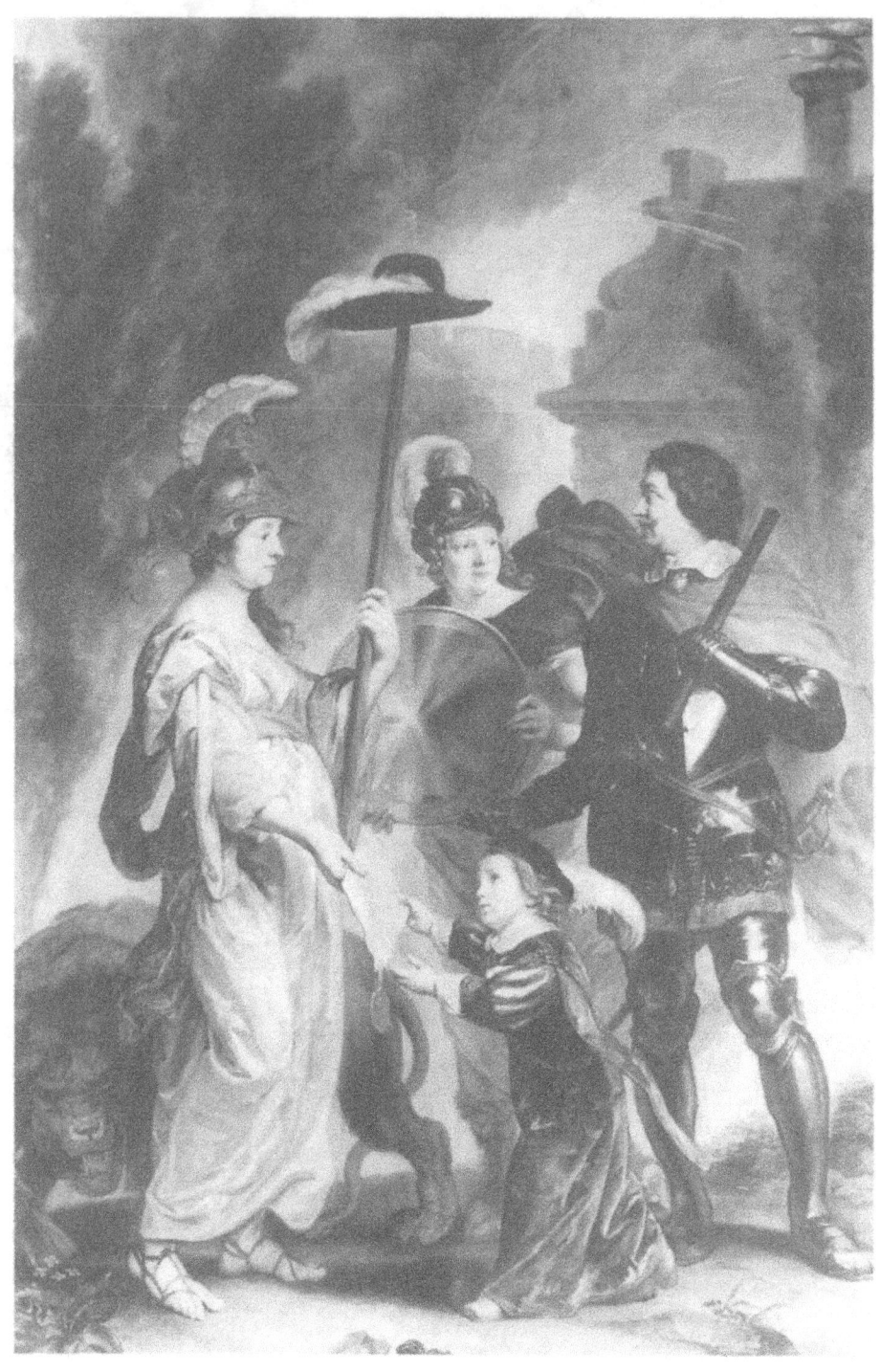

FIGURE 8. Theodorus van Thulden,
*The Naming of the Young William II in the
Survivance of the Stadholder, Captain and
Admiralship.* Royal Collections, The Hague.

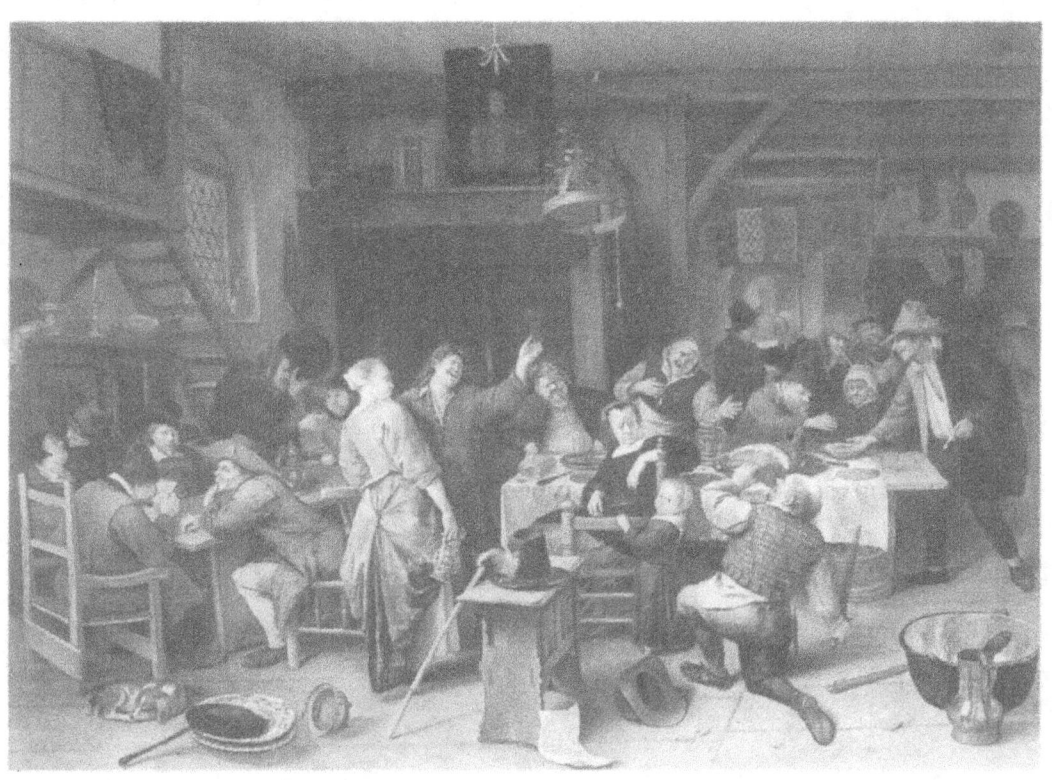

FIGURE 9. Jan Steen, *Prinsjesdag* (Prince's Day: Celebrating the Birth of Prince William III). Signed. Rijksmuseum, Amsterdam.

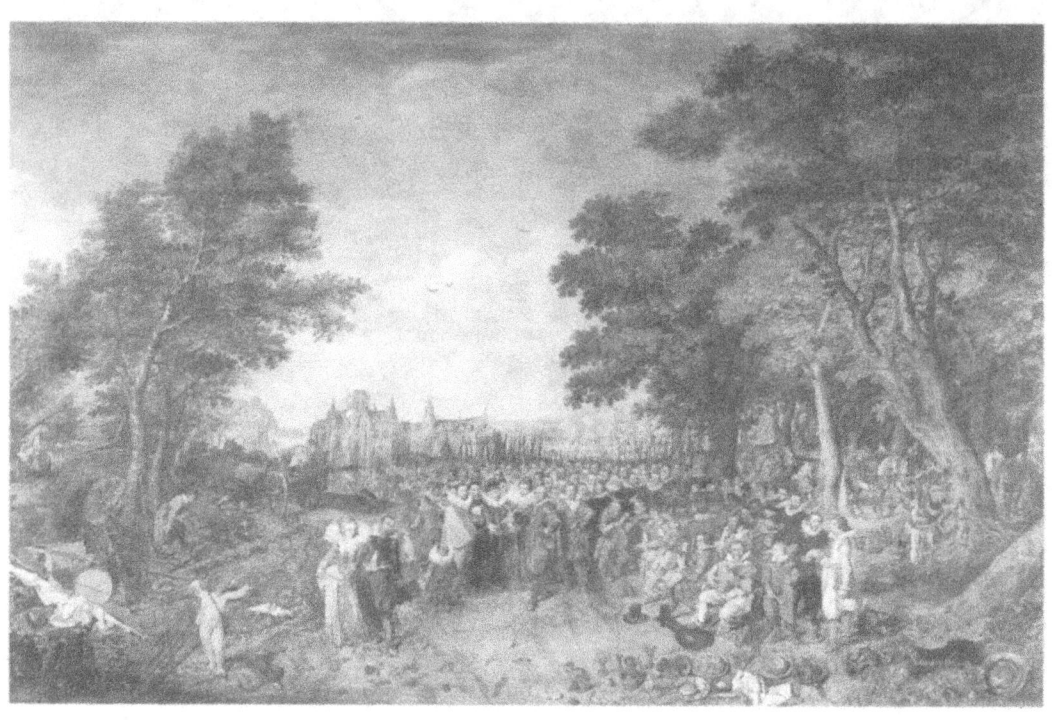

FIGURE 10. Adriaen van de Venne, *Allegory of the Truce of 1609.* Signed and dated 1616. Louvre, Paris. Photograph by Eric Lessing/ Art Resource, New York.

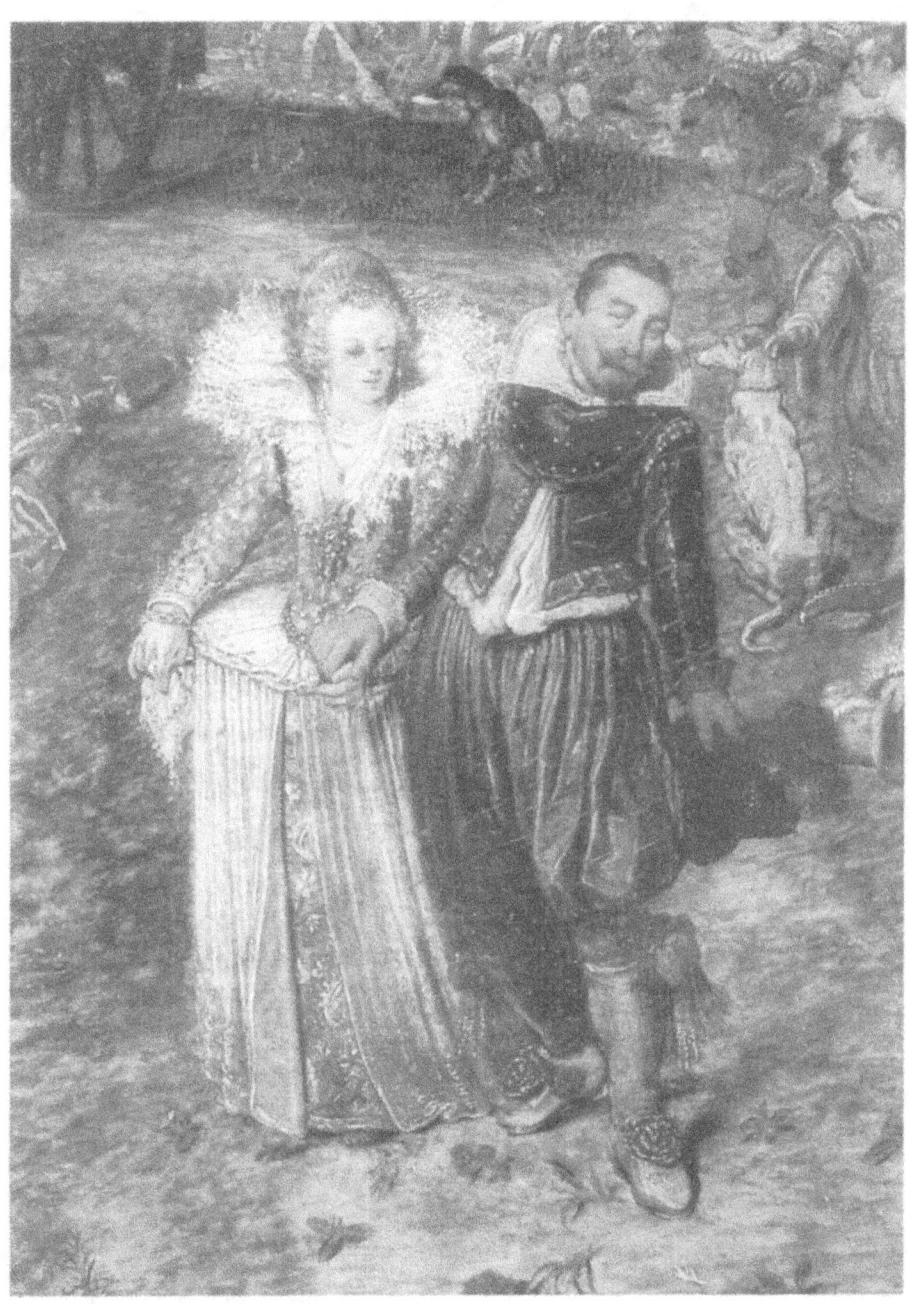

FIGURE II. Detail of Van de Venne's
Allegory of the Truce of 1609.

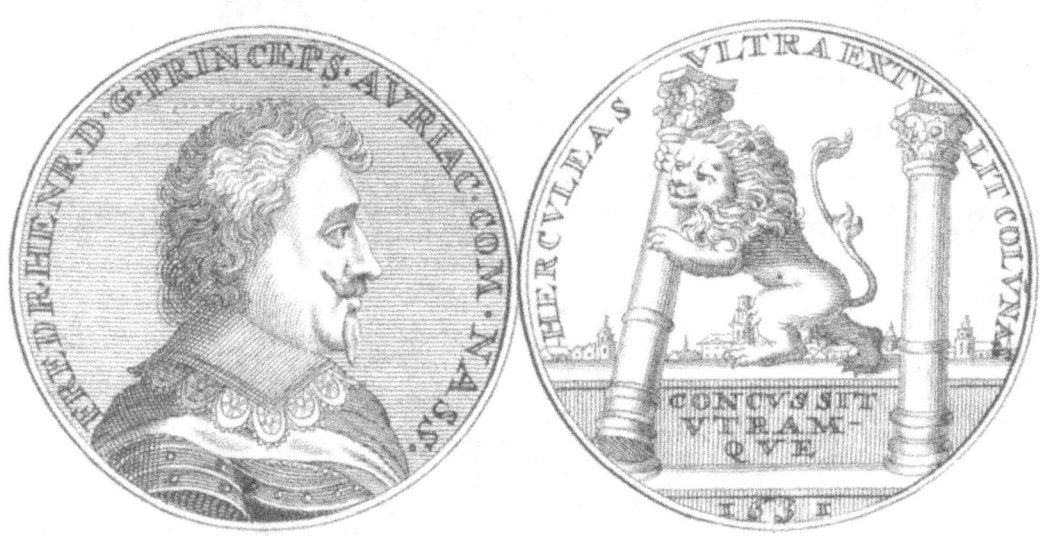

FIGURE 12. Anonymous, Netherlandish coin
of 1631 (from Bizot). Photograph by author.

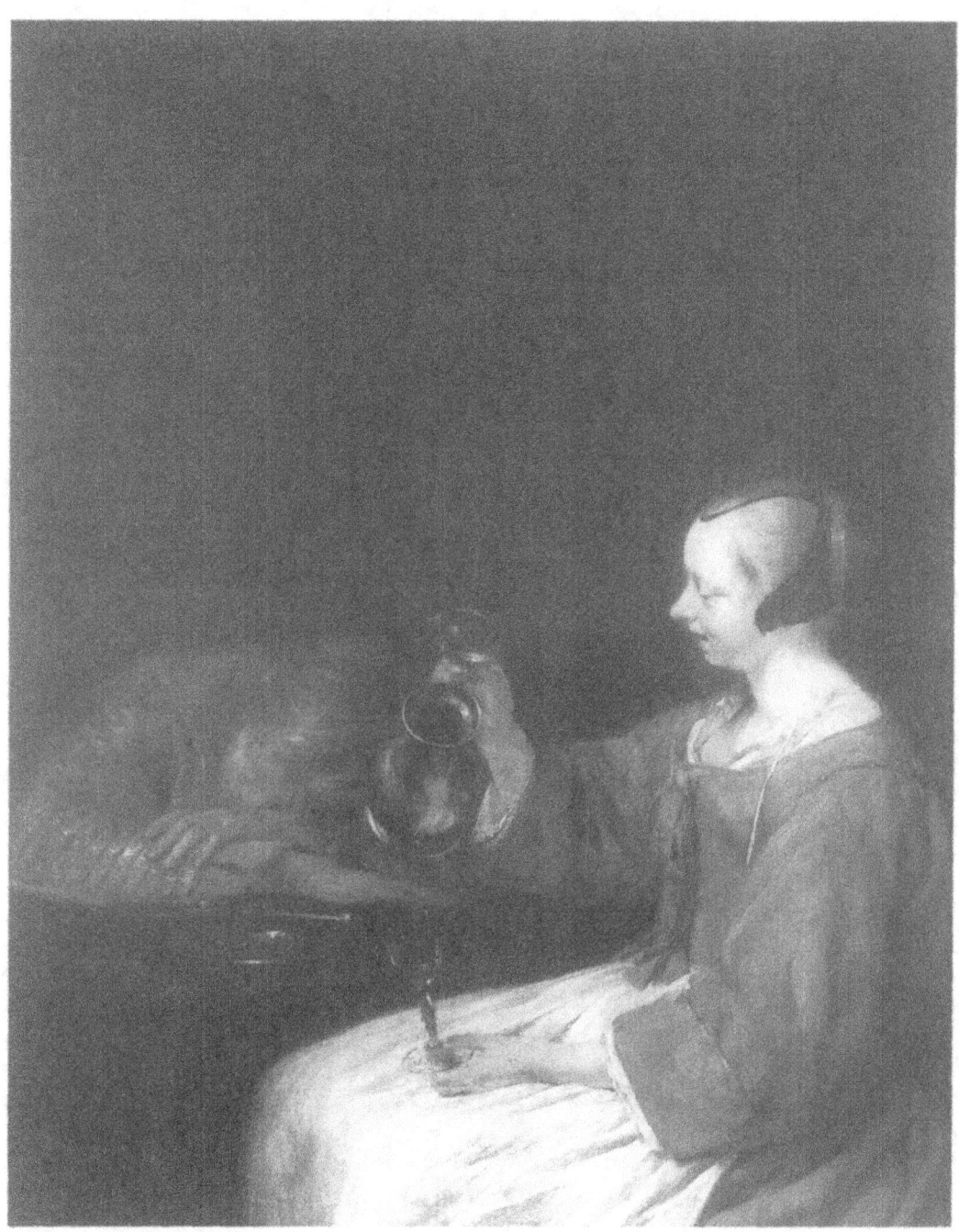

FIGURE 13. Gerard ter Borch, *Drinking Maid with Sleeping Soldier*. Musée Fabre, Montpellier.

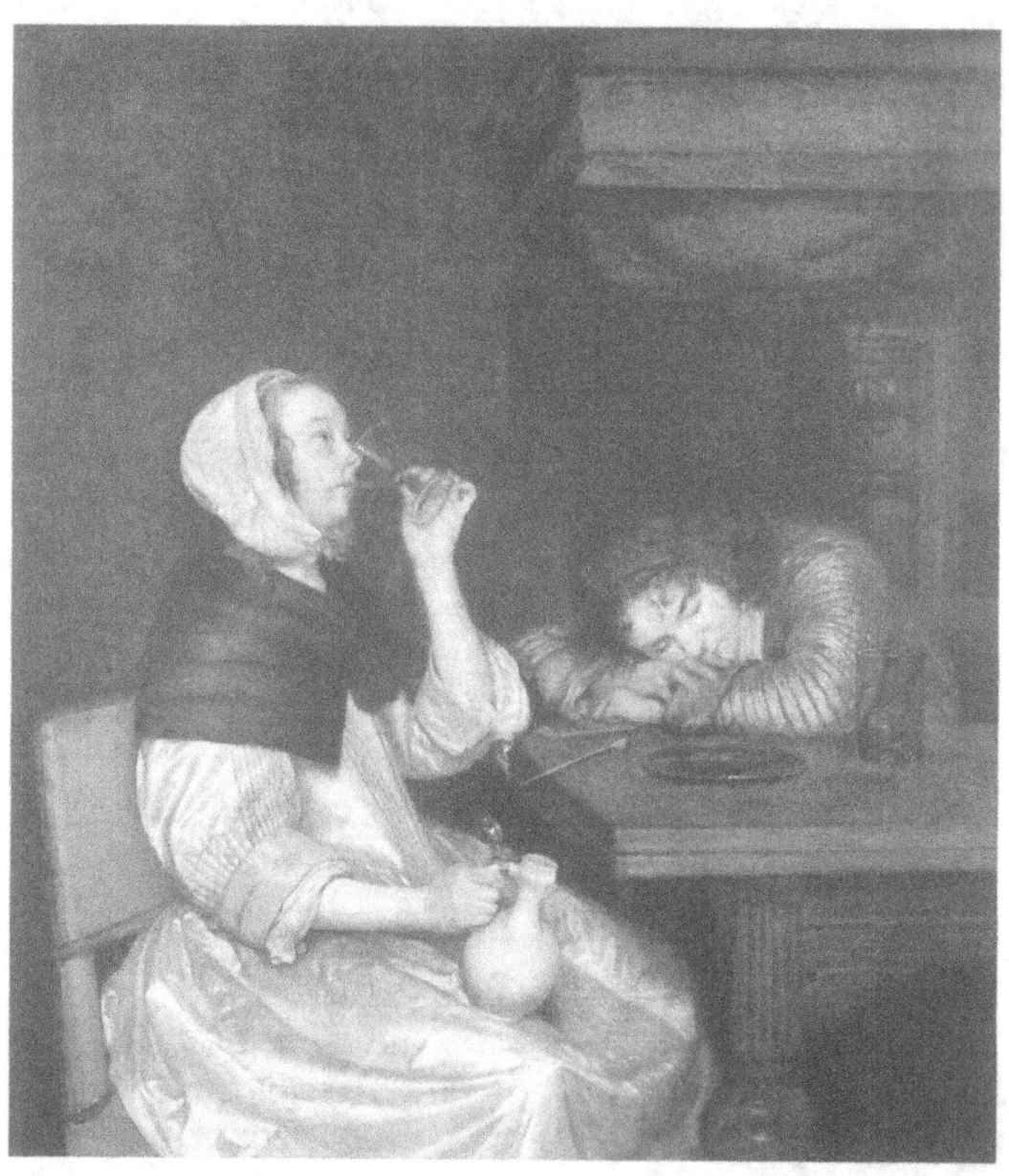

FIGURE 14. Gerard ter Borch, *Drinking Maid with Sleeping Soldier*. Private Collection.

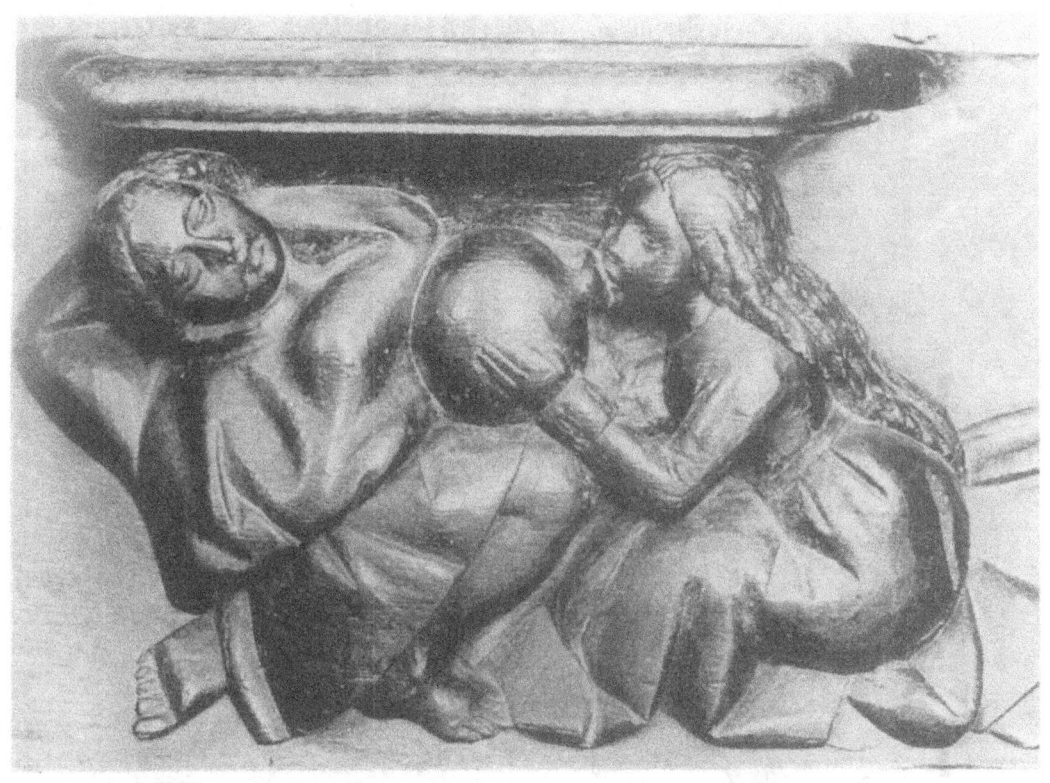

FIGURE 15. Anonymous, *Dissipation*.
Misericord (from Kraus and Kraus 1975).
Church of St.-Pierre, Saumur.

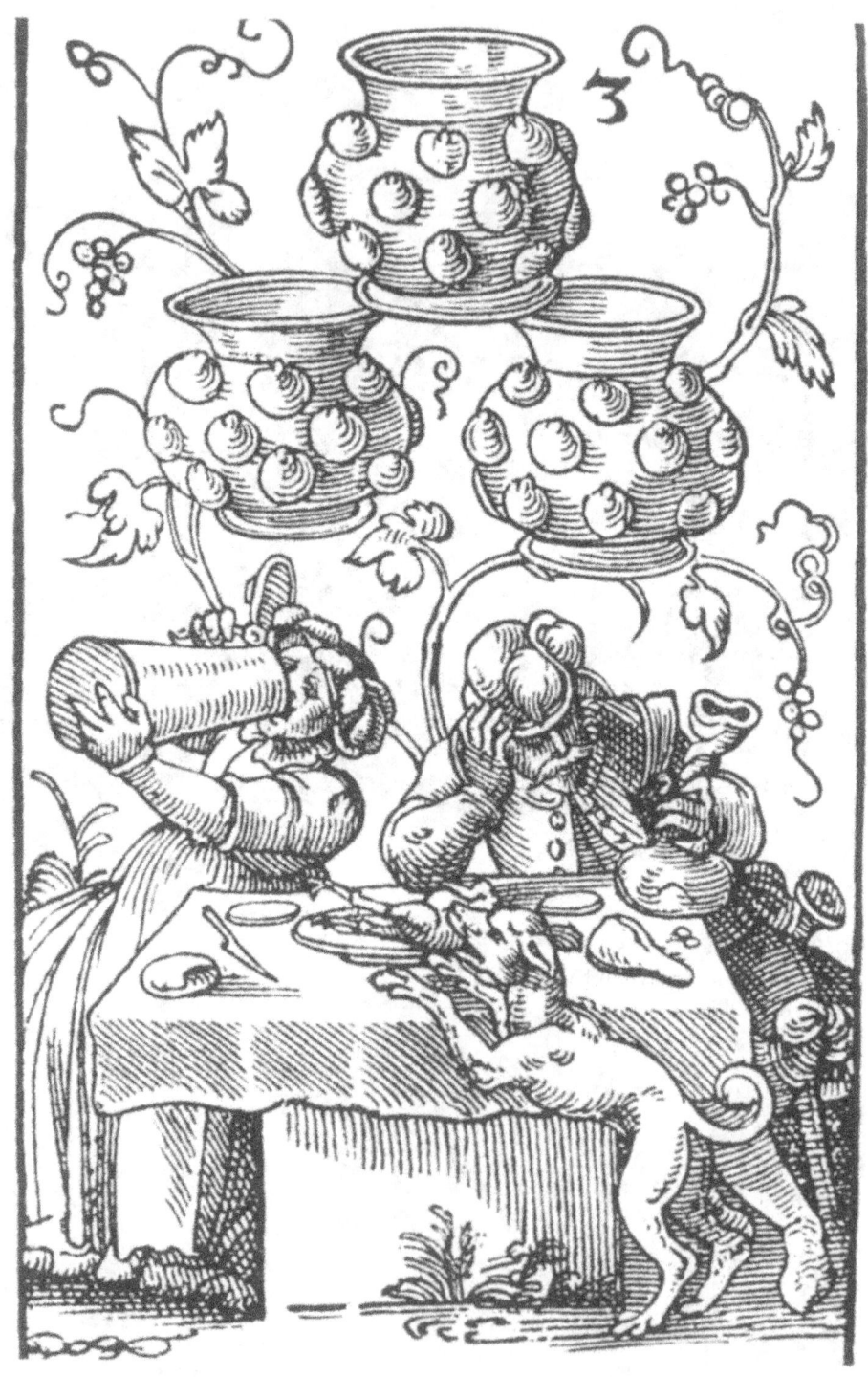

FIGURE 16. Jost Amman, *Kartenspielbuch.*
1588. Photograph by author.

FIGURE 17. German
School, *Melencolious.*
From *Augsburg Calendar.*
Woodcut. Metropolitan
Museum of Art, Harris
Brisbane Dick Fund,
1926 (26.56.1), New York.

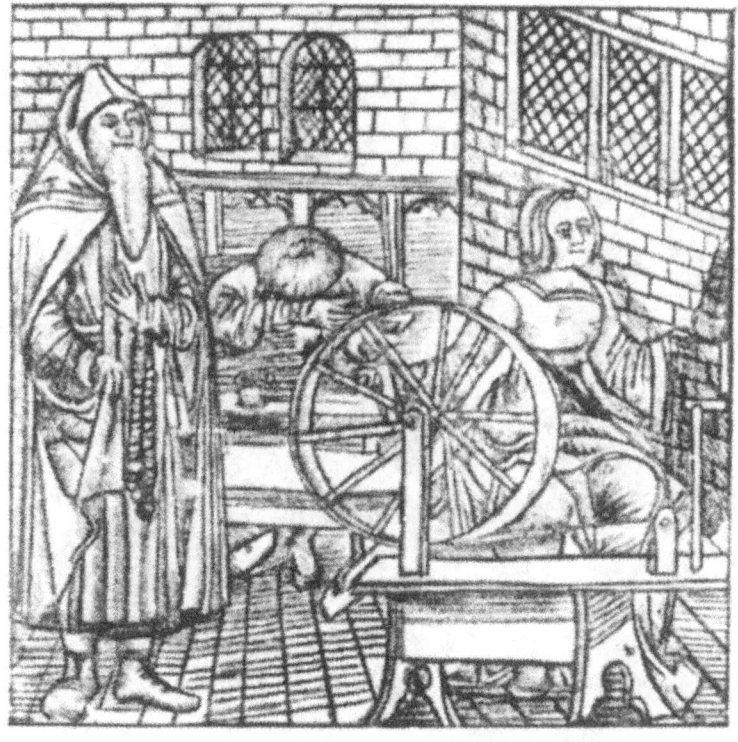

FIGURE 18. Anonymous,
The Lustful Monk (from
Fuchs 1909). Photograph
by author.

Die fromme huszmagt.

Ir Hauszmägt sond hie mercken eben/
wend ir verdienen ewigs lebén.
Nemen von aller buszmagt leer/
So überkumpt ir gůt vnd eer.

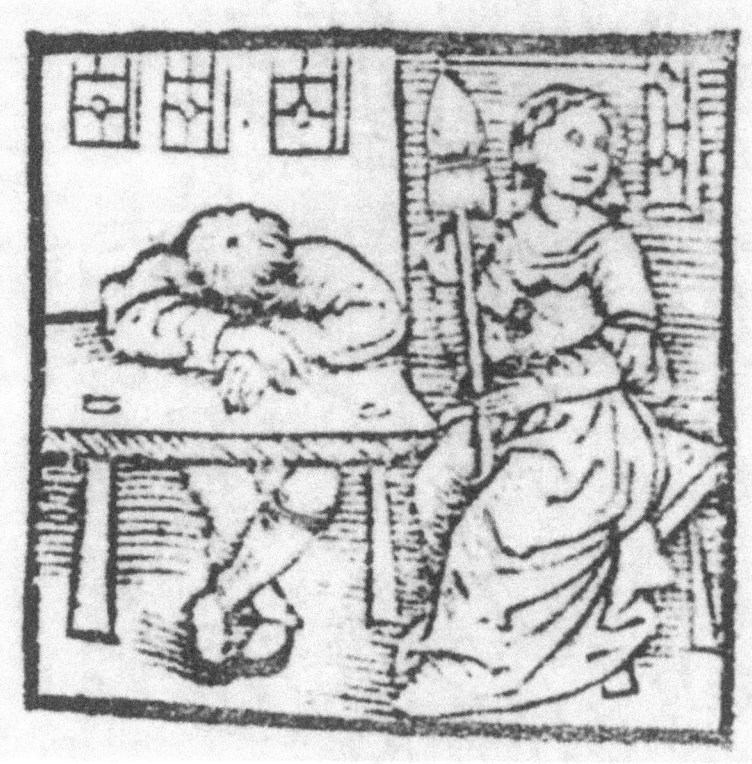

FIGURE 19. Anonymous, *Die Fromme Hausmagd* (from Spamer 1970). Photograph by author.

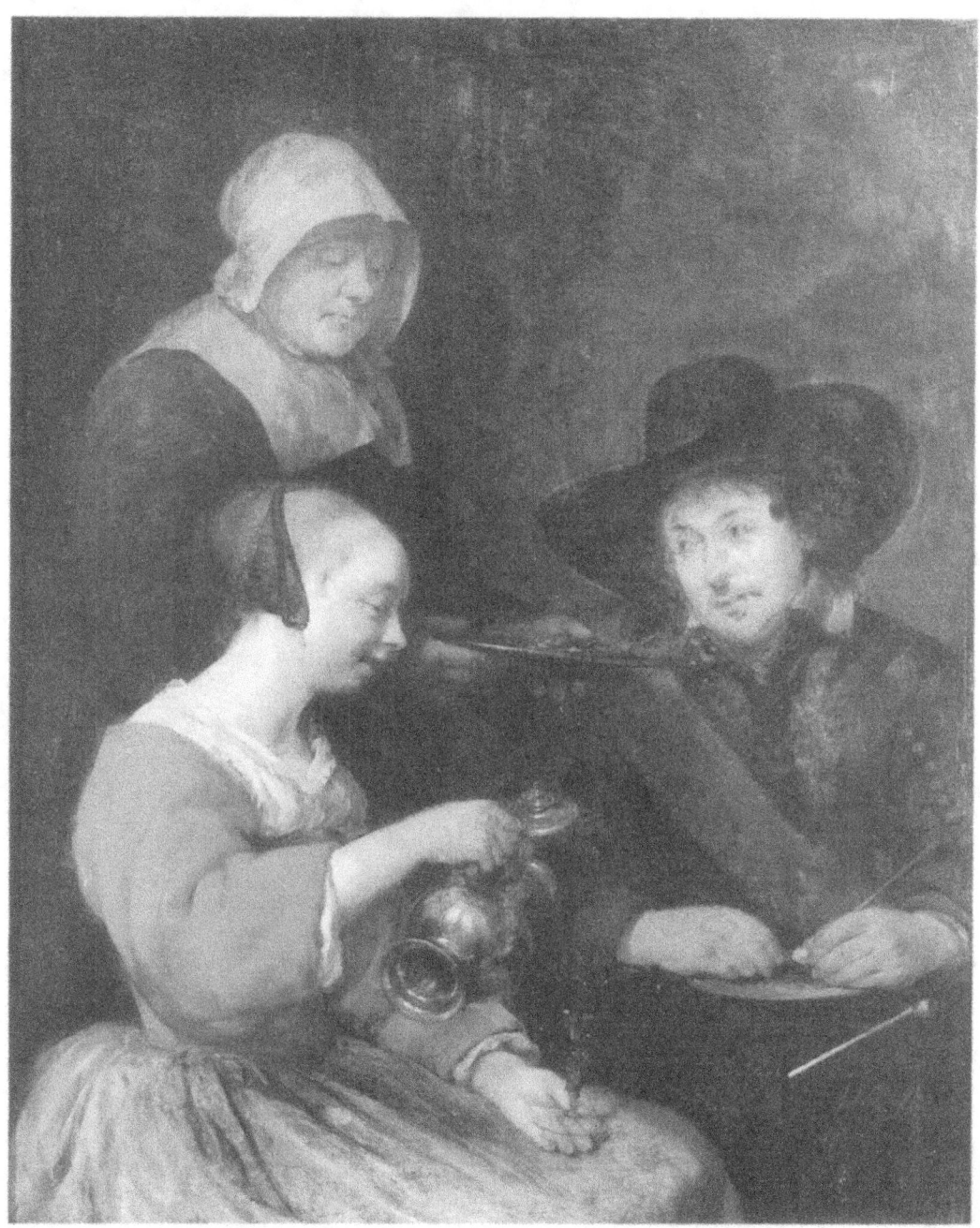

FIGURE 20. Gerard ter Borch, *Woman
Pouring Wine.* Brooklyn Museum of Art,
Gift of the Friedsam Executors through the
Metropolitan Museum of Art., 34.494.

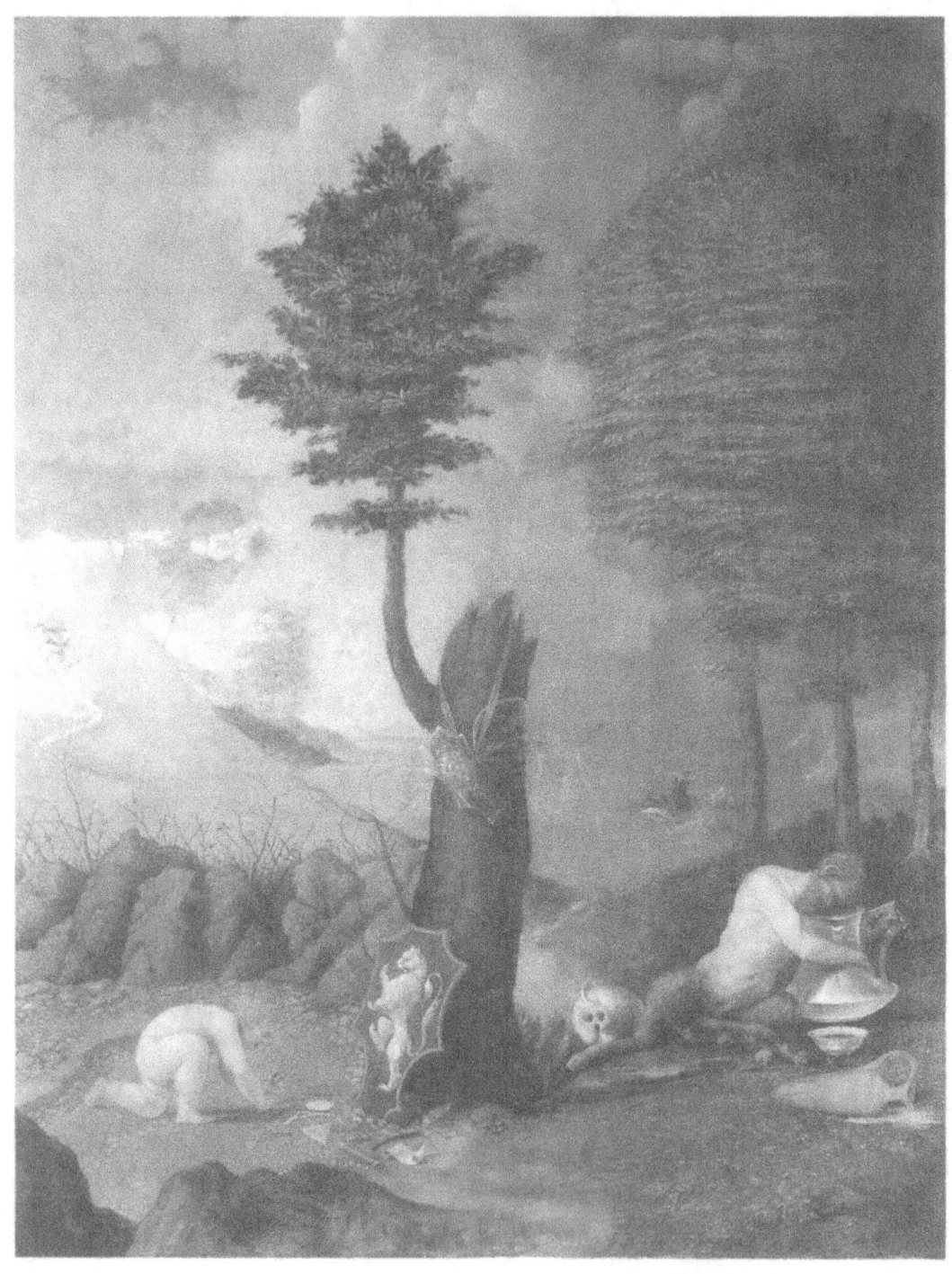

FIGURE 21. Lorenzo Lotto, *Allegory of Virtue and Vice*. National Gallery of Art, Samuel H. Kress Collection, Washington, DC.

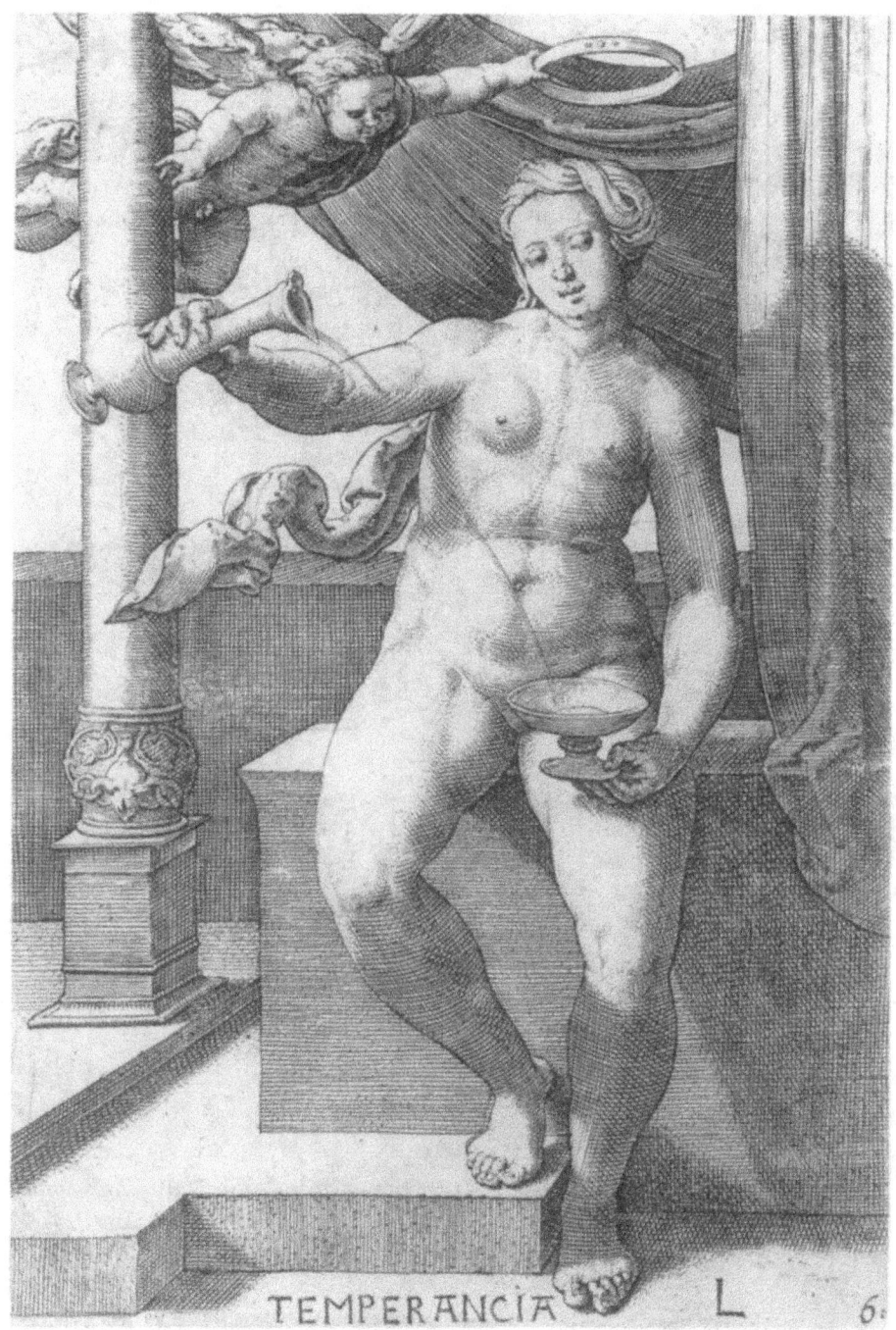

TEMPERANCIA   L   6:

FIGURE 22. Lucas van Leyden, *Temperancia.*
Metropolitan Museum of Art, The Elisha
Whittelsey Collection. The Elisha Whittelsey
Fund, 1957, New York.

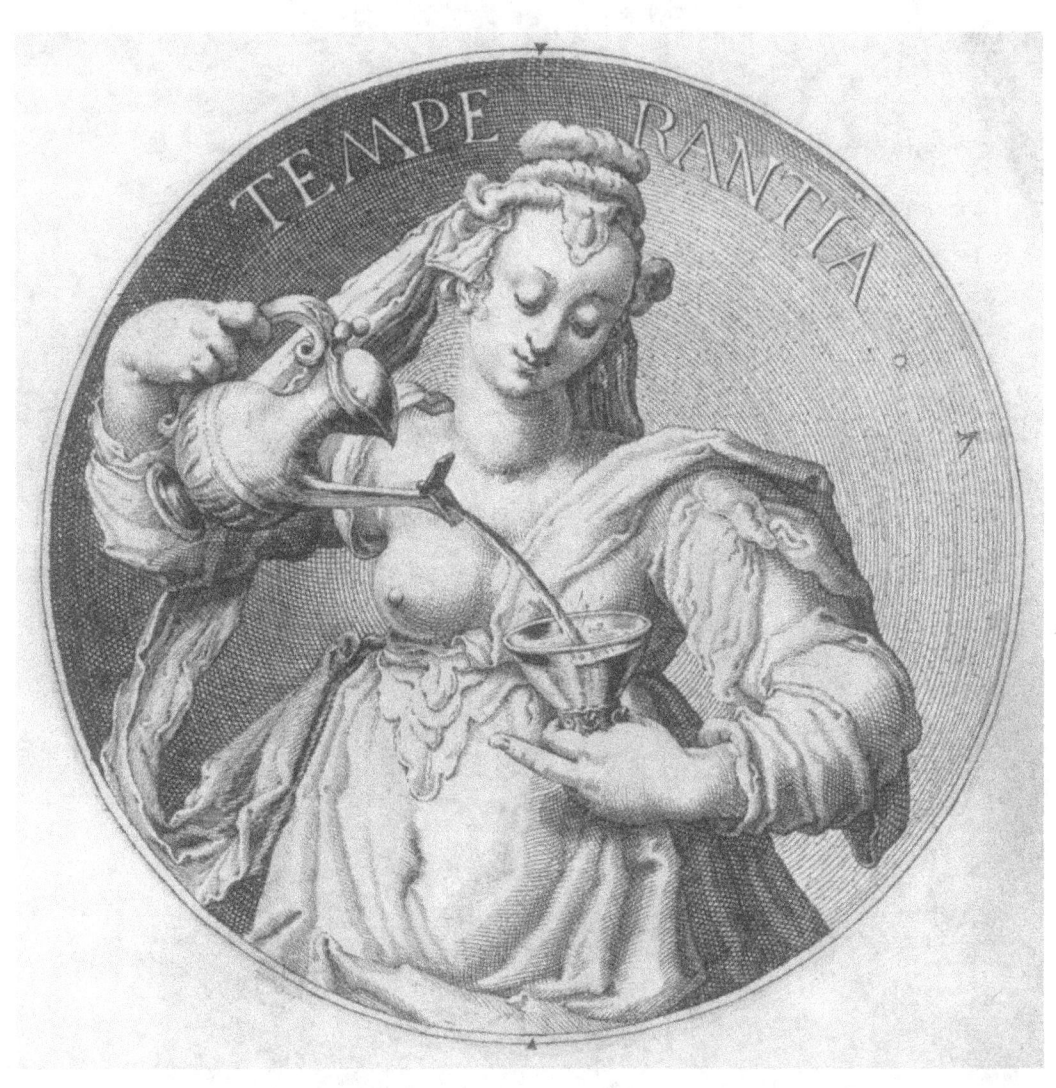

FIGURE 23. Jacob de Gheyn II, *Temperantia.*
Rijksmuseum, Amsterdam.

II.

ABVSVS TRISTITIAM, VSVS VOLVPTATEM PARIT.

Si oculus tuus fuerit simplex, totum corpus tuum luci-
dum erit: si autem oculus tuus fuerit nequam,
totum corpus tuum tenebrosum erit.

Matth. 6, 22.

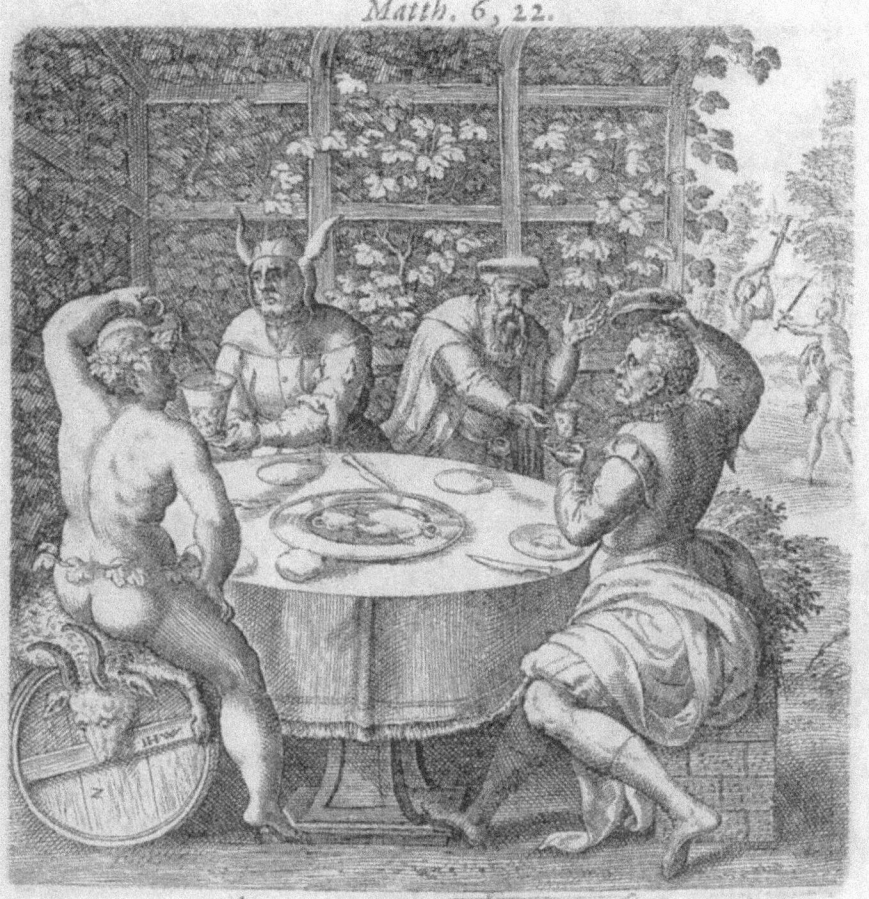

Diuitiis locuples Dominum collaudat Iobus,
Oppressus pleno laudat & ore Deum.
Vtilis in cunctis pietas est : omnia puris
Pura, sed impuris sunt malè pura nimis.

QVID

FIGURE 24. Jan Wierix, "Abuse breeds sadness,
proper use, pleasure." From D. V. Coornhert,
Recht ghebruyck ende misbruyck van tijdelijcke have,
1585. Spencer Collection, New York Public Library,
Astor, Lenox and Tilden Foundations, New York.

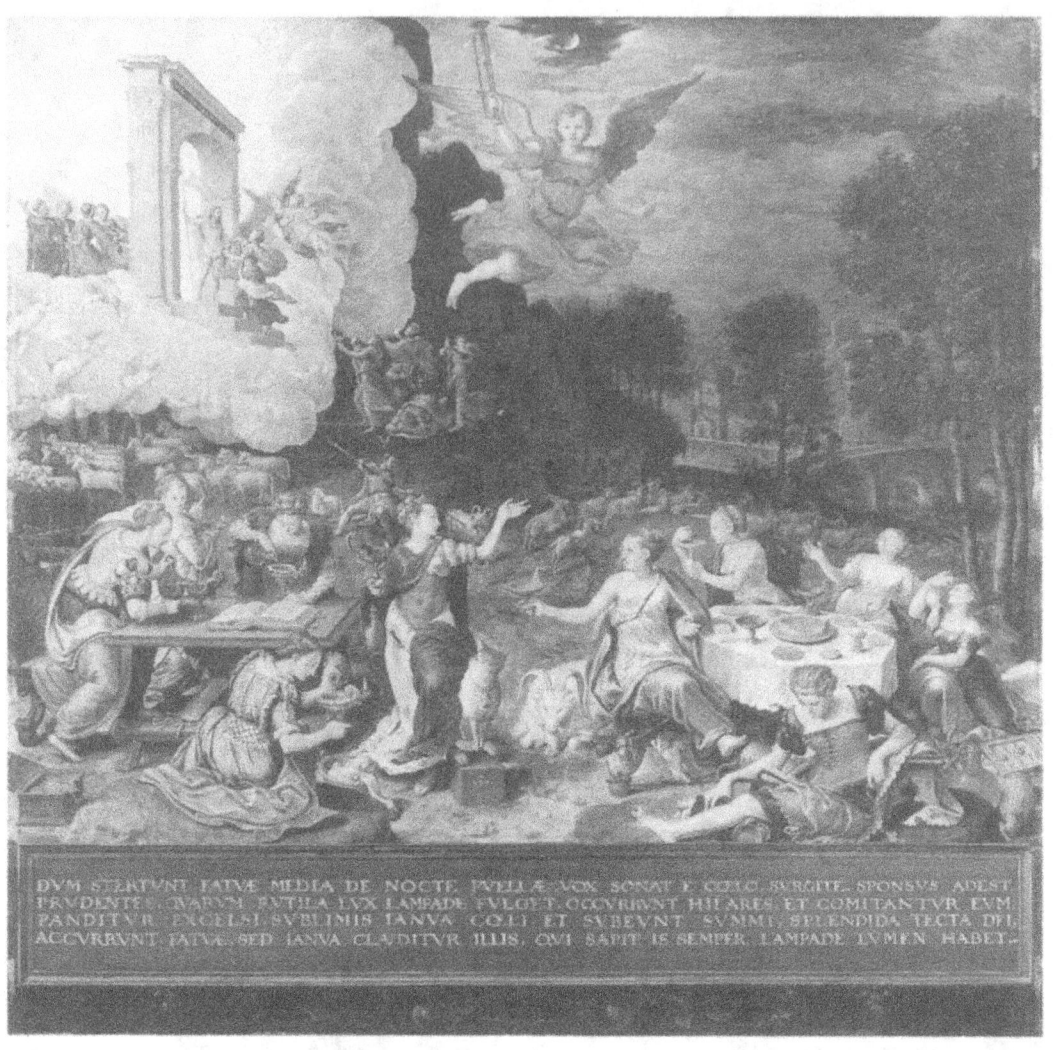

FIGURE 25. Hans Ewoutsz., *The Wise and Foolish Virgins*. Royal Museum, Copenhagen.

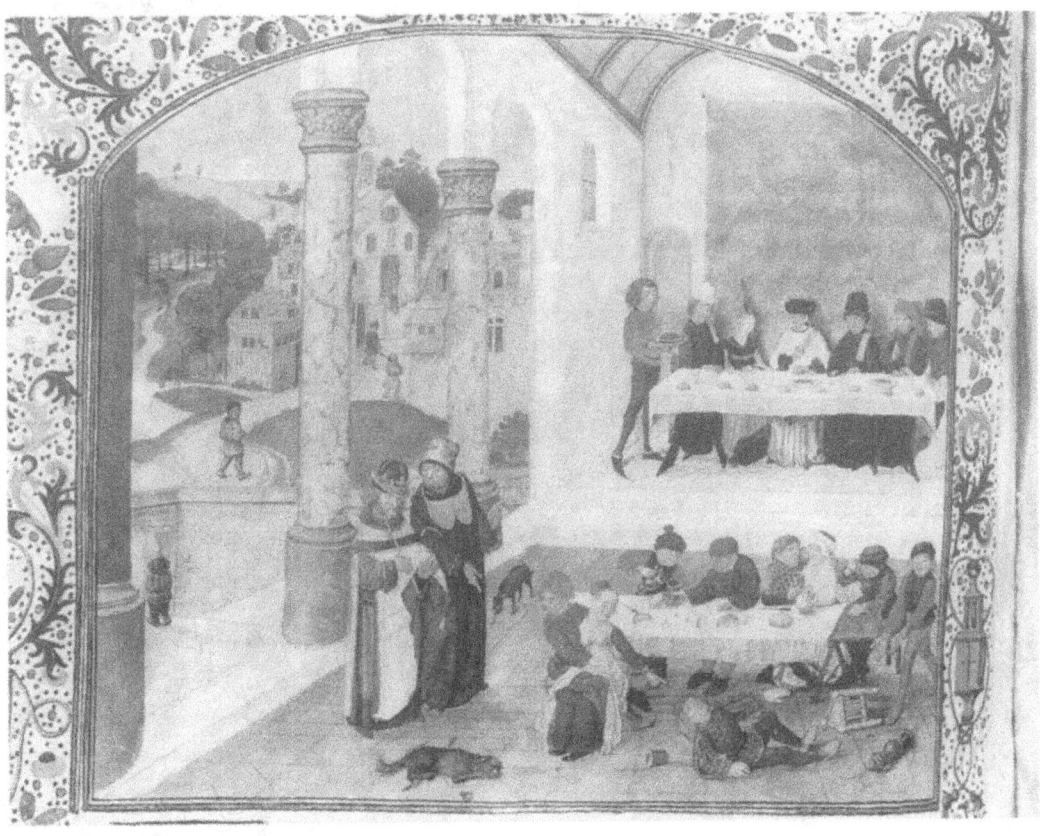

FIGURE 26. Flemish school, *Tables of the Moderates and Immoderates.* From fifteenth-century edition of *Valerius Maximus.* Universitätsbibliothek, Leipzig.

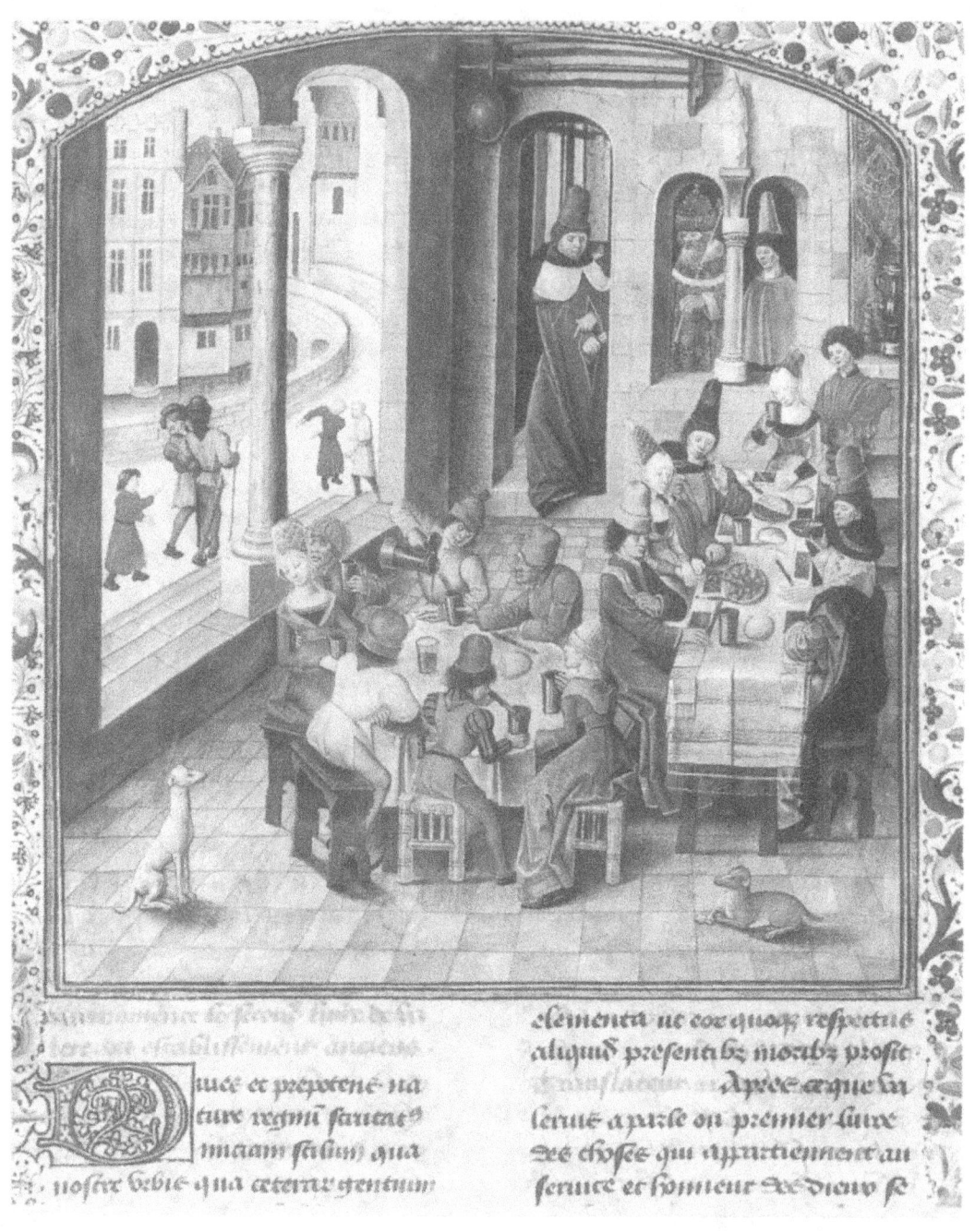

FIGURE 27. Flemish school, *Tables of the Moderates and Immoderates.* From fifteenth-century edition of *Valerius Maximus.* Staatsbibliothek zu Berlin, Preussischer Kulturbesitz, Handschriftenabteilung, Berlin.

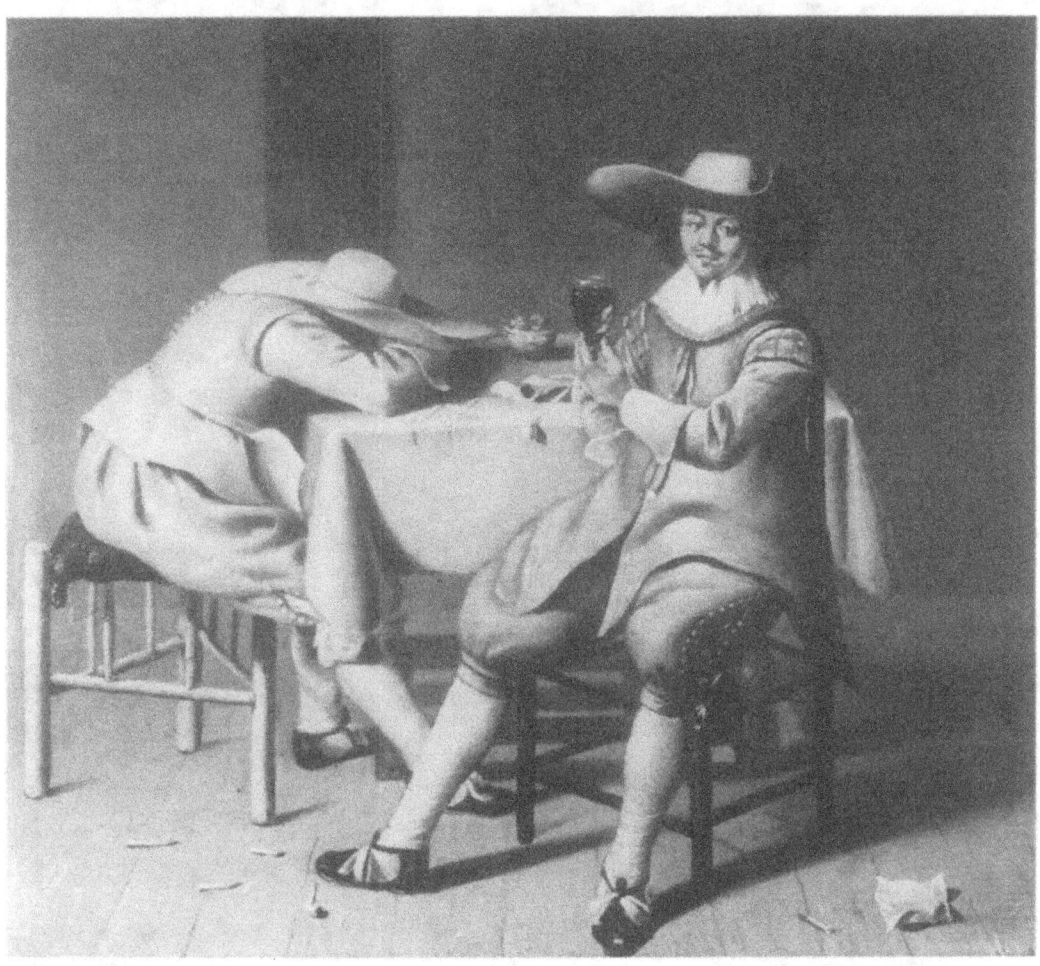

FIGURE 28. Jan Olis, *Two Men at a Table.*
Location unknown. Photograph from the
Rijksbureau voor Kunsthistorische Documentatie,
The Hague / The Netherlands.

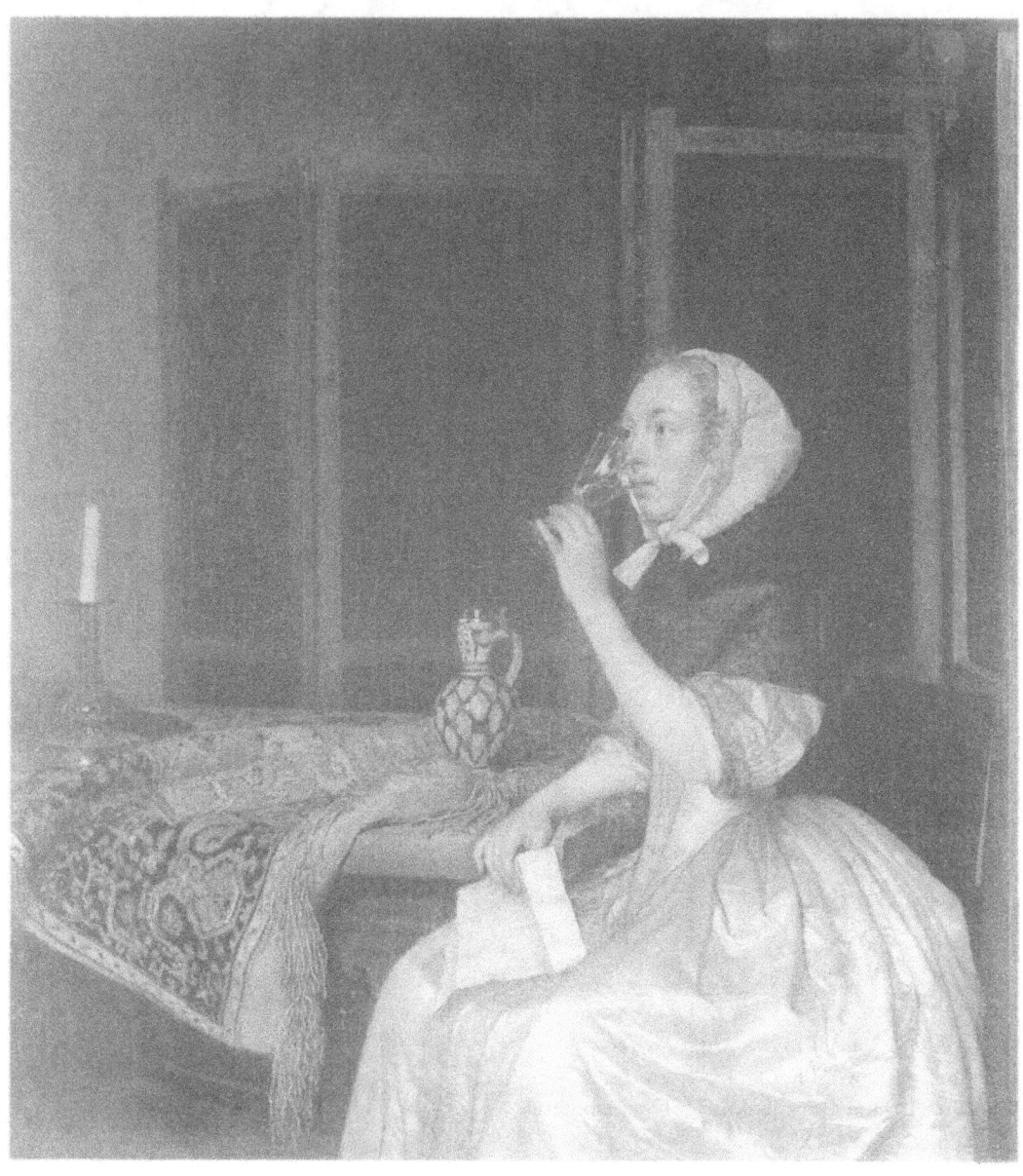

FIGURE 29. Gerard ter Borch, *Woman Reading a Letter*. Sinebrychoff Art Museum. Photograph by Central Art Archives, Helsinki.

3

Pendants and Meaning Making in the Paintings of Gerard ter Borch

By the time the Dutch painter Gerard ter Borch began his career, most of the important categories of genre painting had already been well established.[1] Among the most popular was the *cortegaerdje*, or guardroom scene. Its earliest forms had been developed by the Amsterdam painters Pieter Codde and Willem Duyster in the 1620s.[2] Further, the subject had been modernized and given new meaningful and moral implications in the 1630s by the Utrecht artist Jacob Duck.[3] Ter Borch's earliest paintings of this subject, which date from the late 1630s and early 1640s, run the full gamut of types previously developed in this tradition, from the descriptive ambience of Codde's work to the more self-referential, didactic guardrooms by Duck. His personal contribution to the cortegaerdje genre came shortly after his return to Holland from Germany, where he had contributed to the documentation of the Peace of Munster of 1648. An analysis of Ter Borch's strategic moves in transforming the guardroom tradition is useful because it sheds light not only on his own particular artistic progress but also on the broader issues of the changing nature of Dutch genre painting after mid-century, which in turn both reflected and shaped the changing terms of Dutch social life in general.

These issues come into particular focus through the examination of Ter Borch's two sets of pendants or companion paintings made in the decade from 1650 to 1660.[4] Two of these paintings (one from each set) share an essentially similar composition, a shallow interior space with two half-length figures, a drinking maid and a sleeping soldier, seated at a table (figs. 13 and 14). The earlier of the two is in the Fabre Museum in Montpellier, and the later one is in a private collection.[5] In both, the figures are organized on opposite sides of the table, which provides the primary spatial definition in each painting. The figures are identified by their costumes as soldier and maid, and the setting is an inn or tavern by implication.

On many levels these paintings offer a point of departure from the conventional guardroom depiction. Their intimate interior setting, their close-up views, and the condensation achieved by the reduction to a single couple are among their most innovative features. The minimalized visual language of Ter Borch's paintings calls for a different kind of interpretative spectator response than the more expansive multifigured narratives by Codde or Duyster. Jacob Duck's painting in Cambridge of about 1635 that depicts a soldier and a laughing girl seated around a table in a room with a window comes closest to the Ter Borch in composition.[6] Yet Ter Borch's figures are clearly more normative, less caricatured; they are conceived more realistically, and their relationships appear more "natural."

Even more than their compositions, the activity of the figures in Ter Borch's paintings appears, at first glance, to be virtually identical. In both, a young couple is shown to have consumed large quantities of wine and tobacco. Their excess is accentuated by the passed-out state of the soldier while his female partner, on the other hand, continues to outdrink her mate.

Ter Borch's paintings are richer and more complex than the guardroom tradition he inherited because they participate in and make reference to a broad range of northern European pictorial tropes. Generally, they belong to the endemically popular theme of a drunken company, a subject treated with tremendous humor in Netherlandish art of the sixteenth and seventeenth centuries.[7] And within that genre they even more specifically participate in those images that play on the humorous inversion of established gender stereotypes where the man is drunk under the table by his female partner. Just how long this joke had been told visually is indicated by the fifteenth-century sculpted misericord from the Church of St.-Pierre in Saumur (fig. 15).[8] Again with a minimum of means the early sculpture brilliantly illustrates a sprawling drunken couple and the humor implicit in the juxtaposition of a woman who continues to drink with gusto while her male companion is already far beyond his limits. Their instability and the inebriation that is its cause are figured through the seesaw composition as the bodies of the couple are visually joined by a large round jug the woman brings to her lips.

This joke is represented again in the sophisticated and very influential *Kartenspielbuch* of 1588, by Jost Amman (fig. 16).[9] Amman's engraving once again emphasizes the humor of the situation by exaggerating the large size of the woman's beer mug, one that she hoists heftily to her mouth. Her partner has fallen asleep while holding his moneybags with one hand and supporting his head with the other. The joke on them is further elaborated by the popular motif of a dog, who takes advantage of their drunken state and steals the roast from the plate before them.[10] Characteristically, the text above and below the image mixes humor with a commonplace moral. The German text below the print reads:

Weil herr und frau sein voll und blind
Vom Wein: Schau jr best haussgesind
Der hund / so auch sein theil wil han /
Dest braten huns sich masset an.
Derwegen sich nur niemand wunder /
Dass gross Reichthumb offt gehet under:
Was ihm der herr schetzt sein gerecht /
Dem will auch folgen nach der Knecht.[11]

The text and image express that a life of excess without moderation will inevitably lead to the dissipation of worldly goods and ultimate ruin. This "message" had an endemic popularity in the sixteenth and seventeenth centuries, and certainly both of Ter Borch's paintings can be understood as part of its discursive proliferation.

Viewed in this way, the misericord, Amman's print, and Ter Borch's paintings communicate on the level of the well-established medieval paradigm of narrative exempla, in this case negative exempla.[12] And it is this aspect of Ter Borch's work that is most frequently offered as the explanation of its singular "meaning."[13] Without discarding it as at least contributing to some part of the images' effect, we can go further in our understanding of this complex image by situating it within other Netherlandish visual conventions and paradigms. In this way subtler levels of nuance and meaning for the knowledgeable historical viewer are gained when the paintings are placed in the scheme of other traditions.

One such tradition connects Ter Borch through a formal rather than a strictly iconographic typology. Indeed, his compositions have several important formal prototypes found in the realm of popular imagery of the fifteenth and sixteenth centuries. For example, an arrangement identical to Ter Borch's can be found as early as 1480 as an illustration of *Melancholia*, one of the four humors from the *Augsburg Calendar* (fig. 17).[14] This woodcut shares all the same essential compositional components with Ter Borch's paintings; a woman and a man organized around a table set in a shallow stagelike space, with the woman on our side and the man at the far side, sleeping on folded arms with his head on the table. In the distribution of the figures on opposite sides of the table, and especially by putting the woman on our side of it, this work is even closer to Ter Borch than the similar composition by Jost Amman discussed above.

Genrelike representations with the remarkably successful conceit of figures seated around three sides of a table as an organizing device—with the outer side of the table open to the viewer to produce the effect of his/her inclusion in the fictive space—are ubiquitous in Western culture. They can be found from the early-fifteenth-century book illustrations through to Cezanne's *Card Players* and are even common in contemporary television sitcom scenarios. Within this history the formulation of the figures seated around a table with a woman on our side stands out as exceptional. This, together with the reduction to a single heterosexual couple, brings these examples together as related.

Yet unlike the drunkenness that is figured with this conceit in Ter Borch, Panofsky's research on Albrecht Dürer has shown this print and another very similar one (fig. 18) to be expressions of the related human trait of sloth and sluggishness, which was associated with the melancholic humor.[15] That the sleeping man is an expression of slothfulness is clear; the woman, however, is shown to be slothful in a more convoluted way. She "turns away," physically as metaphorically, from her duty, which is figured as her spinning.

This formulaic composition was, however, not confined to exclusive use as the representation of sloth or melancholia or drunkenness. It recurs at least once more as an illustration in the 1520 edition of a popular German religious tract, *Die Fromme Hausmagd* (fig. 19).[16] This fascinating literary exempla, one that was reprinted innumerable times, takes us through the average day of a highly religious maid who experiences and re-experiences the trials of Christ as she enacts her daily chores. Thus, for example, when she makes dinner, she experiences the Lord's Last Supper; when she puts out new linens, she sees Christ's face on the cloth of St. Veronica; and so on.[17] Oddly, although the woodcut does account for the positive image of the woman required by the text, since it shows her now actively engaged in her work, there is no textual explanation for the man who is asleep there. His presence can be explained only by the practical fact that he was part of a woodcut that was available to the publisher as a stock image. The suitability of this print was *sufficient*, even if it was not perfect, for the specific text needing an illustration.

In each of these printed cases the popular composition of a sleeping man and seated woman became appropriate, that is, took on specific meaning, only in direct relationship to the printed text presented in conjunction with it. Newly created markets for printed images and printed texts sprung up with such rapidity in the sixteenth century that often the two were paired in what seems to us today somewhat spurious and generic ways.[18] The restrictive expectations of a patron's specific and controlled meaning heretofore characteristic of works of art were not applicable to these new circumstances.

The same kind of flexible, more playful attitude toward any given configured meaning was structured into the subjects of Ter Borch's paintings as well. This was accomplished through his working process and mostly through his use of pendants or companion paintings as a structure that provided the defining frames of reference. Among the strong innovative qualities of Ter Borch's works is the way he allowed meaning to be constructed by occasion-specific circumstances. Just as the earlier woodcuts took on meaning in a case-by-case situation, Ter Borch's couple told a different story, depending on the pendant they were matched with.[19] Further, and at least partially as a consequence of his work, this more flexible, playful attitude can be found as a characteristic in Dutch genre painting in general after 1650. This insight speaks to the current debate about meaning per se of Dutch genre paintings and helps to clarify the fact that neither do these paintings exhibit a loss or "erosion" of meaning, as it has been referred to, nor do they continue to present that meaning in the same way after mid-century. Rather, the very notion of meaning itself has been altered.[20]

The Montpellier painting was planned from its inception as one half of a pair. Its pendant is now in the Brooklyn Museum (fig. 20).[21] The two paintings, treated as pendants by Gudlaugsson, have the same dimensions, date from the same time on stylistic grounds, and have matching, complementary compositions. Both paintings have the same minimized background and present three quarter-length figures. Most markedly the female figure in both is dressed similarly and represents mirrored images of the same model, a woman usually identified as Gesina ter Borch, the artist's sister.[22] In each case she holds a decanter (the same one) and a stemmed wine glass. She is absorbed in her activity and smiles to herself, giving the two paintings an air of levity and good humor.

Iconographically, the complementary aspects of the Montpellier painting and the Brooklyn Museum painting as mirror images articulate a meaningful polarity. Although the woman in both of these paintings may seem to the modern eye to be preoccupied with, if not the exact same, at least very similar activities, to the seventeenth-century Dutch eye their activities stood for diametrically opposed concepts. The Montpellier painting shows the woman tipping her decanter toward her so that she can better peer into it. This gesture was a well-known literary and artistic convention that signified the habitual drinker, the lush or tippler.[23] Such a person was called then, as today, a *kannekijker*, which is to say, literally, "one who looks into the can," in order to determine whether or not a last drop can be wrung from the empty vessel. Examples of the kannekijker abound in sixteenth- and seventeenth-century paintings of so-called *Merry Companies*, where the convention could easily set the tone of the picture with wit and humor. These associations also made "kannekijker" eminently suitable as a *shimpnaem* (nickname) for the infamous Rederijkers, the local theatrical groups whose popular street plays and rowdy personal reputations gave special meaning to the rhyme "Rederijker: Kannekijker."[24] Although the kannekijker was usually male, as he is in several paintings by Adriaen Brouwer and Jan Miense Molenaer,[25] women have also been portrayed this way, for instance in Joachim Beuckelaer's *Inn Scene* (1563), which hangs in the Royal Museum of Fine Arts in Antwerp.

One of the earliest appearances of the motif, the allegory by Lorenzo Lotto (fig. 21) of 1505, in the National Gallery of Art, Washington, depicts a gluttonous satyr in the act of "looking in the can," on one side of a divided composition.[26] The split composition of Lotto's painting structures meaning in essentially the same way that a pair of pendants does; indeed, this painting provides us with a close visual parallel to Ter Borch's work discussed here.

As a kannekijker, the woman in Ter Borch's Montpellier painting was rendered a particularly appropriate mate for the drunken and passed-out mercenary soldier on the other side of the table. They belong together as "birds of a feather," or, in Dutch terms, they confirm the proverb "gelijk bij gelijk" (like with like).[27] As fictive "types" they stand outside the constraints of normal society and are given license to act in ways that upstanding citizens could enjoy only vicariously.

The couple of the pendant also represents birds of a feather. Their character is most evident in the woman of Ter Borch's Brooklyn Museum painting. She is, despite immediate appearances, performing an activity that is actually diametrically opposite to that of her mirrored counterpart. She is pouring into her glass, an act that also had strong conventional iconographic implications. She would have been recognized by the seventeenth-century Dutch viewer as part of the tradition for representing the cardinal virtue of temperance or moderation, which had been represented thus since at least the eleventh century.[28] The conceit stems from classical antiquity, where the custom of tempering alcoholic intake by diluting wine with water was common.[29] The representation of "Temperance" figured in this way was popularized in northern Europe during the sixteenth century in emblematic prints and paintings. The specifics of distinguishing both liquids to convey the idea was not always insisted on, as can be seen in a variety of prints of "Temperantia" by, for example, Lucas van Leyden (fig. 22) and Jacob de Gheyn II (fig. 23), which date from the beginning of the sixteenth century and the beginning of the seventeenth century, respectively.

It is clear here that, contrary to the prevailing knee-jerk art-historical interpretation of images of drinking as pejorative, attitudes toward wine in the period under discussion were neither automatically nor exclusively negative. In the early modern period sin or censure came specifically with overindulgence rather than simply imbibing per se. In fact, the belief that drinking some wine actually had a positive physical and social value is expressed again and again in numerous sixteenth- and seventeenth-century emblem books. As early as 1553 we find these verses with an illustration:

En un repas boire un coup, est louable:
Boire deux foys, est besoing: troup, plaisir:
Quatre foys boire, est fureur detestable:
Tout le surplus est honte et deplaisir.[30]

Similarly, Laurentius Haechtanus expresses the benefits of wine taken in moderation in *Parvvs Mundus*, published in Antwerp in 1579, which begins, "Wein recht gebraucht / Das gfelt Gott auch"[31] [Wine properly used / This pleases God too]. In the middle of his poem he writes, "Wieso den Durst viel besser lischt etwa / der Wein mit Wasser gmischt"[32] [He who wishes to quench his thirst / Will mix wine with a bit of water]. Nicolaus Taurellus's *Emblemata Physico-Ethnico hoc est Naturae Morum*, published in Nuremberg in 1595, comes close to Ter Borch's pendants in spirit when he writes:

Der Genuss, den der Natur (des Menschen) an sich sehr angenehm ist,
Schadet, wenn er allzu sehr ubertrieben wird.
Aber guter Wein, der ein wenig zu reichlich getrunken wird schadet nicht.
Wann immer Reichtum, Ehre und Freunde gefallen,
Gefallt auch korperliche Kraft, Schonheit und bluhendes Aussehen.
Du solltst nur wissen, dass das, was nutzt, ebenso schaden kann.
Denn in Guten is Schlechtes und im Schlechten Gutes.[33]

The point of these verses is clearly that it is the abuse of wine taken in excess that is to be avoided, not wine itself.

Ter Borch's juxtaposition of these two paintings can now be seen within a certain paradigm as the contrast of temperate and intemperate behavior. And although the binary format of the pendants relates to the medieval structure of contrasting cardinal virtues with cardinal vices, and more specifically Temperantia and Gula, civility rather than sin is at issue here.

Interestingly, this is also the point of the comparison made in the previously mentioned painting by Lorenzo Lotto, an interpretation whose specifics have escaped notice until now. There, the putto who occupies the side of the painting opposite the drunken satyr acts as a contrast. He holds a compass and is at work measuring; that is, he is performing acts of regulation and control. *Misura* as temperance, announced as early as 1359 by Brunetto Latini, is found on Andrea Orcagna's tabernacle of Or San Michele, where she appears also holding a pair of compasses.[34] These had been commonly included among the signs of temperance in medieval and Renaissance imagery including Pieter Bruegel's large print of the subject.[35] Thus, within the same panel Lotto effectively contrasts corresponding virtue and vice, temperance and gluttony, a compelling binary that, as I have said, had been in use throughout the medieval period.[36]

Many works structured around this binary were produced between the time of the painting by Lotto and those by Ter Borch. A theatrical figure joins a mythological figure to convey the same opposition in Bernard Gebraud Furmer's *De rerum usu et abusu*, published in Antwerp in 1575 and subsequently translated from Latin to Dutch by Dirck Coornhert as *Recht ghebruyck ende misbruyck van tijdelicke have*.[37] The book describes with image and text the proper and improper way to behave in company. Jan Wierix's illustrations include one of interest to us here of a strange foursome seated at a table (fig. 24). The two men to the left relate exclusively to each other, as do the two men to the right. The scene is no ordinary "merry company," since the figure in the left foreground is Bacchus himself, who sits almost nude on a large barrel and is handed an enormous glass of wine by a man in a fool's costume. The couple on the right is clearly more formal. They are dressed in contemporary gentlemanly attire, the glass exchanged between them is decorously small, and the man in the foreground politely tips his hat. In this context Bacchus and the fool play out the role of gluttonous behavior comparable to Ter Borch's soldier and maid in the Montpellier painting. The two gentlemen at the right correspond to the polite company of man, woman, and servant in the Brooklyn Museum painting.

A sixteenth-century example of contrasting virtue and vice that has particular relevance for Ter Borch for its emphasis on women is Hans Ewoutsz.'s painting of *The Wise and Foolish Virgins*, in the Royal Museum in Copenhagen (fig. 25). Aside from the fact that the wise virgins are represented as pouring (albeit they are pouring oil to keep their lamps filled) and the foolish virgins are represented as overindulging in drink and sleep, Ewoutsz.'s painting sheds light on Ter Borch's imagery through its formal distribution of right and wrong. The wise virgins occupy the right field of the painting, and the foolish virgins occupy the painting's left field. The artistic convention of placing the more positive subject in the right field and the lesser one in the left field was a visual means to assign value through "dexter/sinister" differentiation, a convention once again established as early as classical antiquity.[38] It manifested itself throughout the medieval period in Christian iconography and in courtly heraldry.[39]

The convention survived through the seventeenth century not only in such religious subjects as the wise and foolish Virgins but, significantly for Ter Borch, also in the more contemporary genre of the guardroom scene. It is, for example, the structure utilized by Jacob Duck in the 1630s in his *Call to Arms*, now in the Minneapolis Institute of Arts, as one of the many instances in his art where older religious conventions are reworked and modernized to express secular concerns.[40] The contrast in the Minneapolis painting may be seen as that of the "good" soldiers on the right, beautifully uniformed and ready for action, with the "bad" mercenaries on the left, drunk and slothful.[41]

These paintings address an area of concern that may best be called social decorum. Culturally they operate in the realm of the so-called civilizing process, bringing into a coherent visual program positive and negative social behavior that has bearing on class status.[42] Notions of social propriety and decorum were concerns of great importance for the upwardly mobile Dutch middle class, who, no doubt, viewed these paintings as confirmation of proper behavior and as the affirmation of class status.

The amazing and prodigious fifteenth-century illustrations for the *Facta et Dicta Memorabilia Romanorum*, written by Valerius Maximus in the first century A.D., are among the earliest overt visual expressions of these concerns. The manuscript was copied, translated, and illustrated many times from the thirteenth through the sixteenth century.[43] The illustrations made in the Netherlands in the mid-fifteenth century introduced at least two sets of images remarkable for their prophetic characterizations of social decorum as a function of class.[44] The eating scenes from the manuscripts in Leipzig and Berlin depict a meal of civil and disorderly companies quite unrealistically convened in the same room but at different tables (figs. 26 and 27). Their relevance here is clear in the contrast they provide of table manners "in bono" and "in malo." In both the Valerius Maximus illustrations and Ter Borch's pendants the works establish characteristics for negative social stereotyping, the peasant in the case of the former, the mercenary in the case of the latter. The fifteenth-century terms for the stereotyping go further still in the contrast of styles used to portray peasant and aristocrat. The upper-class characters are idealized and undisturbed by any display of emotion. Moreover, the shape of the tables themselves and the disposition of the figures around them differ in accordance with the activity figured by them. Significantly, the table of the orderly company is open on the side of the viewer, inviting access and participation, whereas the figures of the disorderly table are placed all around it, leaving no open access to the viewer.

As a final precursor to Ter Borch the small painting by Jan Olis (fig. 28) painted around 1635 reiterates and condenses even further the ideals represented in these examples.[45] In a single image two men are seated at a table with a bare minimum of background description. The space is a neutral, nondescript one and works as an abstract foil for the "message." One of the men has fallen asleep in a drunken heap on the table, while the other gallantly toasts the viewer with a small upraised glass of wine. The two protagonists are dressed identically, and, in fact, like Ter Borch's doubled use of Gesina, Olis presents a double image of the same persona, "generic social man," one figuring overindulgence and the other displaying gentlemanly manners.

Ter Borch's paintings, in contrast to those of his predecessors, bring the issue of gender into the mix. The bodies of the two women are essentially the same, but the men in the two paintings are pointedly different. Gender, then, functions to differentiate the issues at stake in the pendants. Significantly, Ter

Borch's pendants introduce the concerns of class and status through the varied military identifications of the men within them, indicating once again how viable the military was as a microcosm of Dutch society at large. The soldier in the Montpellier painting is a mercenary. His demeanor and his wardrobe define him as someone whom the seventeenth-century viewer would have recognized as the lowest kind of soldier imaginable. The man in the Brooklyn painting is clearly presented in more dignified terms. The bandolier across his chest was an article of military clothing officially used for hanging charges for a musket, a purse, or a sword. It thus belonged to well-appointed soldiers or *schutters*. In the Minneapolis painting discussed above Jacob Duck shows his "good" soldier in the act of putting his bandolier on. The bandolier and his clothing in general define Ter Borch's soldier here as a proper one; one who contrasts with the excessive behavior of the soldier in the Montpellier painting. He is a man of stature represented as a gentleman, well dressed and attentive to his mate.

The sameness of the woman, like the sameness of the man in Olis's painting, works to make her a universal statement about womanhood in general, as a sign that supersedes the differences of class. She becomes the fulcrum for discourses of the civilizing process and is closely associated with table manners and proper social deportment, concerns that were especially strong in Ter Borch's time. As a result of the improved financial situation of many Dutchmen these modern guidelines for behavior presented as cultural artifacts helped them to appear suited to the privileged social position to which their newly acquired money entitled them.[46]

The advantages of moderation as a lifestyle are clearly expressed in the Brooklyn Museum painting. Not only do we see the woman lovingly admired by her male companion, but she is waited on by a serving woman. Although it is not clear whether this serving woman is a domestic or an innkeeper, as Gudlaugsson saw her (her simple dress and humble demeanor suggest to me more the former than the latter interpretation), she figures the privilege afforded this woman to be waited on.[47]

This first set of pendants proves to be rich with visual and complex formal and iconographic genealogies. The web of images, and the ideas they participate in, allows for a wide range of meaningful responses, including conservative Christian ideas of sin, as well as progressive, modern ideas of civility. In his second set of pendants Ter Borch definitively tips the balance toward the latter. When we look again at Ter Borch's later rendition of a drunken sleeping soldier and his mate in the private collection (fig. 14), we may notice immediately that the significant detail of the kannekijker motif, the very detail on which the difference of the two women hinged in the earlier pendants, is absent here. It has been replaced with a woman who drinks deeply from her glass. She, thereby, presents a more neutral image than the Montpellier maid, since drinking wine per se, as we have seen, was neither a positive nor negative activity in the seventeenth century. Moreover, its position in the pairing has been reversed so that the woman is now on the pictorial right and faces to her left.

The pendant for this work (fig. 29), in the Sinebrychoff Art Museum, Helsinki, likewise reverses an earlier composition by Ter Borch, that is his painting in the Städelsches Museum in Frankfurt.[48] Whether the companion paintings were conceived at the same time or matched by Ter Borch later, he clearly meant for them to be pendants.[49] The fact that they are the same size, use the same model, and have complementary compositions all testify to this. Further, they were engraved in the eighteenth century as pendants and spent almost two centuries together as such in various collections.[50]

In the end it is their iconographic relationship, which I here develop, that confirms their pendant status. The Helsinki painting shows a woman in the same activity as her counterpart, that is, drinking deeply from her glass. She is represented alone in front of a table with a letter in her other hand. The key to the connection between these two paintings lies not in their contrast, as was true in the previous pair, but in their similarity. Just as the activity of the two women is the same, the situation in which they find themselves is also comparable.

The fact that in the Helsinki painting Ter Borch has painted a single woman alone underscores the significance of the letter she holds. Reading and writing letters was a common subject for Dutch painting in the seventeenth century. Many of these letters have been interpreted as communications of romance and love from a distant lover whose whereabouts is sometimes alluded to by a map or painting within the painting.[51] Examples of this kind of picture can be found in the oeuvres of Dirck Hals, Vermeer, and numerous others. The love letter, with its heritage going back to chivalric practices, became such a fashion in the seventeenth century that it evolved into an artistic genre in its own right. Manuals were written to provide prototypes for gallant love letters, and the literature of emblem books further popularized the subject as a genre.[52] Emblematically, as, no doubt, in reality, letters conveyed thoughts of love and eased the pain of separation. Otto van Veen's *Amorum Emblemata* conveys this sentiment in picture and text:

> La lettre parle.
> l'Amour impatient de route longue absence,
> Inuenta le moyen pour se joindre d'esprit,
> Ores qu'absent de corps, par un papier escrit,
> Auquel il peint le mal, qui sa poitrine eslance.[53]

Love letters were not exclusively used to communicate the purest form of love, since they also figured prominently in the history of courtesan literature. As a separate type the representation of these letters also had a visual history of its own, including the message sent from King David to Bathsheba.[54] The idea that there were various possible interpretations of the love letter in Dutch painting is particularly important here since, like the image of a woman drinking, the image of a woman reading was, without further cues, a neutral one. Among its various implications it could be lascivious, or it could be romantic. Ter Borch's second pendants, therefore, unlike the first set, were of images lacking activities that could be locked into a good/bad binary. Their concerns seem, rather, to be more modern in the sense that they move even further from the older, more traditional, didactic discourses.

A meaning that has been forwarded in association with these images and one that fits well here refers to the consolation afforded by wine. This turns out to be not only the common denominator of the two paintings but the hinge on which their connection turns. Wine as a consolation for disappointment in love is a timeless and universal concept. It is often expressed in seventeenth-century Dutch literature, and it can be found in as close a source to Ter Borch as a poem by his half sister, Gesina, who presumably is the model for the woman in all four paintings under discussion. She writes:

> Wreede Venus oorzaek aller Smert
> 'K verjaegh en ban U geheel uyt mij Hert
> Want ghy niet anders baert dan droeve Pyn
> Wech geyle min. 'K verdryf U uyt myn sin
> En hou het met de wyn.[55]

The women in these two paintings are equally in need of consolation as each is in a lamentable situation. Each has in a sense been left alone but not entirely. In the painting of a sleeping soldier and a drinking maid she is neglected by her companion, who has passed out from too much drinking and smoking. In the Helsinki painting she is alone but this time with a letter, a letter that brings her thoughts of love from her mate. In essence, then, as Otto van Veen framed it, he is present in spirit.

In the former painting the woman consoles herself with wine, for her lover is physically present but spiritually absent; in the latter she consoles herself, for her lover is spiritually present but physically absent. With the two Ter Borch has effected a witty conceit concerning the plight of women who are unfortunate in their choice of lover. Here the joke is on the women, who love well but not too wisely. Since their condition seems for all intents and purposes to be temporary, the joke is well taken.

The two paintings by Ter Borch of drunken sleeping soldiers and drinking maids with which we began this investigation, and which initially looked so similar, can now be seen to have had very different kinds of effect. The issue of importance of context is not new for seventeenth-century Dutch art, nor does it seem remarkable that the context created by pairing two images together would consequentially affect the meaning of each. What is noteworthy is that Ter Borch would have used such similar images to such different ends. These modern pictures, like the very early printed book illustrations that had bearing on the stock type from which Ter Borch's images were chosen, were seen by him to be flexible in their ability to convey content. Moreover, the very nature of that content was not fixed, neither in the realm of a didactic moralism nor in that of social or class definition. What remains constant is the humor that is essential to all of the paintings.

Ter Borch's first pair of paintings with a sleeping soldier presents a modern interpretation of a traditional subject. Rich in allusions to visual and literary conventions, they strike the spectator as humorous and are cloaked in an edifying discourse. They differ from the paintings of sleeping soldiers by, for example, Jacob Duck as "humorous" differs from "comic" and "edifying" differs from "didactic."

Ter Borch's pendants speak to the problem of a changing orientation in Dutch genre painting of the seventeenth century. They provide a sliding scale of concern with and reference to the older and more traditional standards of good and evil toward more modern secularized concerns of class definition and the humorous foibles of the human condition. The change is not an abrupt one, nor is it an exclusive one; but rather, like all history, it is a slow scenario of shifting priorities.

II
Re/visions

Jan Steen's Formulation of the Dissolute Household: Sources and Meanings

The seemingly random chaos and keenly observed realistic details of Jan Steen's *Dissolute Household* paintings have led more than one writer to see them as true reflections of his disorderly home and life, an idea abetted, no doubt, by his recognizable presence in many of them.[1] Indeed, Houbraken, Steen's first biographer, made a direct connection between Steen's riotous lifestyle and his initial impetus to paint these images as a means of staving off bankruptcy.[2] It was, however, also Houbraken who first called the *Dissolute Household* a *zinnebeeld* [meaningful picture], and this more interpretative approach to the paintings has dominated the recent literature on the subject.[3] In it, moralizing messages culled from sixteenth-century traditions, such as proverbs and popular prints, are successfully discussed in relationship to his art.[4]

Here I would like to add to these interpretations by pointing out some specific sources for Steen's masterpiece in this genre, *In Weelde Siet Toe* (fig. 30), of about 1663, now in the Kunsthistorisches Museum in Vienna.[5] Although it is known that he incorporated popular art of the past into his paintings, the multifarious and sometimes self-conscious manner in which he did so is the further topic of this essay. This may, then, serve to indicate how the painting's meaning was arrived at and elucidate the nature of the meaning itself.

Generally speaking, the dissolute household, as a subject formulated by Steen, recalls the artistic conventions of the sixteenth century rather than the seventeenth, for there is precious little in his own century that is comparable.[6] One of the sixteenth-century precedents often referred to in relationship to Steen's work is the "topsy-turvy world," popularized in prints and constructed on the conceit of stating what is, or what should be, by what is not.[7] The symbolic inversion of cultural standardized norms was, in fact, an age-old device of satire and irony and dates back to antiquity.[8] However, the kind of specific topsy-turvy inversion characteristic of this type of imagery appears unambiguously only rarely in Steen's work, as in the stained glass in the Linsky Collection painting (now in the Metropolitan Museum in New York), where a boar carries a hunter's rifle.[9] A similar yet not quite identical idea is represented by the transference of aberrant adult behavior to children, as is clearly seen in details, for example, of the painting *As the Old Sing, the Young Pipe After* in The Hague. One may say that, in concept and somewhat in form, the transposition of activity common in prints and paintings of tavern life to the locale of the sanctified Dutch home can be seen as the major inversion of the subject taken in its entirety.[10]

Closer examples of subjects with comparable concepts to Steen's *Dissolute Household* are the sixteenth-century prints of disordered homes created by German and Netherlandish artists. In one, published by Hieronymous Cock (fig. 31), we are presented with a mythic personality called *Sorghelos* and his wife, *Verlega*, in avid avoidance of their work. They idle away their day with the rationale, explained in the central caption, "What we don't do today, we will do tomorrow."[11] The consequences of their attitude are apparent in the wild children and general disarray of their home and business, all ideas that recur in Steen's work. Equally indolent, the characters of Bartel Beham's woodcut of the *Spinnstube* (fig. 32) are preoccupied with all manner of excessive behavior. Here, as in Steen, intemperate sexuality, eating, and drinking are presented in wild abandon, all in the confines of a domestic interior. These are, of course, activities much better suited to scenes in taverns and bordellos, as were represented in various paintings and prints of the sixteenth century. We are indebted to Konrad Renger's book *Lockere Gesellschaft* for the insightful exposition of these images.[12] As he has shown, sixteenth-century interpretations of life in public places were both numerous and varied, ranging from the presentation of the biblical parable of the prodigal son to that of folk heroes and drinking brothers. They all, however, shared the same essential concern for the wasteful dissipation of fortune through careless and excessive indulgence in gambling, wine, and women. An example of this genre, which serves well to illustrate Steen's connection with it, in both concept and form, is the woodcut by Cornelis Anthonisz. of 1541 (fig. 33). The second in a series of prints that plots the rise and fall of another *Sorghelos*,[13] this image provides us with a significant number of concordances with Steen's painting. To begin with, both take place in fairly shallow, boxlike rooms with a *doorkijkje* through to a kitchen on the right revealed through an arch. The doorkijkje schema, although applied to domestic interiors in Dutch paintings of the 1650s and 1660s,[14] had initially been invented for tavern and bordello interiors in the sixteenth century; and this particular formulation, with a fireplace to the right, probably still had that connotation for Steen.

Further, both print and painting combine the didactic strategies of word and image. Although this was a common phenomenon in prints of the sixteenth century,[15] it was not for large oil paintings of the seventeenth.[16] The words themselves and, consequently, the main concepts of the two images are analogous, hinged as they are on the idea of *weelde*, or luxury. In the print weelde is personified and labeled; in Steen's painting it is written on the slate on the stairs to the right, *In Weelde Siet Toe*. It is the very warning that gives the painting its title. Both artists have conceived of luxury in very similar terms: elegant, high living signified through an abundance of food, drink, and worldly possessions. A comparison with Adriaen van de Venne's two visual essays on weelde —one a monochromatic painting from the Boijmans van Beuningen Museum in Rotterdam (fig. 34)[17] and the other an illustration for Jacob Cats's popular *Spiegel van den ouden ende nieuwe tijd* (fig. 35)[18]—serve to underscore the similarities between Steen and the sixteenth-century sources rather than those of the seventeenth. Yet by comparing Anthonisz.'s print to Steen's painting, we can see that the compositional structure of Steen's work is at once more centralized and cohesive. What seemed initially random and chaotic is in the end tightly organized around a central motif, that of the amorous couple who are surrounded by a splay of figures forming a semicircular arch.[19] The source for this configuration comes from an entirely different stock of images.

Steen's figures so disposed can be read from left to right, that is, from the infant and the young boy by the window, to the old religious couple by the door, as a progression from youth to old age. This particular design and its associative meaning had long been popular from sixteenth-century broadsheets as the *Ages of Man* (fig. 36).[20] Despite the variations in the older interpretations of the subject, the primary schema for the popular prints remained unchanged, that is, in the form of an arc-shaped bridge across which man or woman traveled, aging a bit with each successive step. They each held an attribute that alluded to an activity appropriate for that particular age. The idea was related to that of *Vanitas* and to the moralistic notion that each stage of life had its proper preoccupations, collectively giving a universal sense of human life in its entirety. Significantly, the same or similar ideas had been expressed in different forms in paintings of the sixteenth and seventeenth centuries, of which I illustrate only two, Titian's *Allegory* (fig. 37) and Valentin's *Four Ages of Man* (fig. 38), both in the National Gallery in London. They serve to emphasize the formulation particular to the prints and to accentuate their boldly distinguishable form as a type in Steen. Aside from the Vienna painting, Steen's appreciation of this type is documented by its presence in his painting of the equally old-fashioned subject of the *Choice Between Wealth and Youth*, in the National Museum in Warsaw (fig. 39).[21] Here a simplified drawing on the wall recalls its design and suffices to conjure up the prints and their message. As a print within a painting it serves as decoration and as a commentary on the main subject.[22] We may say that its essential structure functions similarly in the Vienna painting.

Yet in its new and altered context its meaning takes on a particularly ironic twist. This new meaning must surely depend on the central couple, who act as the nucleus for the configuration. They are represented as a fun-loving couple, placed conspicuously facing out at the spectator. The encircling element of the figures behind them is extended by large objects that lie to the left and right of the couple. These figures and their attributes also have their precursors in the print imagery of the sixteenth century. In fact, in the prodigious print by Bartel Beham of the *Spinnstube* (fig. 32), a couple in the lower left-hand corner grope and grapple one another in a similarly lustful way. An overturned pitcher with its contents spilling out lies on the floor in front of the woman and alludes to her licentiousness and unchaste state.[23] The man, for his part, has a discarded hat thrown on the floor behind him, connoting similar character weaknesses.[24] Steen has thus taken up a constellation of similar motifs in his centralized couple, now, however, turning them in space to face the viewer. For the couple's combined posture he had tapped another visual tradition, one that developed in the context of mythological imagery and is sometimes called the "slung leg motif."[25] Its role in this mundane setting, as in its more elevated settings, is as a signifier of sexual intimacy. This point is further emphasized by the woman's gesture as she toasts her companion with a full glass of wine between his legs. Steen's connection with Beham and the sixteenth-century world of emblematic imagery, despite these changes, remains clear.

The couple represents lust, kindled by drinking and characterized by recklessness.[26] The man and woman revel in carnal desire; they and all the world around them, as the encapsulated collective embodiment of humanity, women and men, from cradle to grave, dance perennially around the vanity of the sensual world. The image is a playful and jovial one but not completely carefree or without reservations. A note of warning is issued in the compelling basket with objects situated ominously over the scene as a whole.

The basket contains objects associated with illness and poverty, such as a crutch, a leper's clapper, a whip, cards and a sword, all of which relate to the life of those who have fallen on hard times.[27] The objects act to prophesy the doom that awaits these wasteful characters. Similar warnings had been issued by many sixteenth-century images of reveling, including those of the prodigal son and the series outlining the demise of *Sorghelos*. In fact, one may say that the particular condensation of the cause and consequence of the events compressed into a single image was structurally more common than not in sixteenth-century representations. A few of these may be interesting in comparison with Steen. In a print resembling the 1541 *Sorghelos* tavern scenes the prodigal son is seen dissipating his fortune, while hovering over him a seven-headed monster appears in a cloud of smoke (fig. 40).[28] It is accompanied by a caption that designates the characters as sinful fanatics.[29] Its presence goes unacknowledged by the characters below, just as the basket of impending poverty and illness goes unacknowledged in Steen's painting.

Another comparison can be made with an illustration from Dirck Coornhert's translation of Furmer's Latin text, *The Use and Abuse of Worldly Goods, Recht ghebruyck ende misbruyck van tijdelijcke have*,[30] a book whose recurrent theme is relevant to an understanding of the Vienna painting and one to which I will return. In this context the section entitled "*The Prodigals*" (fig. 41) is comparable as an emblem of tavern life.[31] It represents a young man throwing away his money to a gambler, a musician, and women of easy virtue. Behind him, and slightly above his head, an old thin woman sits and weeps. She, we are told by the label above her, is poverty, *Egestas*. She too looms, unheeded, as the prophesied doom of this prodigal, not unlike her still-life counterpart in Steen's painting.

A last example of this phenomenon is chosen from Otto van Veen's *Emblemata Horatiana*, a work from the early seventeenth century (fig. 42).[32] Gambling and merrymaking occupy the figures in the foreground, and the disastrous consequences of their evil actions are represented in the right background. There, an old man and young boy beg for alms while a doctor examines a urine sample behind them, a sign of either pregnancy or the general loss of good health. The doctor's visit was a subject portrayed by Steen in its own right.[33] Once again, the merrymakers pay no attention to these warnings and continue to dance, drink, and gamble in the same blithe fashion as Steen's figures.

To return now to Coornhert, his influence is an appealing one to consider on several levels. He was among the most influential moralists working in Holland in the sixteenth century,[34] and the emphasis in his writing on moderation, temperance, and diligent labor was essential as the foundation for the social and moral preoccupations of Steen's day.[35] Furthermore, he was a man who appreciated irony and wit and often incorporated them into his own work. I have already said that the general tenor of his book related to Steen, yet there is another specific illustration that has particular relevance here. Section 5 shows us a fool who empties his purse between Venus and Bacchus, the goddess of love and the god of wine (fig. 43). To the left of the main event an idler sleeps with his hands buried in his coat and pocket[36] while the cat eats a fish off the table and a dog dips into the pot on the floor. A careful look at Steen's painting reveals a similar constellation and disposition of objects and ideas. The central subject involves the dissipation of wealth through love and wine, and to the left an idler, this time a mother, sleeps while a dog eats a pie from the table.[37]

The connection between Coornhert's illustration and Jan Steen's painting is a complex one, involving structure, form, and meaning, replete with numerous associations and connotations. Mischievous, thieving domestic animals had been represented in abundance in the realm of popular art and popular language, going back at least to fifteenth-century proverbs[38] and illustrated on misericords in northern Europe.[39] Another example of the subject contemporary with Coornhert is Jost Amman's playing card of the 1580s (fig. 16).[40] In a state of drunken stupor the overindulgent couple neglect their possessions, which then get stolen by the dog. In the seventeenth century, a few years before Steen's painting, Nicolaes Maes had tapped into this rich tradition and incorporated the idea in his witty representation of *The Idle Servant*, now in the National Gallery in Washington. There it underscores the subject of sloth as the lack of domestic vigilance. And Steen himself had used the device more than once under similar circumstances.

Steen had, in fact, placed it in the center of another *Dissolute Household*, last known in the Percy B. Meyer collection, where the main subject is that of domestic negligence (fig. 44).[41] Since it is essentially an abbreviated form of this painting that is found on the left of the Vienna painting,[42] it will be useful to examine it a bit more closely. The self-indulgent sleep that has overtaken the adults provides an opportunity for the children and animals to wreak havoc on the home and its contents. One child even picks his mother's pocket, illustrating the popular Dutch proverb, "De gelegenheid maakt de dief" (Opportunity makes the thief) that had been illustrated earlier by Otto van Veen in his *Amorum Emblemata* (fig. 45).[43] He had, in fact, produced an image in the same unthreatening terms, with little putti stealing food and drink. Steen's and Van Veen's works are both quite different from Mitelli's interpretation of this motto as highway robbery.[44] Theft of this sort had been frequently found in bordello scenes of the sixteenth and seventeenth centuries, of which I show a print after Cornelis Massys of circa 1560 (fig. 46) and Steen's own so-called *Bad Company* in the Louvre in Paris (fig. 47). The point is the same. The indolent and overindulgent sleeper is the responsible party, bringing on him- or herself all sorts of misfortune, especially poverty. To quote from the biblical proverbs cited by Coornhert, "For the drunkard and the glutton shall come to poverty, drowsiness shall clothe a man with rags, and slothfulness casteth into a deep sleep and an idle soul shall suffer hunger."[45]

Significantly, the theft occurring in the Vienna painting is somewhat removed from the mother, and the gesture of blowing smoke at her replaces it. This gesture has its own history as a form of derisive mockery and is often especially connected with lewd thoughts, as in the detail of Albrecht Dürer's engraving *Dream of the Idler*, where a devil blows into the sleeping man's ear with a bellows,[46] and in Steen's own *Tavern Scene*, now in the National Gallery in London (fig. 48). This special nature of the *oorblazer* affirms the main subject of Steen's Vienna painting, that of lustful abandon.

The inclusion of the Meyer painting vignette within the Vienna painting has several implications. It fixes the subject securely in the genre of the dissolute household, for, aside from this detail, all the other activities could equally well be taking place in a tavern or a bordello. The abbreviated form of the Meyer painting is, thus, essential as a sign of the domestic locale of the scene as a whole. Furthermore, as a representation of sloth it provides one of the causes that allows, one might even say encourages, the ongoing events to take place. The sub-subject, sloth, can be specifically related to the main subject, lust. The traditional implications of this union were discussed by Panofsky in his interpretation of Dürer's *Dream of the Idler*[47] and by Stridbeck in his interpretation of Pieter Bruegel's design for *Accedia*.[48] Lust and sloth are also conjoined here in Steen's painting, although they are not given equal importance. Such equality was, however, achieved in the last of Steen's large *Dissolute Household* paintings, the one in the Wellington Collection in London (fig. 49). Compositionally split down the center by the awkward and unusual placement of the chair, the painting has, in fact, two centers of focus. On the left, in a reiteration of the main components of the Vienna painting, carnal lust is portrayed; on the right, in a reiteration of the main components of the Meyer painting, domestic sloth is portrayed. Together the two are presented as equally responsible for the breakdown of society's rules and standards as the Dutch ideologically constructed them in the idealized notion of the home.

Taken in its entirety the Vienna painting appears as a complex nexus of old ideas and new ones created from older material, all presented in various degrees of self-consciousness and visual recognizability. Some of its precedents are so only in general concept, others in the specific formulation of their ideas, and still others in the formulation of both form and concept. For them Steen clearly drew from the storehouse of forms and ideas of the previous century. He was particularly sensitive to the power of popular art of the sixteenth century, with its bold and directly expressive designs and its immediate, visually available structures. It is worth remembering at this juncture that the majority of these images were produced in large editions and were indeed "popular," that is, known to the grandparents, parents, and children of Steen's Haarlem. In incorporating this art into his own he was often consciously referential. His understanding of the past included both an appreciation of its implicit authority and the comic consequences of its transference to a modern, ironic context. Sins become follies, both human and ludicrous. His painting is, thus, less a moralistic admonition than a statement of the human condition in its entirety. In this it is similar to the universal statement made by Steen's large painting in the Mauritshuis in The Hague, painted about ten years later, that presents *The Life of Man*.[49] Considering the human condition, Steen, like Democrates, would rather laugh than cry. In the end the nuances of meaning in his work are akin to those in the work of Erasmus, and, like Erasmus, Steen praises folly with a degree of ambivalence.

To conclude, Steen's Vienna painting *In Weelde Siet Toe* is a product of a complex, deliberate, and thoughtful process. If it does not appear so at first sight, that is all the more to the credit of Steen's power as a storyteller.

5

"There's No Place like Home": Jan Steen and Domestic Ideology

The study of family life in early modern times has become *the* popular subject in recent academic publications. Historians from various schools, including social historians, the Annales, and those who study the history of mentalities, have probed the changing structural and social conditions of family life in this unstable period. Undoubtedly, this newly intensified interest in the structures and ideologies of the family reflects certain modern anxieties about that institution in our own time. It seems clear this recent exuberant desire to analyze its past is itself an expression of wanting to understand and control its present. Paintings on this subject created in the seventeenth century—and still on view today—are the perfect bridge between these two enterprises. Not surprisingly, then, the study of Dutch genre paintings that seem so casually to depict "the home" and "the family," two separate but interrelated constructions, has ridden the popularity wave of these recent interests. In large measure a result of its prevalent artistic strategies of the realism that lies first and foremost in the fiction of its informality, Dutch painting is often used to illustrate certain "truisms" evinced through written documentation; and conversely, literary documents are frequently invoked to organize and explain painted representations. All are deployed with simplistic assumptions that both informational sources bear a direct and positive relationship to historical reality, usually with greater privilege and credibility assigned to the written text.

Even the paintings by Jan Steen, whose impetus seems so obviously centered in the conventions of comic and farcical visual traditions, have been subject to the sort of analysis that intends to unearth certain "realities" of his life and time.[1] My intention in this essay is to reassert the *synthetic* nature of familial representation as affective, discursive visual tropes in Dutch painting in general and in

Steen's work in particular. I want to show how these works, operating within a particular visual language, were far from disinterested and accidental reflections of contemporary mores but rather worked actively within a discourse of social construction to fabricate the shifting terms of the norm. I want to re-emphasize their place within the history of the Netherlandish genre imaginary, to show how their rhetoric is visual and their logic pictorial, and finally to suggest that as works of Dutch culture they acted as signs that shaped the contours of modern life as much as they reflected them.

To do this effectively, it is first of all necessary for me to dislodge the idea of domesticity in the visual arts from its implausible position of bearing a singular, hard-and-fast meaning. Its potential as a multivalent construct in producing social value can be mobilized only after a critical analysis of its larger ideological position. Then the visual construction of domesticity, providing as it does aesthetically authorized cultural norms, can be situated within the production of various social mechanisms, paramount among them the so-called civilizing process.[2]

In my essay "Jan Steen's Formulation of the Dissolute Household, Sources and Meanings," originally written in 1984, I focused on a number of sixteenth-century print sources that Steen had structurally incorporated in various ways into the type of his paintings generally called "dissolute households."[3] My intention at that time was to illustrate how whole sets of visual constellations, initially introduced and circulated in sixteenth-century paintings and prints, were virtually quoted in Steen's domestic interiors and particularly in his masterpiece in Vienna, *In Weelde Siet Toe* (see fig. 30). The sources he chose were those that particularly addressed and, in a real sense, composed a Netherlandish "genre" formulation of public life. I attributed Steen's insertion of a "public" iconography into a "domestic" space to the early modern comic strategy of topsy-turviness. What I had not yet seen in 1984 was precisely the conceptual artificiality of the larger Dutch social project of fabricating a notion of the "domestic" and the early modern desire to create a feeling of nostalgia for it. One of the most effective ways Dutch genre painting after 1650 does this is by defining domesticity as a sort of representational opposite, a countersign, as it were, of the tropes of public interior spaces such as guesthouses, taverns, and bordellos. By transposing many of the previous century's established inn/bordello visual structures into interiors that are clearly meant to be understood as private and familial, Steen makes particularly transparent the reciprocity between the two—visually fabricated social notions of "itinerancy" and "domesticity."

It seems clear to me now that both of these terms need explication and critical analysis—the former because it has fallen so far out of the modern consciousness of acceptable positions (having been replaced by concepts with very different social and cultural implications, such as homelessness and vagrancy); and the latter because we are far too familiar with it, so familiar, in fact, that it has become normalized, and thus its artificiality is invisible to us. The Dutch literary scholar D. Th. Enklaar was still in touch with the notion of itinerancy when he wrote *Varende luyden*, meaning *Roaming People* or *People on the Go*, in 1937 and *Uit Uilenspiegel's kring*, or *From Uilenspiegel's Circle*, in 1940. Both books track the course of a compendium of late medieval mythic literary wandering types, such as the members of the *Blaue Schuit*, a fictive guild of drinkers and rogues, vagrants, students, and other colorful characters.[4] In recent times the scholarship of Herman Pleij has once again focused on this historical Netherlandish literary genre and in the process also addressed some particular visual examples of early modern images.[5] My own work has treated, but perhaps not stressed enough, the overarching project of early Netherlandish genre imagery in terms of itinerancy.[6] Once the early history of genre is understood through this frame, we can then appreciate the full extent to which the visual fabrication of domesticity in the second half of the seventeenth century is, indeed, itinerancy's final development.[7] What I am proposing is clearly a project of daunting dimensions, and the best way to begin here is by exploring a sample case explicated through close reading and comparative analysis.

Jan Steen's *Dissolute Household* of circa 1668 (fig. 49), in the Wellington Museum in London, seems a propitious site to begin such a critical analysis. This painting works well as an exemplary model precisely because in it Steen revels in the sort of self-conscious artistic quotation and self-quotation that brings the notion of comic transpositions so evidently into the forefront of his process. It is a work whose composition, as noted in my previous work on Steen, looks unusual because one of the central figures (possibly Steen himself) turns his back on one-half of the painting. The resulting awkwardness suggests that there is more to understanding it than as simple mimetic realism. I have suggested that it may be seen as a reiteration of the compositions of two of Steen's earlier works in this genre, the Meyer painting and *In Weelde Siet Toe*.[8] However, this splitting affect opens onto a far greater field of associations, as we will see.

This painting by Steen is the one that gives the name to the type since Steen inscribed the words "Bedurfve huishow" on the slate in the lower left.[9] Although the phrase "bedurfve huishow" is usually translated as dissolute household, the seventeenth-century meaning is more literally a ruined or spoiled household, much like a ruined or spoiled piece of fruit, or man or woman.[10] In this sense it conjures a notion of "household" that is far from real but rather one that is pure, pristine. The title also allows that something or someone has ruined this perfect,

virginal condition, a something that I am here proposing can be found in the practices and conventions from the outside, specifically the tavern/bordello tradition.

Despite its initial chaotic appearance—which describes the activities of no
less than eight figures, a dog, and a monkey—Steen's hand in carefully orches-
trating the composition and meaning soon becomes evident. The multilayered
structure of the composition as a whole underscores its sense of parts. These parts,
or sets, hold the potential to trigger various associative reactions in the visually literate viewer—ranging from references to sixteenth-century paintings and prints
to those of other works by Steen himself. Quotation and self-quotation work together here to produce what is ultimately a highly reflexive image. And, as will be
demonstrated, among its clearest ploys is the incorporation of "public" activity as
conceived in representation (by which I include both the disorder of the room
and the comic sense of the painting) into the private realm of the home. In the
end the rhetoric of the painting calls the viewer to sum it all up, a dictum literally
given in Steen's Vienna painting *In Weelde Siet Toe*, where Steen wrote "Soma op"
on the chalkboard under the proverb that gives this painting its title. With this he
refers on one level to the internal narrative—that is, to the tally of drinks one
would characteristically keep in a tavern—and on another level to a final reckoning on a moral order, and finally on a third level, externally, to the viewer, suggesting that the most propitious way to grasp the image is by summing up its various parts. Moreover, vision and viewing, as acts, are also wonderfully enunciated
in the title proverb itself, *In Weelde Siet Toe*, literally "in luxury see to it," which
directs us as well to the "seeing to it" of the detailed opulence (*weelde*) of Steen's
scene. The additive visual language of Steen's painting is clearly not unique to him
and has as a strategy (in the whole as a sum of its parts) a direct relationship with
a particular strand of sixteenth-century Netherlandish imagery. Indeed, the way
so many figures are distributed throughout the available pictorial space—frag-
menting the composition and creating multiple focus points for the viewer—
immediately recalls the great Netherlandish genre innovator Hieronymous Bosch,
although clearly Steen's figures are larger, and there are considerably fewer of them.
Closer still to Steen's effect, as discussed in my earlier essay, are the works by
Bosch's celebrated heir, Pieter Bruegel the Elder. Bruegel's encyclopedic paintings
such as *Children's Games*, *Proverbs*, and the numerous kermis scenes share the pan-
oply effect with Steen.[11] And even closer still, indeed in my view closest, in this
generational chain, are the paintings of Bruegel's illustrious if under-recognized
follower Marten van Cleve.[12]

For me the most rewarding comparison to be made with Steen's London
painting is Van Cleve's *Peasant Interior* (fig. 50), in the Kunsthistorisches Museum in Vienna. It is with this painting, as with Van Cleve's oeuvre in general,

that Steen self-consciously and productively opens a visual dialogue and critique. Within traditional art history this might be viewed as a classic case of influence, but it is most beneficially treated as a unique opportunity to track the shifting sands of ideological terrains in the course of the early modern period. We can appreciate the progressive and progressively modern needs of the Dutch burgher populace by evaluating the changes Steen, for one, introduced into the regulatory frames of Netherlandish visual conventionality.

The uncanonical works of Marten van Cleve have heretofore been overlooked as an important source of imagery and information for the history of Netherlandish genre painting in general. This is despite the fact that his place in Netherlandish art history has been secured by no less a source than Van Mander, who lauded both Marten and his brother Hendrick in the *Schilderboek*.[13] His work is represented in several prestigious seventeenth-century collections, including that of Rubens and Leopold Willem.[14] For us this inventive sixteenth-century artist's paintings are of interest on many significant levels, including the formal, the iconographic, and the ideological—and in all the ways these three can be interwoven with one another. He was an especially fitting model for Steen; for, as his paintings show, he was himself acutely aware of the effects of different stylistic modes and of the potentially meaningful implications of trying on diverse stylistic models. His oeuvre reveals his intelligent and effective management of the two prevalent, yet radically different, sixteenth-century Netherlandish artistic modes; that is, the Romanist, best exemplified by Van Cleve's official teacher, Frans Floris, and the Bruegelian manner of painting, which he adopted in his later works.[15] The combative/contrastive relationship of these two modes, as David Freedberg has shown in his discussion of Abraham Ortelius's and Lucas d'Heere's writings, articulated more than the parameters of artistic possibilities in the late sixteenth century; it also provided the basis for an important aspect of Netherlandish art theory after midcentury.[16] My interest here, as I have said, is in Van Cleve's early painting the *Peasant Interior*, in Vienna, a work that combines both paradigms. This large and impressive picture was particularly well known and appreciated in the seventeenth century. At that time it was part of Leopold Willem's collection, where it is noted in the 1659 inventory.[17]

As is often the case, the first detail to signal the connection between the two artists is a seeming inconsequential one. Each artist had placed a pig rather conspicuously in a large interior scene; Van Cleve in his *Peasant Interior* (fig. 50) and Steen in *In Weelde Siet Toe* (fig. 30), both today in Vienna. Within the logic of a realist mode the pig arguably belongs more naturally in Van Cleve's farmhouse/barn interior than in Steen's urban home, although even in the farmhouse its prominence might be questioned. The pig's "out of place" presence, like that of the monkey in Steen's Vienna domestic interior, requires us to understand each within the frame of a visual logic that makes sense on levels other than mimetic "reportage." In contemporary art history they have been interpreted in Steen's work as belonging to the Bruegelian tradition of paintings of proverbs. For example, the Dutch proverb "Strooit geen rozen voor de varkens," literally "Don't spread roses before swine," was particularly popular in this period and was often represented by Bruegel's son.[18] In Steen's *Dissolute Household* (fig. 49) and Van Cleve's *Peasant Interior* (fig. 50) attention is drawn to animals eating off the floor by their placement in the center foreground—the pig and hen eating roots in the Van Cleve and the more domestic cocker spaniel eating from a rich still life featuring cheese and a ham in Steen's London work.

Once one realizes that the connection between Van Cleve and Steen goes deeper than these shared motifs, a richer kind of sense can be made from both, and meaningful dimensions of greater social complexity become available from them. This larger connection between them is apparent once the two paintings are surveyed together. Both paintings are ambitious; they are physically large, horizontal formats filled with a plethora of figures and details in an opulent display that, again, at first glance seems somewhat fragmented, disordered, and chaotic. The interior architecture of both Van Cleve and Steen effortlessly accommodate these impossibly expansive companies, with space to spare overhead and in the foreground. Van Cleve's painting implausibly contains over twenty figures, as well as various animals. Significantly, it is itself an already reduced version of another picture by him of a peasant inn whose present location is unknown.[19] Both Van Cleves are indebted to a painting, again in Vienna, and again coming from the collection of Leopold Willem, representing the *Prodigal Son in a Whorehouse*; a painting that in the eighteenth century was attributed to Marten's brother, Hendrick, and is now attributed to the Master of the Prodigal Son (fig. 51).[20] What the three works have in common is the strange structure of a dividing wall in the center of the composition, which, like Steen's turned-about character, cleaves the composition in half, separating two distinct companies. The wall in Van Cleve's Vienna painting also has a "realistic" function as it contains an area used for the storage of hay. Similarly divided compositions were not in themselves uncommon in the sixteenth century. They were at times set in landscapes and, as heirs to a medieval mentality, were employed to encourage a contrast of the groups in each half, with the discourse of a Christian morality as the organizing force of the comparison. Examples survive from the workshops of Van Cleve's teacher, Frans Floris, and from Lucas d'Heere, representing, for example, the *Parable of the Wise and Foolish Virgins*.

Within this typology Van Cleve's painting is exceptional and prophetic not only because of its contemporary interior setting but because its point does not readily fall into the exposition of moral dichotomies. He seems rather to be explicating conditions of class, gender, residency, and itinerancy—at the points of their interaction.

In the painting by the Master of the Prodigal Son in Vienna, dating to the early 1550s, the wall also awkwardly separates an interior and a landscape space. The transition from outdoor to indoor is achieved, again somewhat awkwardly, through the change from grass to tile floor. Marten van Cleve's scene is decidedly located in an interior proper with a view to a landscape allowed only through an open doorway. The transposition of the peasant from the outdoors to the indoors has among its more critical consequences his separation from his single most redeeming attribute, the land, and in so doing opens the peasant up to a whole new series of judgments and expectations. The fact that Marten specialized in figures, whereas his brother, Hendrick, specialized in landscapes, may inform but does not explain this shift.[21] In the end it was Marten van Cleve's containment of the sprawling, multifigured kermises-like scene into an interior that ranks as one of the most important moves toward the "modernization" of that image type.[22] It ultimately leads the way to the modern formulation of peasant imagery in the seventeenth century in, for example, the paintings by Adriaen Brouwer and others, which implicitly situates the peasants in an urban rather than rural environment.

Moreover, by applying the bifurcated architectural structure to a more secular narrative Van Cleve already changed the terms of engagement. Rather than the overdetermined moralism explicitly proffered by the narrative of the Prodigal Son parable, Van Cleve constructs a scene with a mélange of social functions and classes located in a nonunitarily defined farmhouse/hostel. The painting was described in 1659 as no. 266 in the inventory of Archduke Leopold Willem, as a "piece of oil paint on wood," representing a "Bauerngasterey," that is, a peasant guesthouse, as an "original by Martin van Cleef, Netherlandish painter."[23]

The conditions of this space allow for a series of simultaneous narrative vignettes, with the two sides clearly designed to encourage their comprehension as different. Although such peasant guesthouses surely existed and form part of the social history of the time, it was his visual inventiveness that allowed Van Cleve to give shape to various social groups and articulate their relationships as part of this fictive environment.[24] He, in fact, depicted several kinds of interaction between the resident peasants and their itinerant clientele housed by this interior. Characteristically, the precise nature of these relationships remains ambiguous. For example, in the right part of the painting Van Cleve quotes a subject dramatized by him as the main subject in several of his other paintings wherein a peasant woman with a single exposed breast nurses a baby while an upper-middle-class couple attend in some manner.[25] The subject has been identified as the *Visit to the Wet Nurse*—in which case the scene would be one where an upper-middle-class couple comes to visit their baby with the peasant wet nurse.[26] More recently Van Cleve's subject has been titled "Der Besuch bei der Wochnerin" (Visit to the woman who has just given birth) and "Der Besuch des Grundherrn beim Pächter" (Visit to the lessor).[27] The scene has also been connected to a painting by Marten van Cleve mentioned in the inventory of Pierre Wynants in Antwerp in 1669, "De Voesterheer," a related subject about which I will have more to say in the next chapter.[28] In the end it is unclear what the precise relationship is between these figures of different social standing, except to say that it is congenial and that the painting stresses the sense of well-being of all.[29] Indeed, weelde, as abundance and fecundity, is the most apt characterization of the scene.

Abundance and fecundity are also evident in the more public left side of the painting. Yet the relationship between the classes is not as convivial. Among its most prominent details, a well-dressed man grabs a young female peasant by her blouse while she resists him. This detail is itself reiterated by Steen in both larger compositions, for example in the *Inn Scene*, in the Rijksmuseum, and as the primary subject of the painting *Inn Scene*, in the Städel Museum in Frankfurt. It is the kind of detail that is today easy to dismiss as merely a realistic and "natural" occurrence—the plight of women who serve in the public sphere—one that surely took place "all the time" and needs no iconographic precedent to "explain it." I see this detail as it passes from Van Cleve's generation to Jan Steen's as a perfect illustration of the way historical culture works to normalize certain social acts of power and aggression, reinvesting them with ever-greater authority. The fact that Steen's reworking of the subject places it within a comic setting and includes a degree of self-complicity only makes it more effective.

A common denominator of the two sides in Van Cleve's composition is the focus on various forms of exchange taking place around sustenance or nourishment. In and through these exchanges the boundaries between social groups are visually fashioned, framing social issues of great urgency given the burgeoning social mobility in late-sixteenth-century Antwerp. The works of Norbert Elias and his followers are as relevant here as they were for the pendants (another form of compositional splitting) by Ter Borch discussed earlier. Here, as there, social eating and drinking works in the realm of the so-called civilizing process, bringing into a coherent visual program social behavior that reflects class status.[30] However, unlike the earlier pendants by Ter Borch, notions of morality, positive or negative, cannot convincingly be seen as the primary discourse motivating Van Cleve's compositional split.

The prodigious fifteenth-century illustrations made for the *Facta et Dicta Memorabilia Romanorum*, written by Valerius Maximus in the first century A.D., are perhaps closer to Van Cleve in spirit (see figs. 26 and 27).[31] As previously discussed, the eating scenes from the manuscripts that are now in Leipzig and Berlin depict two meals, one civil and the other disorderly, and both quite unrealistically convened in the same room but at different tables. Among their multifarious meanings these illustrations, as those of Van Cleve's paintings, establish characteristics for social stereotyping.

By now it is clear that Jan Steen's London *Dissolute Household* shares a great deal in visual structure, iconographic motifs, and ideological implication with Van Cleve. It is also clear that their similarities enable us to appreciate more precisely their differences and thus obtain some means to measure the shifting social priorities addressed by visual culture in the second half of the seventeenth century as opposed to the second half of the sixteenth. Although Steen maintains the artificial device of a strongly enunciated bipartite division, issues of class seem far less relevant for him. For although his household includes servants, as well as, ostensibly, the master and mistress of the house, they are all described by their clothes and hairdos as belonging to the same urban middle class.

Investigating the iconographic details in Steen's painting reveals it to be paradoxically both more archaic, or more precisely archaistic, and more modern than Van Cleve's. It is more archaistic in the sense that Steen openly ruptures the realistic premises of his painting by including overt emblems such as the basket filled with, among other things, a leper's clapper and a crutch, the instruments of social and physical demise. These prefigurations of poverty and illness to come had been performed, more naturalistically, by a cripple and infirm beggar in the lower left corner of the *Prodigal Son in a Whorehouse* of c. 1550 discussed above.[32] His work is also more archaistic due to the anatopical appearance of the monkey, clearly not a pet of "everyday life." Central among the "old-fashioned" devices of Steen's painting are the references to the above-mentioned well-worn proverbs, another being "De Hoeren hebben de kaart" (Whores hold all the cards). Similarly archaistic is the invocation of the seven deadly sins, especially, in this instance, sloth and lust—constructs that conjured a late-medieval mentality—a way of thinking that by 1660 was being fashioned as clearly belonging to a distant past.[33]

I believe that by their very invocation these archaisms functioned to incur feelings of nostalgia, a key emotion in the myth of the "home" and its comforts. Significantly, the term *heimwee*, meaning a longing or yearning for home, appears for the first time in Dutch literature in 1688.[34] Pierre Nora's ideas on the "Places of Memory" may serve us here. As he wrote of nineteenth-century France, "tradition is memory that has become historically aware of itself."[35] If Nora's "Land,

Cathedral, Court" were the compelling sites for the formation of French identity, then "Land, City, and Home" are surely the formative sites active in shaping seventeenth-century Dutch identity. Steen's paintings of the home in particular participate in constructing it as a place in memory (both national and personal) of morality and order, portrayed by its loss. Oddly the relentless repetition of moral iconography by contemporary art-historical scholarship services similar conservative nostalgia and desire that things remain unchanged.

At this point it must be said that although this kind of "moralizing iconography" has made many a twentieth-century art historian's career, mine included, and we may all be enchanted with our ability to recognize it, for the seventeenth-century Dutch burgher, and particularly for Steen's level of sophisticated clientele, these old-fashioned and outmoded moralizing tropes were socioreligious categories that had long before become old-fashioned platitudes. To the avant-garde they were humorous by their very invocation; to the rear garde they were nostalgic reminders of the good old days. If they were still believed in at all, as some aspects of Dutch society must have continued to do, for Steen's class of clients they surely functioned as rhetorical truths. To understand this is to understand the difference between moralizing impulses and works that take on moralization as a representational posture or frame. Rather than intending to be didactic, Steen takes the representation of didacticism itself for his subject, and he makes sport of it at that.

In the *Dissolute Household* Steen not only availed himself of an important artistic quotation from a past master, one that spoke to the defining powers of visual culture in the construction of social relationships, but also brought the dialogue of past and present into play with the alterations he introduced into the formula. As an example in detail, Van Cleve's interior opens to a landscape, to the outside world; Steen's room, by contrast, opens only to a secondary interior space, that of the kitchen. The change emphasizes the shift from a preoccupation with itinerancy and transiency in the priorities of sixteenth-century visual myth-making to the late-seventeenth-century preoccupation with a mythically virginal domesticity and grounded permanency.[36] In Steen's interior the outside world is tellingly represented only by a small detail of a figure seen through the large double windows on the left. As he leans out of an open window of an adjacent building and looks in on our scene, he is a hilarious reminder of the closeness of urban living and of the visual access people have into other people's "private" lives in the modern world. The grist for "gossip" given the irregular activities of Steen's household is boundless.

Steen's modern interest in delineating a humorously framed conception of the masculine and especially the feminine are perhaps the most compelling and strike at the heart of his interest in "difference." Steen's painting participates in the articulating discourses of the second half of the seventeenth century, which sought to shift paradigms of woman from the sexual to the civil. His primary strategy is the incorporation of the sexual/public/outlaw into the percept of the civil/private/lawful. Moreover, his constructed heimwee is predicated on the mother and child relationship. Woman and home are interchangeable concepts, only confused by the presence of man. The right zone of Steen's painting is inhabited by the mother and children and revolves around petty theft: the young boy robs his neglectful, sleeping mother; the dog steals the roast.[37] The left zone, inhabited by the father, his lover, and servants, deals with adultery at worst, lasciviousness at least.[38] The fine form of the father's slung leg in a beautiful red-orange stocking makes the connection with the crutch above his head all the more poignant as signs of crime and its punishment.

Steen's notion of representation is, further, thoroughly permeated by a paradigmatic individualism or personalism. The sign of this individual as "elck" is the person of Jan Steen himself, expressed through his insistent systems of self-referentiality, including references to his own work, his own recognizable portrait, and those of his family. Again, as noted in Chapter 4, both sides of the Wellington painting reiterate formulations that must have been well known to the Steen cognoscenti. The right-hand side of the painting quotes the center group of the Vienna painting, and the left-hand side quotes a painting last known in the Meyer collection. In the humorous wink of an eye the viewer gets two Steens in one.

Surely Steen's own recognizable portrait and, to a lesser extent, those of his family and dog, as has always been remarked on, is another driving aspect of his self-referentiality. But rather than speaking to the reality of his images, these, I would argue, secure the *Dissolute Household*'s place within the history of the Dutch imaginary rather than within the history of the real. The gambit begins with Steen's inclusion of the male within the female-defined domain of the home. As I will discuss in detail in the final section of this book, primary among the visual tropes of seventeenth-century Dutch genre painting, which fabricated bourgeois domesticity (as opposed to that of the peasantry), is the singular absence of the father. Steen's image comes into dialogue with Van Cleve's painting, therefore, on a complex of levels. For instance, as aberrant father he also takes the part of the itinerant traveler, with one foot out the door so to speak. By his sheer inclusion in the scene he recalls the peasant (not bourgeois) origins of his referent. Steen's presence as a man is itself a sign of exteriority, as is his activity as sexual or erotic in character. His presence as the artist who fashioned the work further partakes of the northern tradition of the artist as profligate. The often-cited examples (all three remarkably in the same museum in Dresden) are Vermeer's early *Procuress*, Rembrandt's *Self-Portrait with Saskia in the Tavern* of 1636, and Metsu's *Self-Portrait with His Wife*. Indeed, the last two, significantly, are considered self-portraits as the Prodigal Son.

In the end the thrust of Van Cleve and Steen is neither the censure of the public sphere nor the commendation of the private but rather the cultural regulatory definition of both. By creating a sense of nostalgia for a place filled with comforting old homilies and a myriad of in-jokes Jan Steen appeals to the child in every adult who, like Dorothy in *The Wizard of Oz*, yearns to return to a safe and dependable state; yet, alas, there truly is "no place like home."

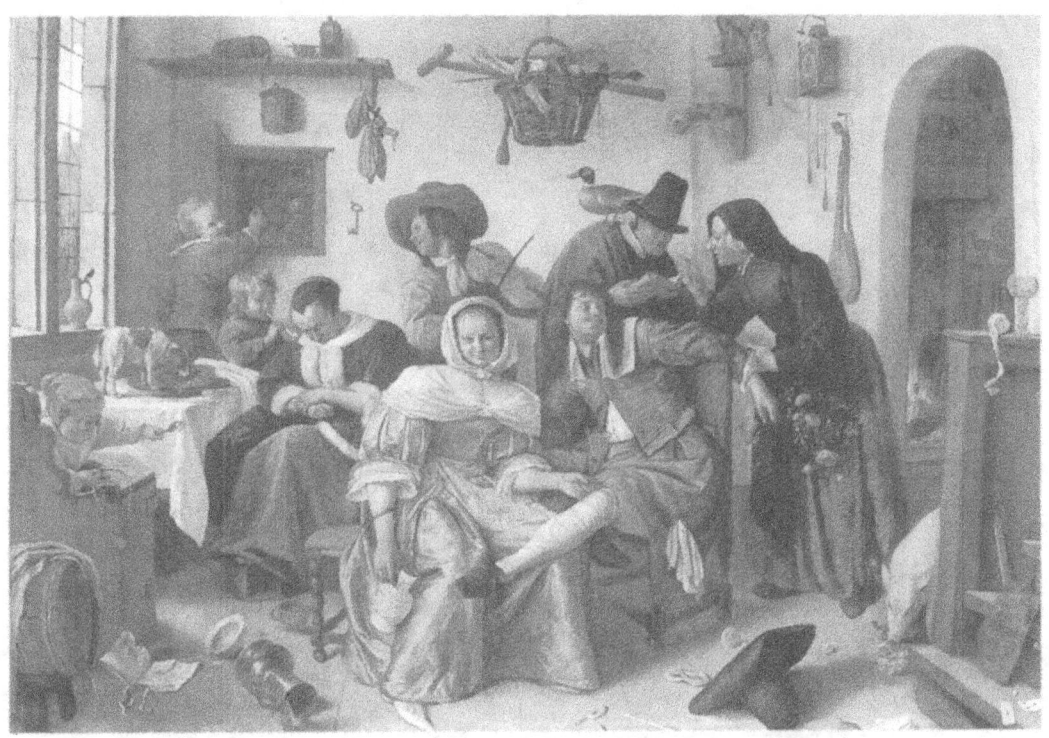

FIGURE 30. Jan Steen, *In Weelde Siet Toe*
(Die verkehrte Welt). Kunsthistorisches
Museum, Vienna.

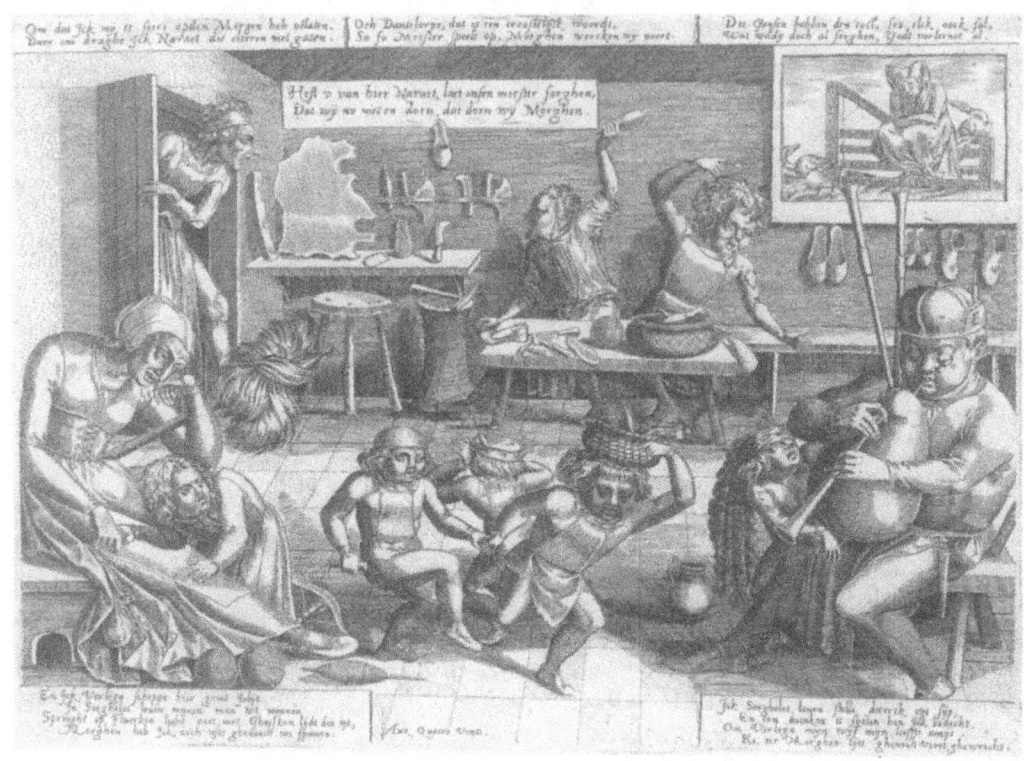

FIGURE 31. Netherlandish (Hieronymus Cock, exc.), *Verlega and Sorghelos*. Rijksmuseum, Amsterdam.

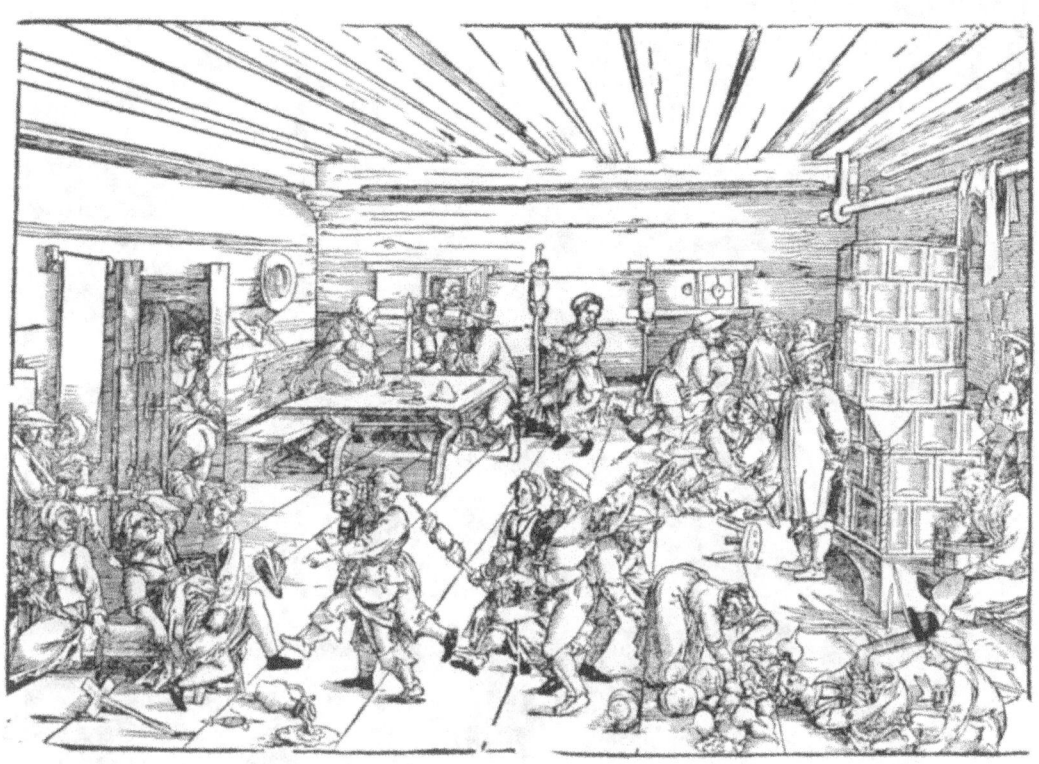

FIGURE 32. Bartel Beham, *Die Spinnstube*.
Facsimile. The Metropolitan Museum of Art,
Harris Brisbane Dick Fund, 1929, New York.

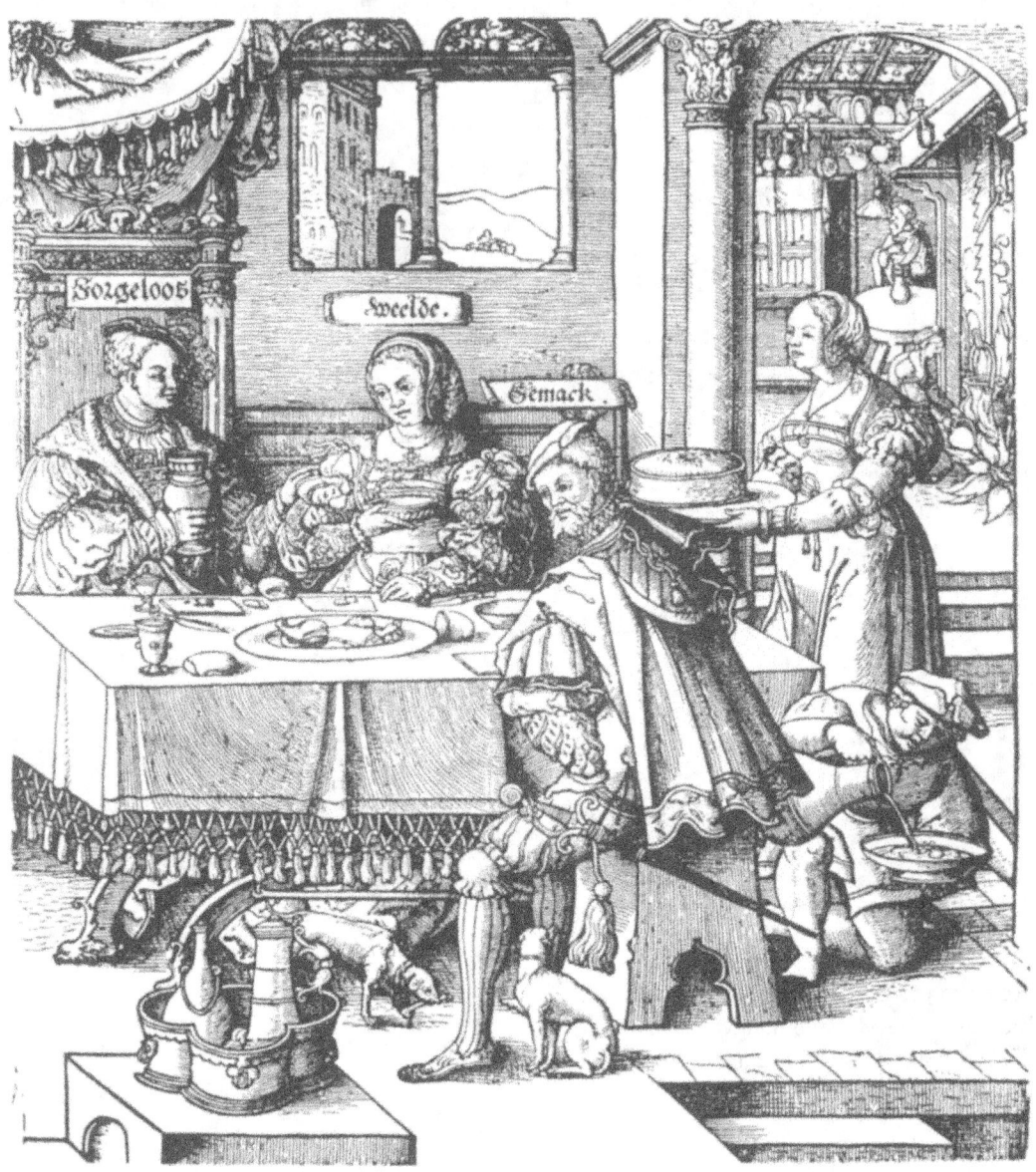

FIGURE 33. Cornelis Anthonisz.,
Sorghelos in a Tavern. Facsimile.
The Metropolitan Museum of Art,
New York.

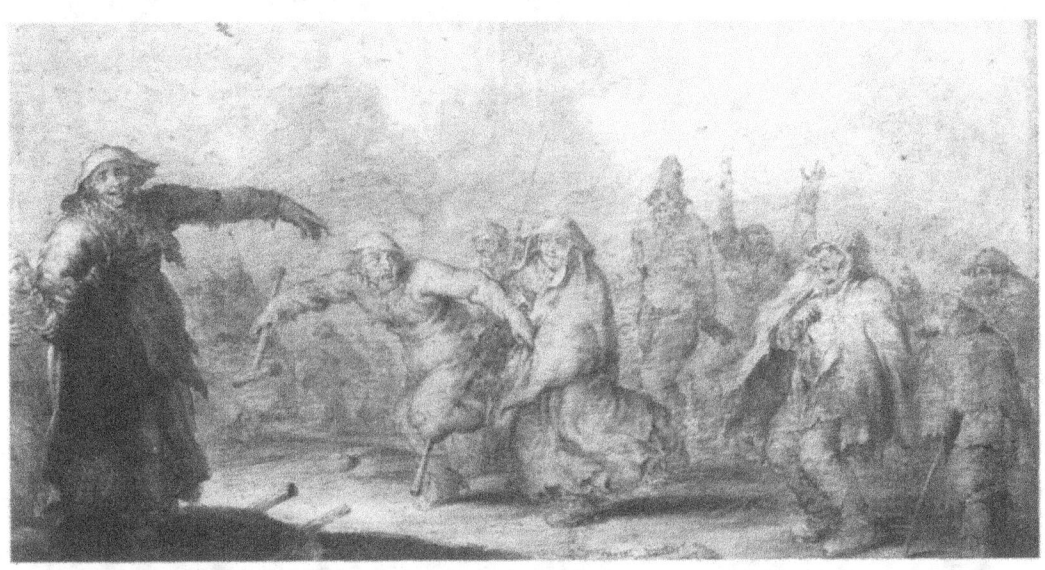

FIGURE 34. Adriaen van de Venne,
Arme Weelde. Museum Boijmans
van Beuningen, Rotterdam.

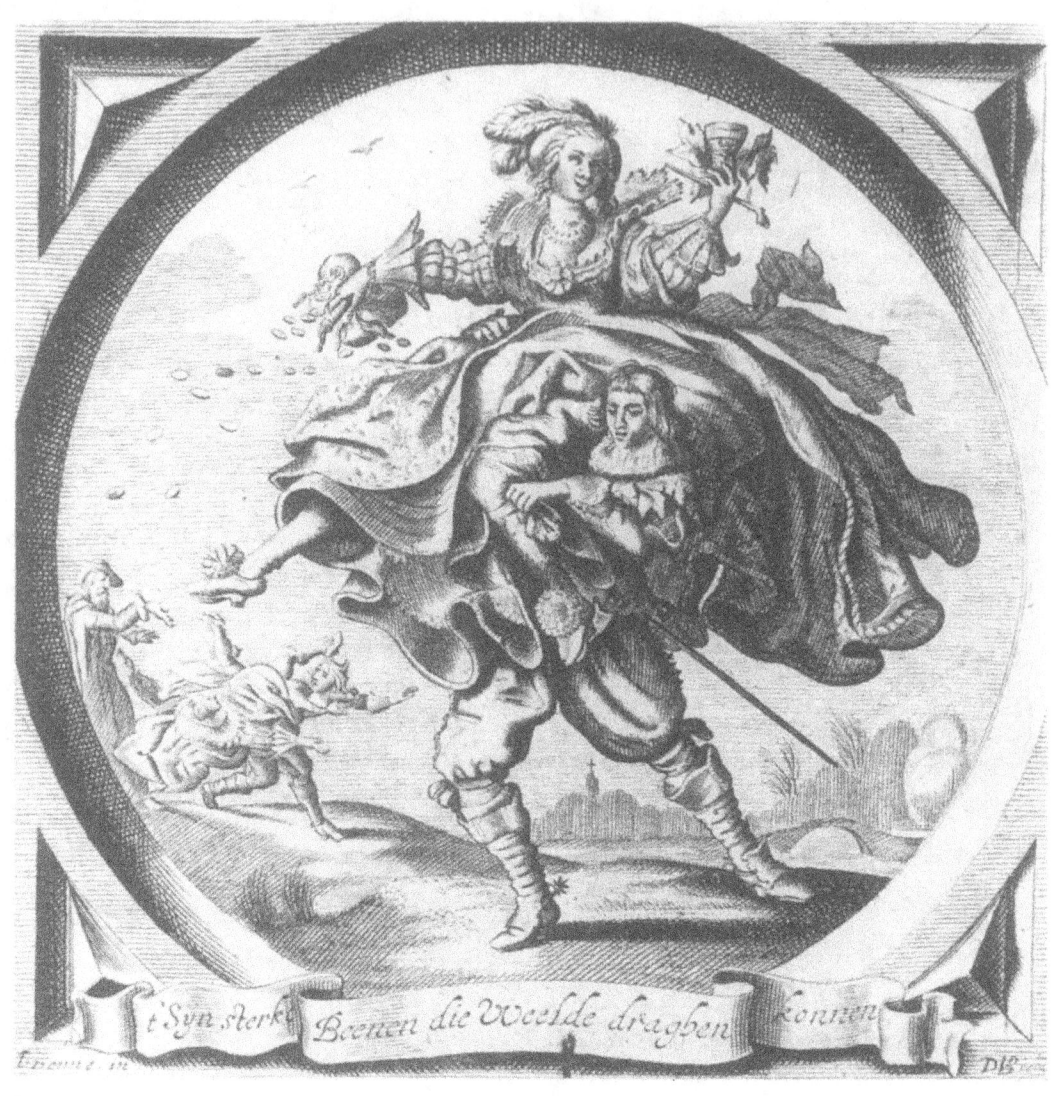

FIGURE 35. Adriaen van de Venne,
't Zijn stercke beenen die weelde dragen
konnen. Illustration from Jacob Cats
Spiegel van den ouden ende nieuwe
Tijd, 1632. Photograph by author.

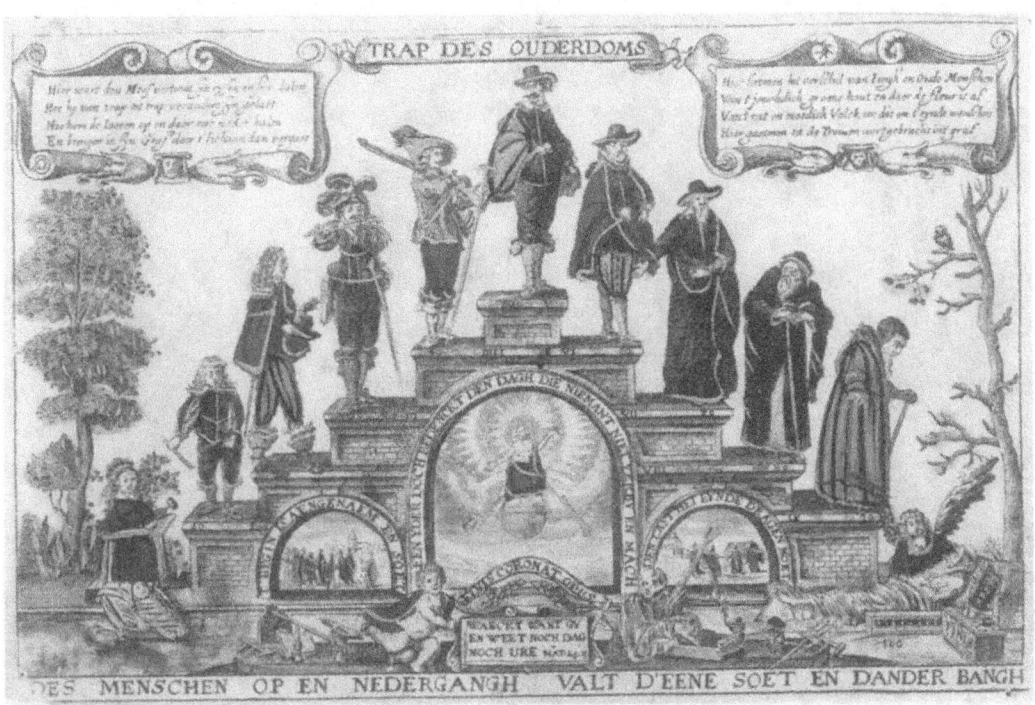

FIGURE 36. Anonymous,
The Ages of Man (*Levenstrap*).
Broadsheet. Rijksmuseum,
Amsterdam.

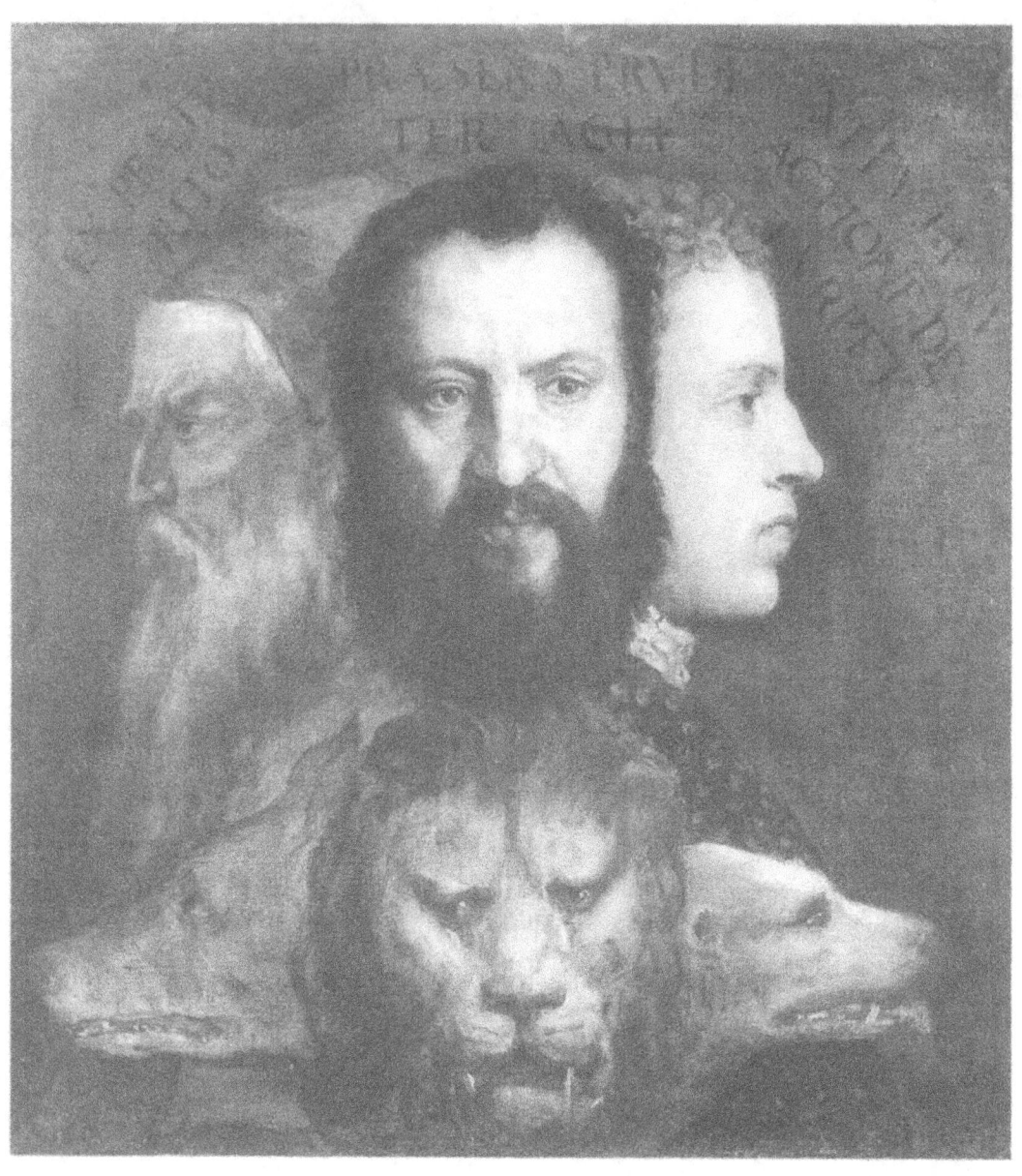

FIGURE 37. Titian, *Allegory*.
National Gallery, London.

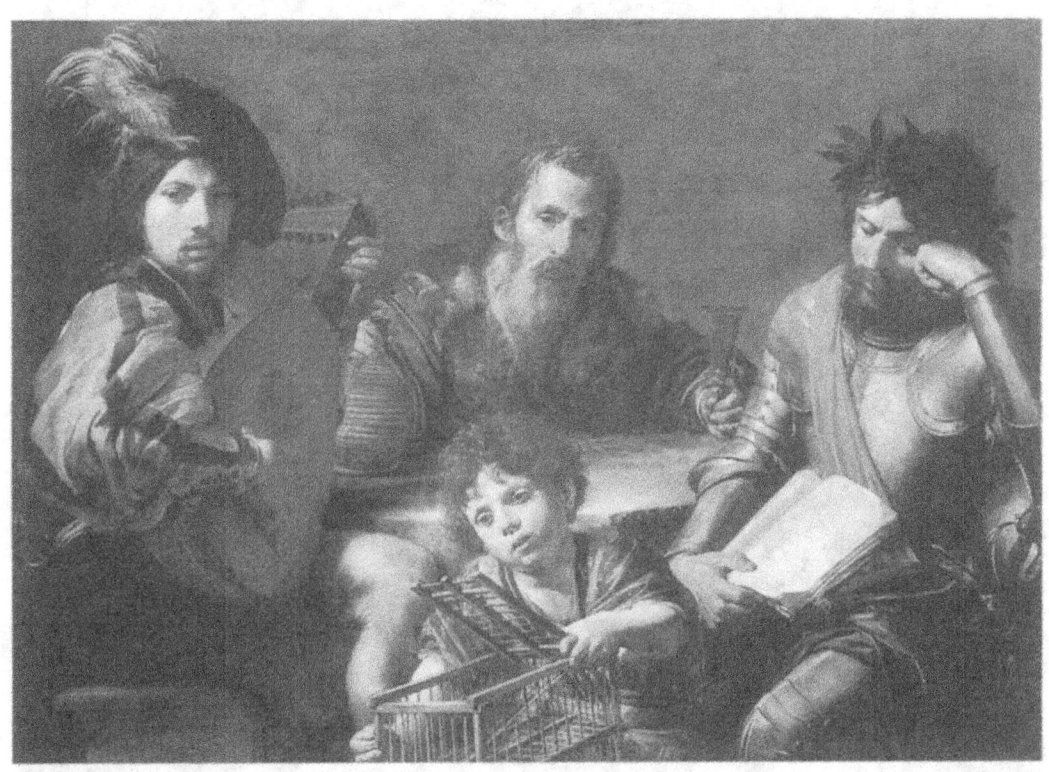

FIGURE 38. Valentin de Boulogne, *Four Ages of Man.*
National Gallery, London.

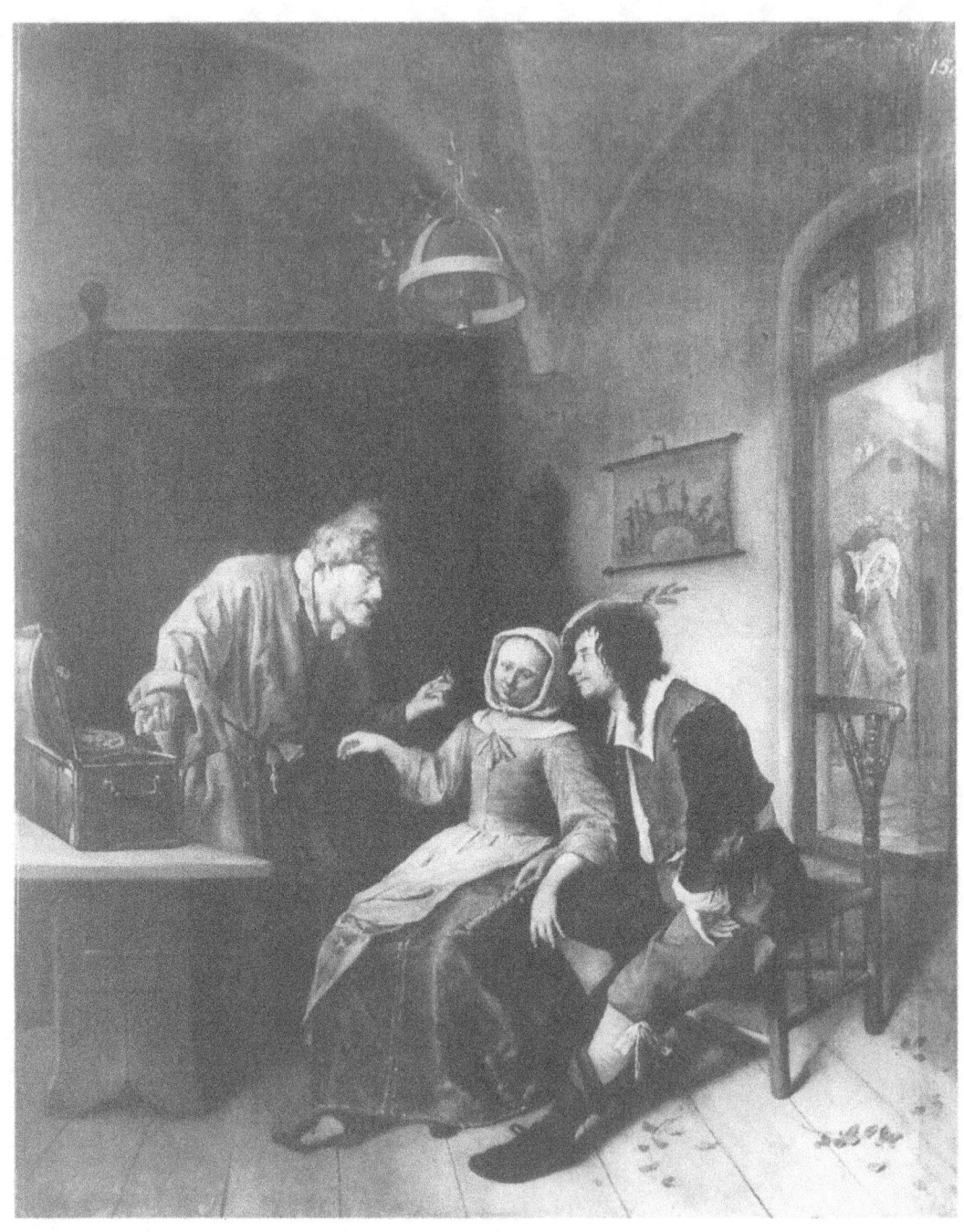

FIGURE 39. Jan Steen, *Choice Between Wealth and Youth*. National Museum in Warsaw.

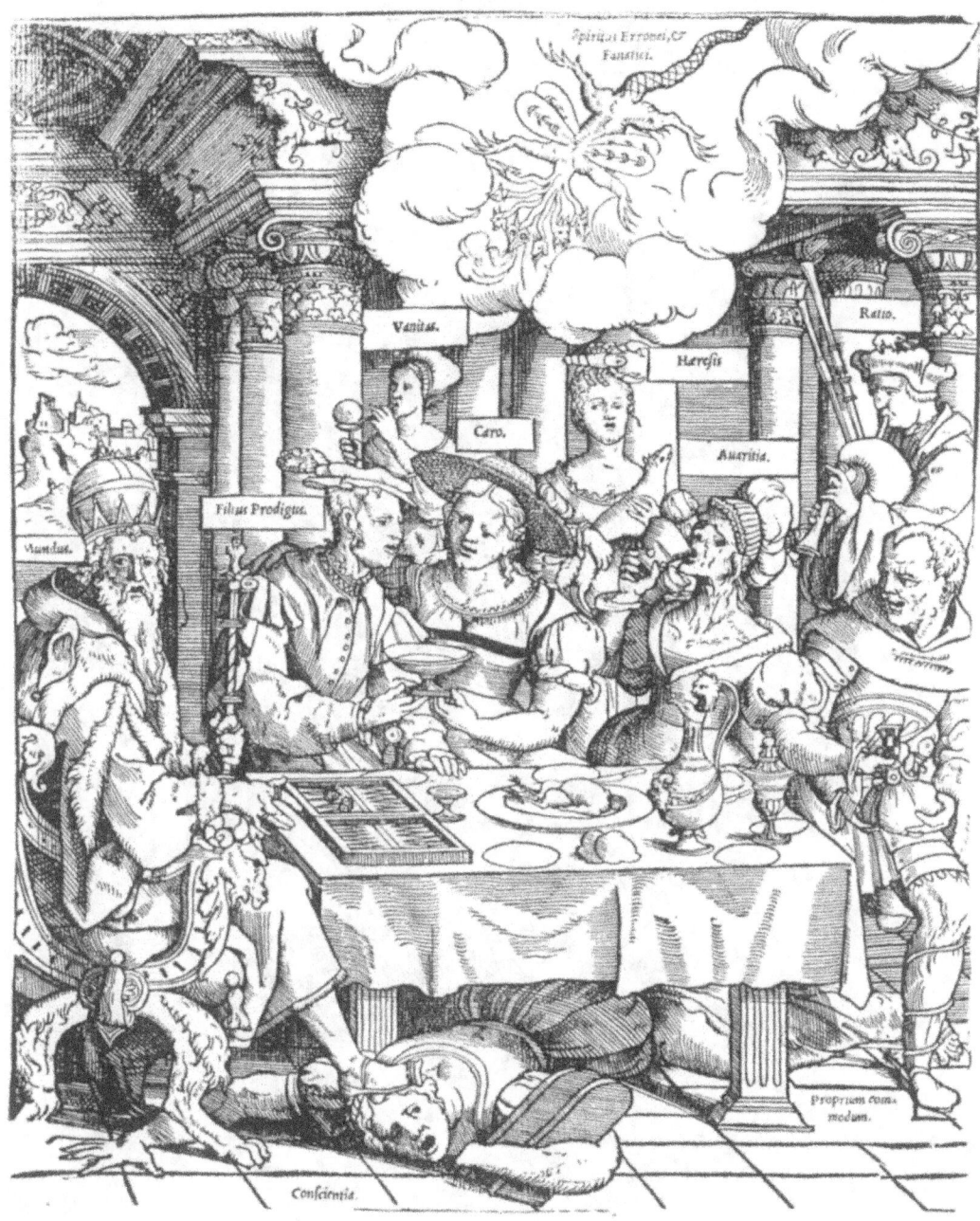

FIGURE 40. Cornelis Anthonisz., *The Prodigal Son in a Tavern*. Facsimile. The Metropolitan Museum of Art, New York.

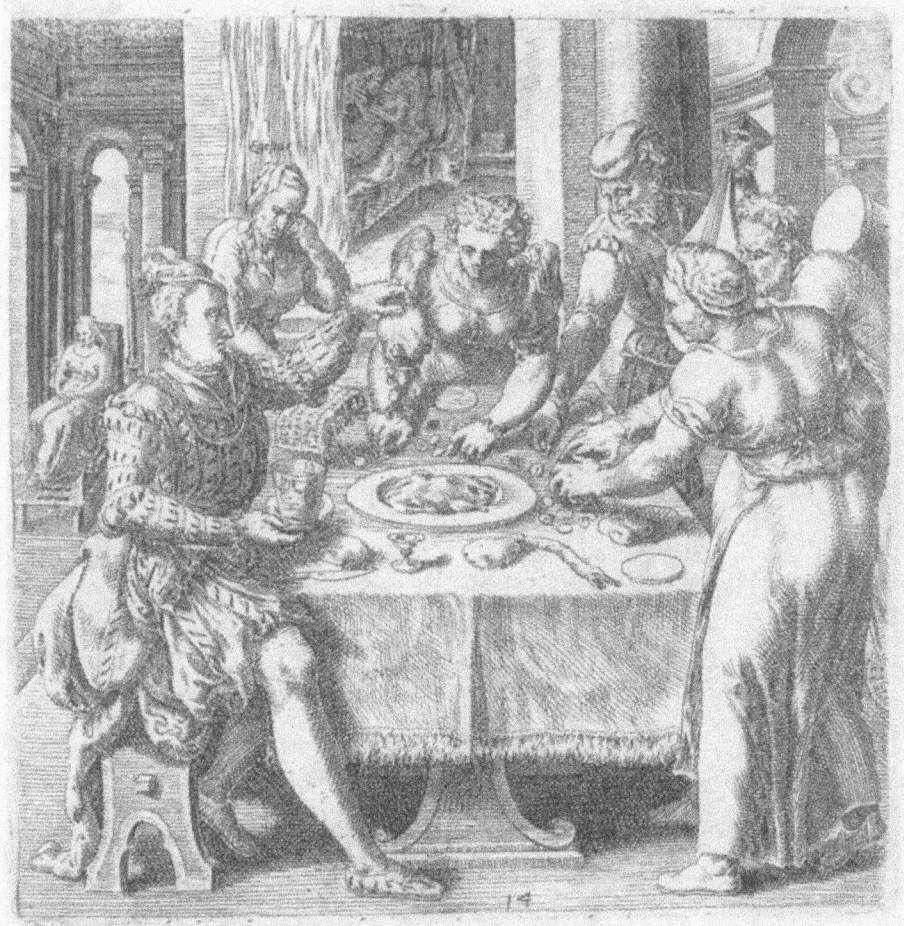

XIIIL

PRODIGI.

Vacantes potibus & dantes symbola, consumentur.
Prouerb. 23, 2.
Qui nutrit scortum, perdet substantiam.
Prouerb. 29, 3.

14

Quid mirum, fundos si prodigus euomat haustos:
Illos comminuit faucibus antè suis.
Græcari solitum tandem diuexat egestas;
Qui vel pauperibus danda alimenta vorat.

AVARI.

FIGURE 41. Jan Wierix, *"The Prodigals."* From D. V. Coornhert,
Recht ghebruyck ende misbruyck van tijdelijcke have, 1585.
Spencer Collection, The New York Public Library, Astor,
Lenox and Tilden Foundations, New York.

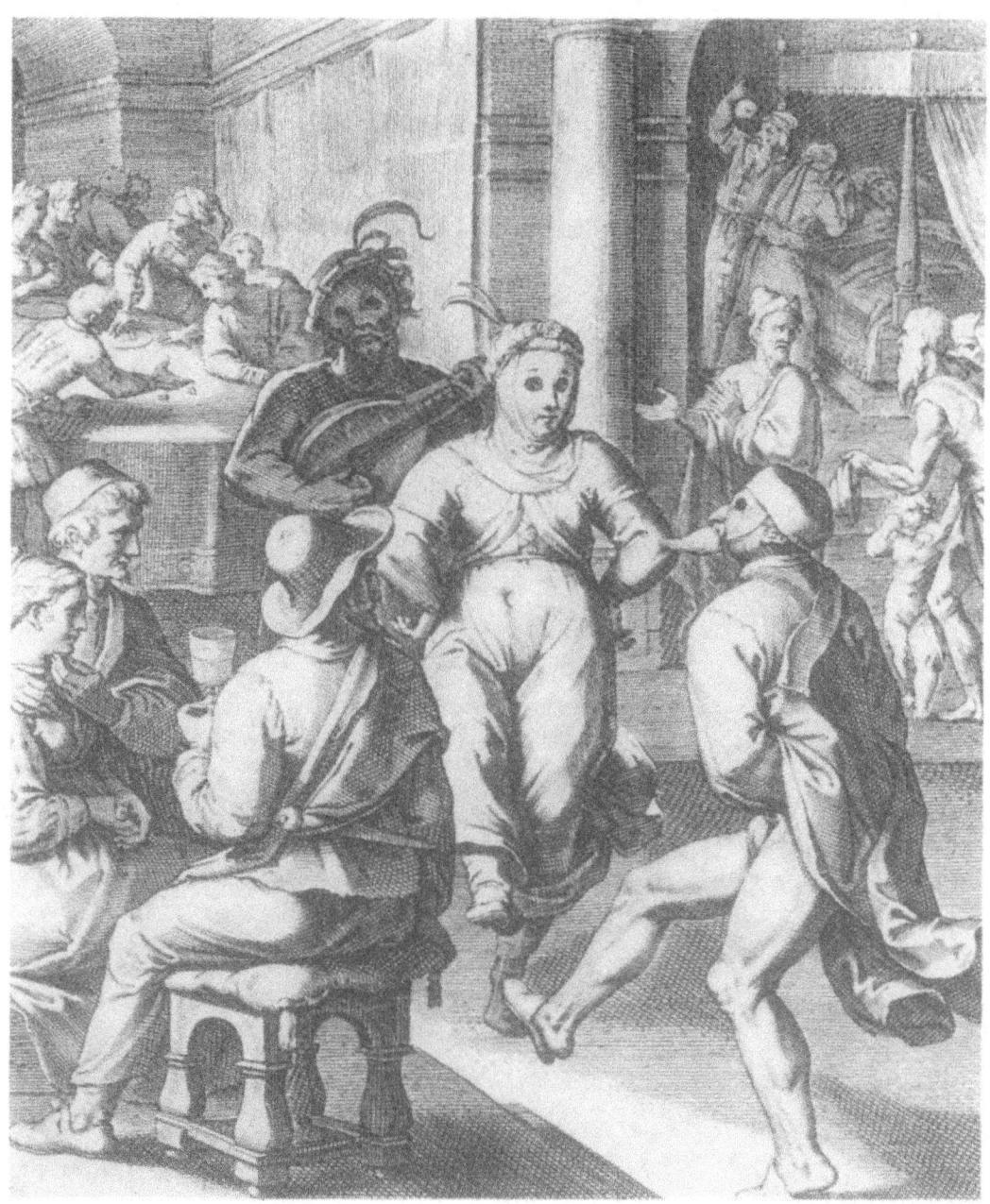

FIGURE 42. Otto van Veen, illustration
from *Emblemata Horatiana*. 1684.
Photograph by author.

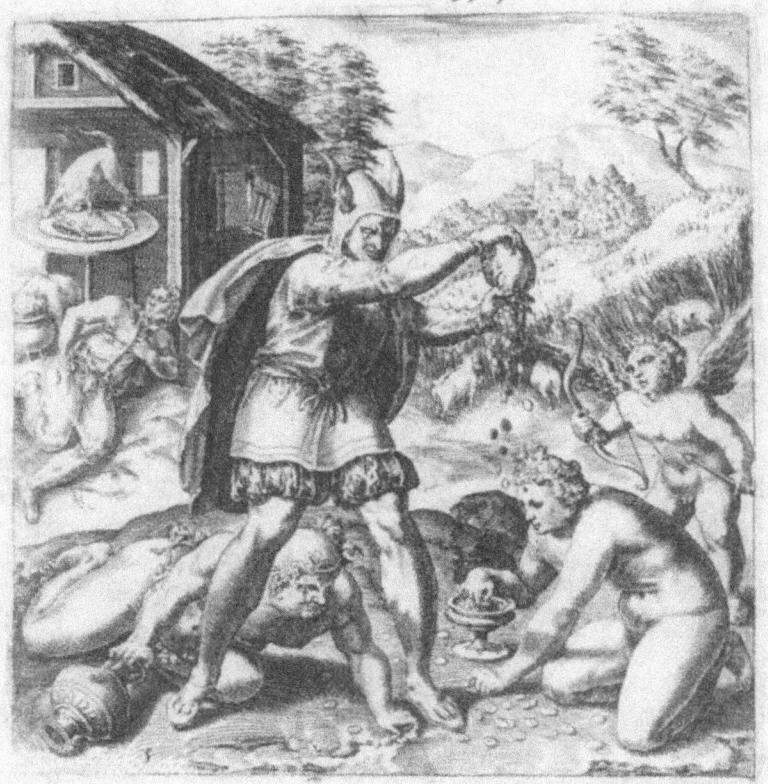

V.

PAVPERTAS COMMERITA.

Vacantes potibus confumentur.
Prouerb. 23, 21.
Anima diffoluta efuriet.
Prouerb. 19, 15.

Prodigus à luxu vitam traducit egenam:
Crefcit focordi farris auena loco.
Oftia virginibus praecludit inertia fomni:
Haec tria pauperies femina digna capit.

MEN-

FIGURE 43. Jan Wierix, *"Well Earned Poverty."*
From D. V. Coornhert, *Recht ghebruyck ende
misbruyck van tijdelijcke have,* 1585. Spencer
Collection, The New York Public Library, Astor,
Lenox and Tilden Foundations, New York.

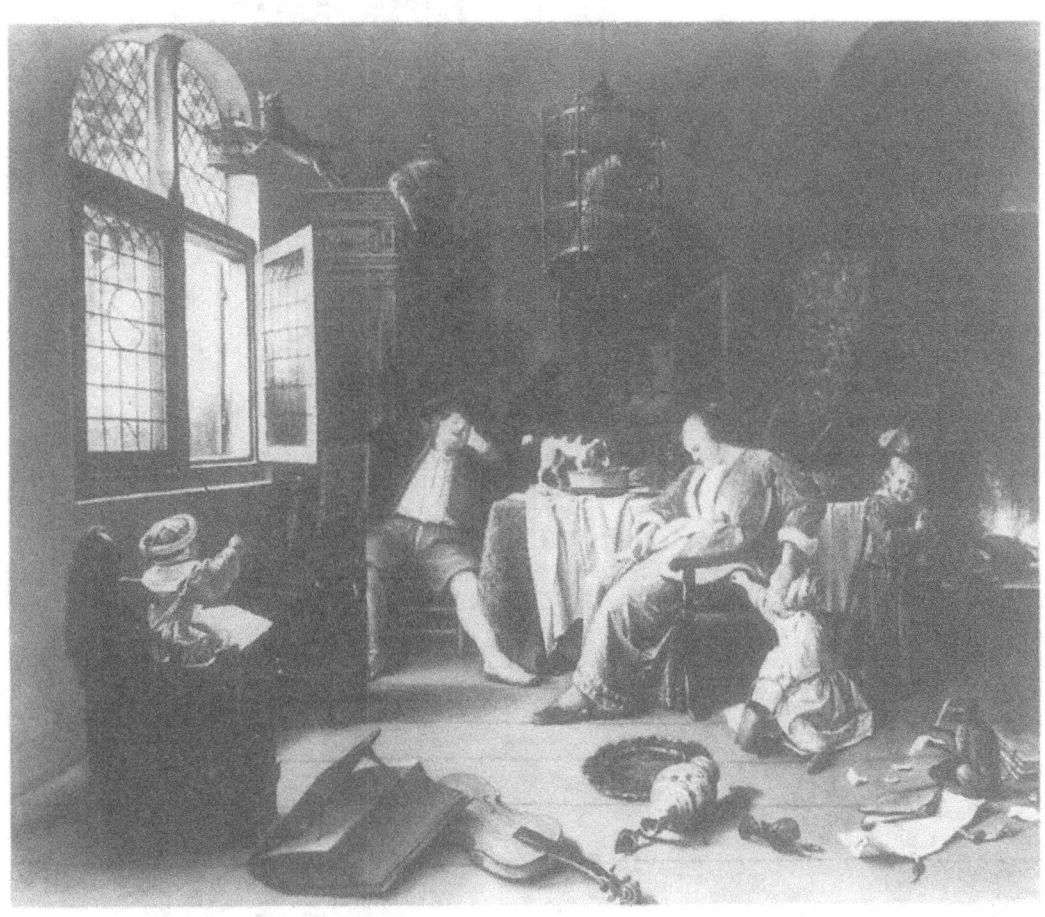

FIGURE 44. Jan Steen, *Dissolute Household*.
Location unknown. Photograph by the
Rijksbureau voor Kunsthistorische
Documentatie, The Hague / The Netherlands.

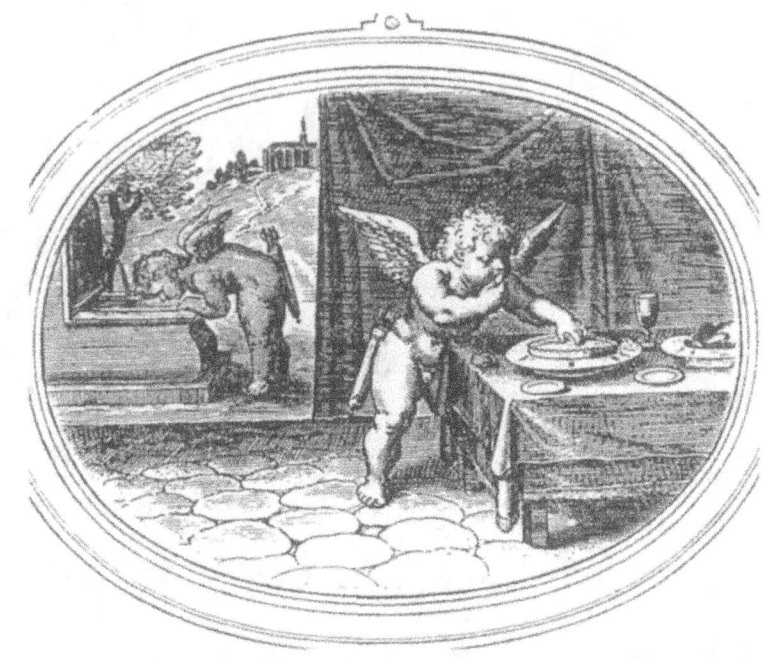

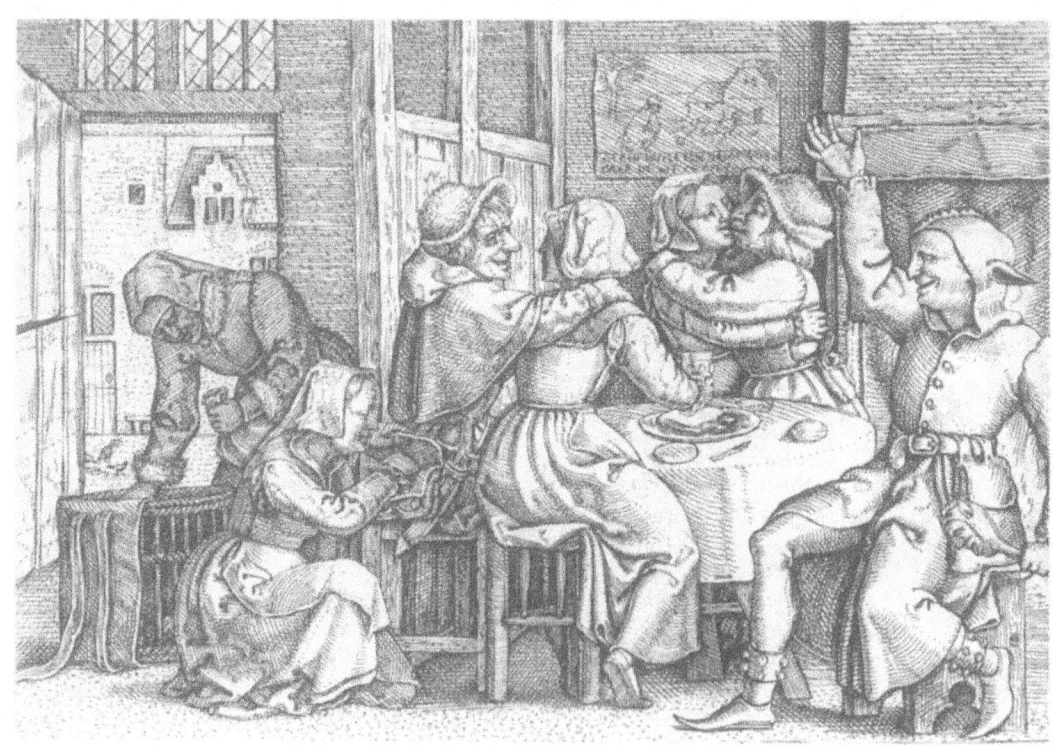

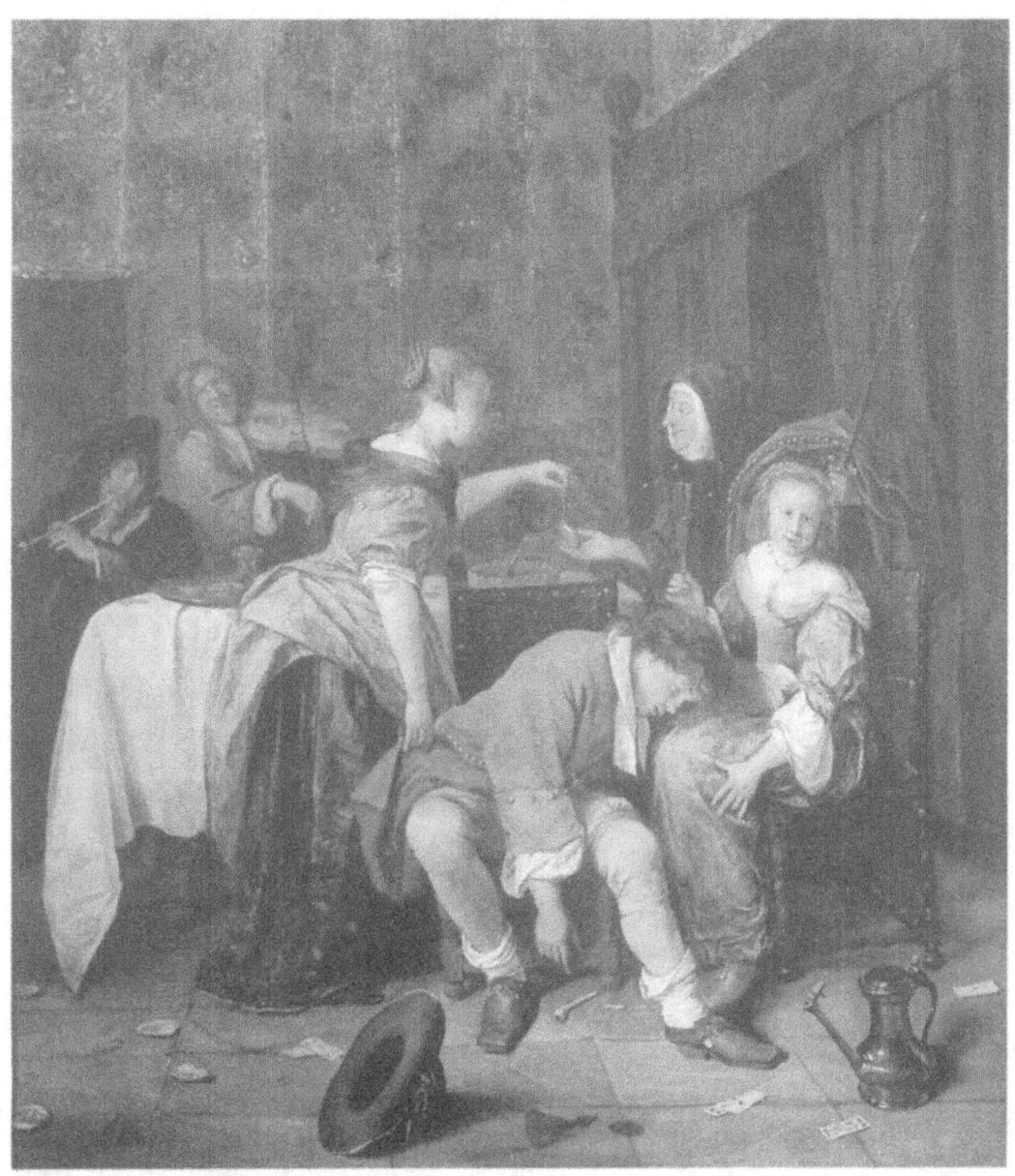

FIGURE 47. Jan Steen, *Bad Company.*
Paris. Louvre. Photograph by Eric Lessing/
Art Resource, New York.

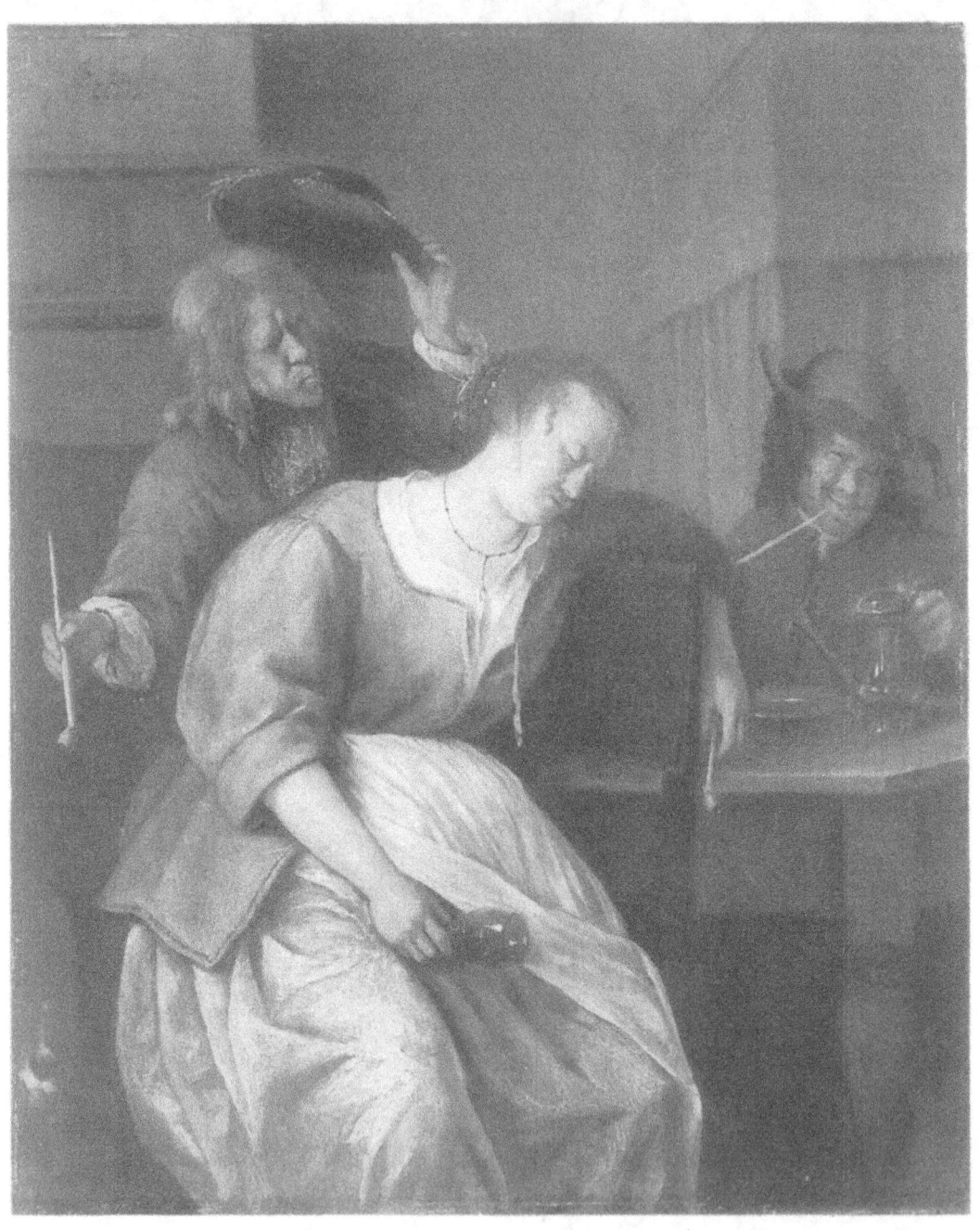

FIGURE 48. Jan Steen, *Tavern Scene*.
National Gallery, London.

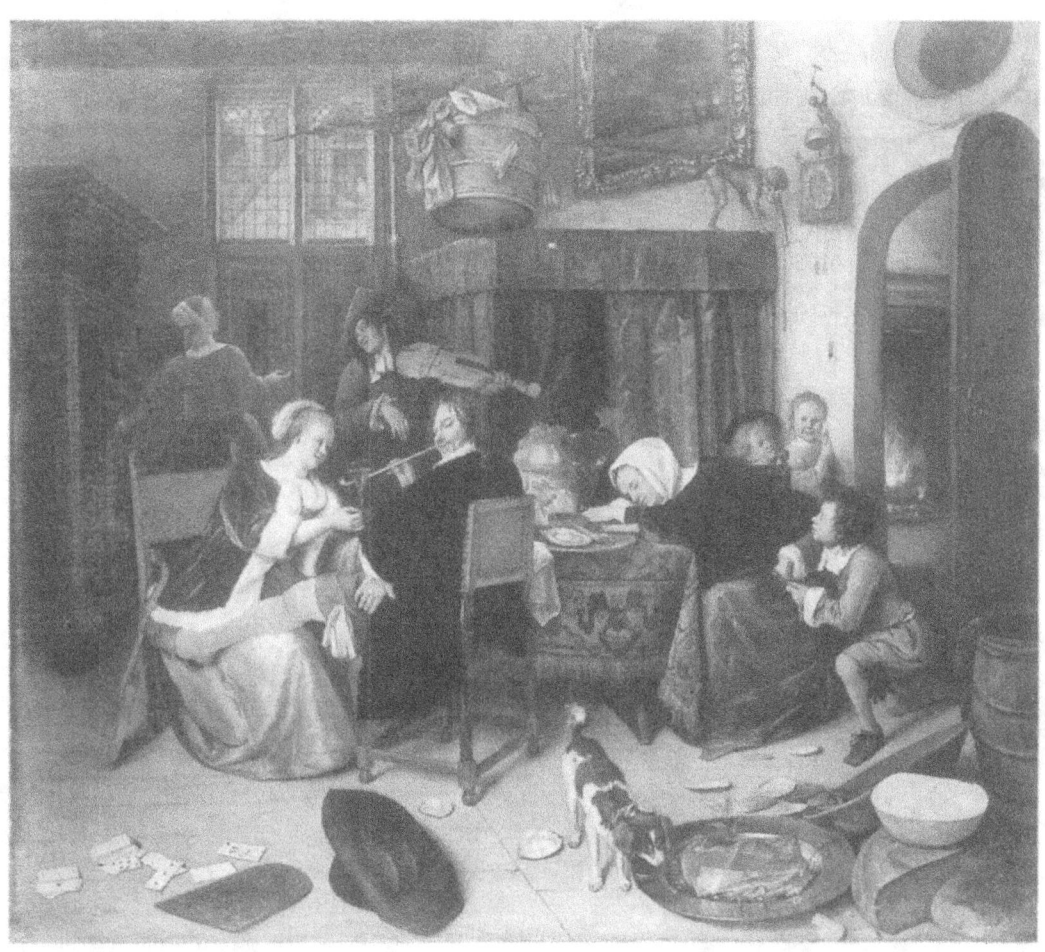

FIGURE 49. Jan Steen, *The Dissolute Household.*
Wellington Museum, London.

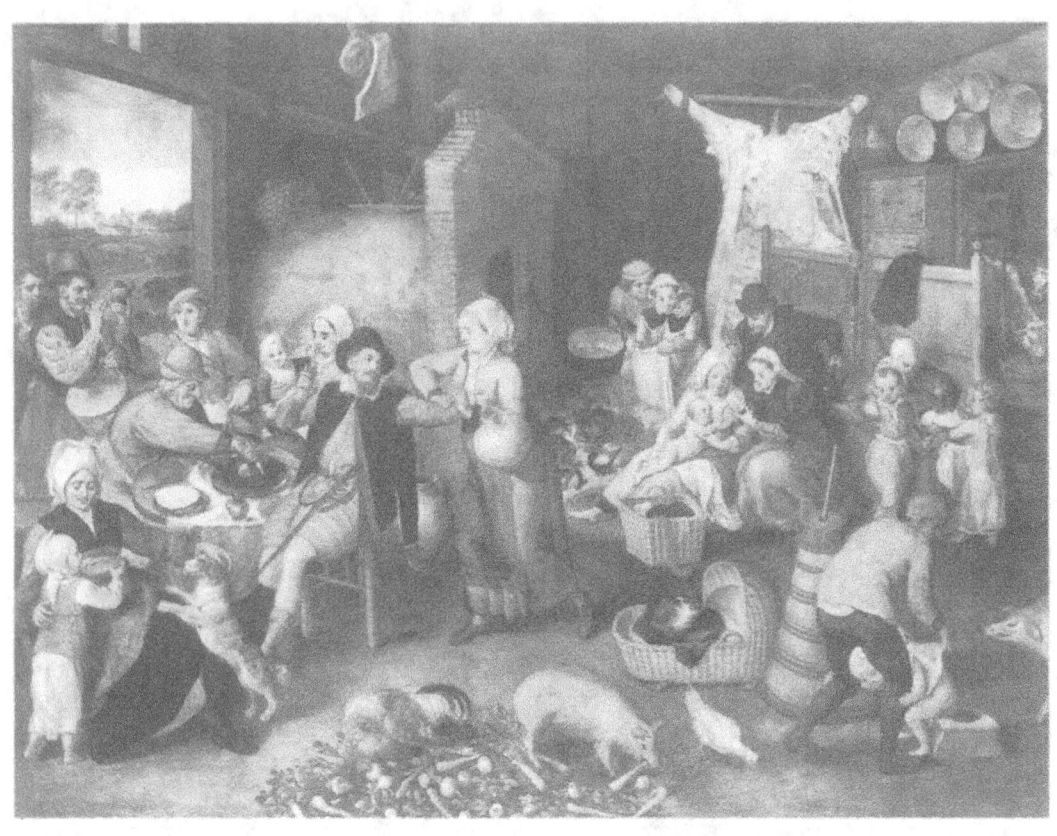

FIGURE 50. Marten van Cleve,
Peasant Interior (*Flämische Haushaltung*).
Kunsthistorisches Museum, Vienna.

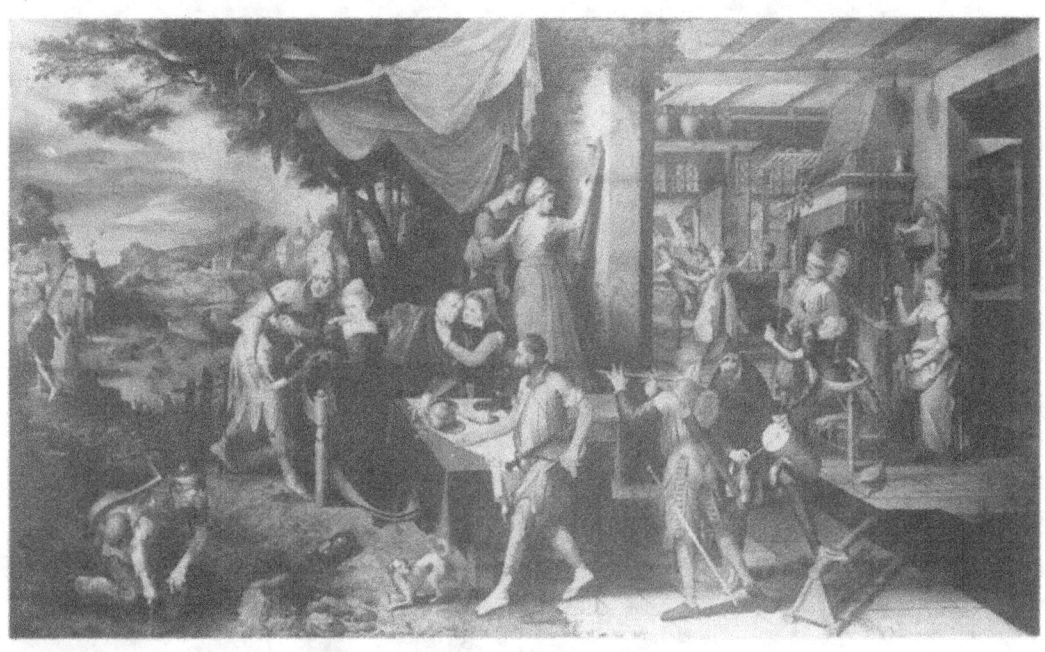

FIGURE 51. Master of the Prodigal Son,
The Prodigal Son in a Whorehouse.
Kunsthistorisches Museum, Vienna.

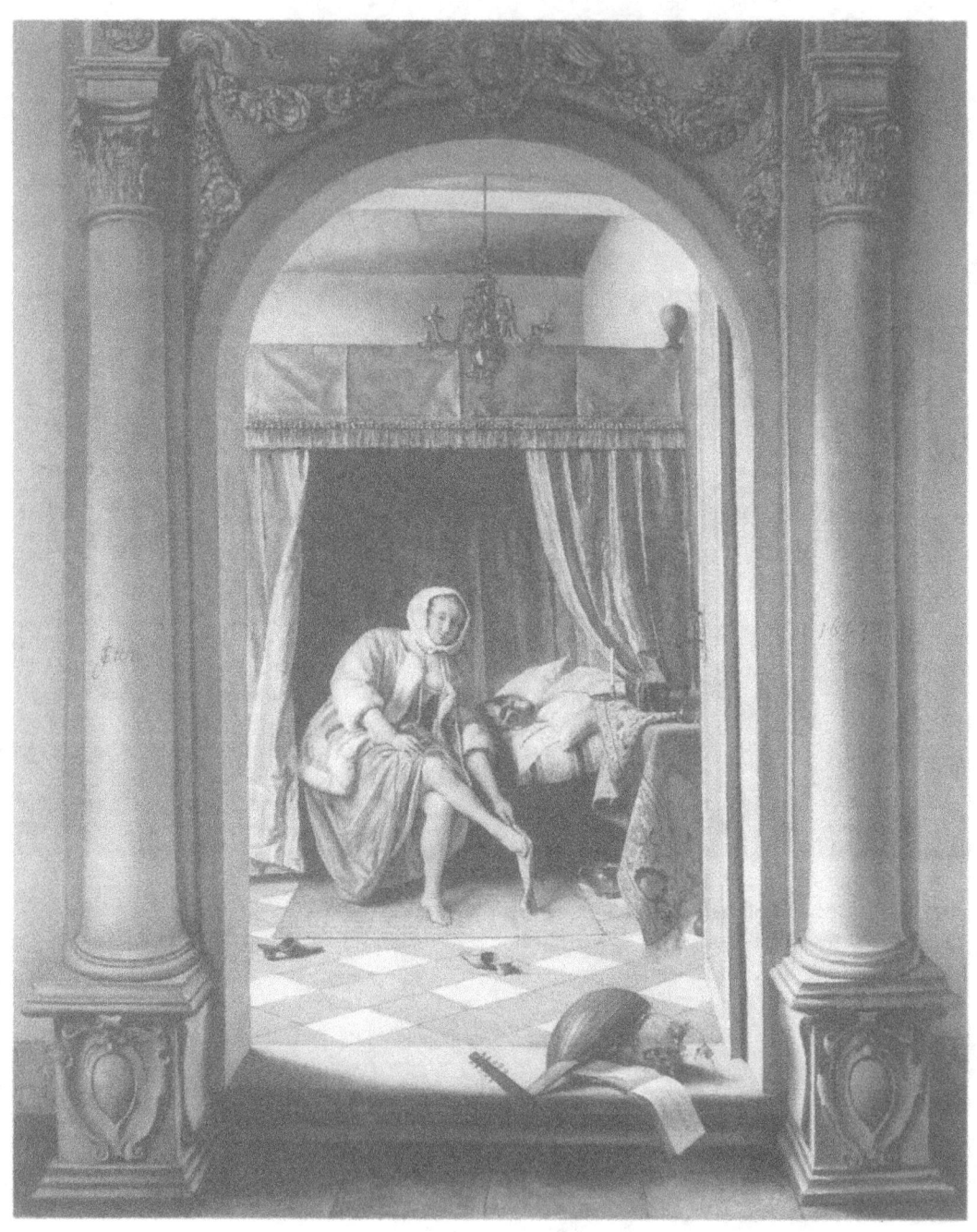

FIGURE 52. Jan Steen, *The Morning Toilet* (*A Woman at Her Toilet*). The Royal Collection, © 2002 Her Majesty, Queen Elizabeth II, London.

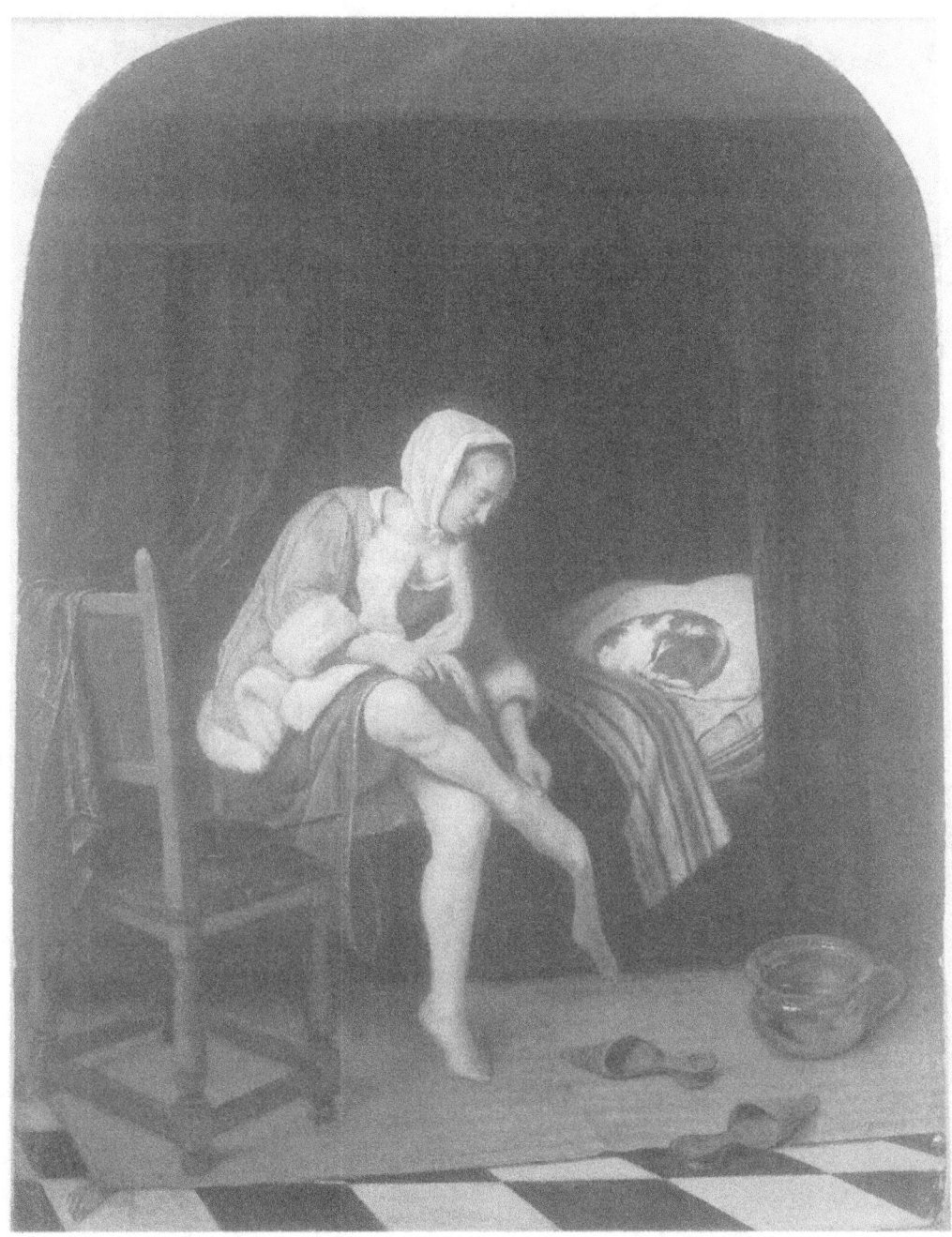

FIGURE 53. Jan Steen, *The Toilet*.
Rijksmuseum, Amsterdam.

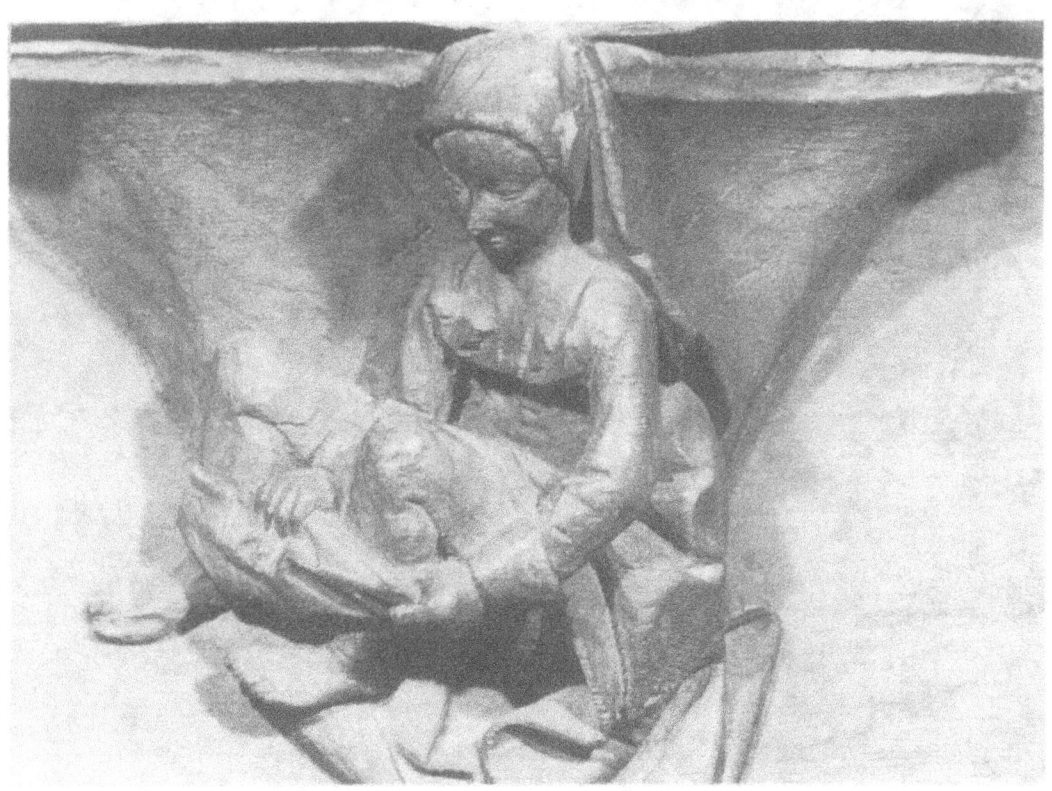

FIGURE 54. Anonymous, *A Woman Putting on Her Stockings*. Misericord (from Kraus and Kraus 1975). Originally from Church St.-Chamant. Photograph by author.

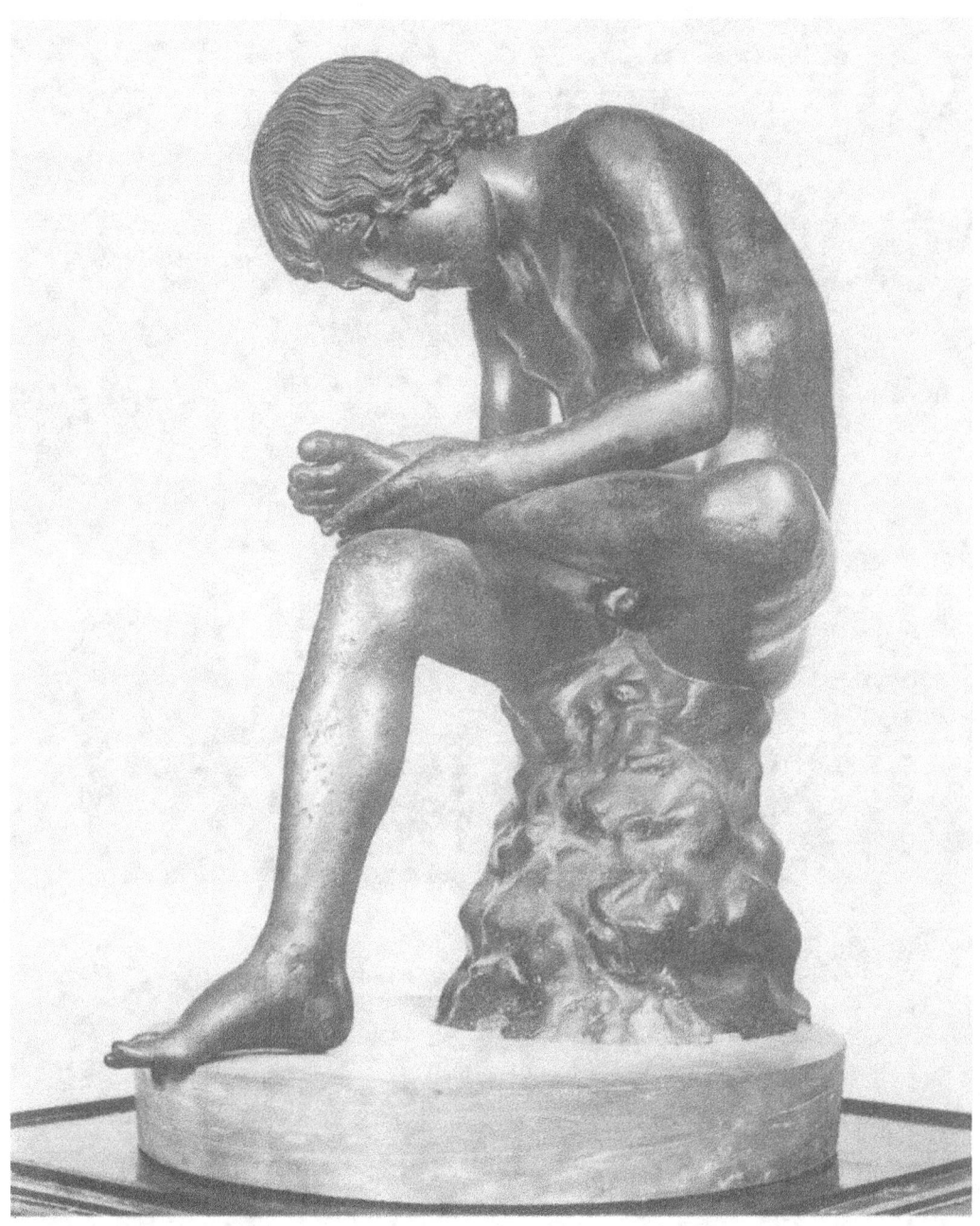

FIGURE 55. (School of Miron), *The Spinario*
(The Thorn Puller). Palazzo dei Conservatori,
Rome, Italy. Photograph by Alinari/Art Resource,
New York.

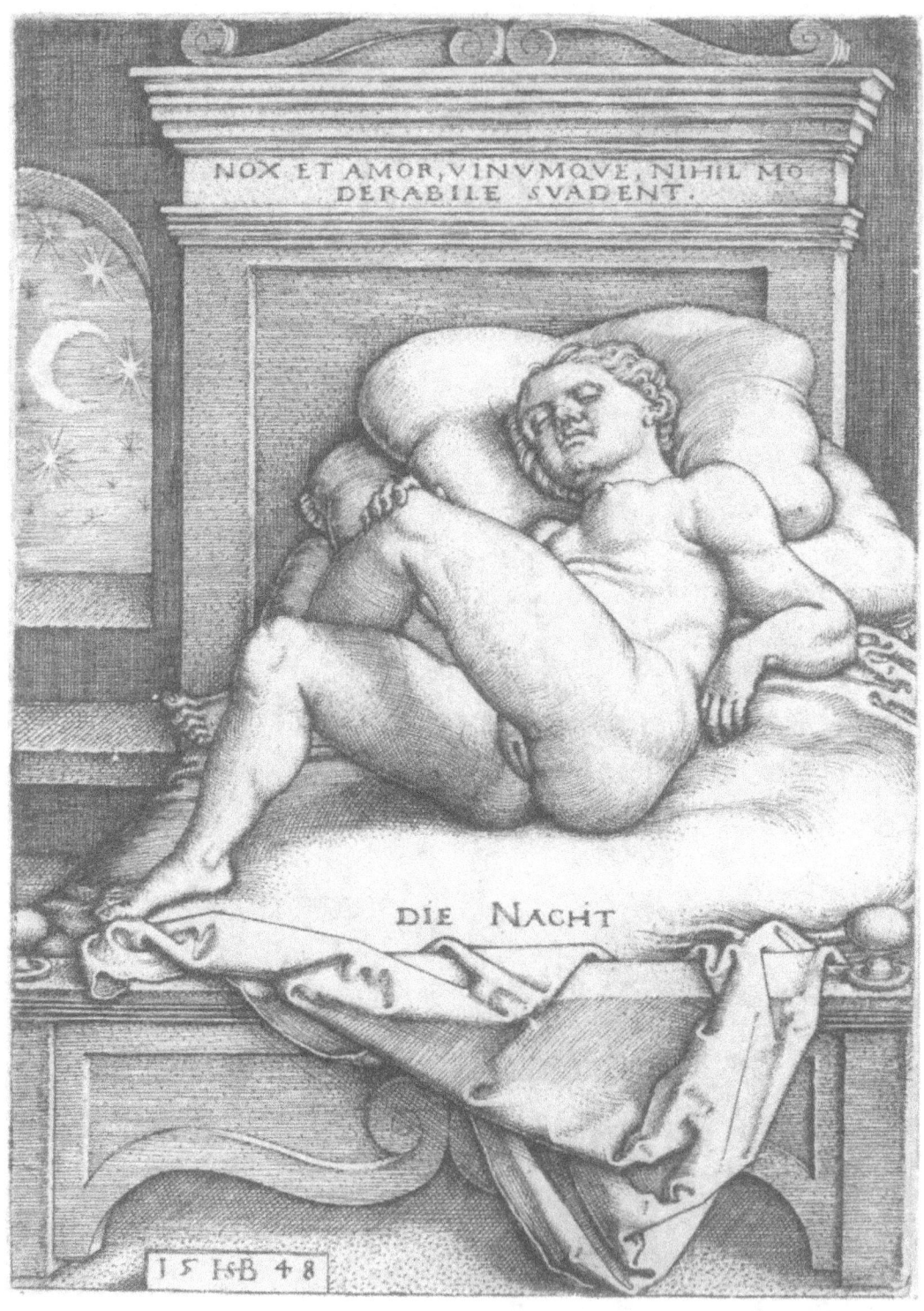

NOX ET AMOR, VINVMQVE, NIHIL MO
DERABILE SVADENT.

DIE NACHT

1 5 HSB 4 8

FIGURE 56. Hans Sebald Beham, *Night*.
British Museum, London.

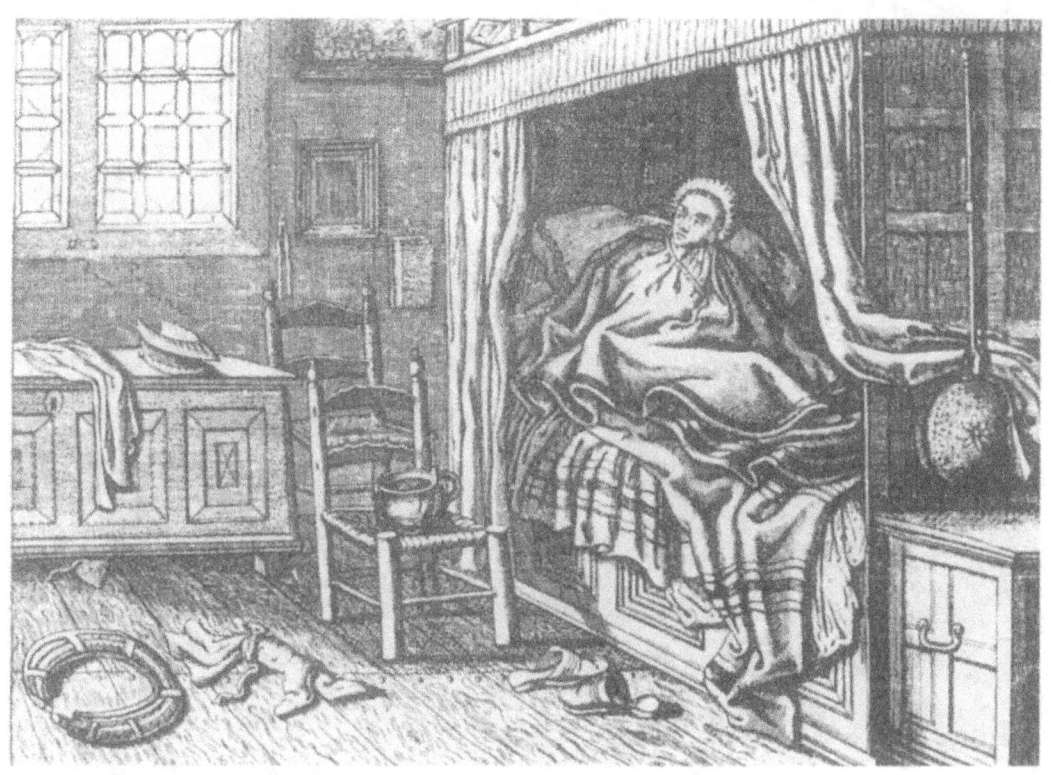

FIGURE 57. Adriaen van de Venne, *"Ledigh en laf, een levend' graf"* (Lazy and insipid, a living grave), from Johan de Brune's *Zinnewerck*. 1624. Republished 1661. Photograph by author.

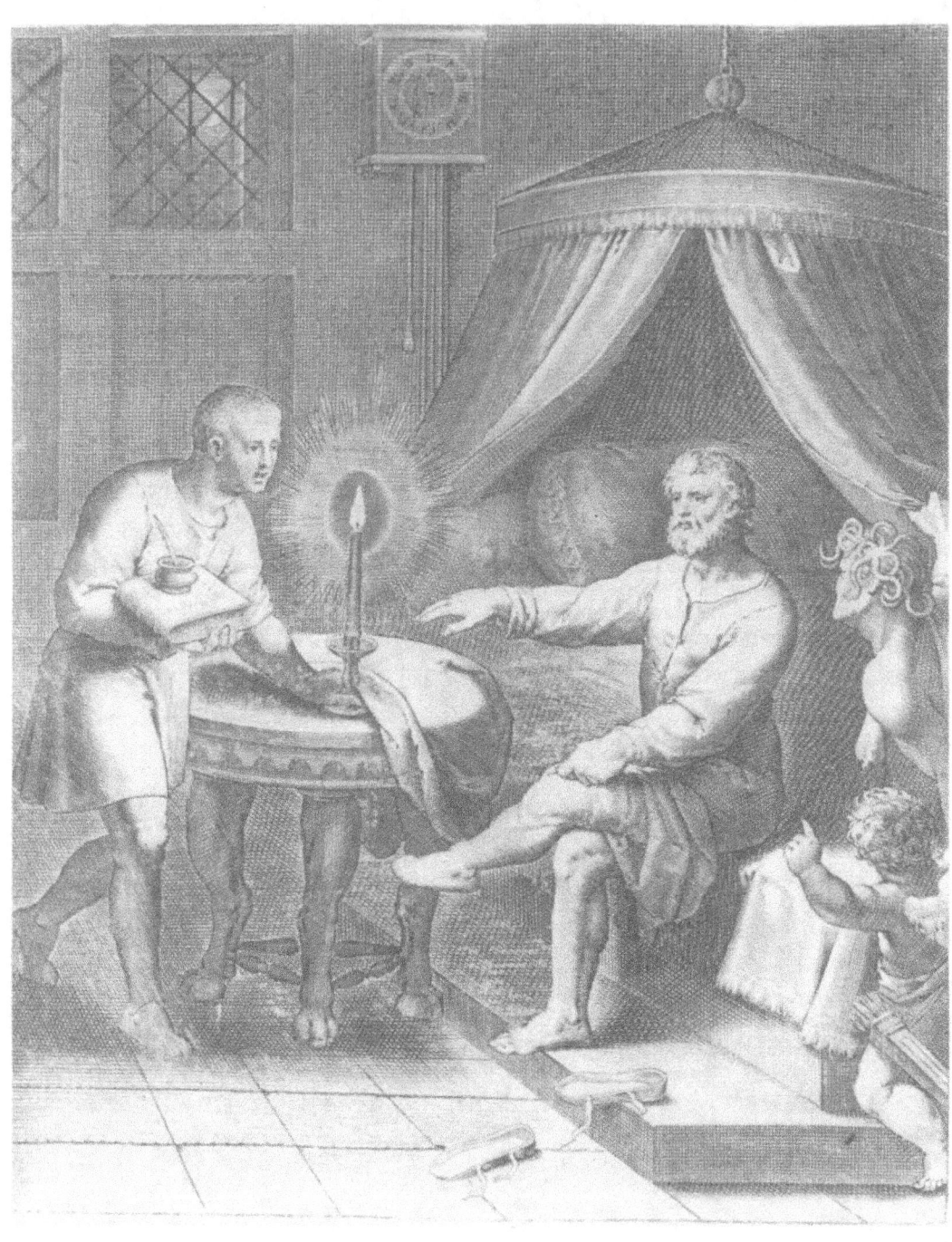

FIGURE 58. Otto van Veen, *"Leedigheit voed ondeugd"* (Laziness is the cause of all evil), from *Emblemata Horiatiana.* 1607/1684. Photograph by author.

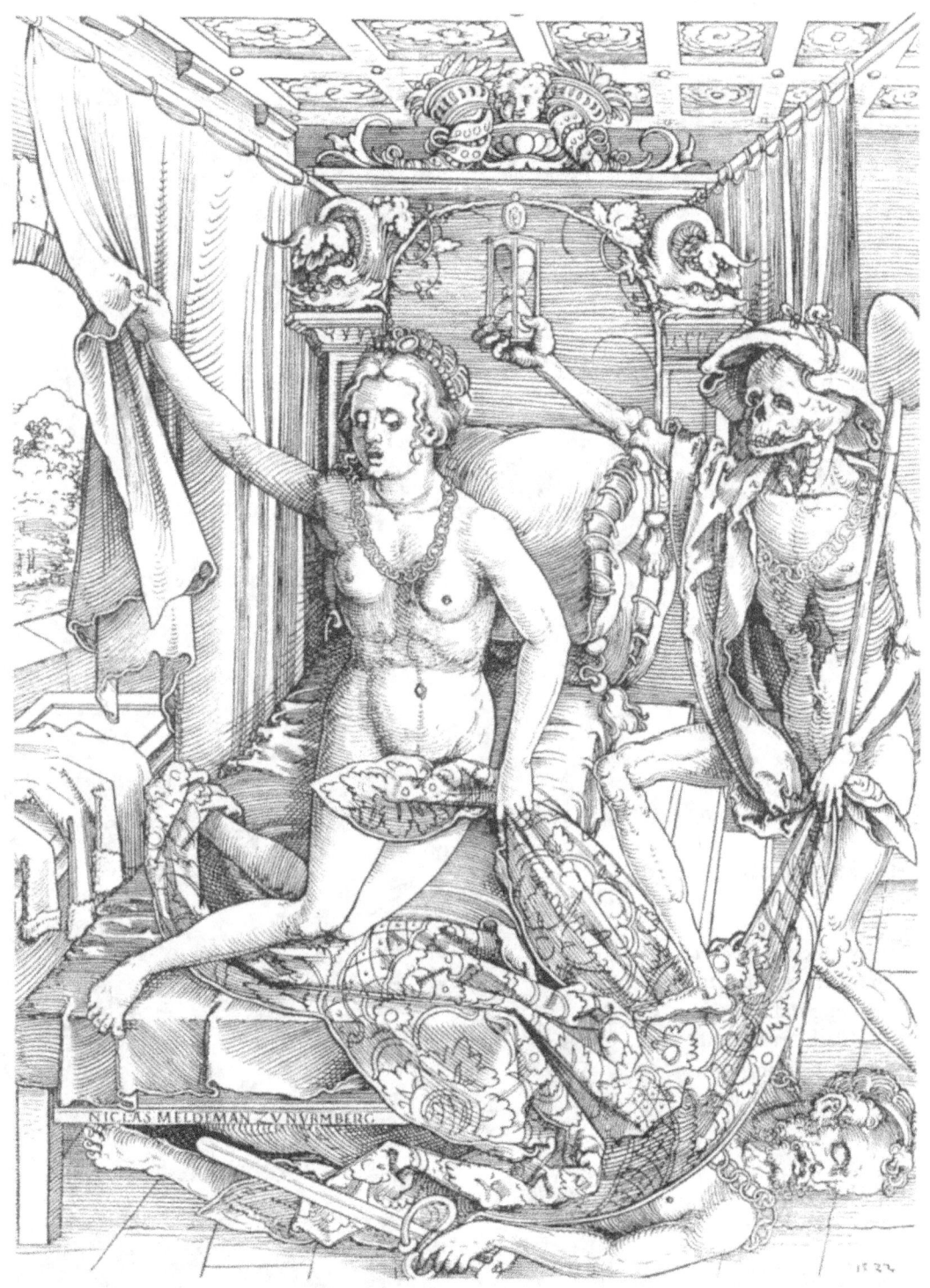

FIGURE 59. Hans Sebald Beham, *The Hour of Death*. British Museum, London.

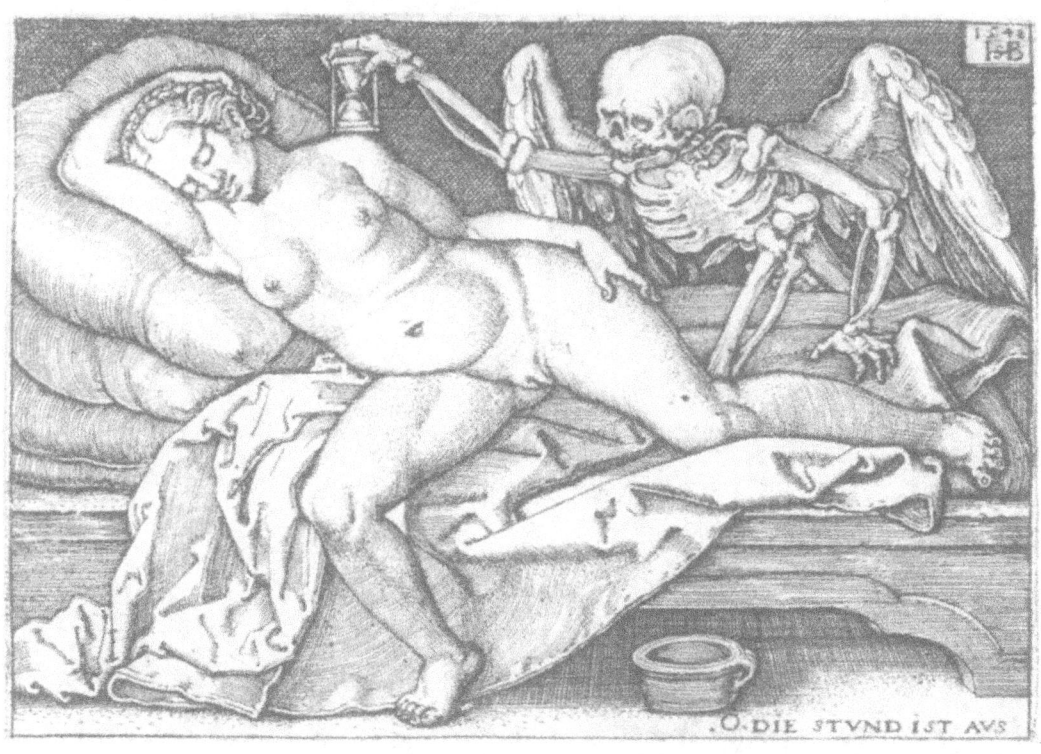

.O.DIE STVND IST AVS

FIGURE 60. (above)
Hans Sebald Beham,
*Death and the Sleeping
Maiden.* British
Museum, London.

FIGURE 61. (right)
Andrea Alciati, *Foedera.*
From *Emblemata.* 1626.
Sterling and Francine
Clark Art Institute
Library, Williamstown,
Massachusetts.

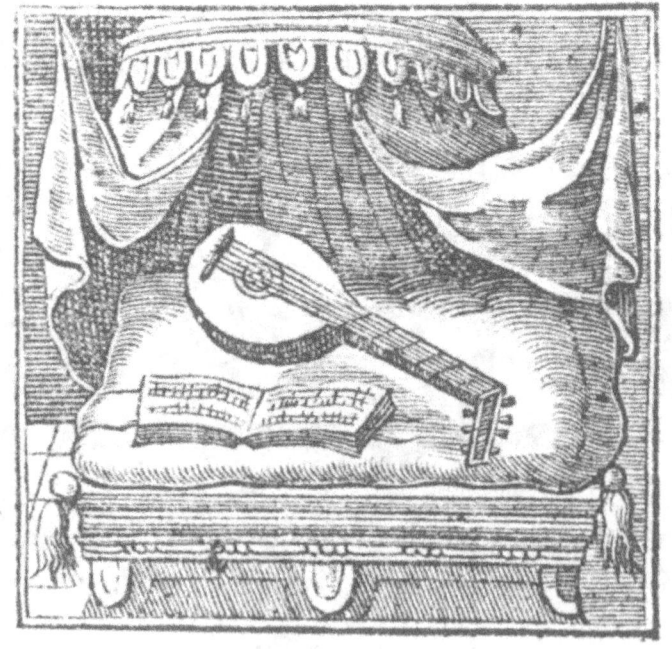

6

Jan Steen and the Invention
of the Modern Woman

Among the more significant achievements of late-twentieth-century cultural analysis was the identification of a set of avant-garde artistic practices that collectively define a movement designated as "modernism." Among the various components of modernism the roles played by the citation of past art and by the co-option of popular culture are consistently acknowledged as central. The maneuvers of modernist art as a reworking of these histories suggests that the past is renewed or reinvented as contemporary; that it is altered, yet retained as blurred, or not so blurred, as cultural memory. Griselda Pollock has insightfully located the moves of so-called avant-gardism in the play of "reference, deference and difference."[1] Yet, far from being truly modern, there is evidence that the history of the visual rhetoric that characterizes these particular components of "modernist" practices, even to the analysts' self-consciousness to name them modern, is at least more than three hundred years old. This insight helps to illuminate the past as well as the present by calling into question what is at stake in holding "modernism" as a prerogative of a more or less contemporary world. For my purposes here, delineating these "modernist" strategies allows for something about the seventeenth century and its negotiating terms, expressed as the culture of the early modern world, to be vitally connected to our own in the present.

This essay will examine how these moves are enacted in the art of Jan Steen, in particular how his formulation of woman is constructed as a sign of this "modernity" in the seventeenth century. My aims are to establish Jan Steen within the discursive framework of a modernist or protomodernist artist; to explicate the reliance of this system on the visual subject of "woman"; and to track some of the seventeenth-century terms of both its subject and system. In order to realize these aims I have chosen to focus on a single work by Steen, the so-called

Morning Toilet (fig. 52), from the Royal Collection of Her Majesty, Queen Elizabeth II, London.

The current art-historical scholarship on this painting, considered one of Steen's masterpieces, is symptomatic of the prevailing treatment of Dutch genre painting in general. The painting has recently been discussed in several highly touted venues.[2] Although they differ on several counts, they agree that the painting is "about" the dangerously seductive wiles of the young girl within it who, by all accounts, is "fully aware" of her exposed state and of the malevolent effects that seeing her body would have on the morals of a male viewer.[3] These sources also invoke the derogatory Dutch slang tradition that uses the word for stocking (the object of the woman's actions) as a simile for female genitalia.[4] In doing so they continue the work of the Dutch art historian E. de Jongh, who established the template for Dutch genre studies in the late 1960s and early 1970s. His work essentially installs a premium on moral education as a primary function of oil paintings and then concludes that the majority of genre images are about naughty, sexy girls who seduce innocent men into immoral behavior.[5] He has worked the endlessly reiterated scenario of victim Adam and seducer Eve into a standard of Dutch art-historical methodology.

"E. de Jonghism," in its reductive understanding of genre paintings, equates this image's meaning with the woman's act of pulling on her stockings. Actually she's taking them off. It was, in fact, de Jongh who first related the image to the popular use of the word for stocking as a slang expression referring to female genitals and/or women in general.[6] Aside from the various disparaging uses of the word *kous*, which reduces women to their genitals, he also points out that the term probably derives from the stocking's association with the foot and that body part's traditional sexual and even phallic symbolism.[7]

Let us try to redistinguish between whole and part, between the painting and the figure, and between the figure and her pubes. If we view the painting as a discursive surface and its work as producing woman as a sign, Steen's effects are set on a course of expansion rather than reduction. Indeed, among its pictorial gambits Steen's painting, as an entirety, references a host of diverse art histories, high and low, to which it lays claim as heir. He enters into a complex discourse with the past, which includes but is not limited to the woman's action of putting on her stocking. As we will see, Steen reworks and renovates the multivalent and highly complex cultural tropes circulating around and through woman as the sexualized subject in the development of modern, urbanized identities marked by consumership—especially as they had been encoded in northern European print culture of the sixteenth and seventeenth centuries. Finally, the painting dialogues with Steen's autograph version in the Rijksmuseum in Amsterdam (fig. 53), which differs from the London painting in many significant details, most especially in its very imposing strategy of framing.

A figure represented in the act of dressing or undressing has a long history in Netherlandish art. A late-fifteenth-century misericord, originally from the Church St.-Chamant, figures among the earliest depictions of a seated woman either pulling on or taking off her undergarments (fig. 54).[8] An initial comparison between this figure and Steen's opens a host of pertinent issues. The anonymous wooden sculpture depicts a seated woman with her skirt pulled up in her lap, with bare legs and feet, grasping what appear to be stockings or some form of undergarment, which is gathered at her ankles.[9] Similar to Steen's figure (or figures, if we include the Rijksmuseum variant), the woman is otherwise dressed, even to a head covering, except for this item. For this reason it seems more likely that she, as Steen's figure(s), is undressing rather than dressing. The realistic detail in Steen's paintings of the trace left by the stockings on the woman's calf further corroborates this reading.

Unlike Steen's figure this woman does not cross her legs, but she does spread them in an open position that is accentuated by the placement of her right arm between them. Her intimate activity and open-legged pose lend her a free, unselfconscious air and suggests that she is not aware that she is being watched. This misericord was made in a moment before institutionalized notions of decorum had fully made their way into hardened prescriptions for gender depictions. Soon after, Leonardo da Vinci's remarks participated in the establishment of these representational gender stereotypes with their assumed state of perennial surveillance when he advised, "In women and girls there must be no actions where the legs are raised or too far apart, because that would indicate boldness and a general lack of shame, while legs closed together indicate the fear of disgrace."[10]

Steen's image, produced a century and a half after Leonardo's remarks, transgresses that stereotypical prescription even more aggressively. As an oil painting rather than a semihidden misericord, it is by all counts more visible and more about visibility. The woman's raised, crossed leg conveys how comfortable she is with her own body. The gesture, combined with her erect head facing out toward the viewer, indicates that that comfort is not just about being alone. In contrast to the woman's down-turned face in the misericord, the full face of Steen's woman constructs an image more self-conscious about seeing and being seen. Interestingly, the figure in Steen's Rijksmuseum version also looks down, naturally absorbed in her activity and oblivious of the viewer. The difference revolves around the construction of the figure as either self-absorbed or self-confident. For the latter we are presented with a female figure in the London painting with the qualities of a self-willed, fresh young woman.

I use the word *fresh* here to be understood in several of its various meanings, as paradoxically cheeky, impudent, saucy, as well as young, innocent, unselfconscious—but then also as contemporary, current, and modern.[11] In the first definition her full face is construed as *not* the demure "downward gaze" promoted by the etiquette of gender and class in this period.[12] We can again turn to Leonardo, who recommended that women should be represented with "their heads lowered and inclined to one side."[13] Steen's decision against this posture is especially pointed here because looking out as she does actually goes against what is the more natural pose for the narrative, that is, lowering her head so that she can see what she is doing.

The definition of *fresh* as new or recent touches on the complex relationship between gender and modernity, which, as an issue, has been extensively explored by nineteenth- and twentieth-century cultural historians.[14] Yet I propose that many of the same social and cultural mechanisms that are brought into play in the conflation of woman and modernism in the nineteenth century were already active in the processes of early modern life in the Dutch Republic. This highly volatile period in Dutch history witnessed tremendous growth in the entrepreneurial sector marked by an equally impressive degree of social mobility, all of which impacts our subject.

The "(early) modern woman" worked brilliantly as the site where many of the nation's new demands could converge and be renegotiated. The richness of the sign can be seen to conjoin urbanized modernity with modern art as urbanized female sexuality with female representation. Linguistically, the association of (early) modern woman and (early) modern art is indicated by a number of conflations of the period. For example, in England the word *painting* referred equally to the cosmetic painting of a face, as well as to the painting of a picture.[15] In seventeenth-century Dutch the word *verciering* (as adornment) was also equally shared between a woman's face and a canvas.[16] More formally and more directly, within Renaissance academic discourses the conflation between a beautiful woman and a beautiful painting had been especially well established in Venice, as Elizabeth Cropper has so cogently demonstrated.[17]

In this context it is also worth noting that in the seventeenth century the currency of the Dutch word *modern* circulated primarily within cultural and particularly artistic circles.[18] Although texts on artists used the word *moderne* as an adjective to designate living rather than dead artists, it was more and more used to designate a particular kind of modern painter, one who specialized in scenes with contemporary figures, that is, with contemporary fashions.[19] In particular, there are a fair number of archival documents around 1635 that use the adjective *modern* in their descriptions of Dutch genre painters. For example, the inventory of Pacras Vos mentions "[a] modern painting by Dirck Hals."[20] The list of works in Dirck Hals's own lottery of 1634 includes "an oval with modern figures by D. Hals."[21] A Haarlem document of 1636 refers to the genre paintings by Jacob Duck as *moderne beeldekens* (modern paintings with contemporary figures).[22] In the same period Gerard ter Borch's father laments that his son had chosen to paint in the "modern manner," giving us yet another important early example of the use of the term.[23] Later, in 1707, Gerard de Lairesse considers artists like Frans van Mieris and Gerard Dou to be among the better "modern artists."[24]

Indeed, as a concept "modern" is most developed in the writing of de Lairesse, who uses the word in a variety of ways in his *Groot schilderboek* of 1740.[25] He consistently takes it to mean "contemporary" and criticizes those artists who practice it for being too bound to fashion and the fashionable, whereby he means clothes and hairstyles. Indeed, there is a good deal of slippage between "mode" (fashion) and "modern" in his text, where de Lairesse calls the same artist a "Modernschilder" in one breath and a "Modeschilder" in the next.[26] I would argue that precisely therein lies one of the primary discursive contractions on which the conflation of art, modernity, and femininity is forged; for as long as modern fashions were a topic of public discussion, their primary association was with the feminine. This is made particularly clear in the advent and proliferation of costume books in this period. It is especially explicit in one of the earliest of these, the *Gynaeceum; The Theatre of Women: Wherein May Be Seen the Female Costumes of All the Principal Nations, Tribes, and Peoples of Europe*, designed by Jost Amman and published by Sigismund Feyerabendt in Nuremberg in 1586. The introduction describes ever-changing fashion that "panders to the passionate lovers of dress, and especially to the more showy of women. That sex (meaning "women") is not only the more inclined by nature itself to the pleasure and beauty of dress, but also . . . takes the very highest account of personal ornament and decoration in order to retain their husbands."[27]

Women's close association with changing fashions is further attested to by the progressively nearly exclusive bond in Netherlandish culture between women and the iconography of *Vanitas* (vanity), one of the most egregious of the seven deadly sins. The combination of a young woman and a skeleton, or simply a skull, often references the vanity of material concerns, represented by the woman's costume and hairdo, and presents the consequences of such vanity for the soul after death. Clearly, the skull on the threshold in Steen's Buckingham Palace painting accesses that tradition on some level. On another level there is little doubt that the stylishness of the costume and accoutrement, as well as the virtuoso articulation of their lush materials in meticulously applied oil paint, accounts for a great deal of the *Morning Toilet*'s lure.

It must be said that the new art of Dutch genre painting in the first half of the seventeenth century depicted somewhat equally young dandies and damsels romping around in contemporary, extravagant costumes. But, as I have discussed in detail elsewhere, with genre's progressive gentrification, from the late 1630s to 1670, its subject became more and more focused as the domain of the feminine rather than masculine character.[28] Jan Steen's contribution to this gentrification is considerable, and the role played in its establishment by his *Morning Toilet* is notable. The performance of this gentrification is best understood by viewing the painting against its various histories.

The image of a young woman seated on her bed and disrobing hardly seems to need art-historical precedents. Yet, as we have already seen, the woman's specific posture ties her to a visual history that deepens the engagement of the visually literate viewer—without excluding the cultural novice. The crossed-legged pose of Steen's figure is a direct invocation of one of the most well-known and emulated works of classical antiquity, the *Spinario*, or *Thorn Puller* (fig. 55).[29] From the time of its inception to the present the artistic pose of legs crossed so high up is a frequently depicted ploy of erotic visual culture. It has had an incredibly prestigious life in canonical art history, from the Hellenistic *Spinario* to endless ancient Roman adaptations through Jan Steen, Watteau, Fragonard, Courbet, and many others. The *Spinario*'s pose is justified by the narrative that he crosses his legs in order to pull a thorn from his bare foot. The pose is particularly revealing when the subject is male because it allows for a titillating view of his genitalia. And in fairness to contemporary interpretations, the posture was soon eagerly co-opted from its homosexual to a heterosexual context and the crossed legs of a woman could access a discourse that served to focus all attention between her legs.

Some early modern northern European artists, such as Hans Sebald Beham or Adriaen van de Venne, stretched the limits of the pose's natural believability for the sake of complete exhibitionism. This is the case of Beham's small print of *Night*, a work also related to Steen's through the framing function of the bed, which creates both a visual and narrative focus (fig. 56). In Beham's small print the woman's perspectival and foreshortened placement allows for an unprecedented view of her vagina. It is, however, important to make the distinction that, by contrast, although Steen's formulation of the woman's posture may recall those erotics, it actually shows very little that is lewd. In fact, the degree of exposure is an interesting point of difference between the Amsterdam and London versions of Steen's painting; the woman in the Amsterdam painting is clearly more explicitly exposed. Here as elsewhere there is a strategic tradeoff between seeing the woman's face or seeing her pubes.[30]

In the primary art-historic examples some realistic narrative premise usually accompanies the crossed-leg posture, which permits the images to operate on respectable levels as cultural constructions. In these the narrative renders the desired area visible to the viewer only as a "felicitous accident," an unplanned, caught glimpse. This is the case with the *Spinario*, the woman of the misericord, the woman in Steen's Rijksmuseum painting, and the woman in Watteau's *Woman Washing Her Feet*, in the Louvre, to name a few examples. They are all unaware of being fetishized and are rather represented as preoccupied with everyday concerns, like pulling a pesky thorn out or taking one's stockings off. They all share, moreover, an implicit, high degree of physicality. The thorn embedded in the boy's foot is obvious in this regard, but Steen insists, too, on bringing viewer consciousness to the female subject's body by the stockings' impression, which marks her legs in a manner that insists on the soft and impressionable character of their flesh.

The markings on her legs also work to indicate, as I have said, that she is taking her stockings off rather than putting them on; that is, she is undressing rather than dressing. This act is given special significance because the light in the room clearly indicates that the scene is taking place in broad daylight. We are, thus, led to read the image as a woman who has been out partying all night and is just now going to bed. In this she is iconologically related to the many "modern" women who populate the public night scenes in the paintings of the Utrecht Caravaggisti with their dramatic chiaroscuro effects. Unlike them Steen's image is pointedly framed, a strategy that sets it apart. Moreover, on the highly charged threshold of the door that delineates the divide between inside and outside, Steen painted a skull and a broken lute overturned on a songbook, all of which set the stage for a metaphoric appreciation of the image. It should therefore not be surprising that the image works so well with a host of different kinds of contemporary Dutch emblems.

For example, Steen's image is structurally closely related to two genrelike emblems that were popular around 1660. And again, although I am not proposing that these emblems were "sources" in the traditional sense for Steen, they do work together with Steen's painting to give us a sense of a popular, ideological discourse that was current at the time. The first and closer of the two emblems is an image from Johan de Brune's *Emblemata of zinne-werck* (fig. 57), initially published in 1624 and republished in 1661, only two years before Steen's dated Buckingham Palace painting. The text for emblem XIII reads: "Ledigh en laf, een levend' graf" (Lazy and insipid, a living grave). It depicts a similarly defined fashionable woman framed by the bed she sits on and surrounded by a plethora of intimate details, including her undergarments, which are recklessly strewn about the room. In his diatribe against idleness de Brune writes, "Men vind-ter, die tot de middagh in haer pluymen uyt-ghestreckt ligghende, gheen ander bezigheyd gehad en hebben, als om te verzinnen, hoe dat zy haer uren best verquisten zullen" (One finds her around midday lolling about, decked out in her feathers, with no other preoccupation than to invent ways to waste away her hours).[31]

The image is striking as a comparison with Steen, despite the very different venues of the two images. Through similar means they share a vocabulary of form that explicates an urban consumerism through the refiguring of the medieval Christian *Vanitas* iconography. The women are rendered normalized by formal systems of illusion. Their effect is expanded through a host of ancillary details that produce a cumulative sense of significance.[32] In both images a fashionable woman of the day is framed by her architectural, rectangular bed, whose curtains are pulled aside. As we will see, this device, again as natural as it may appear, has a history as a sign of emphasis, indicating that metaphoric attention is vested in this area. In both, the left side of the curtain hangs straight, and the right side is draped in a curve. Both women are displayed as a well-lit form against the dark backdrop of the bed's interior. The bedsheets and ticking in both have striped designs that speak of a certain conspicuous consumption. Both images display empty mule or backless slippers by the bed as a reference to the state of dress or undress of the figure, as well as to contemporary fashions. Fashion is also figured in Steen by the expensive materials of her dress and in the emblem by the discarded hoop that, in the fashions of the day, was worn under the skirt. Bodily functions are also indexed in both by the urine pot next to their beds. Midday as the time of day is strongly evident by the light streaming into both rooms and, in the case of the emblem, by the text. By extension, the woman's position in bed at that time is couched as inappropriate.

The shared cultural construction of the "modern woman" encoded in these images comes into sharp focus when foiled against another contemporary emblem found in Otto van Veen's *Emblemata Horatiana* (fig. 58), published in Amsterdam in many editions.[33] The moral frame for the emblem is once again idleness, proclaimed in the caption given in three languages "Laziness is the cause of all evil." The primary subject, however, is male rather than female, and rather than signifying a negative exempla, the figure is posited as a positive role model.

Here, too, the figure is framed by his curtained bed, the canopy now round rather than rectilinear. He sits on his bed drawing on his stockings with his legs crossed. Placed by his bedside are slippers with loose tie strings. The time of day is at issue here as well. In this instance time is indexed by the presence of the moon seen through the window, the burning candle, and the clock on the back wall. The written text then tells us that the clever man gets up and works immediately when he is awake to avoid being tempted by sin.[34] The burning candle, thus, signifies the early hour of the morning rather than the late hour of night.

Another significant difference is found in the emblem's ancillary figures that decisively alter the type of image and thus its reception. The male subject is not alone in his bedroom, and the other figures offer a mixed bag of character types. The largest is a young boy, realistically conceived as a page, who offers him a folio with inkpot and quill. The other two are marginally represented, their backs to the viewer, pushed off to the right side, and cut by the frame. Together they draw aside the curtain of the man's bed. They are characterized by their visual attributes as the conventional personifications of the sins of lust and envy, represented as an Eros and an old woman with a hanging breast and snakes in her hair.

These last two figures breach the realist illusion of the rest of the image and openly announce its metaphoric character. The rising man is, thus, presented as a kind of Hercules at the crossroads situated between virtuous learning and lazy vice; he clearly chooses the former. The visual language of this print suggests that, to be "fully understood," it would require of the viewer a certain amount of conceptual preinformation. The inclination to read realistically is thwarted, and we are, as viewers, thrown into hierarchal structures of those of us who are more and those of us who are less educated.[35]

If the indication of a metaphoric reading appeared in the margins of the Horatian emblem, metaphoric meaning is consigned to a variety of strategies in Steen's Buckingham Palace painting. They are at once more nuanced and more grandiose. On one level they operate in the small details on the doorway where a lute with a broken string, an overturned songbook, and a skull are painted in the liminal space of the threshold. On another level they operate through the larger superstructures of the canopied bed and the marble-columned entranceway. Although the lute and songbook can hold their place in the realist illusion, the specific detail of the broken string will lead us to other ways of comprehending Steen's formulation.

The skull is difficult, if not impossible, to sustain in a realistic reading. The work done by the skull is easily identified as an overt memento mori, contributing that overdetermined early modern association of the vain, beautiful woman and death, a connection most frequently encapsulated under the rubric of *Vanitas* iconography. The skull opens the door, so to speak, to a host of related metaphoric readings. It also overtly, I would say consciously, connects Steen's painting with a venerable northern European art history. Again, German paintings and engravings of this period come to the fore particularly strongly as visual constructions that associate young, sexually defined women with death. Hans Baldung Grien seems to have been especially caught up with the subject. Even closer to Steen's formulation are several prints that show a young, sexually described woman on her bed approached by the figure of death. Of the many examples, the subject seems to have been a favorite of Hans Sebald Beham, as can be seen in *The Hour of Death* (fig. 59) and *Death and the Sleeping Maiden* (fig. 60). In the prints and the paintings by Grien, rather than a disembodied skull, the grim reaper comes in the form of a skeleton to claim the life of the young beauty. In a fascinating variation on the theme, Peter Flötner relegates the sign function of lasciviousness to the extravagant four-poster bed, which carries the coat of arms of death in the form of skull on the headboard.[36] The sixteenth-century and twentieth-century (art-historical) ideologies served by this union of sex and death are legion. Although Steen's reference to death and the maiden is typically nuanced, it is manifest in the image through a multiplicity of associations, the skull being the most overt. Here the formal connection with Johan de Brune's emblem can be recalled and can be assigned deeper significance. In a sense one may say that an equation is drawn in the London painting by equally dividing the viewer's attention between the inside and the outside of the room. The nature of the connection between the two might be suggested by the caption over de Brune's remarkably close emblem, "Lazy and insipid, a living grave." Near the end of his rather long censure of idleness, de Brune repeats his caption and explicates it further, "For idleness without instruction, as is said, is a death, an entombment of a living person."[37] Indeed, the canopied bed and the marble-columned exterior of Steen's painting are common tropes of Italian Renaissance funerary sculpture.[38] They also provide what Michalski termed the aesthetic boundaries of the image.[39]

A similarly canopied bed works to aesthetically or metaphorically proclaim the significance of the lute with a broken string and an overturned songbook in the 1621 (reprinted in 1626) edition of Andrea Alciati's *Emblemata* (fig. 61). In Steen's painting the combination of the lute and songbook together with the skull is positioned at a critical juncture of both the fictive space and the canvas. It heightens a consciousness about the relationship between the room's inside and outside. Because a string is clearly broken on the lute, a visually literate viewer could fairly easily have made the connection. The specific configuration of these items reiterates their configuration in figure 10 of Alciati's *Emblemata*, one of the most famous and most often reprinted early emblem books. Specifically, in the 1621 and 1626 edition, "seated" on a canopied bed, we see a lute and open musical score. The epigram reads: "It is difficult, unless a man is skilled, to tune so many strings. And if one string is not well tuned, or is broken—which can easily happen—the entire pleasantness of the shell perishes."[40] It speaks to Steen's brilliance in modernizing the image and opening it up to a multiplicity of possible readings that he transposed the metaphoric still life to the threshold and placed the more narratively normative modern woman in its place on the canopied bed.

The diaphragm arch also provides the painting with a variety of possible meanings. The diaphragm arch in the history of Netherlandish painting, other than as funerary, but as a "frame of significance" if you will, has its own long, prestigious history, a history that enriches the many levels of associations in Steen's painting. In Steen the arch marks the division between the two spaces. It is positioned only a few inches in from the real frame and scopically circumscribes the interior scene, rendering it a form of shell. The self-reflexive framing device has been connected to the fashion for the diaphragm arch as a dramatic formal device in Dutch art after 1650; this device is especially abundant in the art of Gerard Dou. Dou characteristically uses the arch to cut the figure off, rendering it a dynamic half-length close-up. The history of the fictive arch that frames full-length figures, as is the case in Steen's painting, and as certainly more than simply a formal device, goes back to early Netherlandish illuminated manuscripts and panel paintings of the fourteenth and fifteenth centuries, allowing it a specifically archaistic turn by Steen's usage. The device is amply represented in the paintings by, for example, Rogier van der Weyden and Dierc Bouts. As we may have come to expect, Steen's painting is informed by both the synchronic and diachronic sets of images, giving it the gloss of both a modern and archaistic image.[41] The significance of the diaphragm arch expands to include the fictive exterior architecture of the bedroom and the scene's frame for the real viewer.

Returning to the young woman who inhabits this shrine, we can further appreciate the modernized visual terms of her lazy and languid life (if not yet conspicuous leisure) as determined, at least referentially, by its past histories. Yet if the discourses connecting sex and death provide a conservative net to "catch" meaning, the kernel or shell that makes that connection is only possible once the attributes of contemporary female youth, beauty, and sexual desire are seized on and imbued with importance. The modernity of this fashionable young woman as a sign of contemporary urban bourgeois society is thus identified through the scopically displayed evidence of consumption. The construction of that modernity is built on a series of interconnecting visual references that are retained as memory but are inflected and refashioned in what is ultimately an image very different from the various works that inform it. These histories are referentially pieced together and crafted into a new "whole," which takes on a variety of quite different implications.

The levels at which this image remakes its history are, then, clearly not confined by its referential moves. The qualities of sixteenth-century prints of being "published" and pervasive gave them an authoritative position, which was not easily opened to questioning or accountability. Precisely therein lay their power to inscribe stereotypes and to classify or structure elements of society, such as class and gender. The qualities of Steen's large oil paintings work through what may be deemed diametrically opposite means. The evidence of Steen's "hand," his virtuoso handling of oil paint to simulate the visual and tactile world—his very signature on the marble column playing on the meaning of his name as stone and as the identity of the author/artist—brings us time and again back to an awareness of him and the studio. This is not only as the artist but also as the paradigmatic modern male, one who is gendered and defined by his fine appreciation of a sexy woman. Jan Steen's *Morning Toilet* thus sets the conditions for cultured male cognoscenti who can bond, that is, understand and relate to one another across the artistically appropriated body of a young, sexually attractive, and scopically framed woman.

It is by now well known that Foucault's insights into the explosion of sexual discourses in the sixteenth century have been criticized for not differentiating the roles played by gender in the construction of modern sexuality. This sexual differentiation is, perhaps, nowhere as evident as in the newly formed secular subjects of the early modern painting. Although excessive female lasciviousness as an ideological position has a history that reaches back to the very beginning of Christianity, it is in the early modern period that it becomes a vehicle for the expression of those characteristics that are associated with cities as the site of modernity and modernism. Steen ultimately invents himself as an artistic entity defined by his masculine sexual appetite as a modern man of the city. He does so by participating in the ongoing project of perpetually reinventing the sexualized, modern woman.

III

Tele/visions

7

Early Netherlandish Bordeeltjes and the Construction of Social "Realities"

Early modern culture vigorously produced the legend of Netherlandish prostitution through innumerable books, plays, paintings, and prints. The *bordeeltje*—the very popular, newly created pictorial type that figured sixteenth-century scenes of bordello life—played a particularly dynamic role in generating this legend. Paintings and prints of this subject were made by the period's leading artists, Lucas van Leyden (fig. 62), Jan Sanders van Hemessen (fig. 63), Joachim Beuckelaer (fig. 64), and Jan Massys (fig. 65), to name a few.

The term *bordeeltje* is felicitous on several counts. As a Netherlandish word coined at the time of the pictures, it encourages us to recapture a certain self-consciousness about new categories of secular images. Its diminutive and affectionate *-je* ending helps assess the tone of its reception. Of greatest significance, it indicates that, rather than being character-identified as titles such as *Procuress* or *Courtesan* would indicate, the images were primarily space-identified. As spaces that gave visual expression to the combined conditions of prodigality and itinerancy, bordeeltjes by definition represented newly configured aspects of public life in the Netherlands; the public consumption of food, drink, and sexuality.[1] Indications of their public stance is given by the alternative name for bordellos themselves as "publiek-huizen" (public houses).[2]

Here I explore the various meaningful responses suggested by the bordeeltje. I have cast my net wide to catch the multifarious ways these images fit in the critical transformations of early modern Netherlandish social life, to make connections that have not been made before, and to ask questions that have not been asked before. Traditional art-historical investigations of these early secular paintings and prints have been limited to two kinds of interpretations. The images are typically treated as moralizing texts warning their viewers against lust, greed, and various other canonical sins and/or as reflections of the real condition of prostitution in the Netherlands.[3] This essay looks at the particular pictorial language, the visual rhetoric, of the bordeeltjes to clarify just *how* and *why* both the moralist and realist interpretations that dominate art-historical responses are the very reception solicited by them, that is, how the artworks themselves "intend" to be interpreted in these ways. Further, the examination of the visual language shared by the type as a whole relates it to past Netherlandish artistic conventions and thereby demonstrates how its new forms and messages were presented in familiar settings. These conventional internal structures within bordello images clearly predispose or prefigure (but do not dictate) some of the ways they were and are understood.[4]

Finally, I look here beyond those internal structures to examine other circumstances that effectively contributed to how sense could be made of these images in their time. I want to suggest how various different meanings could be produced when visually literate viewers related the bordeeltjes to other types, visual and literary, and to other concerns from the fifteenth and sixteenth centuries. My aim is to "unfix" these images from the burden of singular, hard-and-fast meanings, to mobilize their potential meaningfulness by examining them in different hypothetical situations, and to see how they work with the period's ideological preoccupations. By locating and relocating bordello scenes in new discursive frames, taking in both synchronic and diachronic texts, the bordeeltje's role as cultural material in the formations of "early modern" identity may be further elucidated.

In a sense I am indebted to several recent related developments in historical research: semiotic theory, which posits the polysemy of the visual sign; reception theory, which locates the constitution of meaning with the individual reader or viewer rather than with the author or artist; and most especially to feminism, which assigns political significance to the first two.[5] Ultimately, Michel Foucault's work on the history of sexuality and its significance in the production of power discourses has inspired me to shift off of a literal interpretation of the subject.[6] In the end this essay is eclectic, applying these new theoretic methods in a broad, rather than rigorous, sense to open the possibilities of historical interpretation.

Netherlandish history in the sixteenth century has been viewed as marked throughout by change and by its need to reformulate social relationships on all levels. The radical alterations within both the economic and political structures, as well as religious and social practices, have been fully studied and often credited as the threshold of what is frequently called "early modern times." These changes included the creation of distinct domains of social life, the public and the private, as constructs that remained mutually dependent and reflexive. Of particular significance to my argument is the refashioning of gender relations and identities across these emergent formations of a public and private sphere. This essay is attentive to the ideological cooperation of Netherlandish artistic culture with other social factors, such as economic, political, and religious practices, as agents of change.

There is evidence from the later Middle Ages that the site of economic production and distribution was slowly shifting from the house to the public marketplace. This process was aided by formalized guild systems and local laws that worked to effectively decrease (if not eliminate) the outer forms that acknowledge women's economic contribution.[7] By the seventeenth century, women were ideologically relocated to a place other than that of the public, to the newly created notion of the private. Different social forces worked to regulate and "naturalize" this shift. Calvinist authors redefined domestic duty as a bona fide Christian vocation.[8] Further, the philosophical revival of Stoicism in the work of the Leiden professor, Justus Lipsius, gave theoretical impetus and Christian value to this newly formed concept of "private" life and thus to the home.[9] In concert with religious and philosophical forces, the visual arts presented the home as an idyll of order and tranquility.[10] Clearly, the itinerancy represented in bordello scenes took on significance as it could be seen as the opposite of domesticity. All in all, the process involved the creation of binary ideological values, the home became the locus of a feminized "private" sphere to counterbalance the loss of a legitimate presence in the masculine-defined "public" sphere.

The bordeeltje was ideally suited to negotiate these changes. Although it is impossible to prove that any particular image could be seen in any particular space in the sixteenth century, some evidence suggests the broad range of places that were, at least, possible sites for their display. This evidence points to the possibility that the bordeeltje, with other secular types,[11] was exhibited in both private and public spaces, that is, in the home and in public inns and taverns.[12] The term *bordeeltje* is most often found in descriptions of domestic inventories.[13] Nevertheless, mention of this type of imagery can also be found as decoration for public spaces in sixteenth-century literature.[14] For example, in Shakespeare's *Henry IV, Part Two* (1597–1598), when Mistress Quickly, the hostess of a tavern, complains that she will have to pawn the tapestry of her dining chambers, Falstaff replies, "and for thy walls, a pretty slight drollery, or the story of the Prodigal, or the German hunting in water-work, is worth a thousand of these bed-hangings and these fly-bitten tapestries."[15] Similarly, in *Vies des Dames Galantes* Brantôme (1542–1614) makes fun of a woman by comparing her to a figure type seen in Flemish genre pictures that were displayed in inns and taverns:

This doth remind me of another lady of the great world, and one I knew, which wishing to imitate the same mode when about twenty five years of age, and altogether over tall and big statured, a great masculine looking woman and but lately come to Court, and thinking to play the gallant dame, did one day appear so attired in the ball-room. Nor did she fail to be much stared at and rallied not a little on her costume. Even the King himself did pronounce his judgment thereon, for indeed he was one of the wittiest men in the realm, and declared she did resemble a mountebank's wench, or still better one of those painted figures of women that are imported from Flanders and set up in front of chimney-pieces in inns and taverns with German flutes at their lips.[16]

The presence of these images in both private and public spaces speaks to the elasticity of their significance. The literary references further establish the works outside of the Netherlands, in foreign lands, an idea to which we will presently return.

The constructed spaces represented within the bordeeltjes can be viewed as liminal, that is, neither completely public nor private. As the space of commercial sexual exchange, the bordello is economically public. As the place of encounters between men and women, it invokes an inversion or subversion of the domestic relations between men and women as they were being formulated by the theological and ideological discourses of the period. The primary subject, then, plays a specific role in determining a gendered definition of *public* and *private*. It provides a site for the construction of "woman" in general and the "modern" Netherlandish woman specifically.[17] As we will see, these images obtain meanings by playing with and against those meanings circulated in earlier Netherlandish religious painting, as well as in contemporary northern and Italian secular art.

It is of no small consequence that the setting of these formative secular works is a space dedicated to the economic exchange of sexual relations. Foucault, looking back at this period's verbal and literary history, noted that "since the sixteenth century, the 'putting into discourse of sex,' far from undergoing a process of restriction (as moralist interpretations would have us believe), on the contrary, has been subjected to a mechanism of increasing incitement; that the techniques of power exercised over sex have not obeyed a principle of rigorous selection, but rather one of dissemination."[18] Indeed, Foucault speaks of a "veritable discursive explosion" in this period.[19] Rather than seeing this explosion as merely about sex, Foucault goes on to ask the crucial questions, "What were the effects of power generated by what was said (represented)?" and "What are the links between these discourses, these effects of power, and the pleasures that were invested by them?"[20]

It is precisely the realist rhetoric of these images that enabled them to perform so persuasively and productively in establishing links with other formations of power hierarchies in early modern relationships. The bordeeltje's apparent realism is achieved by combining early Netherlandish realistic formal advances, such as the material and spatial illusionism made possible by oil paint, together

with realistic modern subjects in contemporary settings, costumes, and hairstyles, both of which were activated by a lively sense of narrative. These pictures'
"reality effect," to borrow a term from Roland Barthes,[21] is still successfully influencing current art-historical interpretations that treat the images positivistically, as descriptions of actual bordello conditions.[22] In fact, unlike actual bordello conditions in the Netherlands, which, as the work of Lotte van de Pol has
shown, occurred across a tremendously varied spectrum of social conditions and
locations, the uniformity of class and type of locale in the bordellos of sixteenth-
century paintings and prints is remarkable in its homogeneity.[23]

I would suggest that that which is seemingly realistic in such Netherlandish
genre paintings actively participated in constructing what is lived and experi-
enced as reality, that is, that the images themselves work as codes that both create and disrupt the myth of what is socially "real" and acceptable. This does not
remove them from the Calvinist sphere but places them within the larger Calvinist project in its goal to establish codified norms that regulate social order. Indeed, the images function on many levels, ordering, containing, and at times,
possibly even contesting prevailing power hierarchies. Rather than documenting
actual bordello conditions, they worked as ciphers for a host of ideological issues,
together with other contemporary texts on sexuality.

The burgeoning category of secular, privately disposed art in all its international manifestations in the sixteenth century was, to a great extent, specifically
concerned with sexual subject matter. It seems necessary to state this, for despite
the volumes that have been written about this period, this simple fact has been
repressed or, at the least, ignored. The energetic interest in sexual imagery in this
period must surely be "linked" to changes in the official Christian views on sexual
relationships as a result of the Protestant Reformation. Early on, Martin Luther
determined the central role to be played by the sexual issue within the Reformation. His position on the value of marriage threw the pervasive Christian censure
of sexuality into question, resulting in, among other events, the reactionary decree of the Council of Trent in 1563, condemning with anathema the doctrine
that the married state was as good as, or superior to, celibacy. At that same ses-
sion obscenity in art was condemned. Although terse, the Tridentine decree generated long, lugubrious tracts on the evils of nudity and obscenity in art. Among
others, Dolce in 1557, Gilio da Fabriano in 1564, the Fleming Johannes Molanus
in 1570, and Gabriele Paleotti in 1594 railed against sexual indecency in contemporary art.[24] Netherlandish bordeeltjes must, then, be seen in the context of this
period's larger obsession with sexuality as a cipher to police and regulate social
life. Sixteenth-century religious and visual imagery worked through the discourse
of sex to naturalize changes in the organization of power and communal alle-

giance. The chronology and dimensions of this discursive "explosion" on the subject of sexuality take on new specifications when reassigned to visual rather than literary data. This is so, at least partially, because of the unique license afforded aestheticized visual representation that allows it to figure ideas that are otherwise often unspeakable for a culture.

Although sexually defined imagery in sixteenth-century secular art produced for private consumption was being developed in many artistic centers throughout Europe, the two most influential places were the Netherlands and Italy. It is instructive to compare the bordeeltje with these other, contemporary forms of sexual iconography. For example, at the very moment early-sixteenth-century Netherlandish artists were creating their bordeeltjes, the more classically oriented Venetian Renaissance was engaged in producing, in equal if not greater numbers, its own form of visual discourse on sexuality.[25] This came in the form of innumerable female nudes with strong mythological associations, most often Venus, the celestial and terrestrial goddess of love.[26] I want here to compare the opposing rhetorical strategies of two representative works dating from the late 1530s, the *Bordello* by Jan Sanders van Hemessen, in Karlsruhe, and Titian's *Venus of Urbino*, in the Uffizi in Florence (figs. 63 and 66). The subjects are, in fact, comparable even if one is not convinced by current interpretations of Titian's figure as a courtesan.[27] The formal strategies have some similarities as well. Each scene is set with emphasis on the foreground of an interior. Windows give access to the outside world and frame a secondary scene that augments the primary one. Both systems convey a strong sense of display; the Netherlandish work effects this through the three-quarter-length close-up, the Venetian work through the tipped-up surface comprising the woman's body and bed.[28] Both stimulate sexual fantasies made "real" through contemporary costumes and furnishings and the tactility of the material world evoked through the manipulation of light and shade.

However, Titian's nude Venus bespeaks the visual paradox of both accessibility and distance for the viewer. The overt visual presentation of her nude body, with her left hand nestled in her pubes in a gesture that both covers it and directs us to it, is geared to titillate and arouse desire. Such sexual arousal is culturally condonable only through the ambiguity of its iconographic philosophical, possibly Neoplatonic, stance that protects "her" under the rubric of allegory. Whether interpreted as a courtesan or Venus, Titian's isolated female figure projected outward has always been understood iconically as "a pictorial demonstration-piece."[29]

The visual language of Van Hemessen's painting produces a different effect. Flesh is only fleeting, and exposure is conveyed by a low neckline and the show of a back and shoulders. Most significantly, rather than a one-to-one relationship between a single nude woman and the viewer, Van Hemessen creates a "company," a *gezellschaft*, meaning essentially a community, albeit temporary and movable. The representation of an internally self-involved social community is, in fact, characteristic of the Netherlandish formulation of the sexual subject. By contrast, in the Mediterranean model, the viewer rather than the internal protagonist consistently has the privileged view of the woman's body, which is isolated and oriented toward the spectator outside the fictive space.

Van Hemessen's company provides us with a range of gender and age. His figures are characterized by broad, almost caricatured, movements. Mostly, the cramped space, the large gestures, and the physiognomic contrasts of expression and physical condition give the paintings a comic, somewhat burlesque, tone. "Realism" here clearly conveys an earthy, somewhat vulgar, physicality. Where the Italian work produces an elevated, aristocratic conception of desire, the Netherlandish work figures desire as a low, mundane manifestation that constructs the base or "low" elements as "comic" and "real".[30]

Sexuality is inferred through the totality of the Netherlandish picture—the setting and figures, as well as the narrative. Sexuality and avarice motivate this gathering, but narrative holds it together. The Venetian visual rhetoric is iconic; the Netherlandish visual rhetoric is narrative. The Netherlandish propensity for narrative is itself an essential strategy of "realism" as it engages the viewer in a set of assumed temporal situations with dramatic focus.

In fact, as the predominant rhetorical mode of the bordeeltje, not just in Jan Sanders van Hemessen but throughout the sixteenth and well into the seventeenth century, narrative provides Netherlandish bordello scenes with their most compelling tactic of realism. The paintings and prints employ a range of narrative codes imbuing their "stories" with contemporary temporality. Narrative time is constructed by various means. It is sometimes achieved by clear reference to the biblical parable of the Prodigal Son, as in the painting by Joachim Beuckelaer in Brussels or in Van Hemessen's painting, also in Brussels, of about twenty years earlier (figs. 64 and 67). The parable, from Luke 15:11–32, tells the story of a younger son who receives and loses his patrimony by squandering it in foreign lands on riotous living with harlots. He experiences degradation in poverty, eventually repents, and receives his father's forgiveness on his return. Although this parable provides many valuable moments as negative examples for zealous Reformation moralists, the emphasis in both theatrical and artistic expressions consistently stresses the scene in the bordello. It is the place where gender relations are sifted through differentiated modes of desire, sex for the male and avarice for the female. The prodigal's financial and spiritual demise is depicted in the background, securing not only the moral but the narrative structure of the main event.[31]

Male sexual desire and female avaricious desire figure prominently in another group of bordeeltjes. Here the strategy for narrative is the inclusion of the prototypical theatrical figure, the costumed court fool complete with fool's cap and fool's staff who at times acts as narrator.[32] He appears in the early bordello scenes engraved by Lucas van Leyden in 1519 and Cornelis Massys (figs. 62 and 46). Whether he addresses the viewer directly as he does in Lucas's work or is integrated into the narrative as he is in Massys's, he functions as a sign of multi-scened theater, that is, a temporal event. He also functions in both instances to align our sympathies with the economically shrewd women rather than with the man, a key point to which we will return presently.

Narration is also central to the work of the so-called Brunswick Monogrammist, identified by some as Jan van Amstel.[33] His unusual full-length figure bordello scenes are characterized by diverse gestural and figural animation. Within these interiors a multiplicity of activities—women fighting; a couple going up to the sleeping quarters; couples caressing, eating, and drinking together—create the conditions necessary for comic theater. The viewer's attention is scattered across the canvas, and we have the urgent feeling that the constellation of events is precarious and will change before we can see it all.

These narratives with their realist connotations render plausible the ideological messages embedded in their structural forms. Primary among these structures is the consistent mise-en-scène of the bordello as a shallow stagelike interior. The pictorial space is structured as an enclosure that is, I propose, defined as both a woman's space and a woman's sexualized body. Its history as such, and thereby the informed viewer's preparation to appreciate it as such, developed over a long period. In particular, a contemporary, interior space was early established as the Netherlandish visual convention for addressing female sexuality by means of the feminine paradigm, the Virgin Mary. Many late-medieval verbal and visual metaphors used to address the holy mystery of Mary's virginity are couched in architectural terms.[34] She was, for example, proclaimed the temple and sanctuary of the Trinity.[35] Visually she is equated with the church in Jan van Eyck's painting in Berlin. In Panofsky's words, there she is "an embodiment in human terms of the same spiritual force or entity that is expressed in architectural terms, in the basilica enshrining her."[36]

More specifically, the completely closed setting conjures the very old and important iconographic Netherlandish traditions of the *Hortus Conclusus*—the "Garden Enclosed"—and the *Porta Clausa*—the "Locked Door"—that alternately signified the Holy Virgin's chastity.[37] The meaning of the latter was made literally concrete for early Christian nuns when Caesarius, bishop of Arles in A.D. 534, bricked in several doors of St. Jean, one of the earliest and most influential women's cloisters.[38] In the visual arts the earliest depictions of contemporary interiors—revolutionizing the history of art—were those used in the repertoire of the Virgin Mary. Among the earliest contemporary interiors in Christian art is Pietro Lorenzetti's *Birth of the Virgin*, in the museum in Siena, which is dated 1342. It clearly relegates Joachim to a separate panel outside Anna's chamber proclaiming Mary's own Immaculate Conception.[39] The implication of purity conveyed by this arrangement was codified in relation to Christ in the *Merode Triptych*, in the Metropolitan Museum of Art in New York, painted around a century later (fig. 68). Here, at the very moment of conception, Joseph is removed from the Virgin Mary's chamber as visual proof of his lack of physical participation in the act.[40] Other works made in the first half of the fifteenth century show how widespread was the convention for including Joseph in the work of art while excluding him from the Virgin.[41]

It was, however, Petrus Christus who, in a slightly later moment of the story, modernized the conceit by moving Joseph from literal exclusion to a pictorially illusionistic one (fig. 69). In his *Holy Family in a Domestic Interior*, in the Nelson-Atkins Museum of Art in Kansas City, he brilliantly met several intricate demands to include St. Joseph, not only in the work as a whole but in the same, real framed scene, at the same time excluding him from the fictive space of the Virgin's chamber and thereby from her body.[42] He did so by extending the depth of the space into several successive rooms using the recently learned Italian technique of linear, one-point perspective.[43] His formulation effectively enabled the convention to operate on more realistic levels for future generations of Netherlandish genre artists in both the sixteenth and seventeenth centuries.[44]

Indeed, the figure *in* the open doorway of the bordeeltje interior must serve as antithetical, defining the bordello space as the opposite of Mary's sexual pure space, which is closed and reserved. Within the structures of meaning in the early modern period, that which held the Virgin pure renders the bordello interior impure, contaminated as it were. By placing figures entering and leaving open doorways, these symbolic spaces emphasize the construct of a penetrated open interior tainted by the insertion of the exterior. An early example of this phenomenon is the late-fifteenth-century painting in the museum in Leipzig in which a male enters the room of a nude woman, identified by some as a love sorceress (fig. 70).[45] The entering figure, strategically placed at the threshold, becomes a common trope for sixteenth-century brothel scenes, for example, those by Jan Sanders van Hemessen, the Brunswick Monogrammist, and Jan Massys. In the sixteenth-century bordeeltjes the trafficked spaces figure the trafficked female bodies.

Eventually, the conceit of an entering figure in an open doorway signifying an open woman—lascivious, sexually defined, and available—became so com-

mon in Netherlandish secular images that it warranted an emblem and is illustrated here in a print from around 1630 showing a woman by the fire, her legs
spread wide apart (fig. 71). The accompanying explanatory inscriptions in Dutch
and French read:

> Compt vry inne, al ist by dage Coppen,
> Het stater al open, en wilt niet op de hage cloppen.
> Entre hardement Pierre, encores quil soit en iour,
> Ne bucquez sur la haye, ouvert trouverez tout entour.

The meaning is, essentially, that "there's no need to knock when the door is always open."[46]

The intruder in sixteenth-century bordeeltjes did not necessarily have to be
male. The endemic, intrusive old procuress could also signal the same sexual im-
purity of the woman/chamber conflation, as can be seen in several paintings by
Jan Massys, for example the one in Stockholm (fig. 72). The idea for the entering procuress may have originated with his father, Quentin, or with Giulio Romano, whose exceptional works reflect his association with the Italian libertine
Pietro Aretino.[47] Romano portrayed an entering procuress twice, once in a print,
the sole impression of which is in the Albertina in Vienna, which is associated
with Aretino's clandestine erotic series *I Modi*, and once in a large oil painting of
around 1525, now in the Hermitage.[48] The Hermitage painting is comparable to
the early-sixteenth-century Netherlandish tradition in the way fabrics are articulated and in its general subject matter, although certainly not in its nudity or
outward orientation.[49] It is specifically the presence of the old crone poking into
the room that identifies the subject of this painting as a bordello scene rather
than a mythological scene.[50]

Within the various iconographic traditions bearing on sixteenth- and early-
seventeenth-century Netherlandish imagery, where the device is most often and
consistently used, the entering and leaving figure functioned in a complex way,
both to establish the space as public for sexual commerce and as a sign of the
trafficked female body. It established a visual language that determined at least
one level of meaning for women in interior scenes throughout the Western European tradition. There were, however, many other levels that could be conjured
by the bordeeltje in the formations of contemporary social life.

Despite, indeed in contrast to, the literal levels of moralizing interpretation
condemning the sexually open women in these paintings, established by reference to biblical authority, fool's regalia, and or *Vanitas* conventions, the tenor of
these paintings and prints presents these women in a very positive manner, in
full possession of their lives. The power relationships described in the communities conjured by the bordeeltje narratives as a whole could be linked to those

described in other northern European visual and literary narratives. These come to the fore when we respect the visually obvious aspects of the imagery. We are encouraged at every turn to empathize with the women rather than the men, who are alternately described as stupid, unknowing, and an easy mark for deception and degradation.

Netherlandish bordello scenes that give women the upper hand over lecherous, desiring men work intertextually with other sixteenth-century representations of "women on top," to use a phrase coined by Natalie Zemon Davis.[51] The latter are included with other symbolic inversions in sixteenth-century enactments of the "omgekeerde wereld" (topsy-turvy world).[52] These inversions were commonly presented in performances at carnivals and other communal festivities, as well as being frequently described in popular literature and the visual arts. Such symbolic inversions have been alternatively argued as either confirming or contesting the social order.[53] Again, I would stress their formulative role throughout as naturalizing agents. These images work dynamically to construct hierarchical relationships along the lines of gender, which is to structure men and women in a binary relationship as either on "top" or on "bottom" by consistently picturing them in this way.

This is the point of many representations in contemporary Netherlandish engraved images drawn from historical, mythological, and biblical sources that illustrate women's power over men, specifically as a result of their sexual attractiveness. They are known collectively as the "power of women" topos and are represented by the Housebook Master's engraving of *Phyllis Riding Aristotle* and Lucas van Leyden's *Samson Shorn by Delilah*, to cite two examples among many (figs. 73 and 74).[54] Interestingly, as the popularity of the more overt "power of women" subjects began to wane in the second half of the sixteenth century, that of the bordeeltje, whose levels of meaning were more complex and whose possibilities for interpretation were more nuanced, increased.[55]

Although the "power of women" and the "women on top" topoi were generally popular throughout northern Europe in the early sixteenth century, the bordeeltje was a form specifically identified with the Netherlands in this period. Significantly, the subject of "de strijd om de broek," the fight for the trousers (or "who wears the pants"), as a struggle for dominance between wife and husband, seems also to have been a particularly Netherlandish subject.[56] It was, in concept, introduced in Erasmus's *Colloquia* and appeared most popularly in comic prints, as in the engraving by Israel van Meckenem.[57] Later in the century the story was expanded into narrative "strips" that visualized the life of a henpecked husband, the most popular of which were *Klaas en Griet* or *Jan de Wasser*.[58] The connection between the "strijd om de broek" and the bordeeltje is made in an early print of the former that takes on some visual conventions of the latter, primarily a large bed to the right and a fool entering the door on the left.[59]

The Netherlandish images of women dominating men in the "strijd om de broek" and the bordeeltje correlate with the popular assessment made by foreigners of the nature of "real" relationships between women and men throughout Dutch society.[60] Contributing to this mythology, and clearly participating in the same frames of reference, Sir John Reresby, traveling in the Northern Netherlands in the early seventeenth century, wrote, "The wives mostly wear the breeches and insult over their husbands with words upon easy occasion, being much favored by the laws of the country."[61] Van Deursen quotes Fletcher's *The little French lawyer*: "Nor would I be a Dutchman / To have my wife, my sovereign, to command me,"[62] and the Englishman Fynes Moryson, "I may boldly say, that the women of these parts, are above all other truly taxed with this unnatural domineering over their husbands."[63] According to a German observer in 1671 Dutch men not only tolerated this behavior but were proud of it.[64]

These consistent characterizations of the Dutch worked with the bordeeltje to construct, on the level of both high and low culture, an initial conceptualization of an "imagined community" of Netherlandish identity. What I am proposing is that the native conditions of sexuality out of marriage presented in bordello paintings and prints produced the signs for a "popular" definition of the modern Netherlands. This occurs just as the secularized *Virgin in the Garden Enclosed* became an official emblem of the Free Netherlands. "She" can be found on innumerable coins and prints from about 1575 onward.[65] Perhaps one of the best-known personifications of the "Hollandsche huyshouwen" (Holland's house, meaning the Northern Netherlands' state) figured as a "Virgin in the Garden" is the etching by Willem Buytewech made in 1615.[66] Although not working on the same levels, "woman," virginal or sexually free, was being produced at this time as a sign of Netherlandish identity.

The phrase "imagined community" is taken from Benedict Anderson, where it posits a nationalism with a small *n* rather than a capital and in so doing suggests that the communal identification or bonding of inhabitants of a region can be produced by a number of what may called "soft" factors, such as culture, before legal or official national status is achieved.[67] This kind of thinking is particularly appropriate for the history of the early modern Netherlands, where a politically determined national Netherlandish identity remained problematic for an exceptionally long period, whereas the recognition of a Netherlandish culture, especially the visual arts, came fairly early.[68] Netherlandish prostitution was, I propose, among the most effective legends produced in native popular culture to construct an imagined community of Netherlandish identity.

My intention with this suggestion is not to displace the work of these images in constructing gender difference with that of national, cultural difference but to suggest supplemental contexts, new frames, in which such obvious definitions of gender as the bordeeltje provided also worked in the delineation of an insider/ outsider status in, for example, the construction of a national (or regional) consciousness.

Informed by indigenous contemporary clothes and settings, the bordeeltje imagery announced the special native attractions of its sexually defined women.[69] In so doing, it joined ongoing European, mostly Italian, discourses that promoted a sort of sexual tourism.[70] These discourses set into motion the interplay between a regional, cultural identity and the particular sexual attraction to be found in their publicly available women.[71] The red-light district in Amsterdam, a popular tourist stop today, was, according to D. J. Noordam, writing in *Een kind onder het hart*, already a teeming tourist attraction in the early modern period.[72] Early travelers to the Netherlands often recorded their visits to the *musicos* or *speelhuizen* where prostitutes could be found.[73] Moreover, visits to *tucht-* or *spinnhuizen* of various Netherlandish cities, where delinquent prostitutes were incarcerated, were standard stops for tourists. The women there were sexual spectacles of derision and fascination.[74]

The international myths circulated about the specific attractions of the sexually available Netherlandish woman belong to a tradition begun in Renaissance Italy, where different Italian regions competed with one another on the desirability of their courtesans. In the sixteenth century the two primary centers of Italian culture and commerce to compete were Venice and Rome, Rome surpassing Venice up to the time of the Council of Trent, when Venice triumphed as the unrivaled courtesan city of Italy.[75] Pietro Aretino describes foreigners in Rome who, after seeing the ancient sites, would then turn to the modern marvels of the city, meaning the city's famous courtesans.[76] Idealized portraits of famous contemporary Venetian courtesans, which shared visual and conceptual terms with Titian's Venus,[77] were formulated in oil paintings by some of Venice's most prestigious artists, such as Titian and Palma Vecchio. They share the conventionalized characteristics of Venetian beauty, blonde or blondish hair and a disheveled state of disrobement that allows one of their beautiful breasts to be displayed, almost as if by accident.[78]

Soon, descriptions of prostitutes from many other European regions expanded the discourse of national sexual treasures glorified and compared. This kind of comparison, for example, runs throughout Brantôme's *Lives of the Fair and Gallant Ladies*, published in Paris at the end of the sixteenth century. It is the subject of his chapter entitled "Women of various countries compared;—de Béze quoted. [*sic*]," where Brantôme explains:

in which provinces and regions of our Christendom and Europe be there most cuckolds and harlots? Men declare that in Italy the ladies are exceeding hot, and for that cause very whorish, as saith M. de Béze in a Latin Epigram, to the effect that where the sun is hot and doth shine with most power, there doth it the most heat women, inditing a verse thus conceived: 'Credibile est ignes multiplicare suos'. ('Tis to [be] believed he doth there multiply their fires).

Spain is like the case, though it lies more to the Westward; yet doth the sun there warm fair ladies as well as ever it can in the East.

Flemish, Swiss, German, English and Scotch women, albeit they dwell more to the Northward and inhabit cold regions, share no less in this same natural heat; and indeed I have known them as hot as dames of any other land.

The Greeks have good reason to be so, for that they are well to the Eastward. So in Italy men do pray for Greca in letto,—or "a Greek bedfellow."

Brantôme then goes on at great length: "As for my fair countrywomen of France . . ." and ends, "In a word, 'tis good to love in this land of France."[79]

In 1631 nationally identified prostitutes were presented in a remarkable little book with verses in French, Dutch, and German entitled *Le Miroir des plus Belles Courtisannes de ce Temps* (A looking glass of the most beautiful courtesans of these times), which was published in the Dutch Republic, with illustrations by Crispin van de Passe.[80] The introduction to the volume is particularly interesting for the way in which the author justifies his text:

Darum ist mein freuntliges bitten undt begheren, diess geringe Buchlein von ihme nicht anders anzunhemen, dan dass allein: Fur erst, die mannigeley arht von Kleydingen, unter scheidliger Nationen da durch aussgebildet werden mogen.

[Therefore it is my happy bidding and pleasure to offer this small book for this reason alone and no other: Above all, to be able to represent the various art of clothing among different nations.]

The combined application of indigenous fashion, customs, and prostitution as identifying signs of nationality is made particularly explicit here and sheds light on constructs shared by the bordeeltje.[81]

The establishment of national or regional identity in general is constructed by oppositional contrast, defining who one is by contrast to who one is not. Native and foreign are thus two mutually dependent and reflexive concepts, each inconceivable without the other. The traveler traverses the boundaries between them and creates the terms by which they are known to one another.[82] The enticements of unfamiliar, exotic, sexual delights are among the most compelling of these terms. Sexual excitation formulated in early modern Europe, and still at work today, compounds illicitness with the idea of the foreign. It should be remembered here that when the Prodigal Son squandered his inheritance on harlots, he did so while in foreign lands. And the literary history of prostitution is, to a large extent, the history of foreign accounts.

The myths of Netherlandish prostitutes were of considerable interest to armchair tourists, as well as to more geographically adventurous ones. Literature and portable works of art worked to bring the lurid foreign into the safety preserve of home territory. Literary works that supported this fiction are, among others, John Marston's London play of 1604 entitled *The Dutch Courtesan* and the English, French, and German translations of the anonymous *Het Amsterdamsch Hoerdom* of 1681, a novelized tourists' guide to Amsterdam's brothels. The quotes from Shakespeare and Brantôme discussed above indicate the presence of these works of art in foreign places as decorations in public spaces.

On a real level, however, even among the Dutch, bordello life was "foreign" from domestic life. Throughout the Netherlands bordellos were physically located on the margins of society figured by the city walls. And as we have seen, these images worked to produce an image of the sociological "other" that contrasted with respectable burgher life. Again, the definition of one was dialogically dependent on the other. This dependence is reflected in the apologies for prostitution as a necessary evil to keep respectable women safe. It was a justification as meaningful for the sixteenth century as it was for Augustine's era. He warned that the elimination of prostitution would result in the pollution of sexual passion and abuses.[83] The long life of this trope relating a sexually pure home and the sexually free bordellos is expressed as late as 1724 by Bernard de Mandeville: "If courtesans and strumpets were to be prosecuted with as much rigor as some silly people would have it, what locks and bars would be sufficient to preserve the honor of our wives and daughters?"[84]

The bordeeltje's work within the emerging ideologies of early modern Europe can thus be seen as participating in the configurations of difference between social groups: Netherlandish men from Netherlandish women, respectable women from disreputable women, Netherlandish prostitutes from Italian prostitutes, the culture of the Netherlands from that of Italy. As it does so, the bordeeltje coalesces the bonds within each of the formative categories. However, as the gleeful exposition of young sexually energized communities of women whose sexual freedom and joie de vivre are all available for a price, it also works to construct larger bonds between men of all nations. The bordeeltje can be viewed as the site, and the public display of heterosexual desire as the medium, for a cardinal male bonding ritual. The fractionalized division of Christian Europe at this time called for flexible, and in a sense, universal sites of fraternal bonding. Neostoicism was redirecting the energies of man, who was no longer capable or effective in shaping the affairs of public life, to develop an inner framework, a private realm in which to exercise control and establish stability. The controlled sexuality of the female body was the perfect private project. The effects of culturally authorized heterosexual male desire overrode white male differences of nationality, class, or age without destroying the power relationships inherent in those differences. In fact, power relations work best among groups of men when they can claim membership in this "manly" club.[85]

I have analyzed the secular paintings and prints discussed here, with their particular focus on human, sexual narratives, presented as realistic and contemporary, as dynamically involved in defining and structuring power relationships between and among social groups. The bordeeltjes constructed what could be considered as "natural" and "normal" within female/male relationships in everyday social life. Moreover, ideologically, they work within the histories of the sexualized female body, institutionalizing private and public, native and foreign, insider and outsider. Seen in these new contextual frames, the images, rather than functioning as mere purveyors of moral virtue and vice, can suggest infinitely more complex connections through the visual construct "woman." The bordeeltje can add insight to the ever-changing formulations of that multidimensional, unstable, yet all-important sign in Netherlandish culture in the early modern period.

8

Domesticating the Peasant Father: The Confluent Ideologies of Gender, Class, and Age in the Prints of Adriaen van Ostade

The focus of this essay is the domestication of the father in three prints by Adriaen van Ostade (figs. 75, 76, and 77). By representing peasant fathers within the home these mid-seventeenth-century prints have an automatic appeal, as they seem to prophetically express contemporary attitudes toward the home and the shared parental responsibility of childcare. Historically, they may be seen as provisional interventions in the dominant construction of Dutch masculinity. In essence, the subject of this essay addresses the social construction of both femininity and masculinity in the early modern Dutch Republic. It does so in the belief that these are two mutually dependent and reflexive fabrications whose definition depends on their socially assigned differences, one from the other. Thus, the social definition of what is natural and normal for "woman" is construed in terms of what is not, that is, the domain of "man," and vice versa. Similarly, this essay addresses the early modern binary in the representation of class expressed through burghers and peasants and their related visual opposition of urban and rural life. Together they would come to stand as signs of a modern versus a bygone world.

The revision and renegotiation these large unstable concepts undergo in the early modern period, with their concomitant reordering of status and power, may become particularly visible to us through adjustments made within those cultural image types that emphasize tradition and are therefore highly conventionalized in their artistic vocabulary.[1] As we will see, Adriaen van Ostade's prints of peasants work especially well to reveal modern ideological shifts for just these reasons.

In fact, paintings and prints of peasants form one of the most cohesive subjects in the development of early Netherlandish secular art. Peasants figure prominently in representations of the months and seasons as early as the medieval pe-

riod.[2] The tradition of the laboring peasant's association with the seasons continued with renewed vigor into the sixteenth century and may be said to have been
codified by Pieter Bruegel's paintings and prints of the subject.[3] The peasant genre
developed more and more into a category specifically identified with the decidedly urban phenomenon, northern European artistic production.[4] Throughout,
peasants maintained many associations incurred in earlier seasonal cycles. For that
reason their representations were consistently bound to the production of that
other popular northern European subject genre, landscape.[5] Peasant and land
went together as concepts that were bound by their mutual definition as "nature,"
a bond continually fostered in German and Netherlandish art.[6] At times the images took sexual and sometimes even brutish turns, especially after the emphasis
moved from peasants at work to peasants recreating in the celebration of religious
festivals and rituals.[7] In the latter the peasant class as a sign of natural propagation
shifted from agricultural production to human reproduction, figured by robust
physical relationships between men and women (and by the presence of children).

In the first quarter of the seventeenth century peasant imagery was "modernized" by Haarlem artists Adriaen Brouwer and the brothers Adriaen and Isack
van Ostade. Brouwer was the first to consistently sequester the peasants from the
land and locate them in communal shanties. These interiors are to be understood as neither public nor private interiors but as urban rather than rural frames
for the figures.[8] By separating the peasant from his single most redeeming attribute, the land, Brouwer opens the subject up to a whole new series of judgments, expectations, and meanings. And, given the developing drive at his moment to define, favorably, city life as modern life, the peasant appeared displaced
not only in place but also in time.[9] He is found not only outside of his custom-
ary environment but also in a milieu where he is a remnant of an older, one may
say even old-fashioned, way of life. Generally, Brouwer's peasants are the same
sort seen in kermis paintings, but they lack the license afforded to kermis partic-
ipants in their celebration of a socially and religiously sanctioned holiday.[10] Where
the rural peasants of an outdoor kermis event may be seen as indulging in a
once-a-year event, Brouwer's urban peasants are indulging in activity that can
only be read as habitual and permanent.

In the second and third quarters of the seventeenth century, Adriaen van Ostade, Brouwer's Haarlem compatriot, continued to depict peasants in an interior
space.[11] Yet the precise location of his massive ramshackle interior spaces can never
be completely determined. The great range and quantity of his work places it at
the intersection of the histories of the subject in Netherlandish art and those of
shifting contemporary social "realities" concerning peasant life as a sign of the rural in the progressively urbanized Dutch Republic of the mid-seventeenth century.

The various historical shifts in artistic emphasis from working peasants to recreating peasants, from landscape to interior, and from rural to urban all signal shifts in the way these images were thought of and the way they worked to dynamically structure social life in early modern culture. These shifts remind us that despite the so-called realism of these paintings and prints they were fabrications of the imagination and that both the artists who produced them and the public who bought them perceived their relevance to modern society on many dimensions and many levels, including, and not least of which was, the delineations of difference within class and gender formations. Such an analysis of these works moves against their persuasive artistic rhetoric, a rhetoric that aims to seduce us with their "realism" and consequently erase or naturalize their social work.[12]

The complex percept of artistic realism in early Netherlandish art operates within the binary play of high and low, individualism and universalism, urban and rural, normalcy and deviance. Insight into the uses of realism and its early association with the construct of the peasant in, for example, the *Trés Riches Heures* of the Duc de Berry of 1416 is furnished by contrasting the February page with the April page of the same manuscript.[13] Realism is here already marked with theoretical assumptions inherited from ancient writers on rhetoric and the theater such as Aristotle, Cicero, and Terence. Ancient theory linked the "real" and the "low" as parts of the definition for *comedy*, essentially defined as the antipode of the ideal.[14] Whereas in antiquity what was "low" could be defined by a variety of characteristics that for the ancients ranged from the merely mundane to the physically deformed and/or ugly, in the Renaissance adulation of Horace's theory of decorum as stated in *Ars Poetica*, "that figures should be portrayed according to their station in life," fixed conceptions of the "low" to a specifically class-defined concept.[15]

The contrasting styles used for different classes in the *Trés Riches Heures* already illustrate what will be a long-lived association in western European art between "idealized" form used to depict aristocracy on one side and "realism" used to depict the "lower classes" on the other. The definition of the latter as basically sexual is revealed by detailed inspection of the image. Finally, seventeenth-century artistic theory further defined *realism* in terms of a socially hierarchical reception by claiming its appeal to the lower classes. Bellori, writing in 1664, claims, "Common people refer everything they see to everyday visual experience. They praise things painted naturally, being used to such things."[16]

Recent interpretations of peasant imagery have for the most part, rather restrictively, vacillated between the opposite poles of condemnation and exaltation for the figures depicted.[17] The debate has all but ended in a stalemate. In my view the phenomenon of peasant imagery can be seen as neither positive nor negative exempla per se but rather as a system for representing social hierarchies in the service of evolving modern ideologies, which are by nature fluid and mobile. Through the changes in peasant imagery as a sign of early modern society, one can look for and examine those priorities of socialization—what Norbert Elias has termed the civilizing process—through which all social relations were filtered in the period under consideration.[18]

Specifically by examining three prints by Adriaen van Ostade that figure the father domestic, a case study can be isolated wherein Van Ostade probes the limits of picturing men within the domestic sphere and its concomitant implications on the normalcy of socially constructed masculinity and femininity as an urban condition in the Dutch Republic. In doing so, we will see the mediating intimations of age on these formulations.[19]

The three prints by Van Ostade are exceptional within the context of Dutch art (see figs. 75, 76, 77). They earn this status by compassionately depicting, within a genre context, the Dutch family, that is, mother, father, and children, in a domestic interior.[20] Despite the fact that the family was a driving concept of self-definition for the Dutch, the visual presentation of the entire family within the home was actually confined, outside of family portraits, to a few rare cases.[21] For the most part the domicile was culturally and socially defined as the exclusive realm of the woman and urban domesticity as the sign of the feminine. By contrast, these three prints by Van Ostade figure the relationships and the activities of the entire family unit, including the father. Moreover, Van Ostade's peasant father is not merely present but fully active in carrying out the responsibilities of family life.

Adriaen van Ostade's earliest print in this novel project is *The Family* (fig. 75), signed and dated 1647.[22] The etching portrays a large dilapidated barnlike interior with five figures: two adults and three children (and a dog). The preparatory drawing for the print is oriented in the same direction and serves comparatively to underscore the effectiveness of the dramatic lighting within the print.[23] Such large interior spaces have long been considered part of Adriaen's and his younger brother Isack's contribution to this genre.[24] The interior of *The Family* is similar in tone and spatial feeling to the so-called *Breakfast* etching (fig. 78) made by Adriaen at about the same time.[25] A comparison with *The Breakfast* alerts us to the experimental nature of Van Ostade's work at this time. The Latin inscription in state V of *The Breakfast*—"We spend time for an untroubled table / After a lengthy wait, a fair day comes"—explains the bounty of the scene as the just rewards of hard work.[26] Despite the presence of cards, smoking, and drinking—all items that produce the almost traditional art-historical interpretation as condemnatory—the depicted subject clearly presents a convivial and civil scene of

generous exchange. Within each compositional group one figure offers sustenance to another; boy to girl, man to man, men to woman. A sympathetic reading also becomes available when *The Breakfast* is related to the subjects of *The
Fat Kitchen* and *The Lean Kitchen*, two peasant subjects in Bruegel's own oeuvre
atypically located in interiors (figs. 79 and 80).[27] Van Ostade's well-off, rotund
peasants are generous and sharing, as a combination of the ample forms of the
former and the message of charity of the latter. The print of *Tobit and the Angel*,
recognizable on the back wall of the chamber, also inflects the meaning in this
direction as among its messages the parable stressed the virtue of giving alms.[28]
Although the image's meanings are open and depend on the various circulating
discourses with which the viewer associates them, the internal signs prefigure a
more sympathetic view of these peasants.[29] With the clearer definition of the
space as a home, a similarly positive shift in associative inflection is even more
pronounced in *The Family*.

The print is frequently offered as evidence of a general change in the perception of the peasant within Van Ostade's oeuvre and in Dutch art in general after
midcentury.[30] The private, domestic sense achieved in this print through the portrayal of parental care and concern have led art historians to connect it specifically with two well-defined Dutch pictorial types. The first, most oft-cited, is the
slightly later development of bourgeois domestic interiors in genre paintings by,
for example, Nicolaes Maes (fig. 81) and others that flourished from the mid-1650s
onward.[31] Yet these differ from Van Ostade's conception on several significant
counts, not only in the more controlled and limited spaces of their interiors but
also in the description of an urban middle class that dictates the final and defini-
tive difference, a powerful paternal absence.[32] The visual lack of adult men is essential to these paintings. As I have discussed elsewhere (see Chapter 7), these images partake of the Netherlandish visual convention that figures the domestic
interior as the pure, virginal space of the woman's body. I am repeating this idea
here for its relevance to the current argument. Pureness was as central a condition
for the construction of the modern, bourgeois woman as it was antithetical for
that of the peasant woman. The bourgeois domestic space as it developed in Netherlandish art was structured as an enclosure that is, I propose, defined as both the
woman's space and the woman's sexualized body. Its history as such, and thereby
the informed viewer's preparation to appreciate it as such, developed over a long
period. Since the beginning of the fifteenth century, the visual representation of a
contemporary, interior space in Netherlandish art worked as a convention to communicate female sexual purity through the paradigm of the Virgin Mary. Architectural terms, particularly those of a closed or sheltered architecture such as the
hortus conclusus (the garden enclosed) or the *porta clausa* (the locked door) domi-

nate the many late-medieval verbal and visual metaphors used to address the holy mystery of Mary's chastity.[33] Paintings by Robert Campin (fig. 68), Jan van Eyck, and Petrus Christus (fig. 69), to name a few, reflect this system.[34] The same visual language was adopted and inverted in the sixteenth century to depict female licentiousness, the opposite of Mary's virginity. Thus the figure entering or leaving the open doorway in countless Netherlandish sixteenth- and seventeenth-century bordello scenes was surely viewed as a sign of the pure "space/body" penetrated and defiled. Within the structures of meaning in the early modern period, that which held the Virgin pure rendered the bordello interior impure and debased. The entering figure strategically placed at the threshold can be seen in many brothel scenes, including some by Jan Massys (fig. 72), for example.[35] In the sixteenth- and seventeenth-century *bordeeltjes*, as these bordello scenes were called, the trafficked spaces figure the trafficked female bodies. As a sign system this motif survives into the eighteenth century where it takes a new turn in, for example, Fragonard's painting of 1777 entitled *L'Heureuse Fécondité*.[36]

In the seventeenth century the construct of the open door with a figure entering, signifying an open woman, lascivious, sexually defined, and available, became so common a trope in Netherlandish secular images that it warranted an emblem and is illustrated here in a print from around 1630 showing a woman by the fire, her legs spread wide (fig. 71). The accompanying explanatory inscriptions in Dutch and French read:

> Compt vry inne, al ist by dage Coppen,
> Het stater al open, en wilt niet op de hage cloppen.
> Entre hardement Pierre, encores quil soit en iour,
> Ne bucquez sur la haye, ouvert trouverez tout entour.[37]

Seventeenth-century bourgeois domestic scenes, for the most part, reinstated the sign system of virginity in a form of metaphoric purity, which is shared by the monogamous Dutch housewife and the urban interior space she inhabits.[38] This system was so pervasive that it appears "natural" and "normal" to us and, consequently, inflects the visual conjunction of a man and woman in a bourgeois interior as compromising, as in paintings by Pieter de Hooch (fig. 82) and others.

Adriaen van Ostade's disengagement from this conceptual system is best understood as a function of the peasant class he depicts, with its rural associations. Clearly, the peasant father could represent what the bourgeois father could not. He could be present where the bourgeois father could not. The former's absence could not be interpreted as "elsewhere" in the production of capital that would provide for his family. Moreover, the lower, "vulgar" subject brought with it its own particular set of sexuality myths that identified it as raw, instinctual, and identified with "nature" and, thus, separated it from the construction of bourgeois sexuality. Again, these associations are amply represented in sixteenth-century German and Netherlandish art.[39] A way of grasping Van Ostade's peasant paternity as present but controlled is given by considering the second, related art-historical connection generally made for *The Family*, that is, Rembrandt's depictions of *The Holy Family*.[40]

In fact, Rembrandt's *Adoration of the Shepherds* of 1646 (fig. 83), in the National Gallery in London, a subject even closer to Van Ostade in form and meaning than the commonly suggested *Holy Family*, works especially well as a general comparison with the painted version of *The Family* in Budapest (fig. 84).[41] The striking formal concordances here support the analogy whose ultimate relationship rests on the class definition of the two subjects. In both, the poor, humble, somewhat chaotically strewn interiors communicate grandeur as well as reverence. Tonal qualities and large structural spaces render both figure groups warm and intimate yet, paradoxically, dramatic and monumental. Rembrandt's subject was the paradigmatic Christian and, on some level, particularly Protestant, expression of reverence for the humblest and lowest classes.[42] Not only are these lowly members of society the first to be told of the miracle of salvation, but also throughout the New Testament Christ himself is often referred to as a shepherd come to guide his sheep.

The poverty and humility of Christ's circumstances provided a behavioral model for the Christian. This ideology was especially strong in northern Europe, in the tradition of Thomas à Kempis's *In Imitatio Christi*, where "worldly vanities" are denigrated from the very first chapter to the last.[43] The value of Christian grace as superior to worldly goods and as a compensation for the lack of material comforts is expressed again and again in Luther and Calvin. Luther's *Sermons on John* can serve as an example: "And though I may appear to be a beggar in your sight, I still own a great treasure, compared with which all your wealth is not worth a penny. . . . On earth we are beggars, as Christ Himself was; but before God we are bountifully blessed with all good things."[44]

A parallel compensatory dissimulation is made in a subscript added to a print after a similar peasant interior by Van Ostade:

> See us work with sweet spindles.
> In view of such phantasmagoric marvels.
> Yet it is with sense that we love
> our little child and not a little.
> Thus we regard our hovel as a most magnificent mansion.[45]

The sentiment of the inscription is the same as Luther's, but the emphasis has clearly shifted. The print addresses a more secular audience, with the hovel transformed into a mansion achieved through the magic of parental love. The appeal to parental love and responsibility accesses a host of circulating discourses on the family, children, and child rearing that were primary ideological issues for the Dutch at this time.[46]

Discussion of Van Ostade's etching of *The Family* of 1647 can, therewith, be invigorated by the evolving discourse on proper child rearing, its compensatory rewards, and, I propose, its implication for class mobility. This discourse is invoked in part by the older boy's pet, the attentive dog. As a convention the dog symbolized *leerzugtigheid*, or Christian aptitude.[47] Its meaning as such is determined by its frequent emblematic use in books and portraits. For example, a portrait by Ludolph de Jongh, *Portrait of a Young Boy*, in the Virginia Museum of Fine Arts in Richmond, combines emblem and narrative to convey this sentiment. The ability to learn, like so many other preoccupations of Dutch culture, has been sifted and sorted by art historians to "reflect" the moral value of formal education ensuring the proper continuance of virtuous behavior. But, then as now, learning also figured prominently in advancing one's economic and social position, the increasingly important terms of class distinction in the early modern era.

Moreover, in discussing other images Simon Schama connected the Dutch word for education, *opvoeding*, with its etymological root, *voeden*, meaning to nourish. Although eating is the main activity of Van Ostade's figures, more is implied than simple nourishment.[48] Norbert Elias's work presents us with a useful model for thinking about the connective links between early modern preoccupations with education, eating, and manners, although the texts he set out to study were courtesy books, not paintings or prints. His ideas, published in two volumes collectively called *The Civilizing Process*, emphasize the development of table manners as a means of artificially creating class-distinctive behaviors at a time when the traditional borders and boundaries between classes were heavily threatened by social mobility.[49] Elias marks the starting point of *civilité* as a concept of social formation with the publication of Erasmus's *De civiliate morum puerilium*, a treatise on civility in children.[50] Although first published in 1530, Erasmus's work went through multiple editions and was enormously influential in the 1640s.[51] Among its many prescriptions for civilized social behavior, the proper execution of table manners plays a particularly prominent role. Although it may be going too far to label Van Ostade's etching of *The Family* an exposition on table manners, the progressive degree with which civilité figures proper behavior around eating in the particular segment of his images of peasant family life under discussion in this study cannot be denied. With this larger significance in mind, the fact that it is Van Ostade's peasant father who heads the enterprise as the visual apex of a pyramid constructed by the nuclear family takes on new meaning. He cuts a piece of bread, not unlike St. Joseph's action in Jan Mostaert's earlier *Holy Family* (fig. 85), in Cologne. The two images may be linked through the northern European visual practice of showing the male as the *voedster* or *voedstervader*, the provisional or nurturing father, a point to which we will return directly.

The so-called *Pater Familias* (fig. 76) of 1648, executed the year after *The Family*, can be seen as an intensification of the tendencies outlined above.[52] Van Ostade settled on a vertical composition after making both vertical and horizontal preparatory drawings for the print.[53] In the end he not only chose the more compact of the two drawing formats but also reduced the dimensions of the domicile and condensed and compressed the family group. By eliminating one adult male figure from the drawing concept, he reduced any ambiguity of the role of the single male adult who remains. Further, and for our purposes most significant, is Van Ostade's recasting of the father's role. He essentially reversed his position and role with that of the mother. In an unprecedented move Adriaen van Ostade produced a genre picture of a father feeding his child as a positive image.[54] The power of this gendered reversal of socially prescribed maternal and paternal roles for the Dutch cannot be overstated.

Normative behavioral prescriptions clearly defining social roles were fundamental to the institutionalized self-fashioning of Dutch national consciousness on almost every level. Indeed, images of reversed normative behavior were not in themselves new but rather had been used as one of the most insidious strategies for instilling that standard. Topsy-turviness, or the world upside down, had, as a tactic, produced an impressive number of satirical images concerning a broad range of social hierarchies.[55] An entire subcategory of the topsy-turvy world was developed specifically to address gender roles, which Natalie Zemon Davis calls "women on top."[56] Pieter Bruegel the Elder's sixteenth-century engraving of the henpecked husband is one of the earliest to address the domestic sphere. In the seventeenth century the concept of transposed domestic roles was expanded into narrative "strips" that serially visualized the pitiful life of henpecked husbands. The most popular of these were *Klaas en Griet* and *Jan de Wasser*.[57] Among the scenes that ridicule Jan de Wasser, and that are particularly relevant to Van Ostade, are those that show him tending to and spoon-feeding his child (see fig. 86). In these "strips" the pressure to behave appropriately, according to gender, is achieved by scurrilously mocking all deviation.

Derisive behavior reversals may even be seen in two images by Van Ostade himself. In two drawings, one in Frankfurt (fig. 87) and the other in Budapest (fig. 88), peasant husbands hold a cross-reel, an instrument used in the last stages of spinning thread.[58] As Wayne Franits has shown, spinning thread in all its stages had become the quintessential sign of feminine virtue in Dutch art by midcentury.[59] And even though the Frankfurt drawing, when later translated into a print, was interpreted positively by the inscription quoted above, Van Ostade himself depicted the men doing this activity in a droll way. They appear farcical not only by virtue of the endemic early modern association of spinning with femininity but also specifically by their humorous physical appearance.[60]

The two comic drawings by Van Ostade alert us to a number of issues. Most important, they remind us that it would be a mistake to see the shared parental responsibility represented in *The Family* and the *Pater Familias* as in any way reflective of Van Ostade's personal progressive attitudes toward male responsibility for child rearing or even to think that he was particularly sympathetic to the peasant as a class group. At any given moment, a full range of interpretations of this material can be illustrated by his dated works. It would better serve our understanding to see these, instead, as moments of negotiation, as experiments in social formation, if you will. What is being negotiated and how is implicated in the nexus of socially constituted categories such as class, masculinity and femininity, and that least studied social category, age.[61]

Age is essential to the meaning of an emblem in Johan de Brune's book of 1624. He illustrates spinning as a means of defining gender difference and underscores the industrious character of an old woman in his *Emblemata* Number XLIV, entitled "Wat rust en ghewin heeft luttel onderwin . . ." (What rest and profit the humblest activities reap).[62] The woman in de Brune's emblem spins while the man whittles into the fire. The explanatory text continues by declaring the rest of the Christian soul to be far superior to the disquiet of those who seek earthly gain. As in the work by Van Ostade, spiritual, Christian behavior brings ethereal rewards that console and compensate the poor for their lack of worldly material goods. De Brune's emblem may be seen to inform our understanding of Van Ostade in the particular emphasis given to the age of the couple. Spinning could be more than merely a reference to a spiritually sanctioned diligence; rather, it could also be a reference to life itself. Spindle, thread, and distaff were often used emblematically in the seventeenth century to express the idea that "Providence alone permits the thread of life to continue,"[63] hence its popularity in images of the elderly. The image of an elderly couple in the comfort of their home draws our attention to the advanced years of the couple in Van Ostade's happy family.

The advanced age of the father and mother in both *The Family* and the *Pater Familias* has not gone unnoticed. In 1914 the mother's age was an issue: "Would the beauty of that masterpiece, *The Family*, have been greater had the mother, fondling her latest-born in that poor apartment, been young and fair of form and feature instead of worn with years of care and toil to the loss of all comeliness? For me, her plainness adds to the simple pathos, and so to the beauty of the picture, showing Ostade's tenderness of perception."[64] The father is also noticeably elderly in both prints. It is clear that the religious tropes associated with advanced years valorizes his activity in both scenes. We have already seen the deference for old age and its connection with poverty signaled by de Brune's emblem. Similar associations are made in a print by Petrus Fedes van Harlingen. On the level of narrative possibilities we may even think Van Ostade has portrayed the grandfather. Yet, ultimately, Van Ostade's conception of the poor, elderly father feeding his child goes back to a prestigious tradition, one that evolved in the devotion of St. Joseph.

From around 1400, as the cult of St. Joseph developed in northern Europe, he is depicted positively as taking a more active role in paintings of the Nativity and the Adoration.[65] Among his most loving functions is as *nutritor domini*, where he is depicted either preparing food or feeding the Christ Child as seen in the painting by Jan Mostaert (fig. 85).[66] St. Joseph's service and nurture in the face of poverty is, once again, surely related to the construction of that economic state as a condition of Christian piety and devotion.[67] Significantly, Joseph's poverty does not keep him from the care of his family, as St. Bernard described Joseph, "a prudent and faithful servant . . . whom the Lord placed beside Mary to be her protector, the nourisher of His human body and the single and most trusty assistant on earth in His great design"; and he further states that Joseph was there to "carry in his arms, to lead by the hand, to nourish and watch over the infant Saviour."[68] St. Antoninus of Florence (d. 1459) corroborates this view: "just as children need providers (nutritii), so He wanted to have Joseph, holy spouse of His mother, as His provider. Hence he is correctly called the father of Christ, not from the effect of geniture but from the task and care of providing."[69] Similarly Van Ostade's peasant paternity can be defined as "not from the effect of geniture but from the task and care of providing."

Although St. Joseph's portrayal as nutritor domini is rare in the seventeenth century, some cases do exist, for example, *The Nativity* by Jacob Jordaens in the Metropolitan Museum of Art in New York.[70] The tradition of St. Joseph as nutritor domini secularized in Van Ostade's *The Family* and the *Pater Familias* constructs the civil image of a poor but solicitous, caring father. It provides a model for neutered paternal involvement within the structures of Dutch domesticity via the evolving justifying norms of nurture and civilité.

The discourse of civilité is prominent in the final print to be considered here, *Saying Grace*, signed and dated 1653 (fig. 77).[71] Significantly, it is the least narrative and the most emblematic of the three. It was also the most influential of the group. *Saying Grace* draws from a slightly earlier visual stock that portrayed upper-class families who were, in fact, antithetical to the peasant. The subject was particularly popular around 1600, represented in prints by Robert Baudois, Jacques de Gheyn, and Crispin van de Passe and in the slightly later French example by Abraham Bosse. The subject *Saying Grace Before a Meal* has received a remarkable amount of attention in recent scholarship, having been extensively studied by Wayne Franits, Pieter J. J. van Thiel, and Eddy de Jongh.[72] They have unearthed the appropriate visual sources with all their biblical references. Whereas Van Ostade's precursors all depict very well-to-do families, his emphasis is the lower end of the social spectrum. His peasants join the moneyed class in their effort to better the lot of their children.

Adriaen probably conceived of the idea of a poor but grateful family giving thanks for their bounty with his brother, Isack, whose drawing of 1644, today in Haarlem, predates Adriaen's print by several years.[73] Again by comparison Adriaen's peasants appear older and thus in greater control over their lives. The father has become plump as has his son. Moreover, the dramatic lighting in the room and the ladder behind them recall and thereby connect this print with the spaces of Adriaen's earlier depictions of paternal involvement. The strong light and geometricized shapes support the signification of the more corpulent figures in projecting an atmosphere of regularity and normalcy. It is this sanitized formulation that would ultimately contribute to Jan Steen's paintings of the peasant poor as a subject with the same mixture of poverty, piety, and dignity constructed through combined Christian and social graces.[74]

From 1647 to 1653 Adriaen van Ostade probed the possibilities of figuring the father within the peasant family unit as an active participant in the responsibilities and pleasures of domestic life. A comparison between the first and last print reveals the staging status of that experiment. In *The Family* the space is larger; the figures and space are mutually dependent and mutually reflexive. The definition of each relies on the other, as had been traditional for peasant imagery since the early sixteenth century. In *Saying Grace* the space has become shallower, and the figures emerge dominant, almost iconic. Eating has gone from an activity of nurture to one of ritual, all of which is reflected in the tighter composition organized around the table in the later work.

Van Ostade's prints from *The Family* to *Saying Grace* became increasingly less narrative and increasingly more emblematic and abstract. Accordingly, their social function shifted from the rhetorical stance of description to that of prescription. The latter spoke to the anxieties of a growing prosperity of the peasant class in the Dutch Republic.[75] The peasant family is encouraged to accept its lot in life as a reflection of a Christian state. To this end the inscription in Steen's Philadelphia painting of a peasant family saying grace (fig. 89), so close in feeling to Van Ostade's etching, is telling:

Three things I desire only and no more
Above all to love God the Father
Not to covet an abundance of riches
But to desire what the wisest prayed for
[Only] an honest life in this vale
In these three all is based.[76]

If subsequent influence is in any way a measure of the social effect of an image, Van Ostade's *Saying Grace* must be deemed particularly successful. Success
for *The Family* can only be claimed for its formal interior design. Indeed, Cornelis Dusart's watercolor drawing (fig. 90), which so closely clones Van Ostade's
interior, undoes its civilizing effects. In Dusart's drawing the buxom mother
stands at the head of the family, and the nourishing old man is redefined as the
grandfather. Moreover, Dusart restores the chaotic, uncivilized squalor of an extended, rather than a nuclear, family. The homey intimacy and restraint of Van
Ostade's *The Family* are completely repudiated.

Although Van Ostade prints of the domesticated father may be seen in the
larger project of upgrading the peasant's image in Dutch art in general after 1650,
at each stage they inform us about the anxieties and negotiations being staged
around the issues of class, gender, and age as models for modern behavior. They
show us what was viable and what was not. His most innovative efforts ultimately
failed, or at least found little resonance for the seventeenth-century Dutch. It was
his most abstract and conventionalized domestic peasant interior that struck immediate resonance. Van Ostade's domesticated peasant father disappears from the
scene, not to re-emerge until one hundred years later in prerevolutionary Paris,
when once again the derangement of power relationships called forth innovative
images to redefine gender and class.[77]

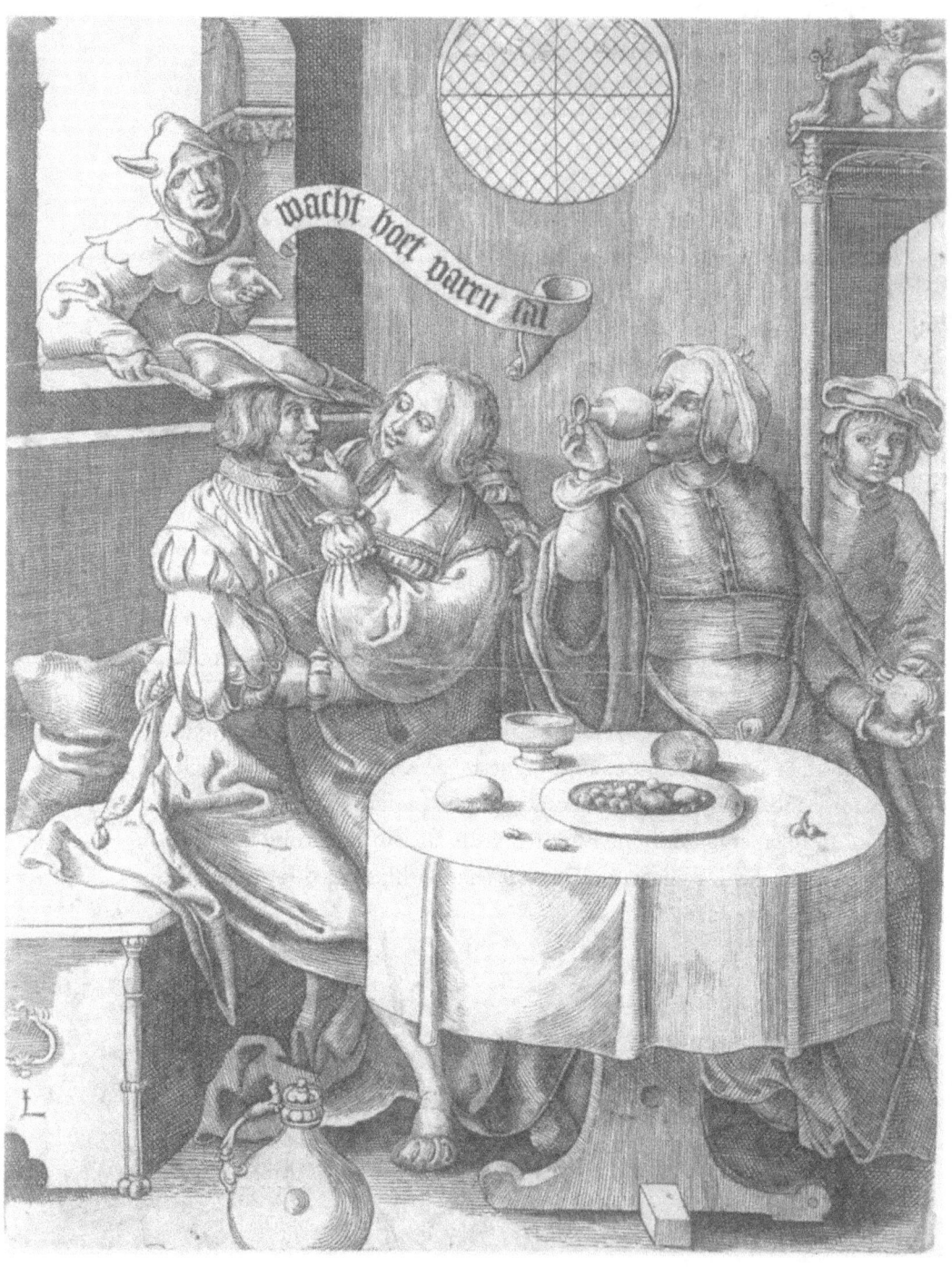

FIGURE 62. After Lucas van Leyden,
[copy in reverse] *Tavern Scene.* 1519.
Rijksmuseum, Amsterdam.

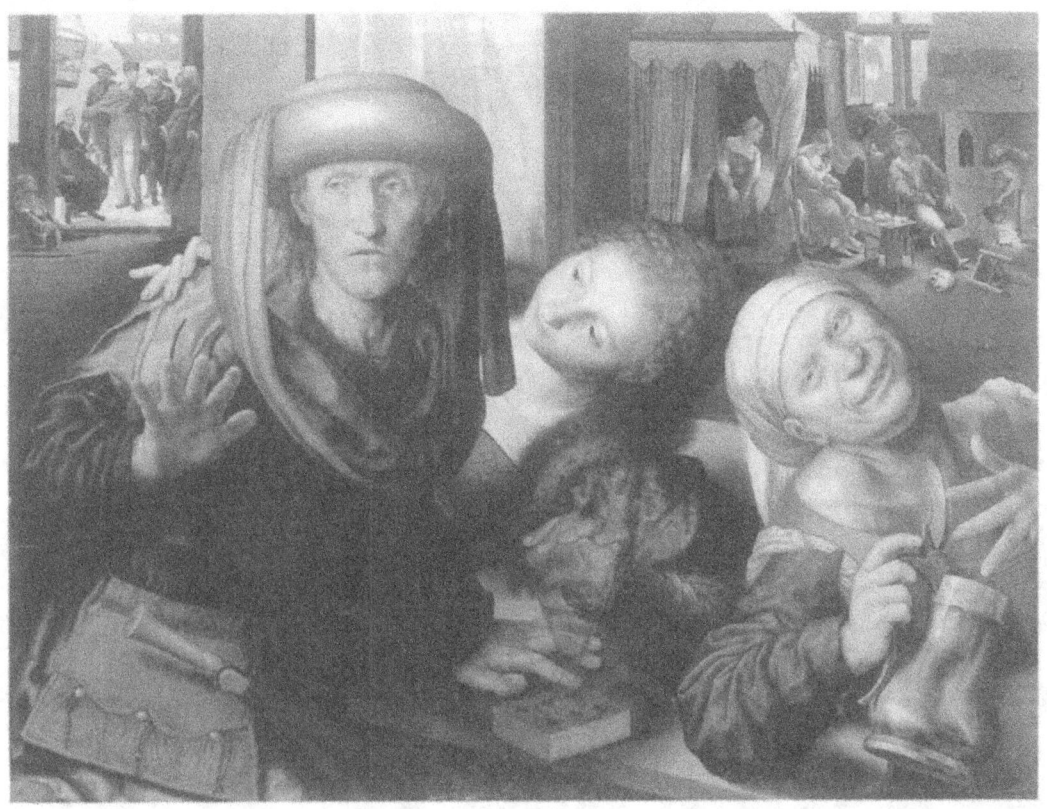

FIGURE 63. Jan Sanders van Hemessen,
Bordello. 1530s. Staatliche Kunsthalle, Karlsruhe.

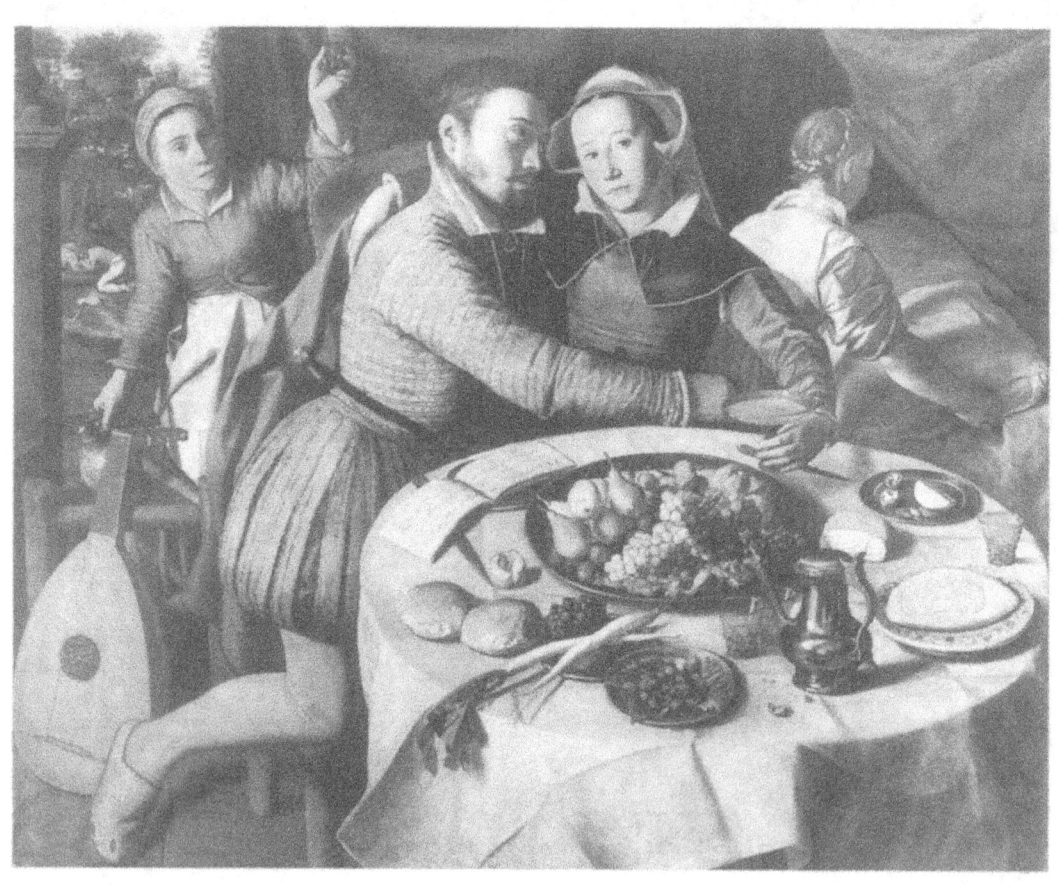

FIGURE 64. Joachim Beuckelaer,
The Prodigal Son. Royal Museum of
Fine Arts of Belgium, Brussels.

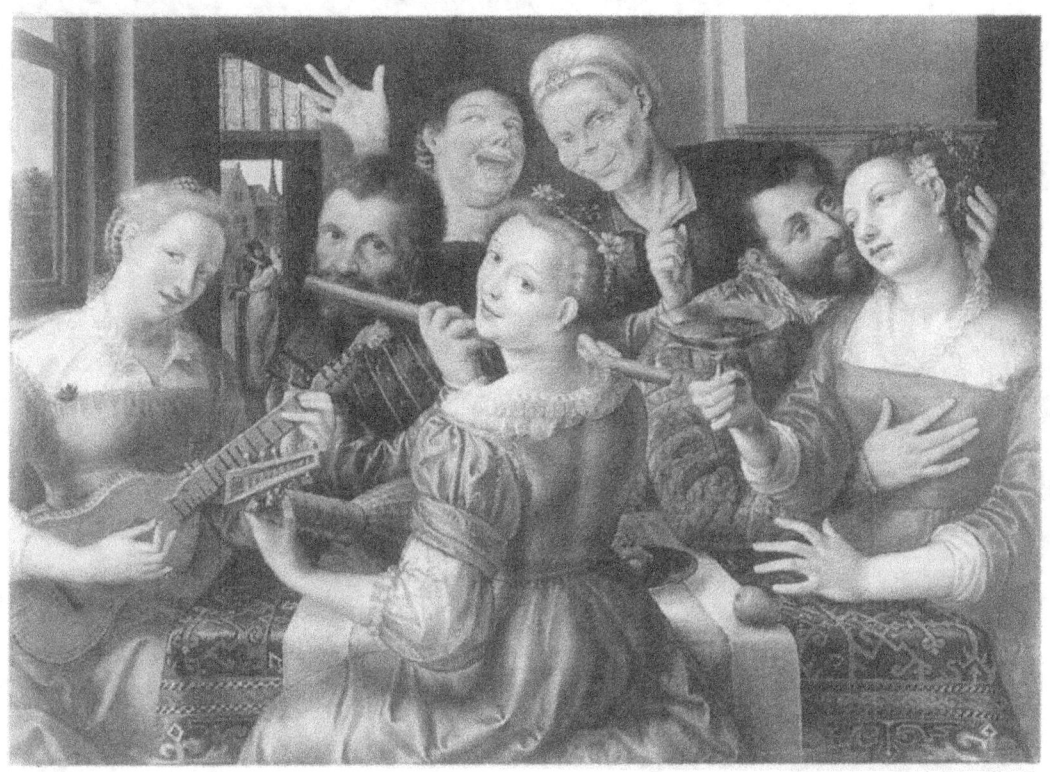

FIGURE 65. Jan Massys, *A Merry Company.*
Nationalmuseum, Stockholm.

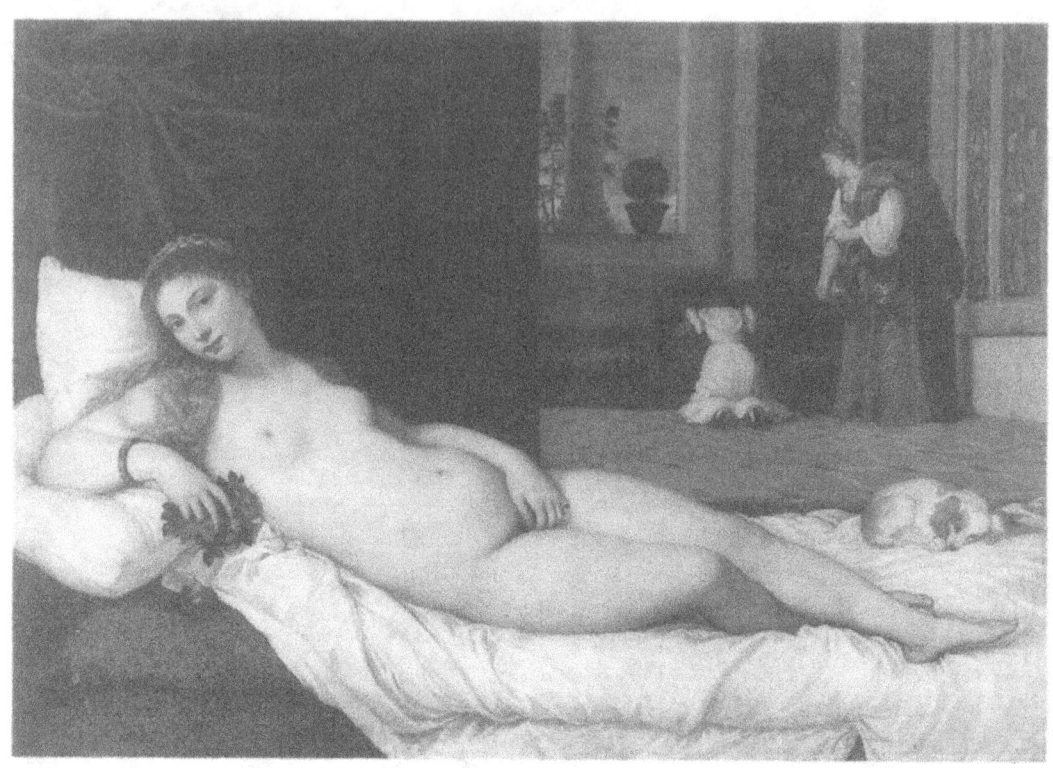

FIGURE 66. Titian, *Venus of Urbino*.
1530s. Uffizi, used by permission of
Art Resource, New York.

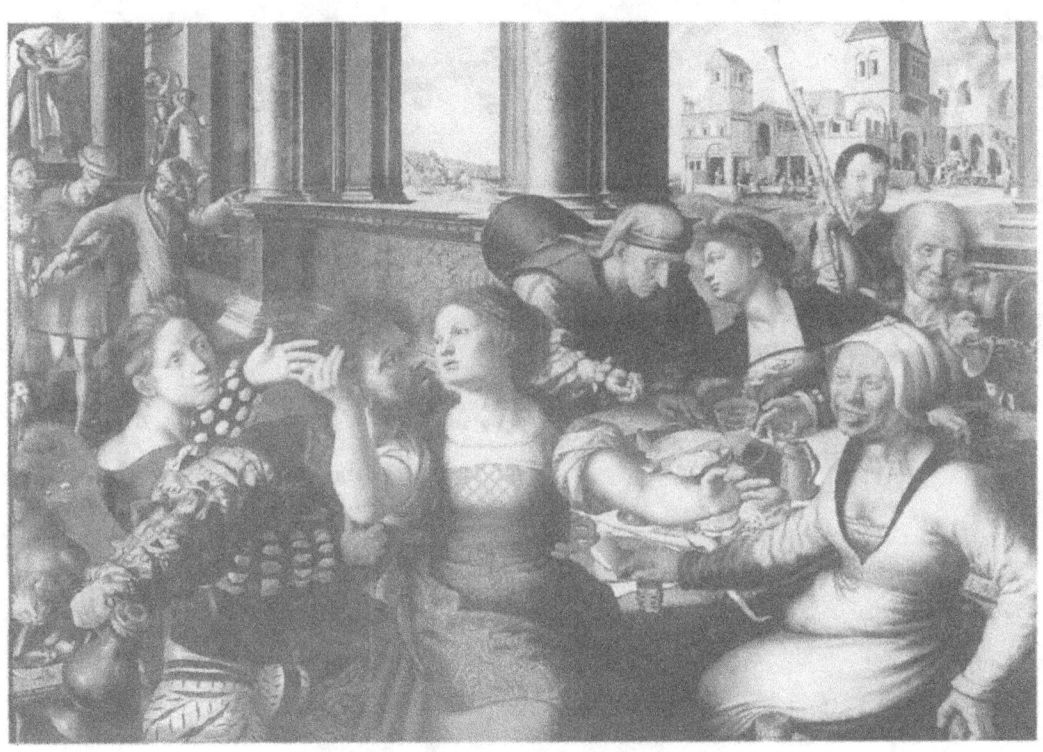

FIGURE 67. Jan Sanders van Hemessen,
The Prodigal Son. Royal Museum of Fine
Arts of Belgium, Brussels.

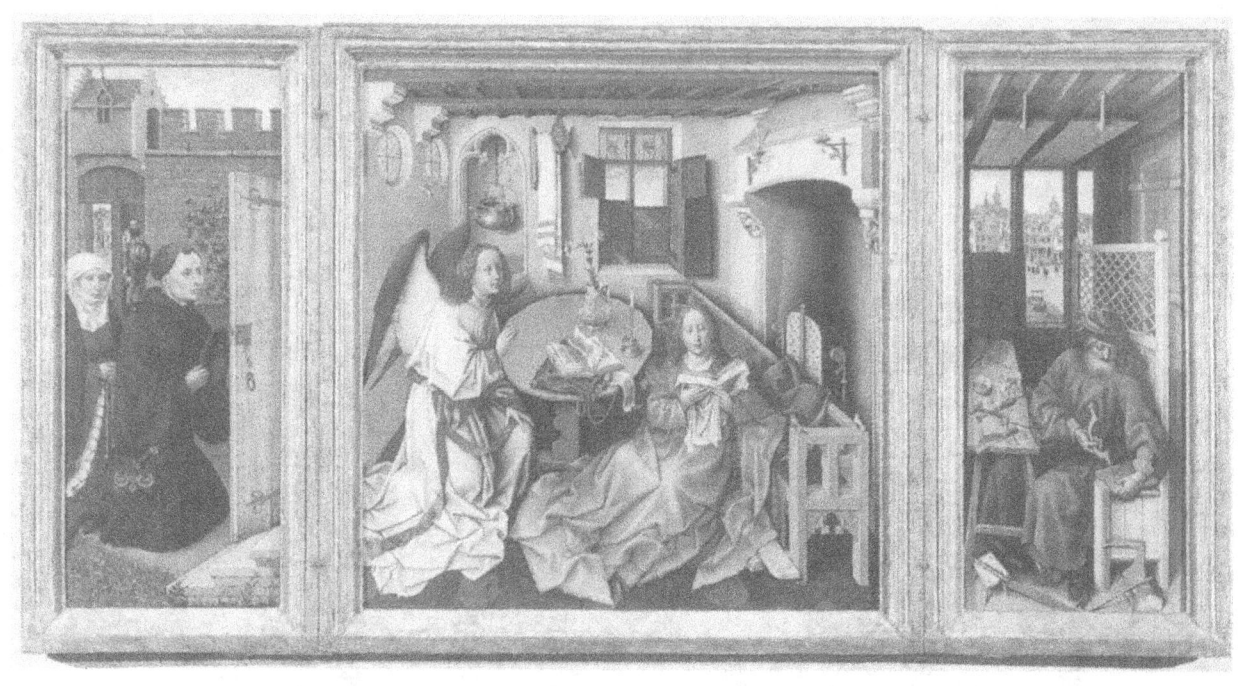

FIGURE 68. Robert Campin, *The Annunciation* [*Merode Triptych*]. The Metropolitan Museum of Art, The Cloisters Collection, 1956, New York.

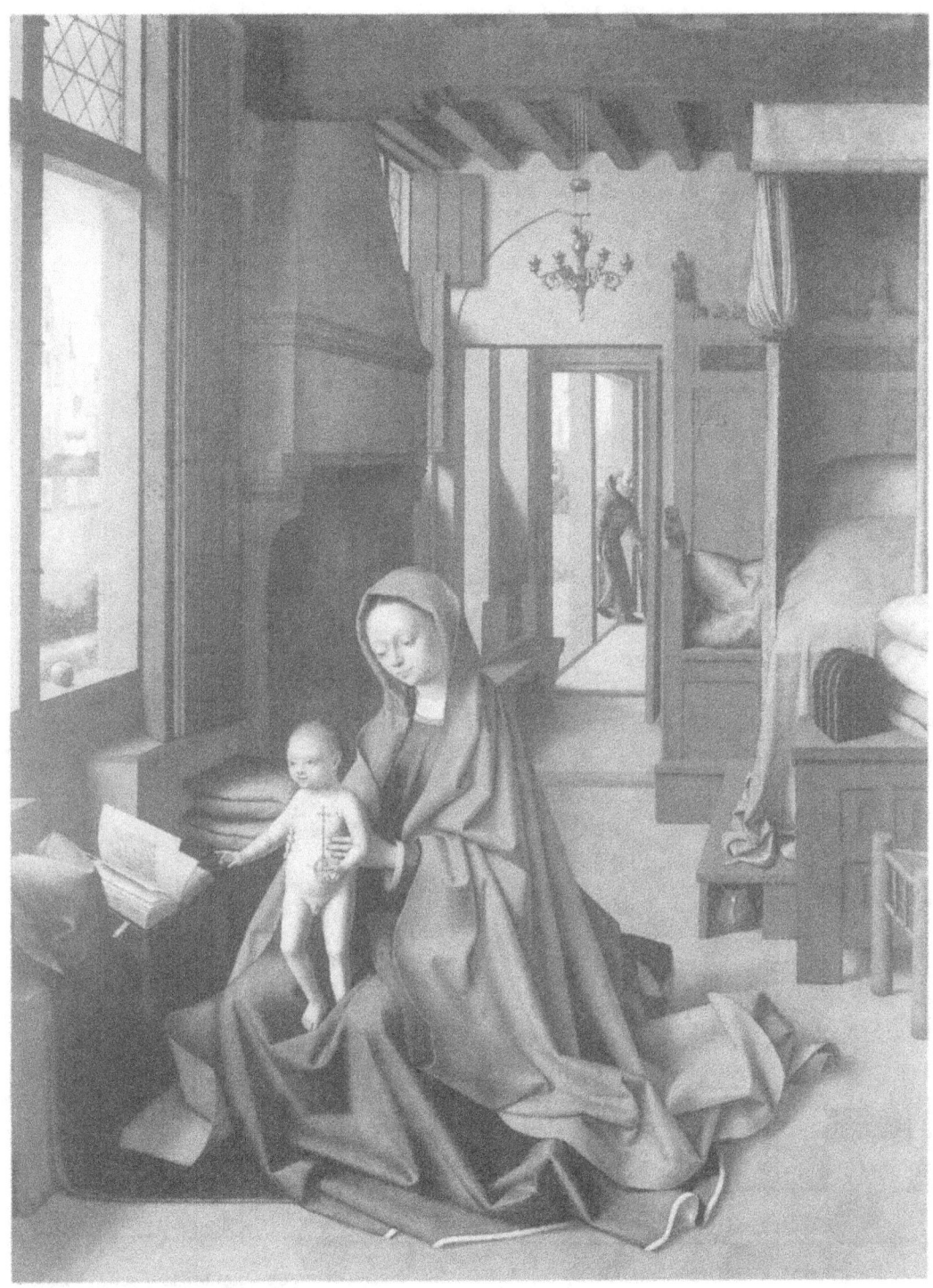

FIGURE 69. Petrus Christus, *Holy Family in a Domestic Interior.* Nelson-Atkins Museum of Art, Kansas City, Missouri (Purchase: Nelson Trust) 56–51.

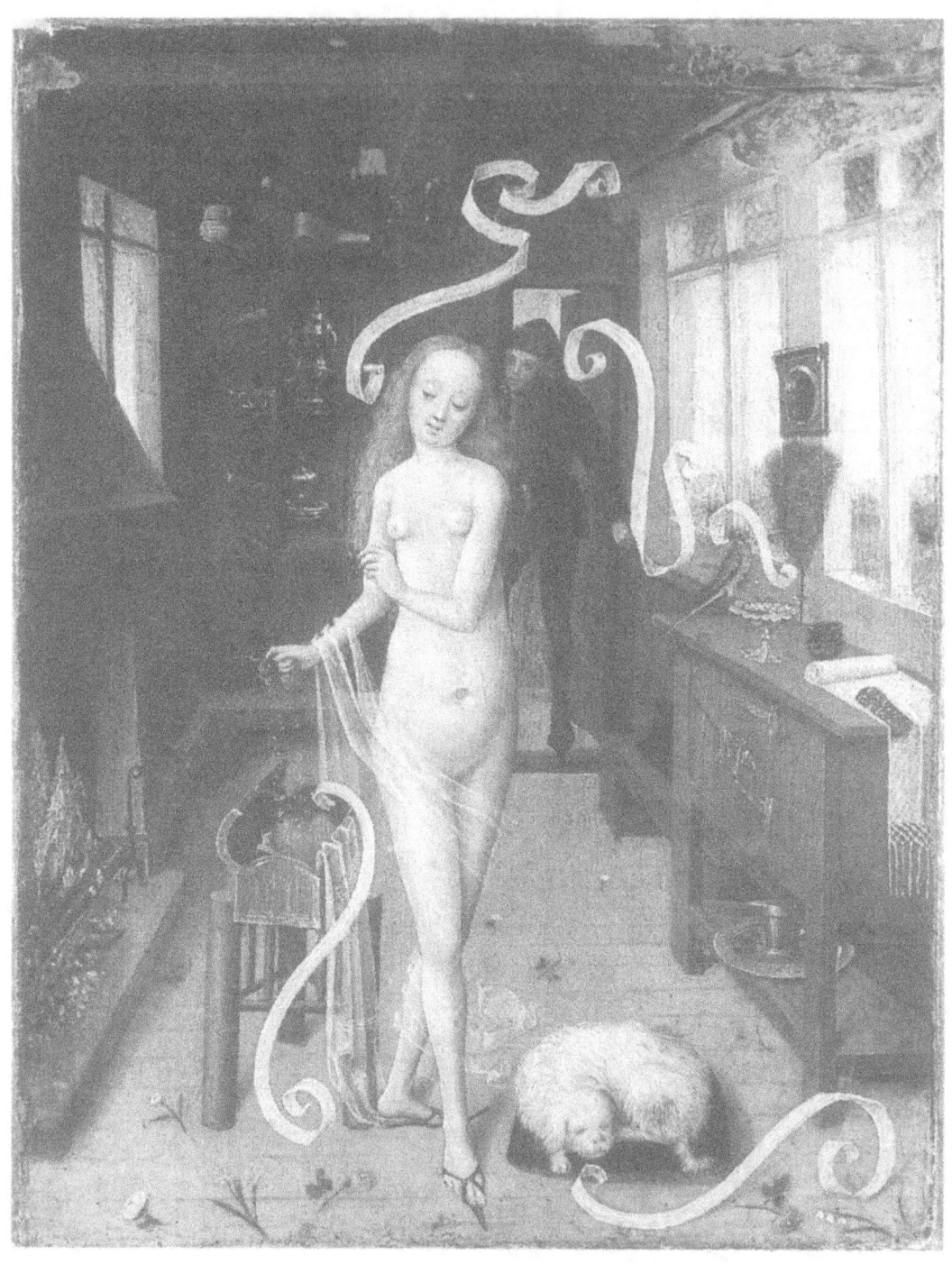

FIGURE 70. Niederrheinischer Master, *Love Magic* (*Der Liebeszauber*). Museum der bildenden Künste. Leipzig.

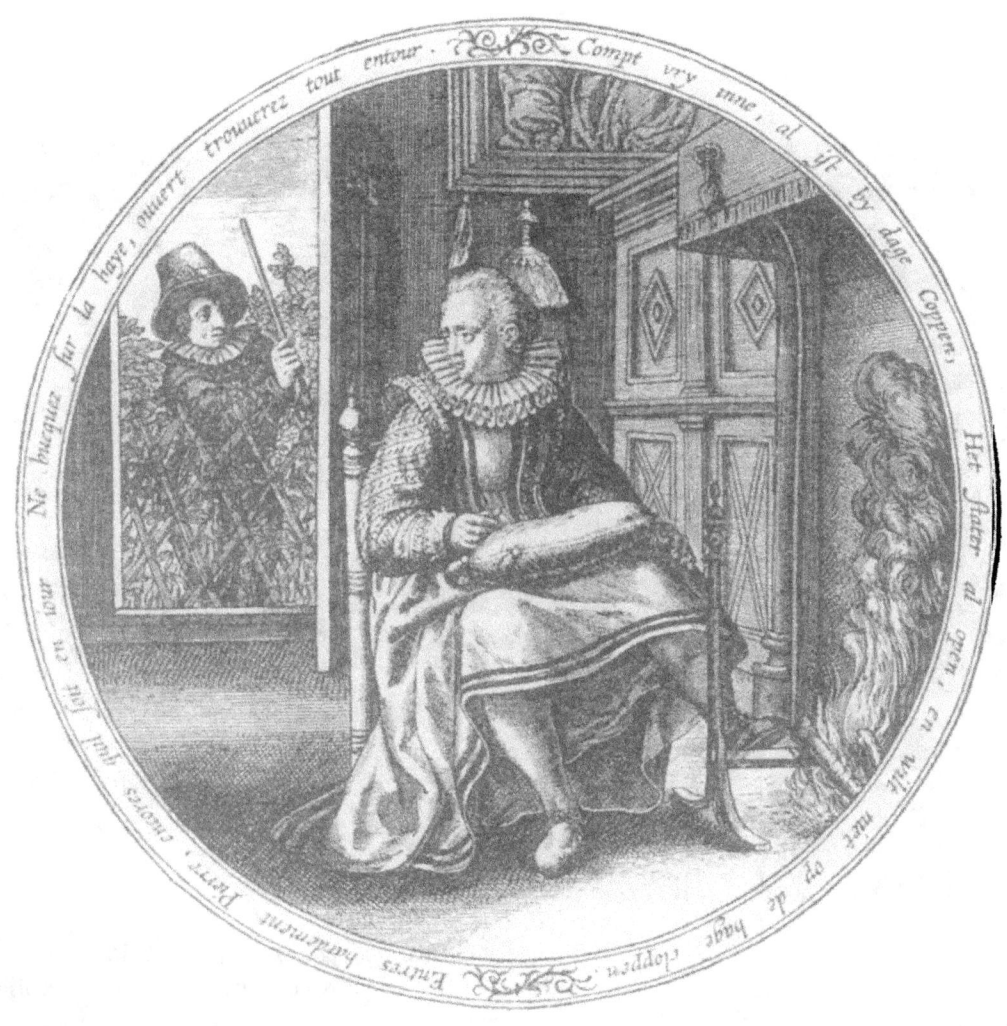

FIGURE 71. Anonymous, *Emblem.*
c. 1630 (from Eduard Fuchs 1928/1973).
Photograph by author.

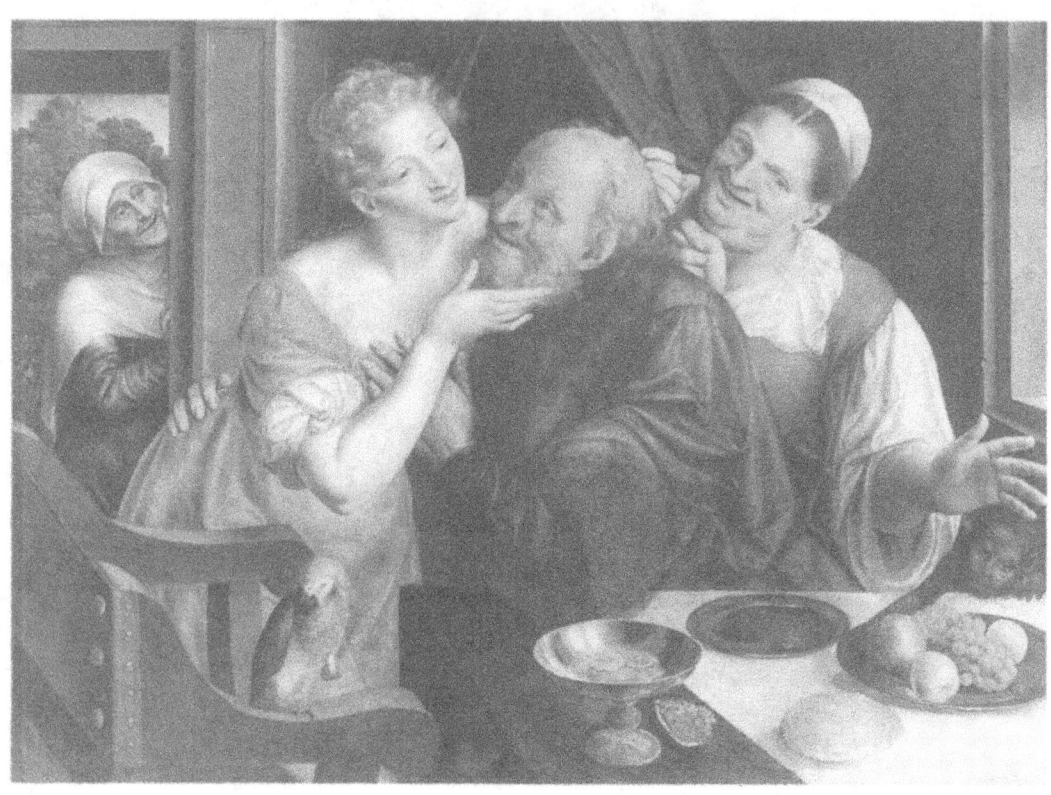

FIGURE 72. Jan Massys, *The Ill-Matched Pair.*
Statens Konstmuseer—National Swedish
Art Museums, Stockholm.

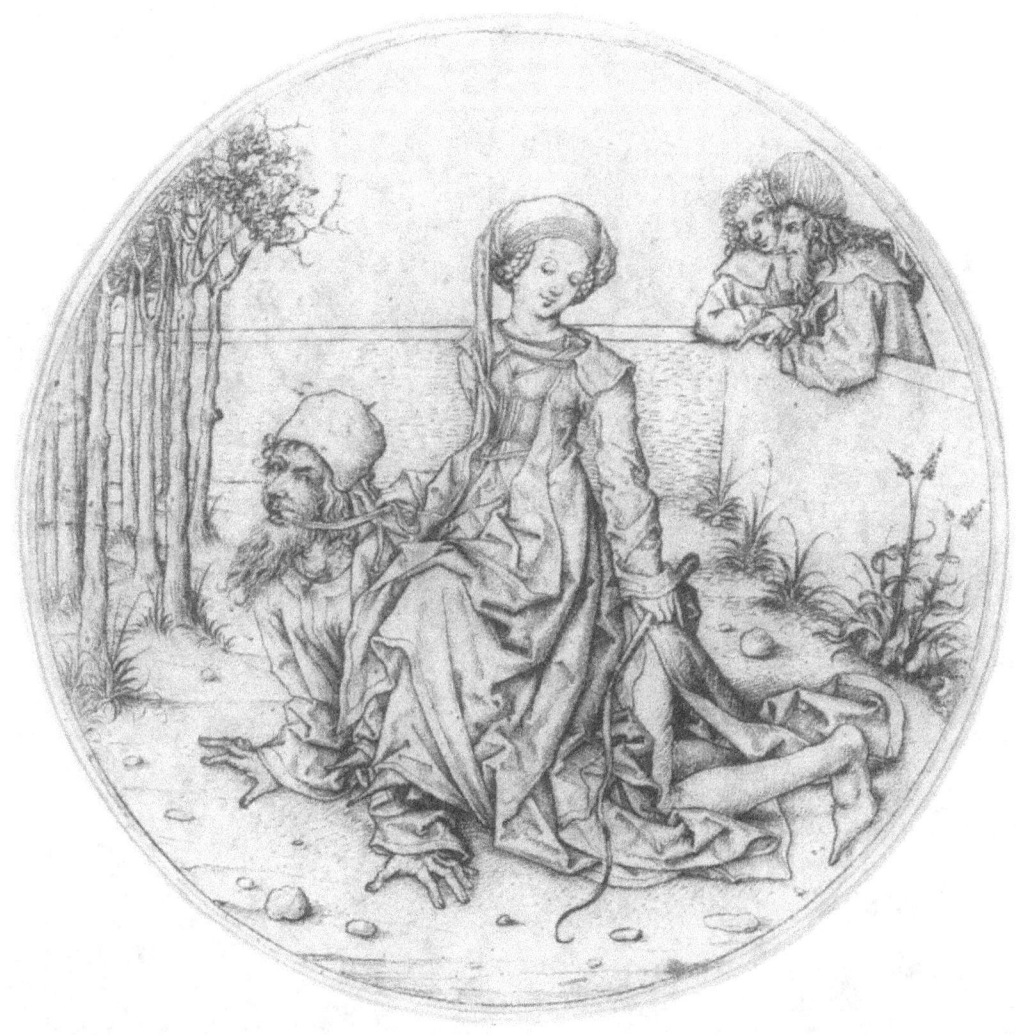

FIGURE 73. Housebook Master, *Phyllis Riding
Aristotle*. Engraving. Rijksmuseum, Amsterdam.

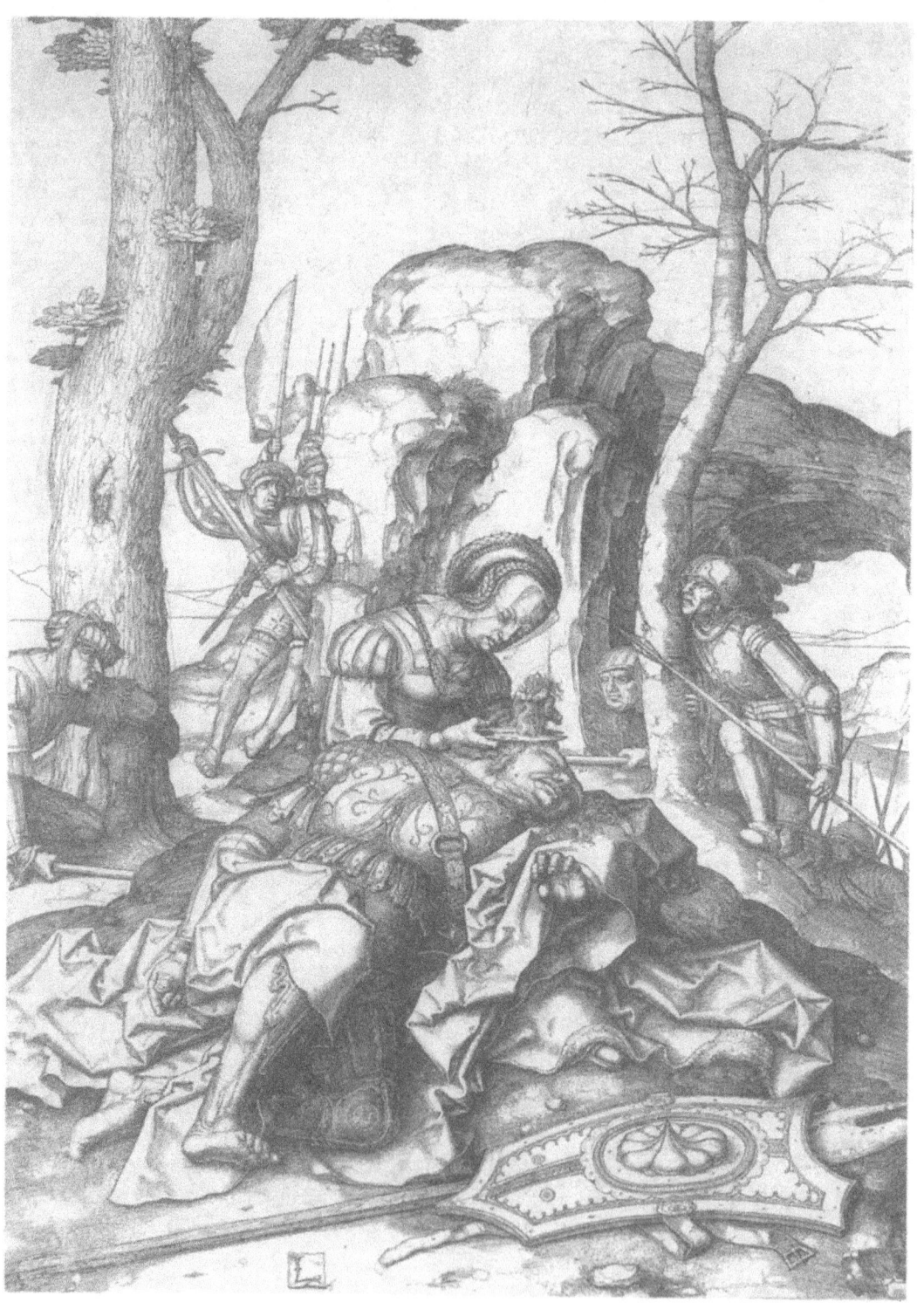

FIGURE 74. Lucas van Leyden, *Samson Shorn by Delilah*. Rijksmuseum, Amsterdam.

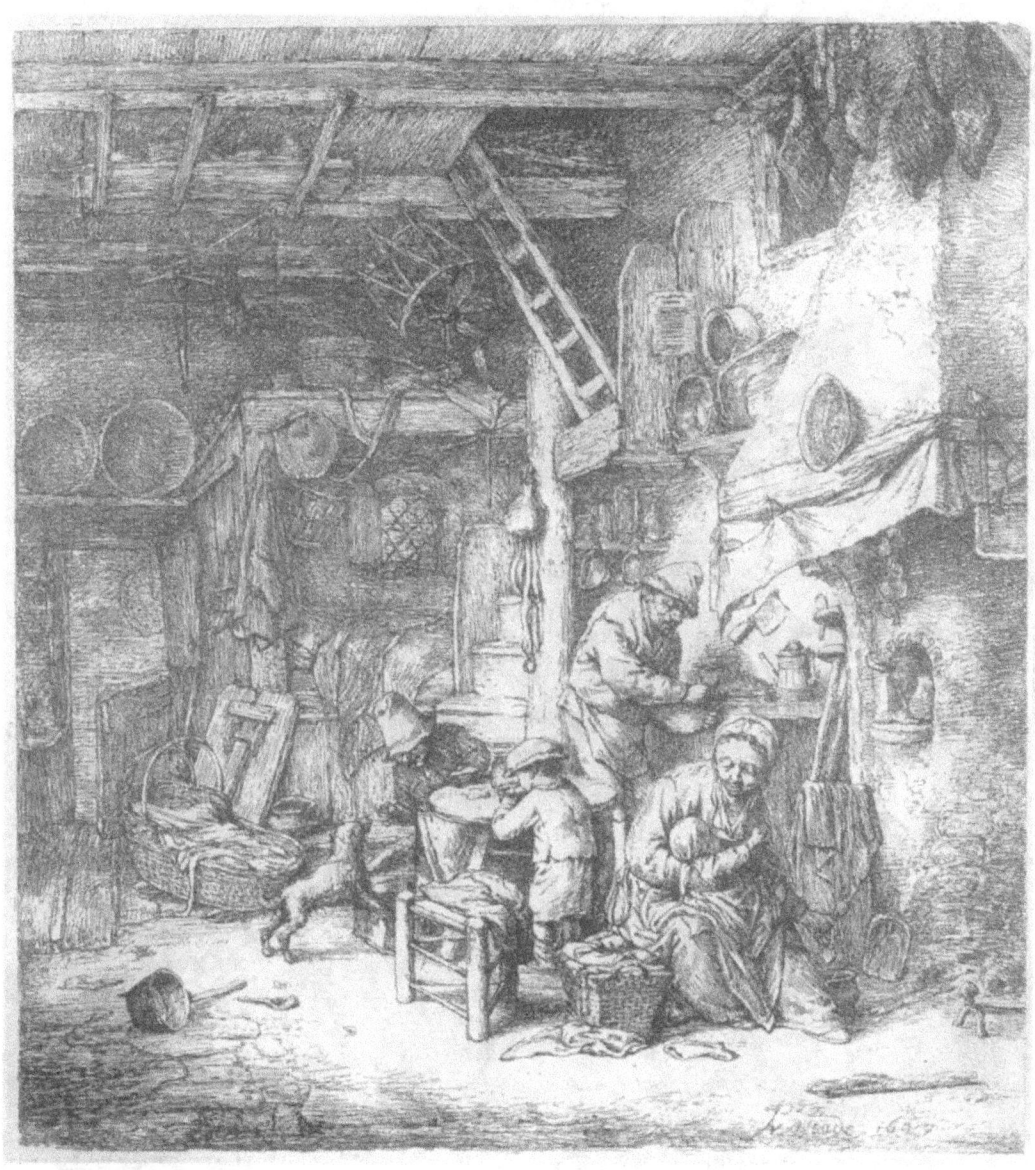

FIGURE 75. Adriaen van Ostade, *The Family*.
1647. The Metropolitan Museum of Art,
Rogers Fund, 1917, New York.

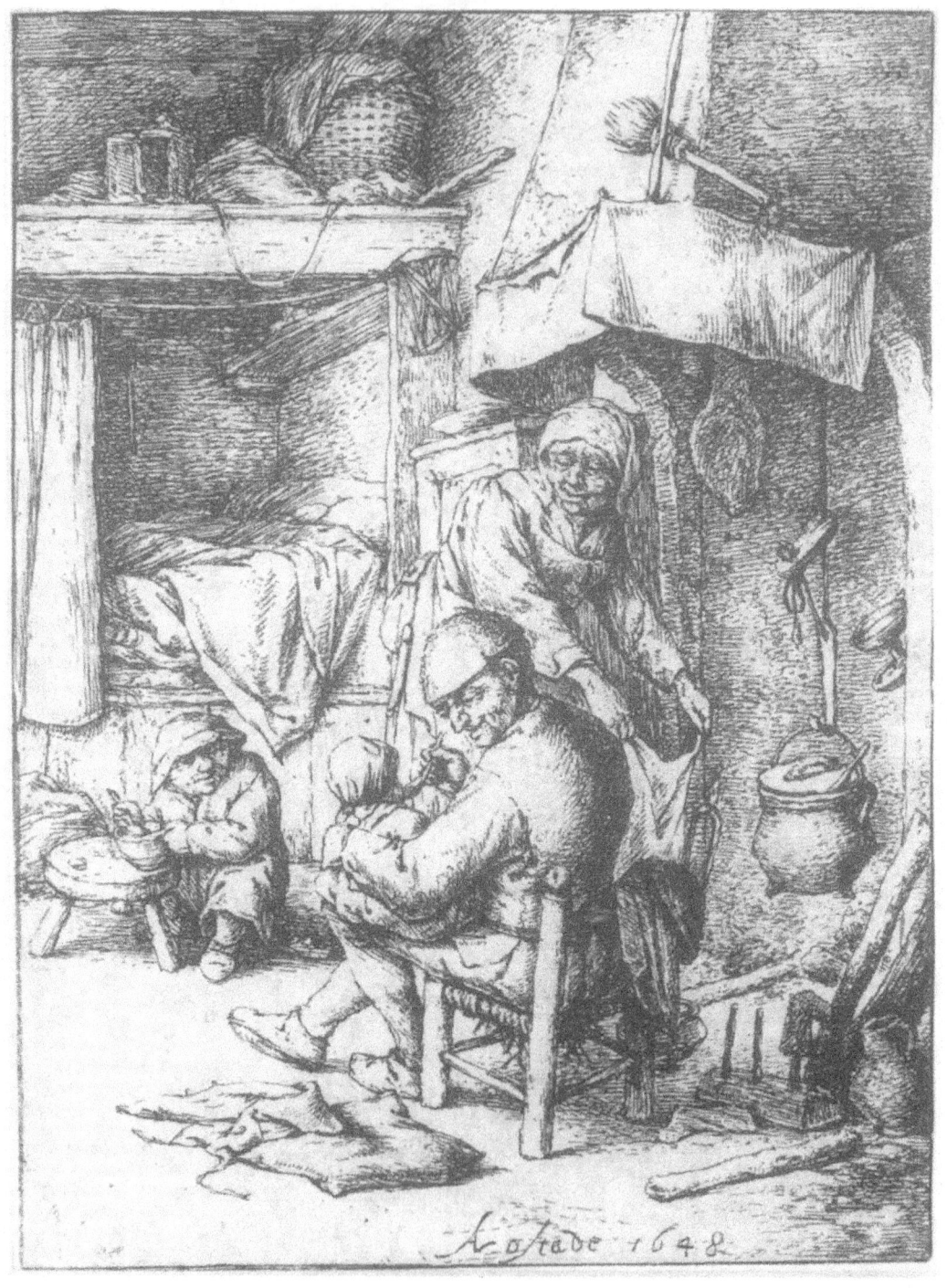

FIGURE 76. Adriaen van Ostade, *Pater Familias.*
1648. Rijksmuseum, Amsterdam.

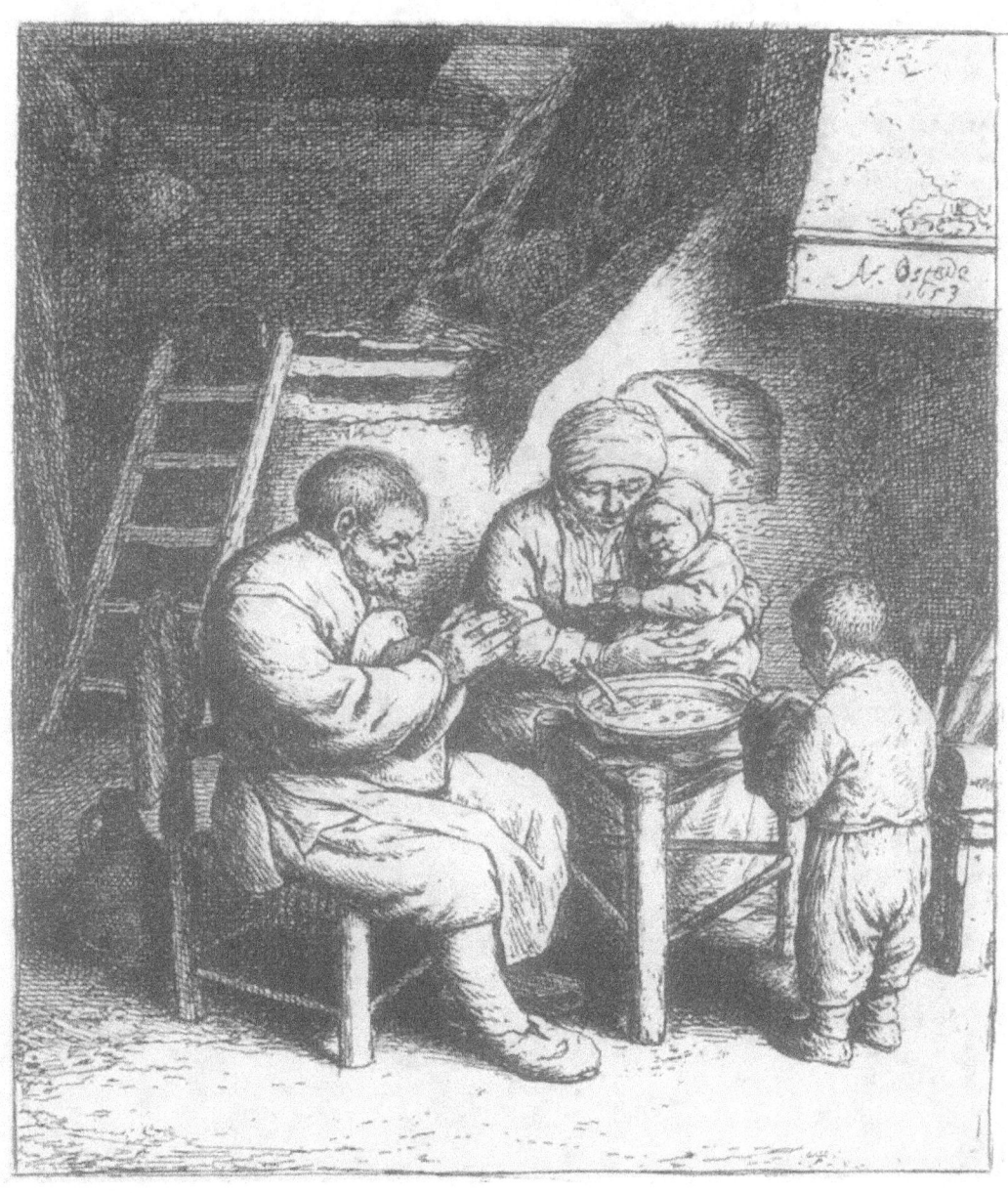

FIGURE 77. Adriaen van Ostade, *Saying Grace*.
1653. The Metropolitan Museum of Art, Rogers
Fund, 1917, New York.

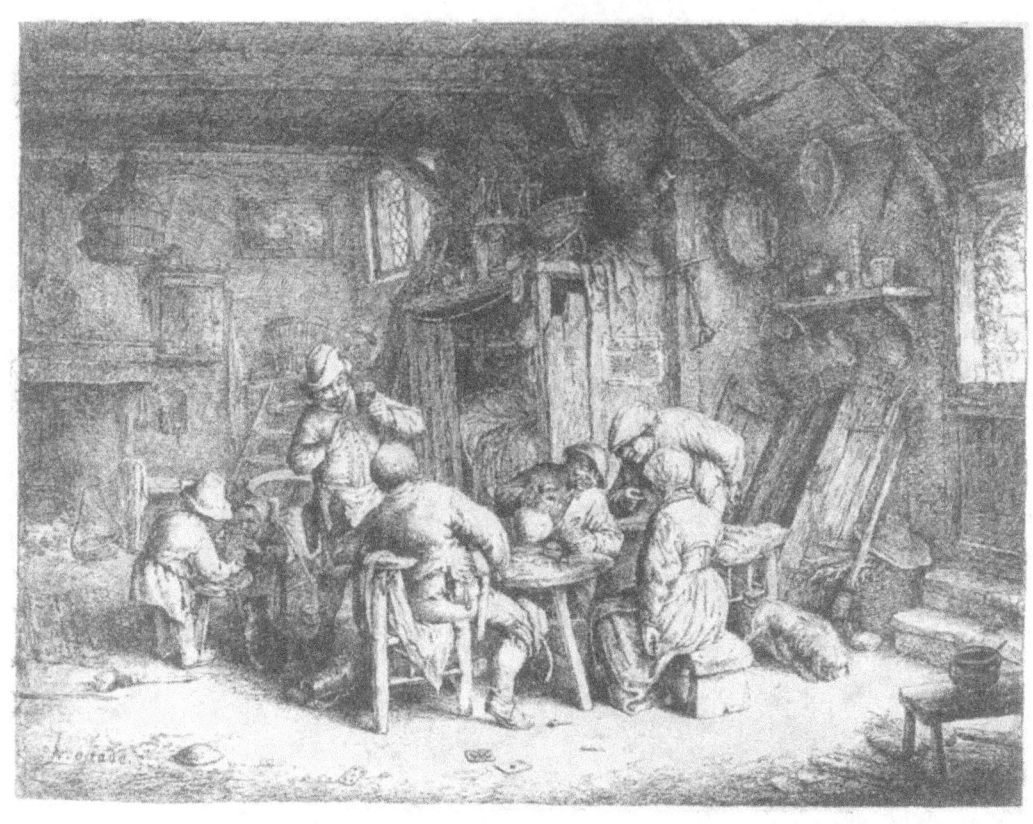

FIGURE 78 Adriaen van Ostade, *The Breakfast.*
1647. The Metropolitan Museum of Art,
Rogers Fund, 1917, New York.

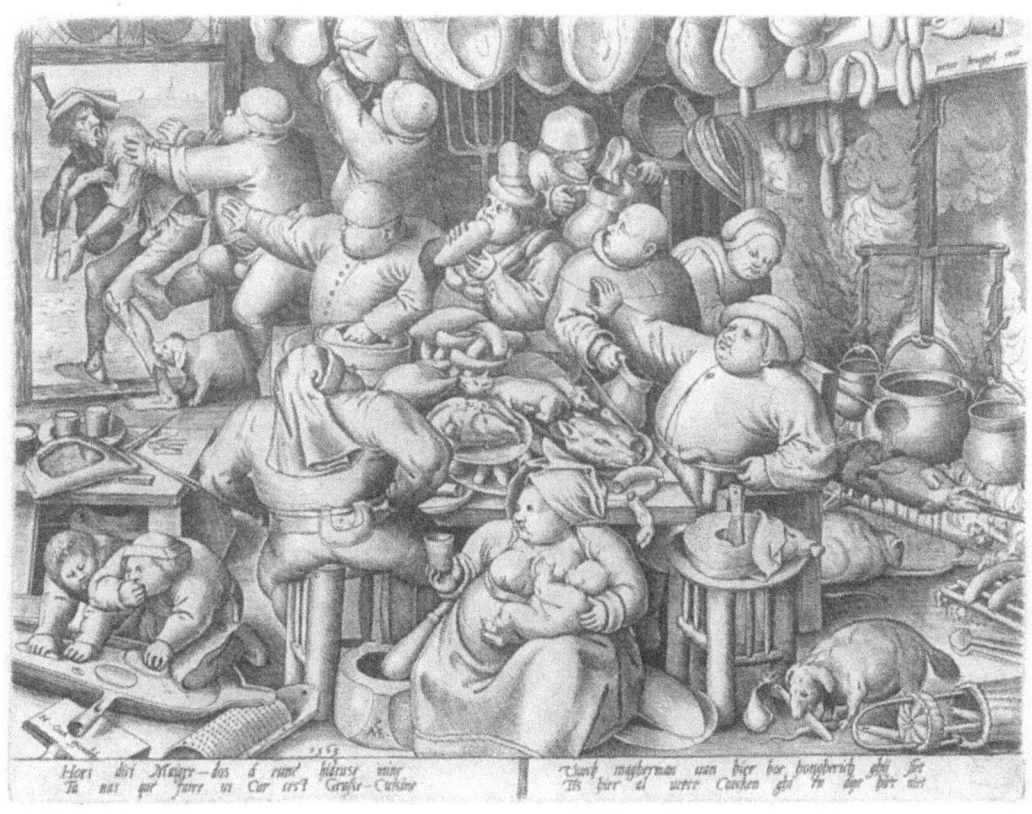

FIGURE 79. After Pieter Bruegel the Elder, *The Fat Kitchen*.
1563. Engraved by Pieter van der Heyden and published
by Hieronymus Cock. The Metropolitan Museum of Art.
Harris Brisbane Dick Fund, 1928, New York.

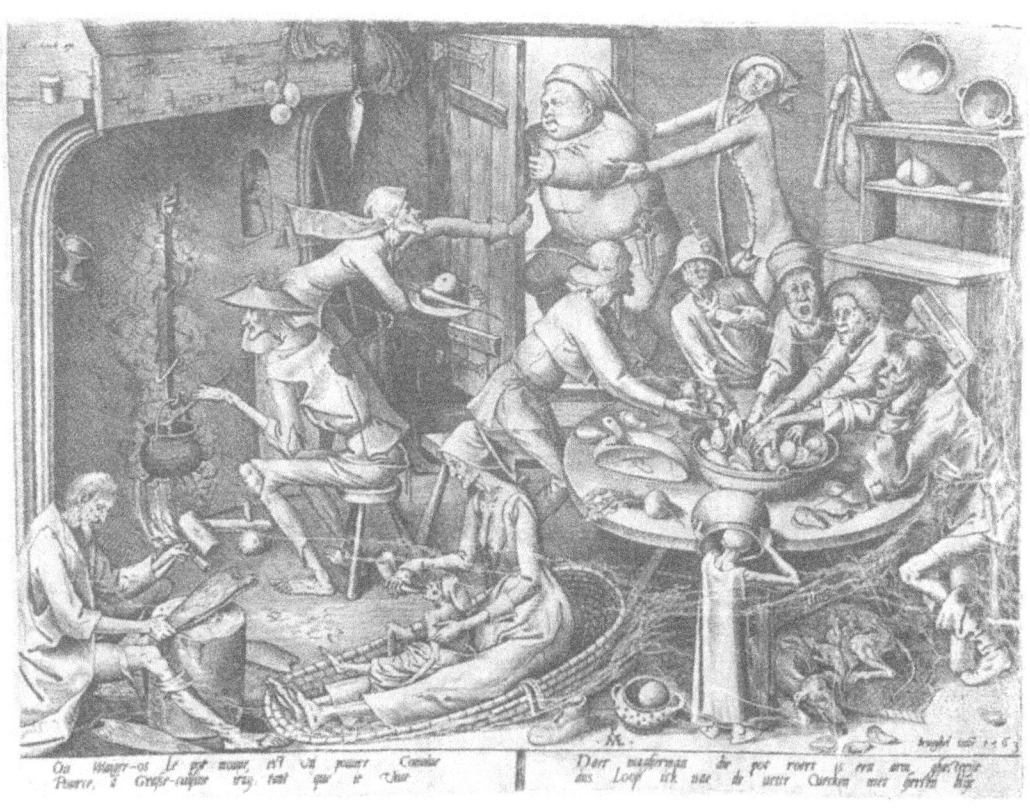

FIGURE 80. After Pieter Bruegel the Elder, *The Lean Kitchen.*
1563. Engraved by Pieter van der Heyden and published
by Hieronymus Cock. The Metropolitan Museum of Art.
Harris Brisbane Dick Fund, 1928, New York.

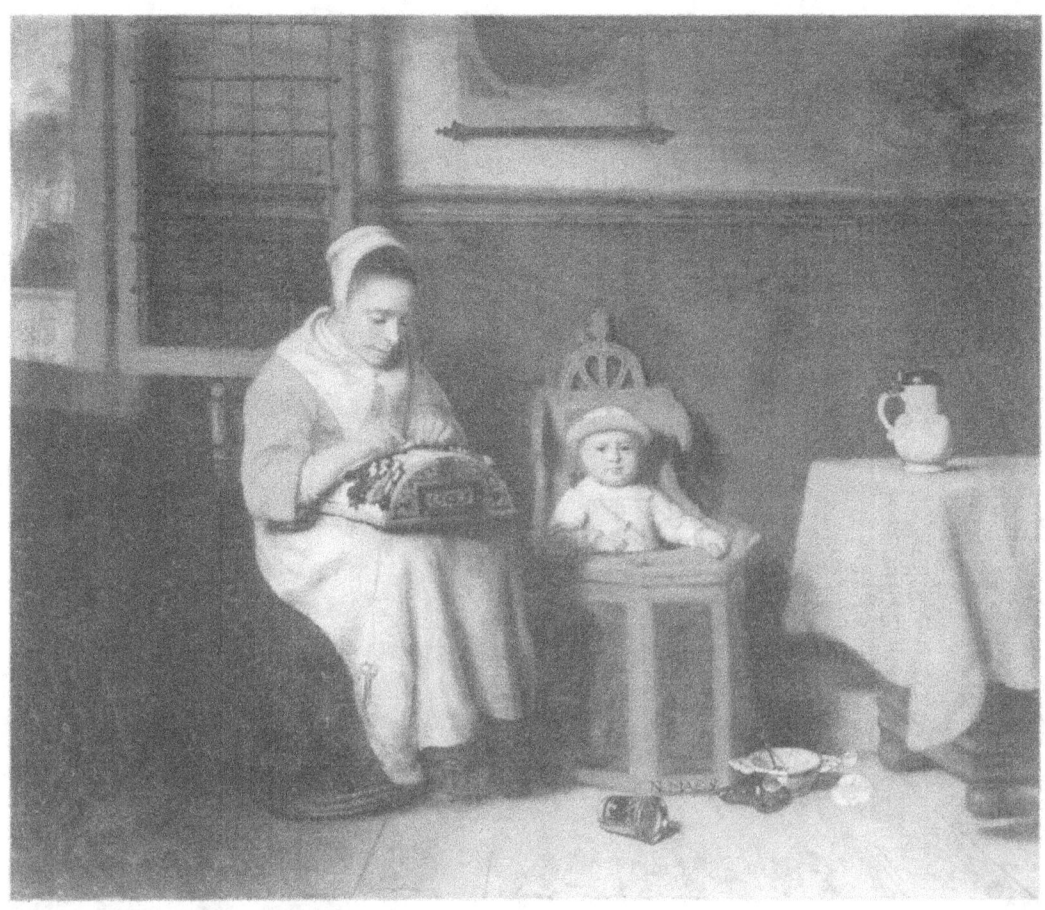

FIGURE 81. Nicolaes Maes, *The Lacemaker*.
Metropolitan Museum of Art, The Friedsam
Collection. Bequest of Michael Friedsam,
1931, New York.

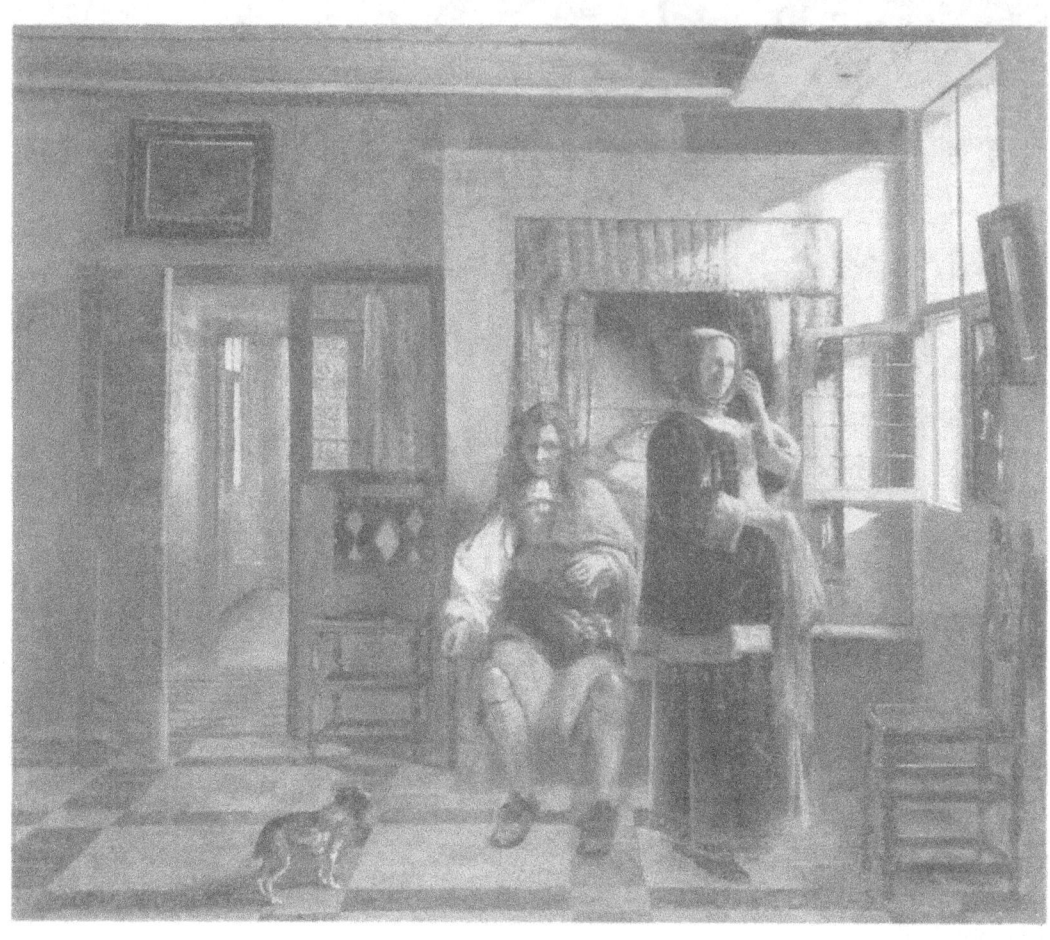

FIGURE 82. Pieter de Hooch, *Interior with a Young Couple.* The Metropolitan Museum of Art. Bequest of Benjamin Altman, 1913, New York.

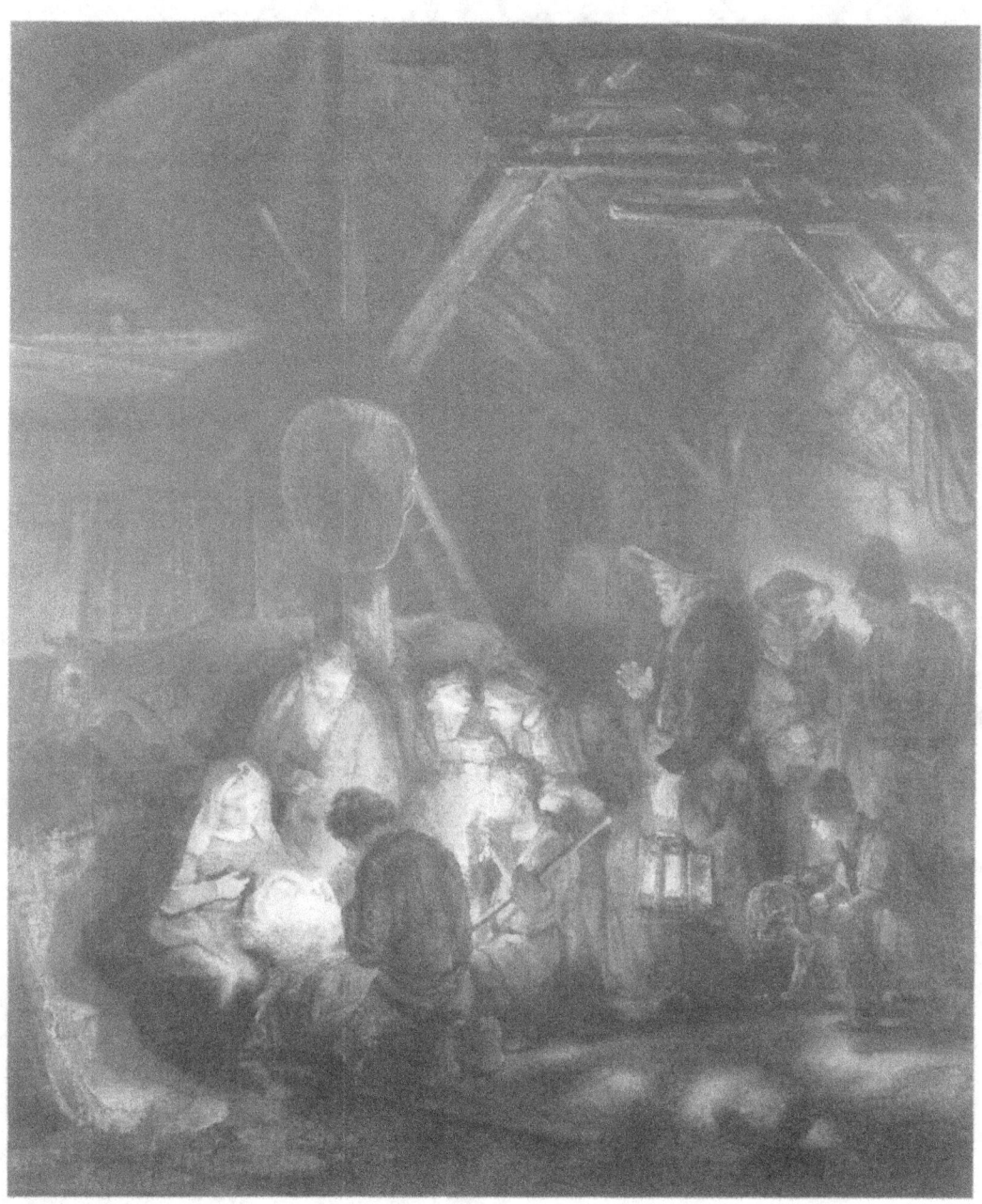

FIGURE 83. Rembrandt van Rijn, *The Adoration of the Shepherds*. 1646. The National Gallery. Reproduced by courtesy of the Trustees, The National Gallery, London.

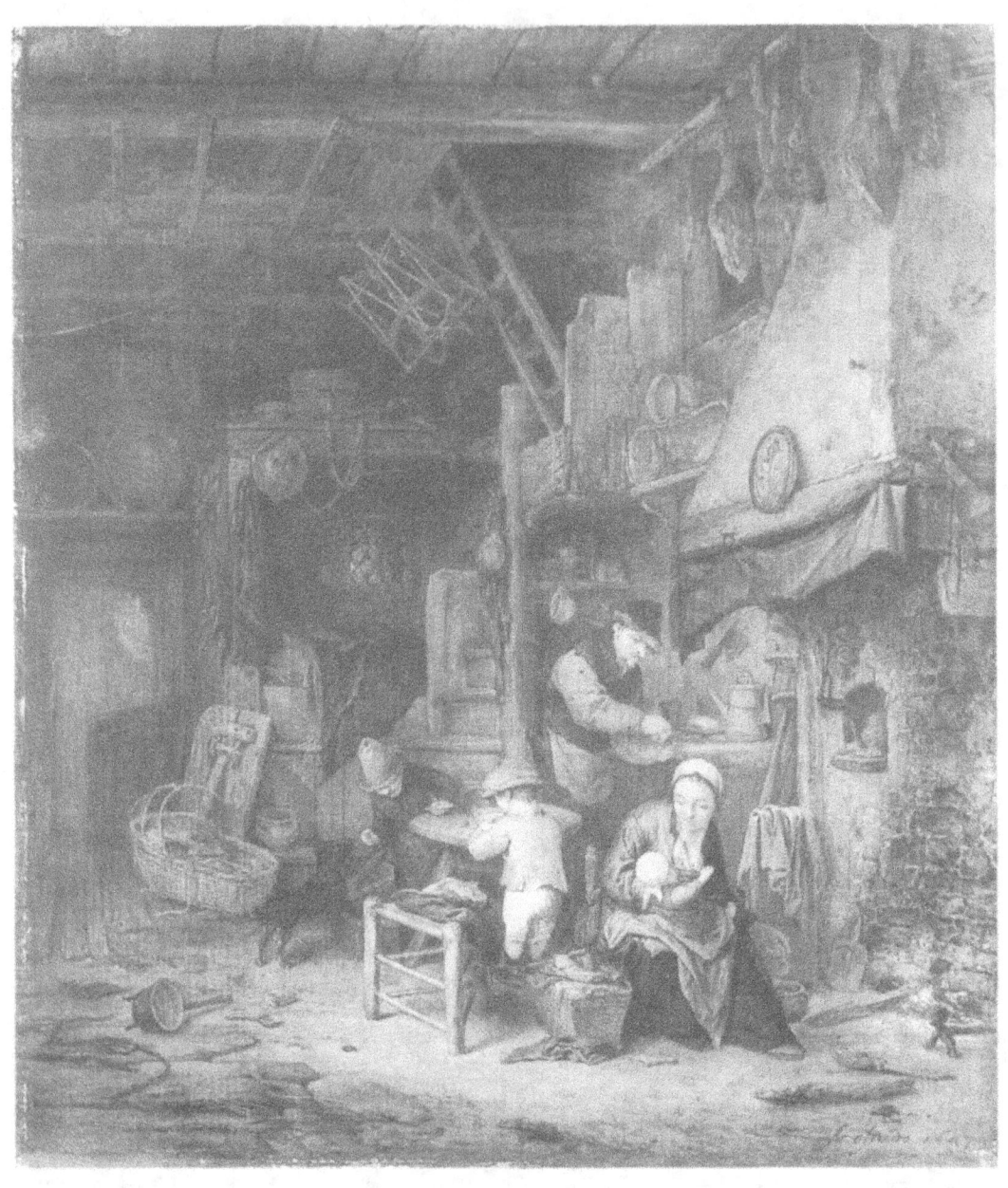

FIGURE 84. Adriaen van Ostade,
The Peasant Family. 1647. Szépmüvészeti
Múzeum, Budapest.

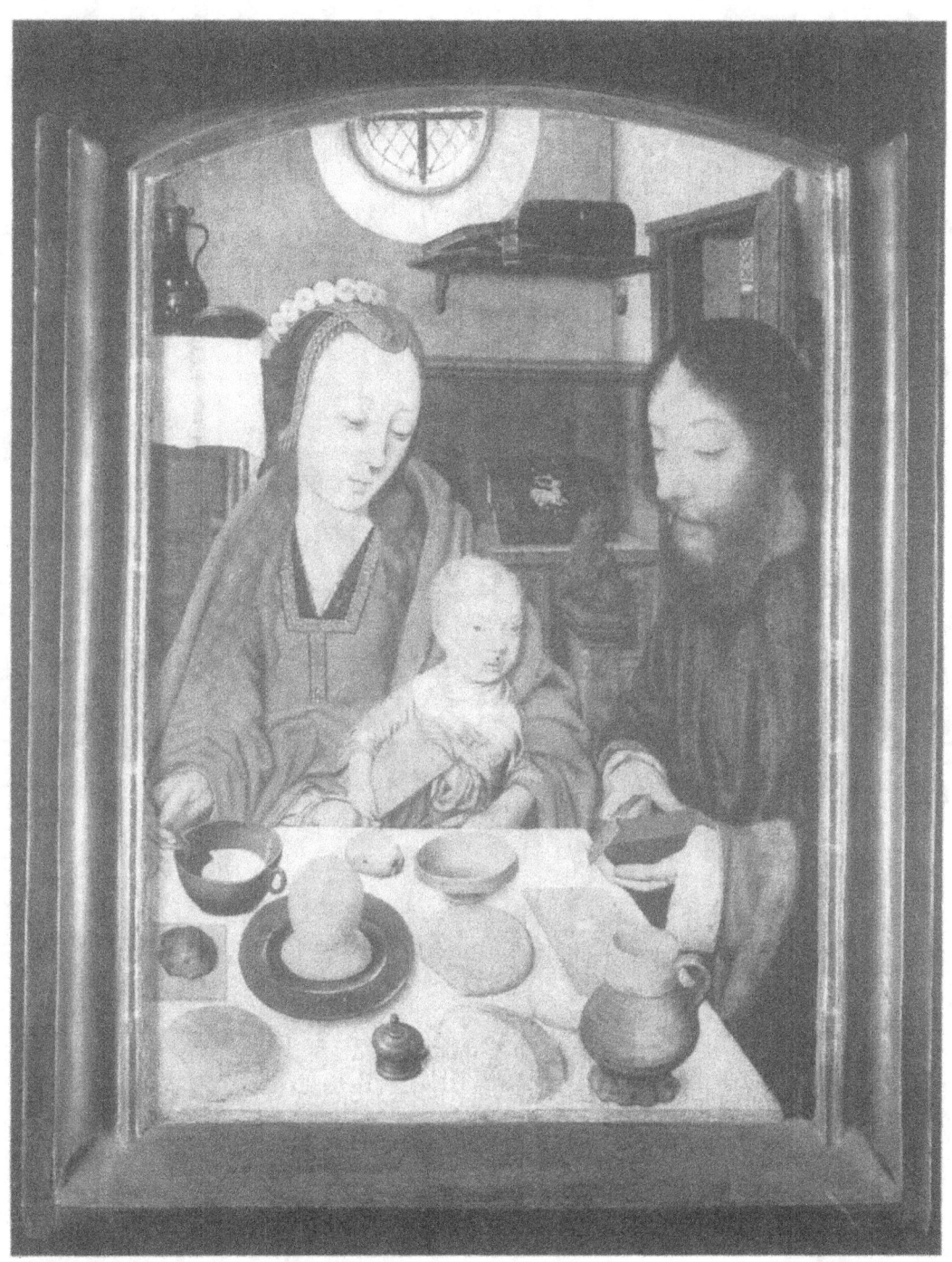

FIGURE 85. Jan Mostaert, *The Holy Family.*
Wallraf-Richardtz Museum, Cologne.

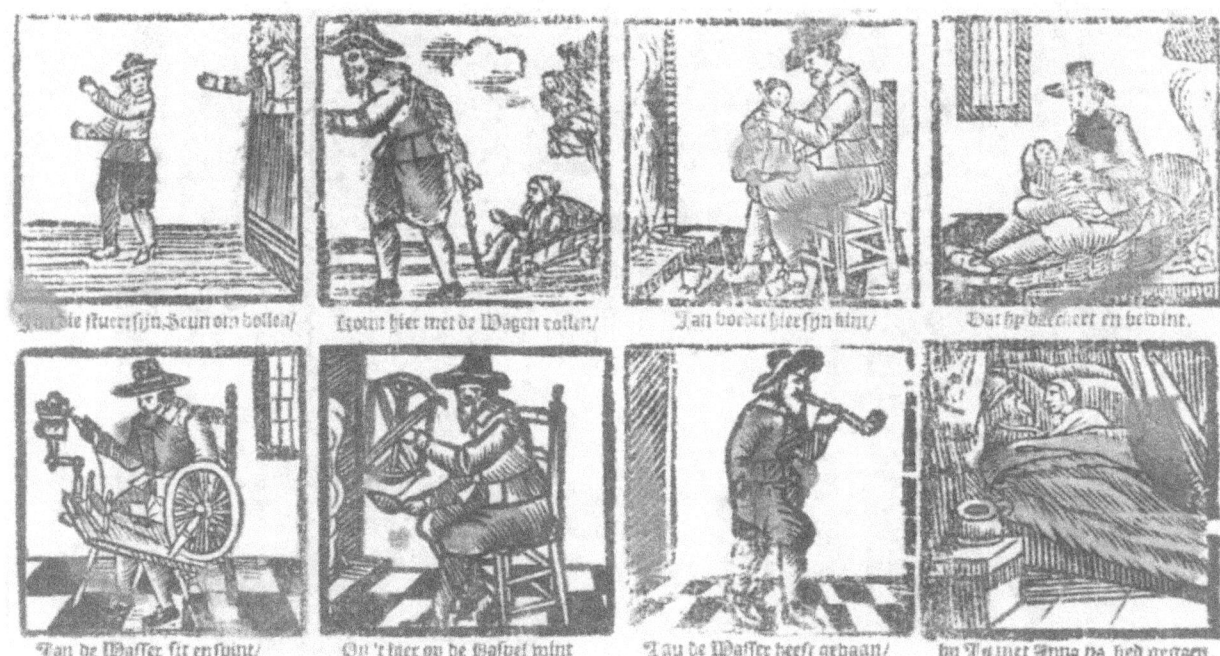

FIGURE 86. Detail of *Het Leven en bedriff van Jan de Wasser en zijn wijf*. Published by Jan Nieuwenhuyzen. Rijksmuseum, Amsterdam.

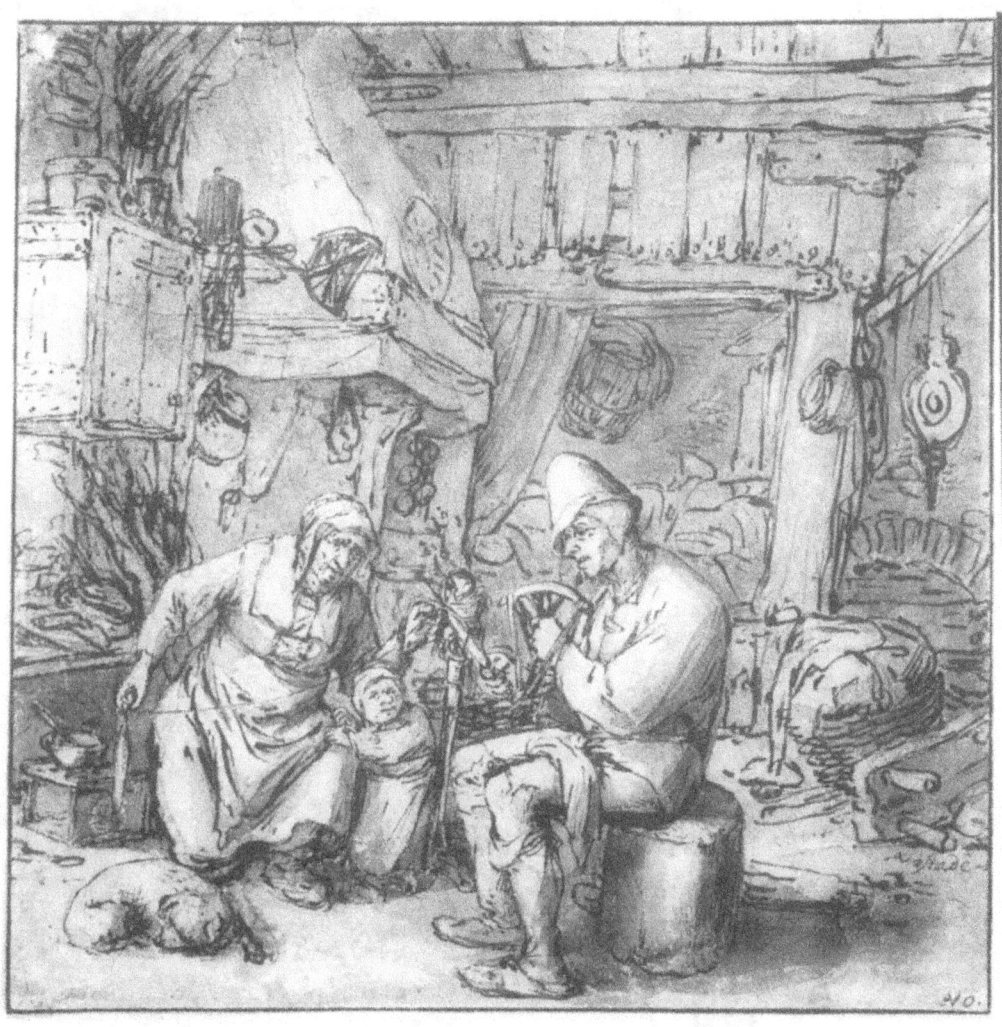

FIGURE 87. Adriaen van Ostade, *Peasant-Husband Holding a Cross-Reel*. Städelsches Kunstinstitut, Frankfurt am Main.

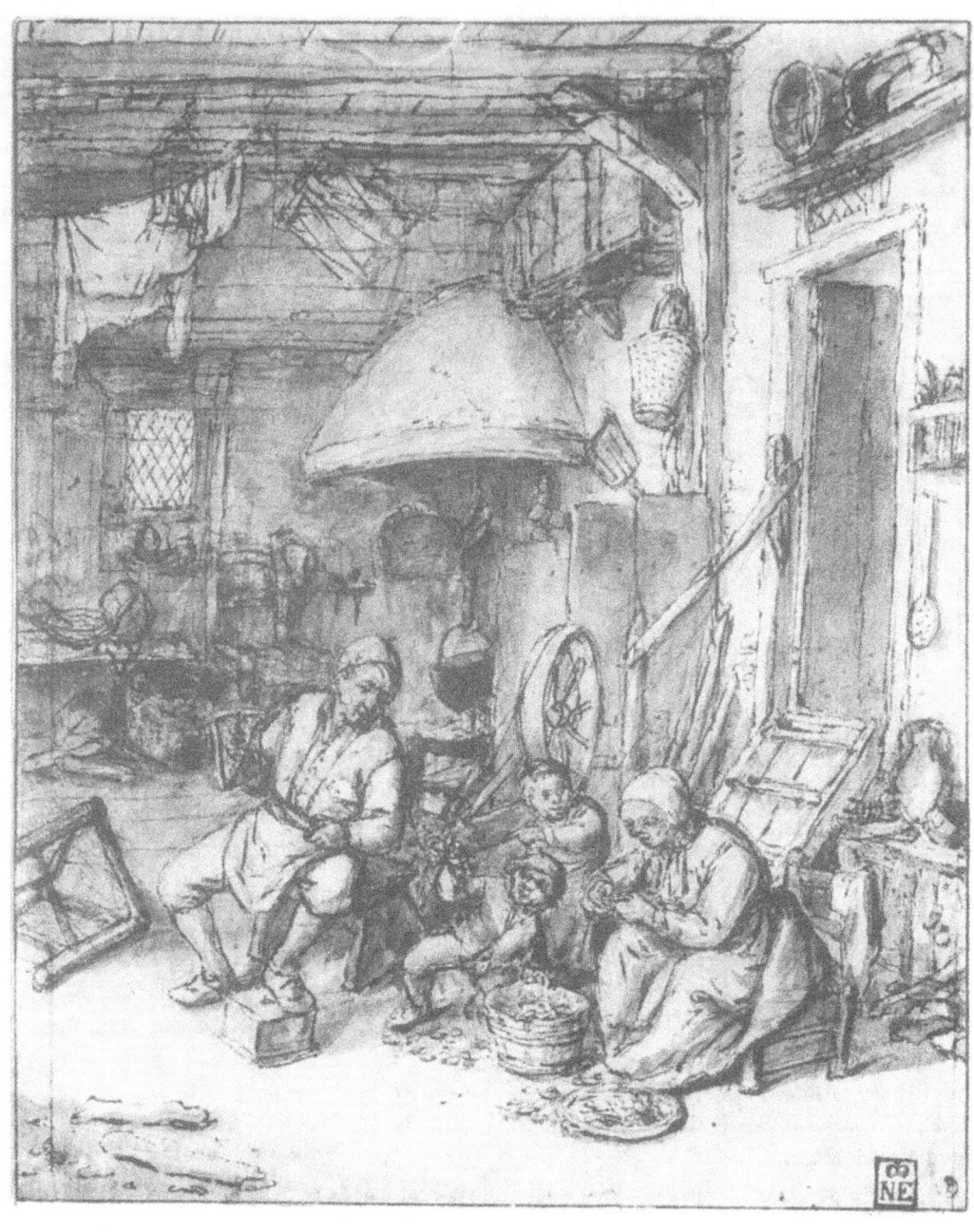

FIGURE 88. Adriaen van Ostade, *Peasant-Husband Holding a Cross-Reel.* Szépmüvészeti Múzeum, Budapest.

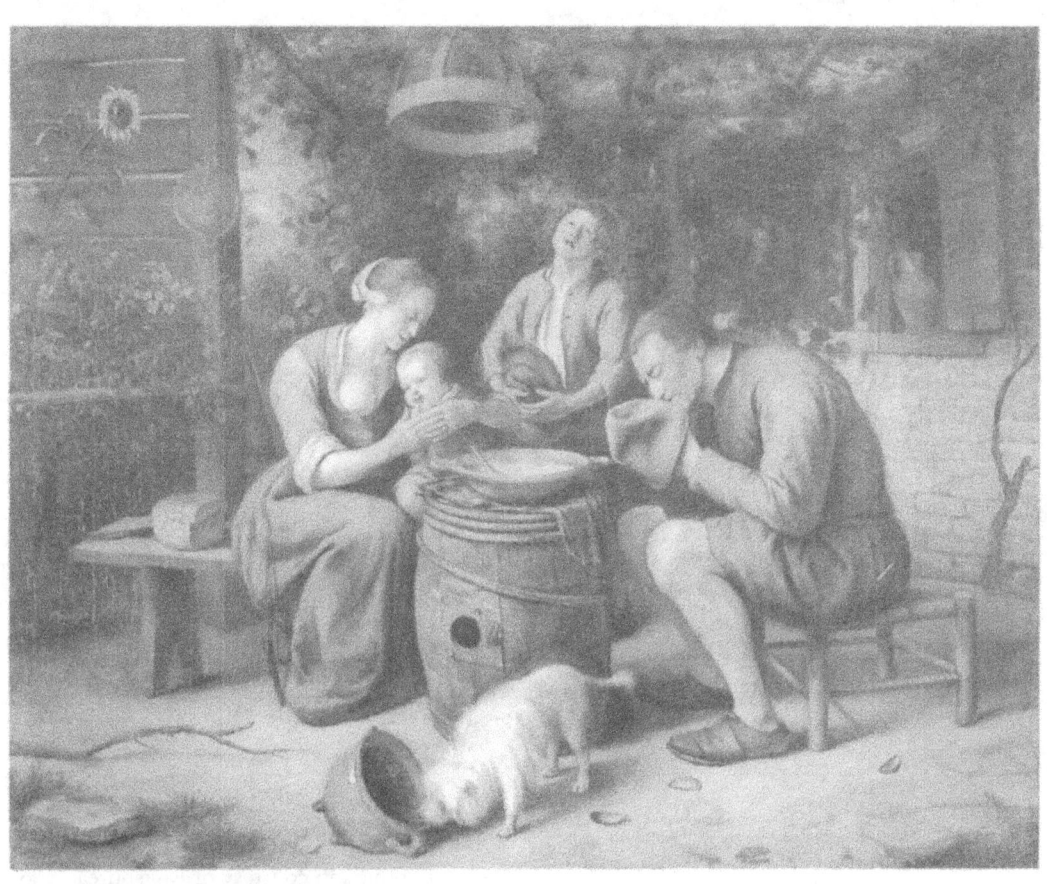

FIGURE 89. Jan Steen, *Prayer Before the Meal.*
Philadelphia Museum of Art, The John G. Johnson
Collection, 1917, Philadelphia.

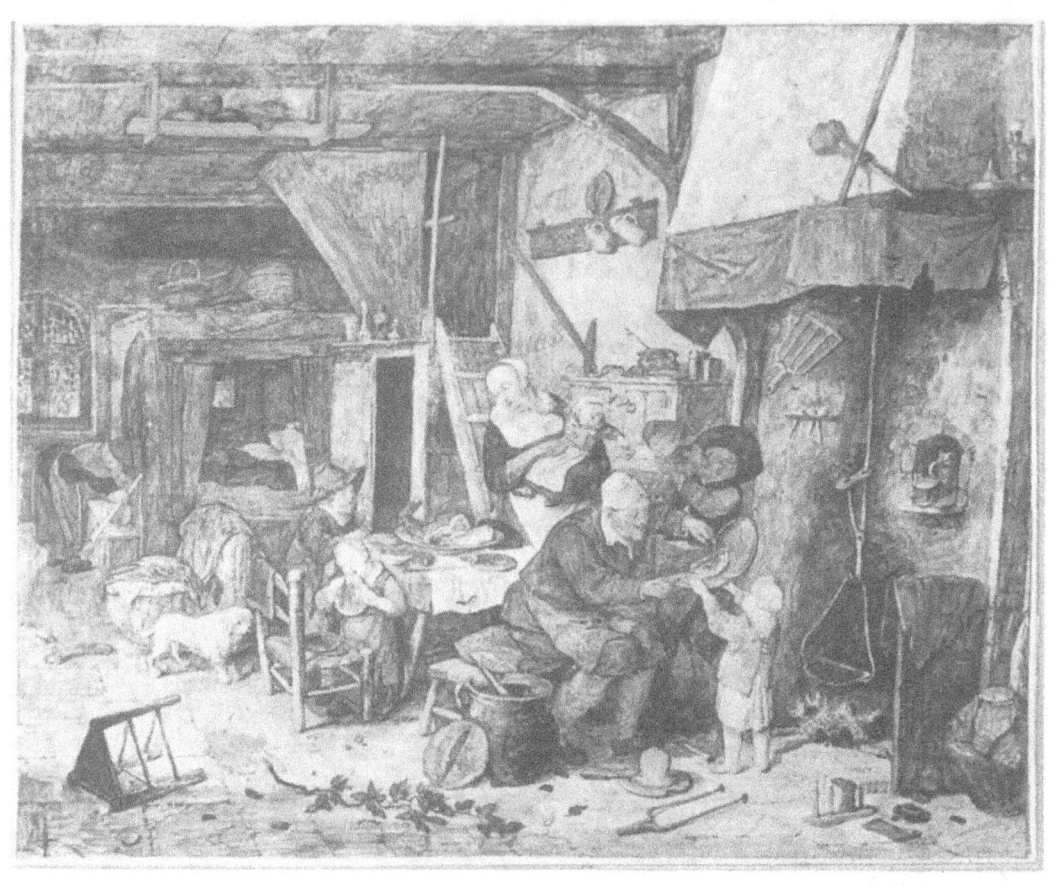

FIGURE 90. Cornelis Dusart, *The Family*.
Photograph courtesy of Rijksbureau voor
Kunsthistorische Documentatie,
The Hague / The Netherlands.

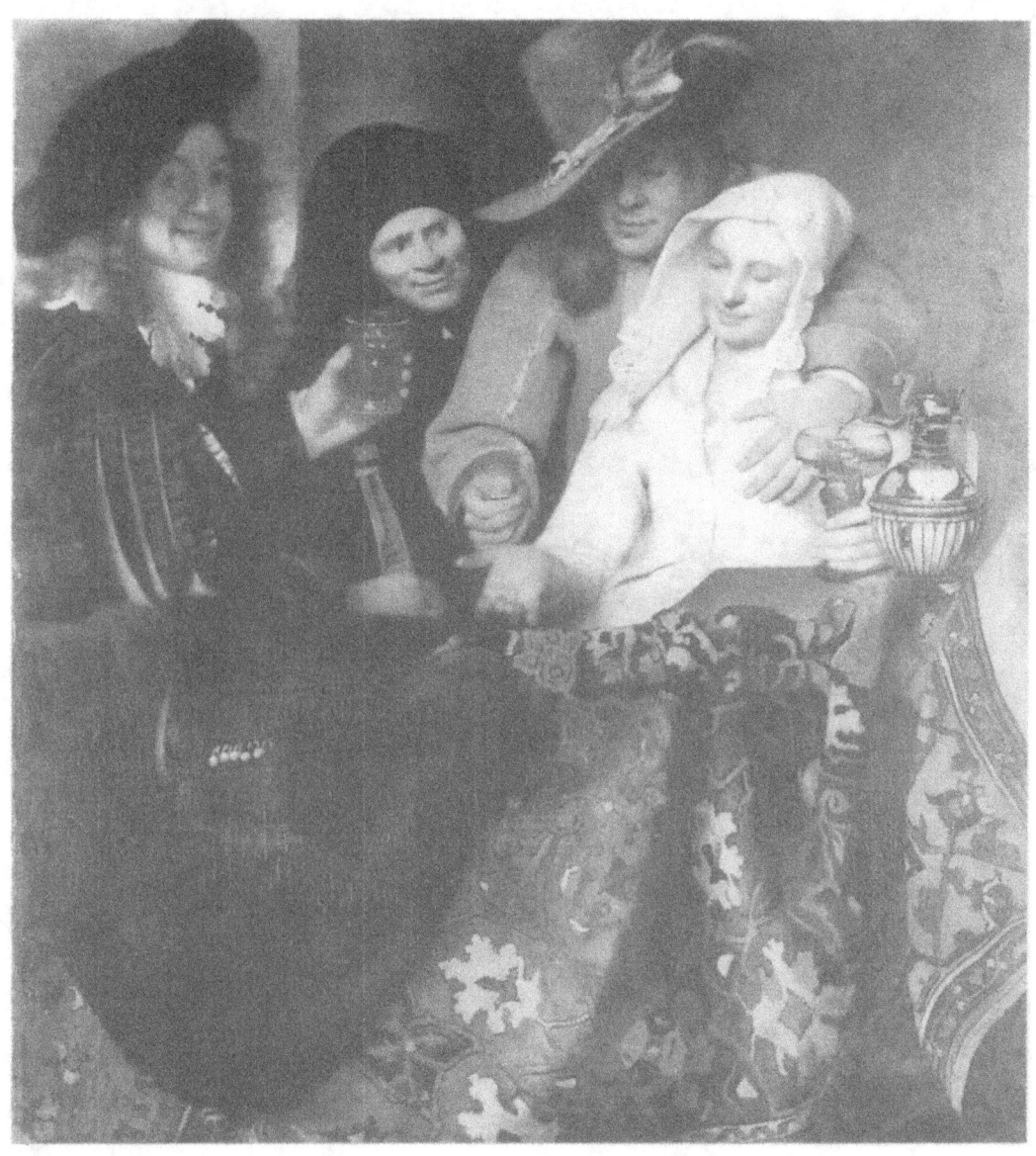

FIGURE 91. Johannes Vermeer, *The Procuress.*
Staatliche Kunstsammlungen Gemäldegalerie, Dresden.

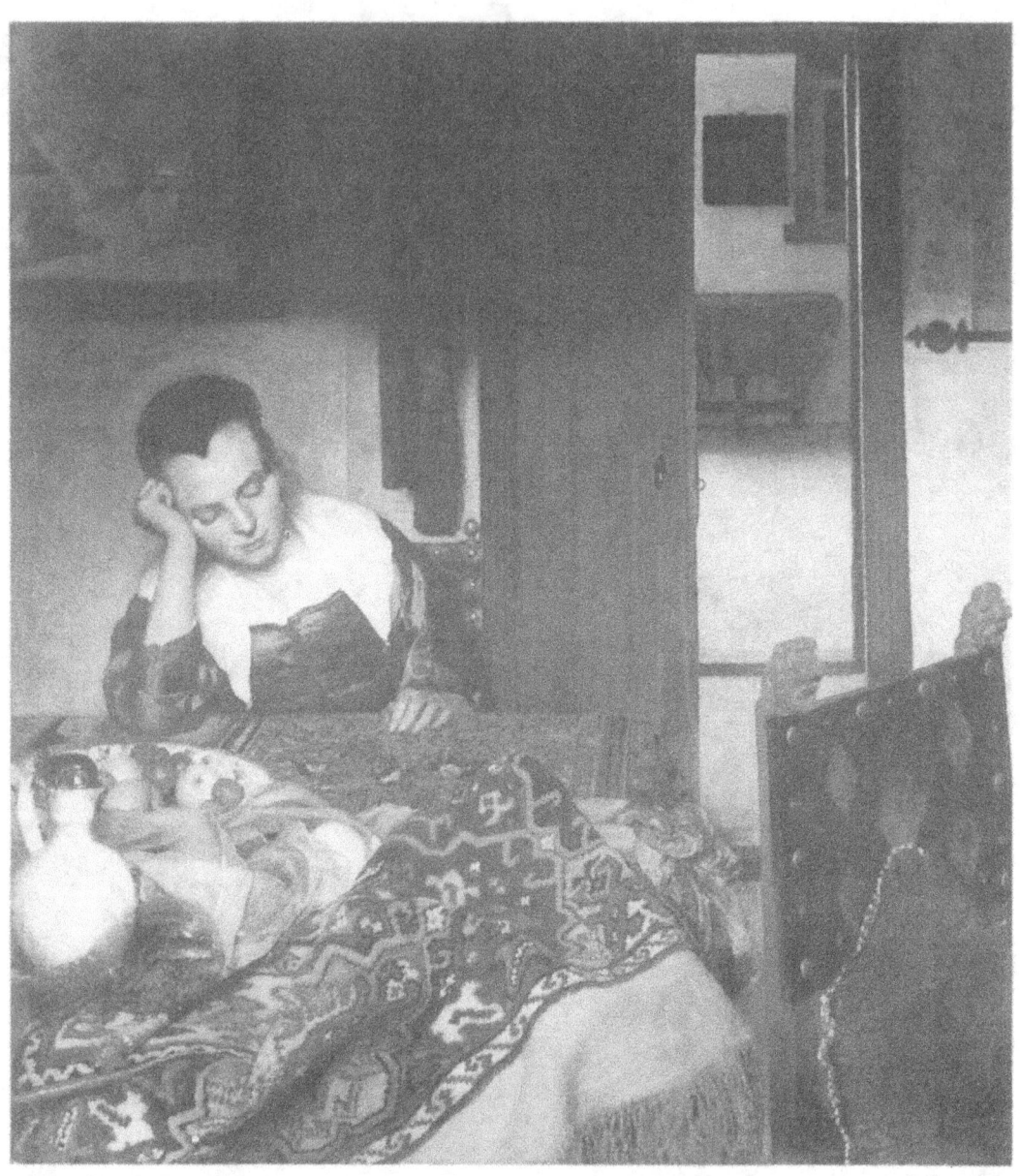

FIGURE 92. Johannes Vermeer, *A Maid Asleep*.
The Metropolitan Museum of Art. Bequest of
Benjamin Altman, 1913, New York.

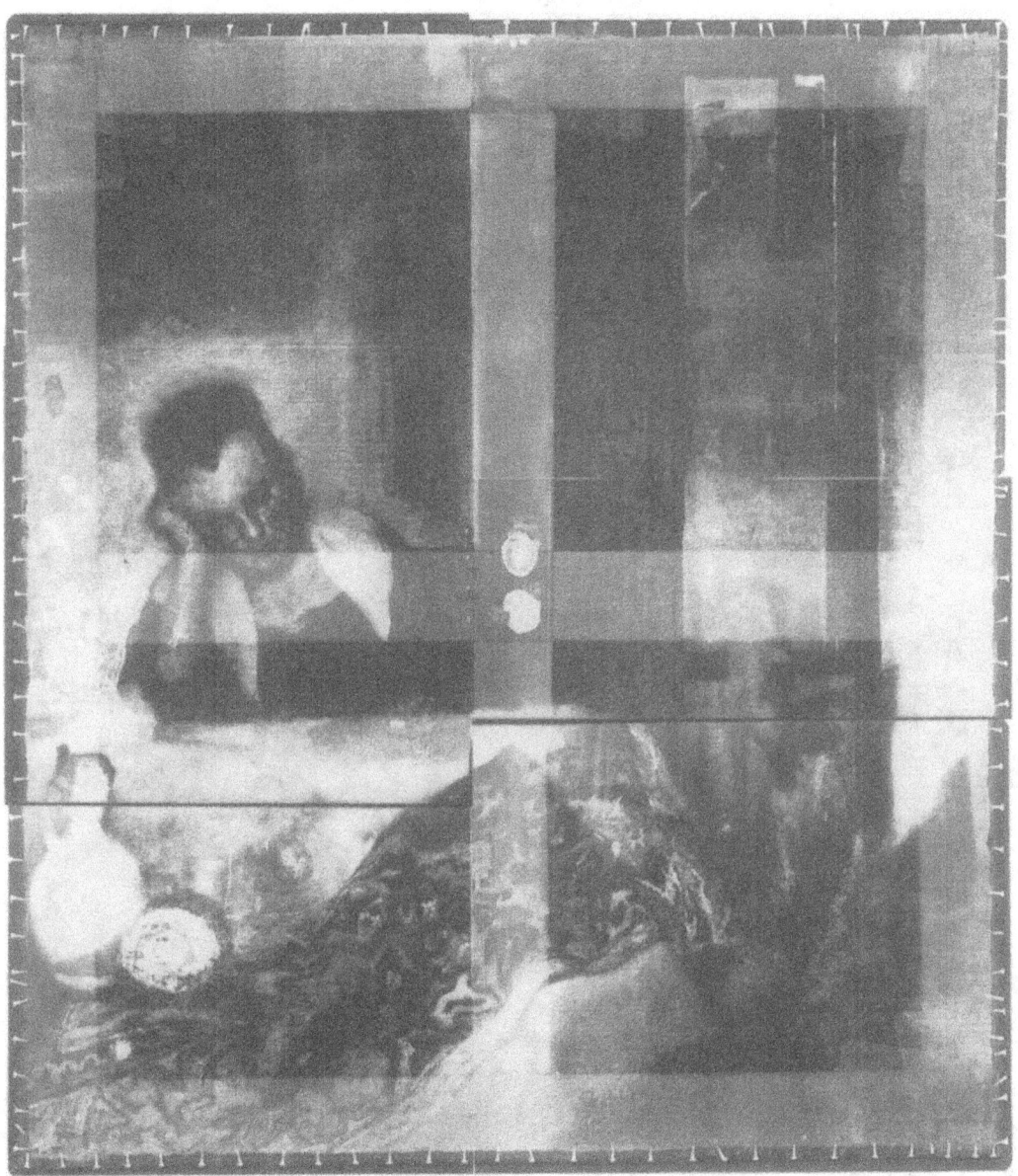

FIGURE 93. Composite X-ray of *A Maid Asleep*.
Sherman Fairchild Paintings Conservation
Department, The Metropolitan Museum of Art.
Bequest of Benjamin Altman, 1913, New York.

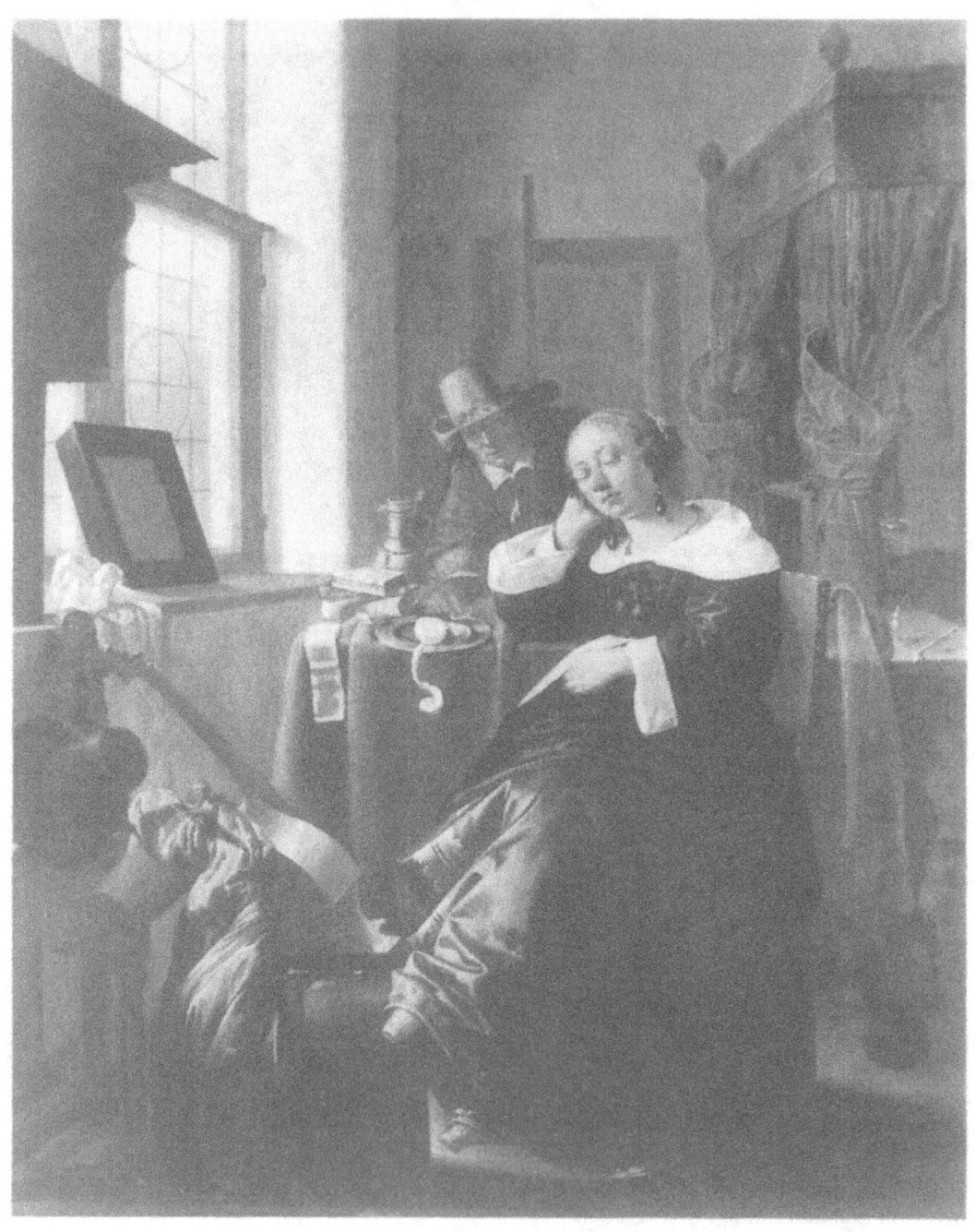

FIGURE 94. Jacob Duck, *A Sleeping Courtesan*.
Location unknown. Photograph courtesy of
the Witt Library, London.

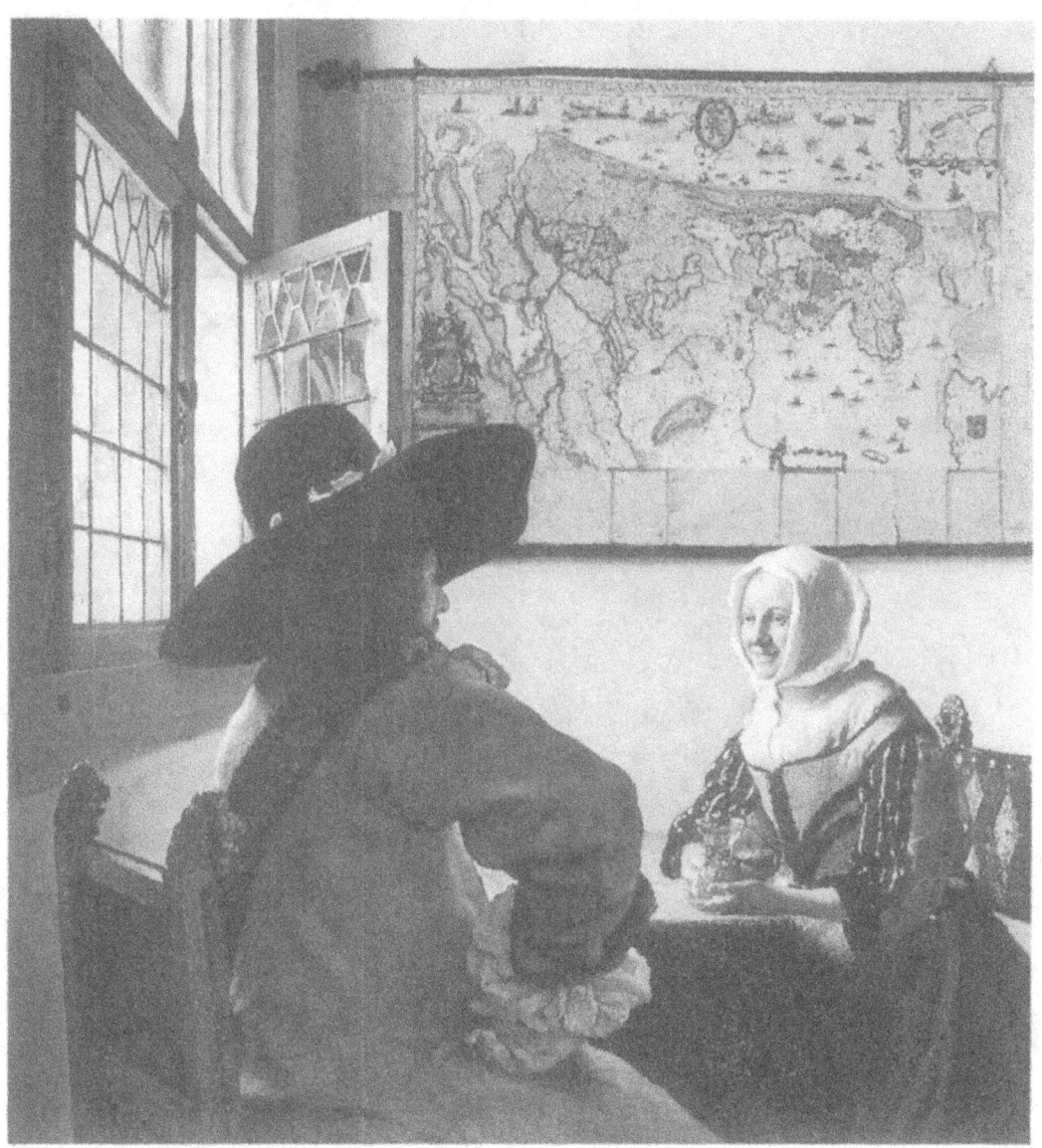

FIGURE 95. Johannes Vermeer, *Officer and Laughing Girl.*
Copyright The Frick Collection, New York.

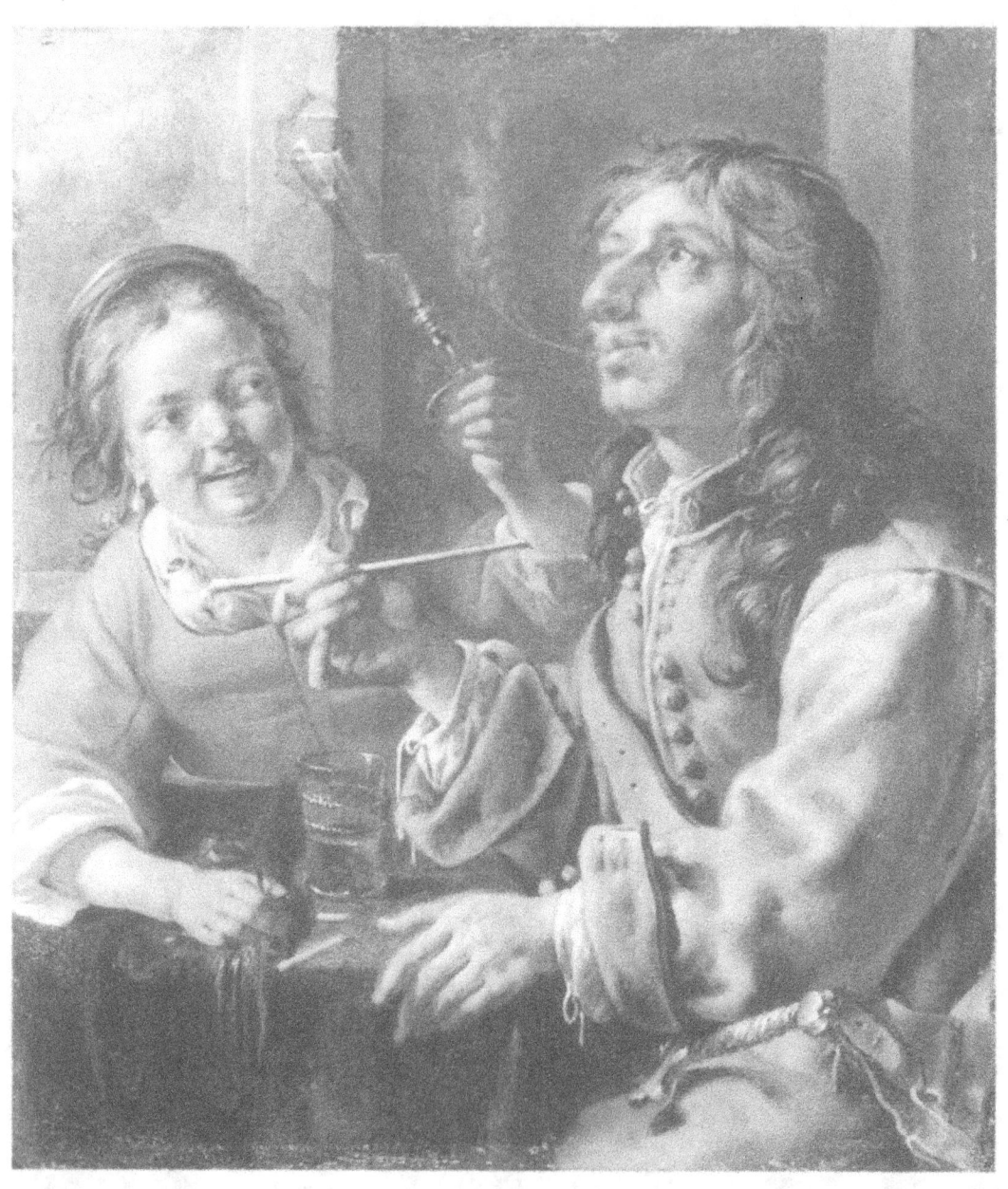

FIGURE 96. Jacob Duck, *Soldier and Laughing Girl.*
Fitzwilliam Museum, Cambridge.

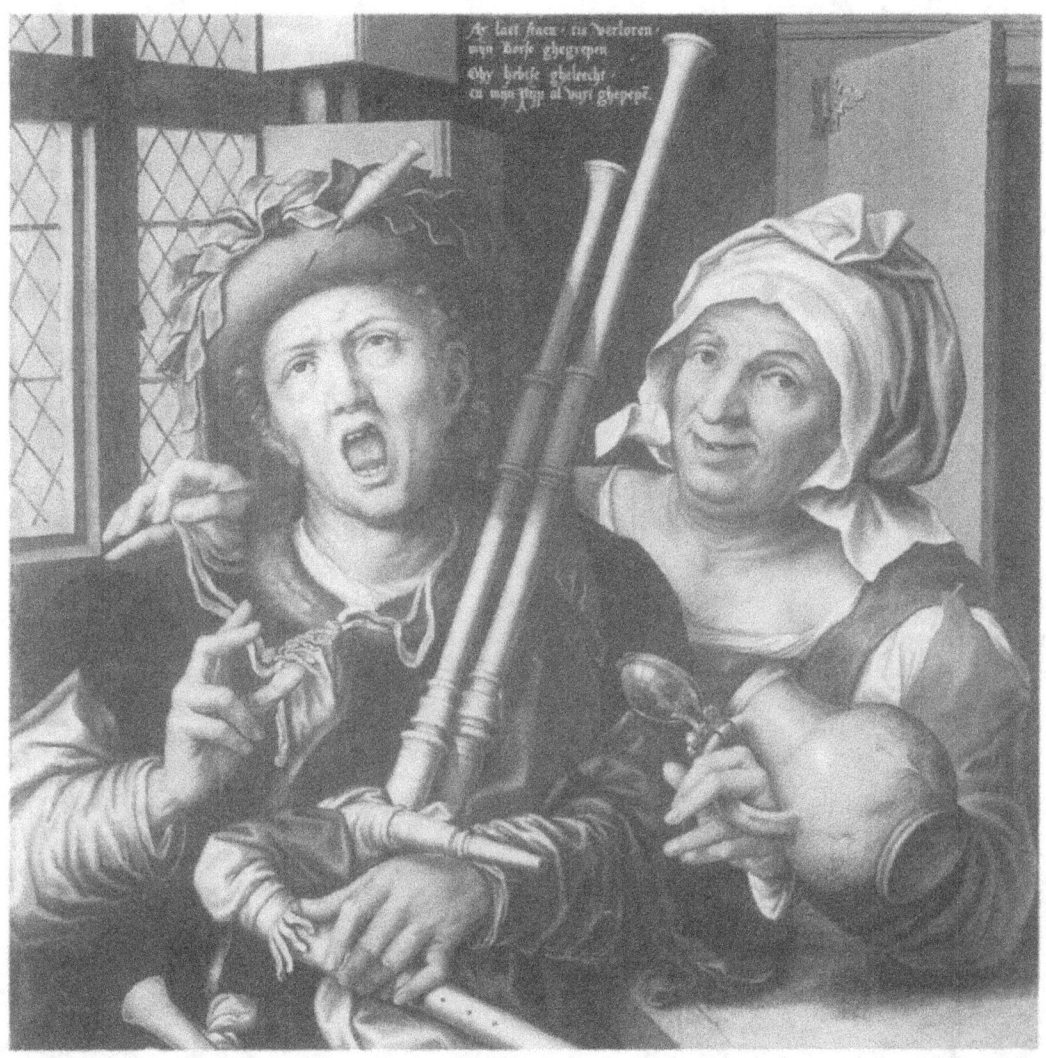

FIGURE 97. Pieter Huys, *Bagpipe Player and His Wife.*
Staatliche Museen Preussischer Kulturbesitz, Berlin.

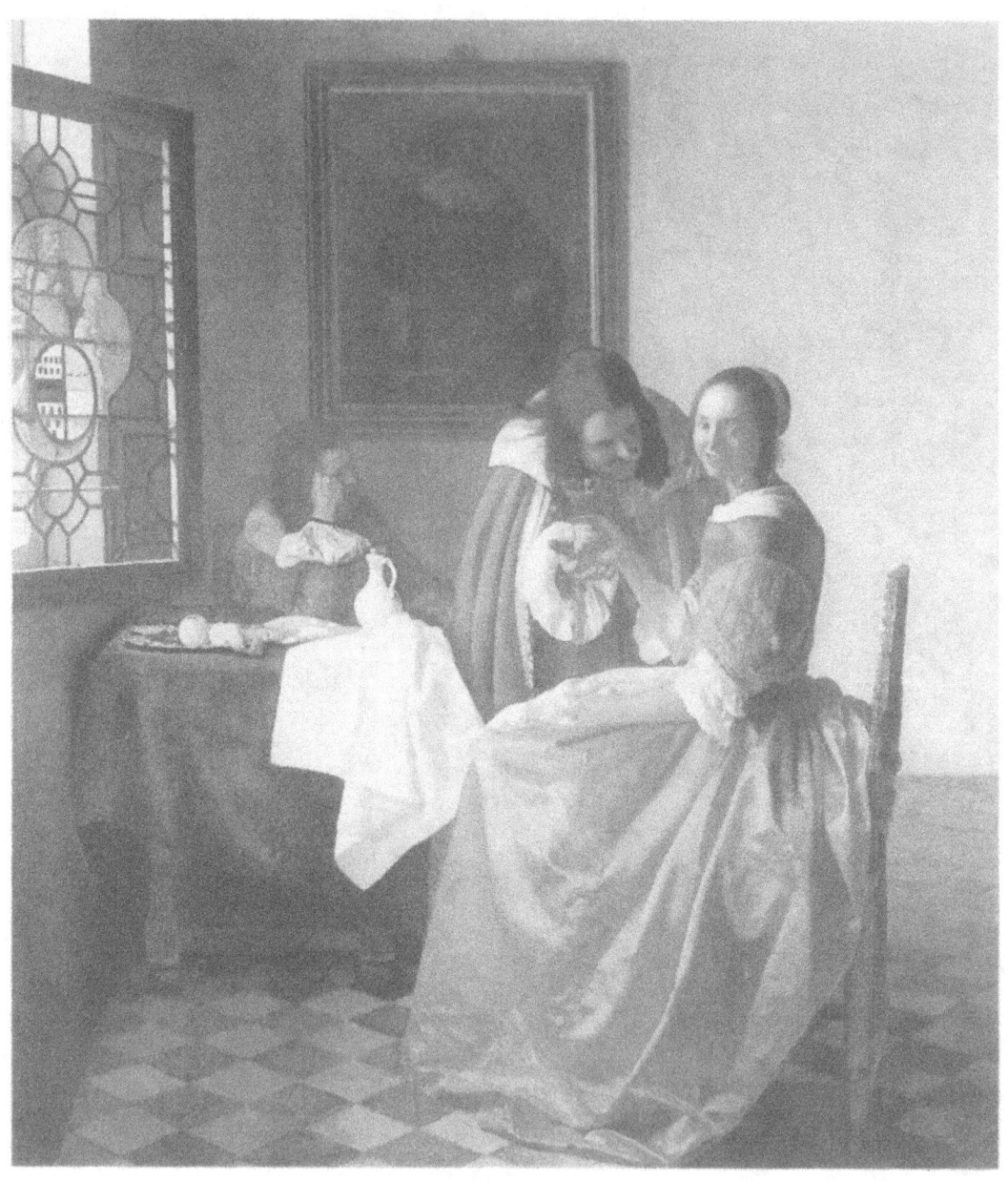

FIGURE 98. Johannes Vermeer, *The Girl with the Wine Glass.*
Herzog Anton Ulrich-Museum, Kunstmuseum des Landes
Niedersachsen, Brunswick.

Vermeer's Women:
Changing Paradigms in Midcareer

Even the most casual study of seventeenth-century Dutch genre paintings reveals a change in tone that occurs sometime just after midcentury.[1] Over the course of time art historians have framed this change in a variety of ways, and the changing terms of their discussions may be taken as a measure of the changing terms of value in the field of historical inquiry in its own right. Before the iconographic revolution initiated in Utrecht in the late 1960s, this change was seen as an issue of quality. As such it was touted as evidence of the greater genius manifested in Dutch genre painting after 1650, especially in the so-called Delft school, with Vermeer as its most outstanding example. Iconographic considerations, with their emphasis on disguised symbolism as a primary pictorial mode and the didactic explication of good and evil as the primary pictorial message, gave genre paintings from the first half of the century a new validity and new terms of appreciation.

As a corollary many have characterized the change after 1650 as the advent or popularization of the home as the site of the new subject in Dutch genre painting.[2] The positive associations of this site are easily made coincident with the interpretive system of Christian morality distinguishing the images along the binary divide of virtue and vice.[3] In the recent past there has even been some discussion about whether this change itself is evidence of a diminishing or erosion of meaning per se.[4]

My interests in this paper are to sketch a new frame for understanding the change in genre after midcentury and to track this change in the early works of Vermeer by focusing on the subject of woman as a culturally produced sign. The exhibitions of Vermeer's painting in the National Gallery in Washington, D.C., and in The Hague have provided new occasion to discuss and understand his art.[5] It may be argued that the two venues of the exhibition of Vermeer's paintings, the

National Gallery in Washington and the Mauritshuis in The Hague (Washington 1995–1996), constitute, in fact, one exhibition, yet from the perspective of cultural analysis the differences in the manner and place of the paintings' exhibition becomes more significant than their shared catalog and curatorial intentions. These opportunities have produced a catalog, symposia, and seminars. They have also allowed for, if not urged, the barrage of historical information embodied in Vermeer's work to be unfixed from its usual order and resifted and resorted through the grille of a modern perspective. Submitted to my art-historical eye,[6] feminist politics, and idiosyncratic curiosity, this historical information is regrouped. It is fashioned into whole new categories, the contents of which cohere in new alliances with newly found similarities. The analogy of poker comes to mind, where a winning hand may be had by cards of the same suit or by cards of consecutive numbers or value. Here a winning hand (that is, plausible claims to historical truths) can be had by renewed and diverse mixing and matching, although the possible combinations are enormous, and, alas, such clear markers as suits and numbers are not so easily seen.

Nevertheless, new plausible historical sense can be made from the work through these new groupings. With this paper I hope to broaden our definition of historical meaning and to relocate Vermeer's early work into what I am here suggesting was a mainstream of Dutch artistic practice that, because of its contemporary relevance, can only now be seen.

Vermeer's depiction of women as a central creative concern has often been remarked upon, most recently by Blankert.[7] Rather than reflecting any real woman (or women), these figures may be seen as formulations of evolving ideological constructs in early modern Dutch society. One of this essay's projects is to locate a change in the terms of these constructs that can be found in Vermeer's early work just after *The Procuress* (fig. 91), in the Staatliche Kunstsammlungen in Dresden; *A Maid Asleep* (fig. 92), in the Metropolitan Museum in New York; and *Officer and Laughing Girl* (fig. 95), in the Frick Collection in New York—all three sorely missed in the exhibition(s). In examining the shift in priorities just after these early genre works, we can see how this all-important, culturally produced sign changes paradigms in the slightly later *The Girl with the Wine Glass* (fig. 98), in Brunswick. Within the changing constellations of Northern Netherlandish burgher culture some issues at stake include, among others, native definitions of femininity and masculinity, as well as the related concepts of artistic mastery and aesthetics.

The three early paintings by Vermeer to figure male/female relationships belong, in my view, to a popular early category of Netherlandish genre paintings, the subjects of which represent illicit trysts. The later paintings, signaled by *The*

Girl with the Wine Glass, in Brunswick, belong to a new, modern pictorial category that represents what we may call for the moment civil trysts. Although not completely analogous, the seventeenth-century terms to delineate the change in women in Vermeer's paintings can be understood as a change from *minne* to *liefde* (eros to agape). The former is a highly developed subject in the burgeoning secular art of the Netherlands throughout the sixteenth and early seventeenth centuries.[8] *Minne* is defined there through a variety of tropes of so-called mercenary love—that is, representations of bordello scenes, so-called unequal lovers, the ruin of the Prodigal Son and others—which found ample expression in both paintings and prints. A consideration of these, if only a very brief one, is necessary here for a clearer understanding of the tradition to which I believe Vermeer was heir. The insightful work of Konrad Renger in his groundbreaking book *Lockere Gesellschaft* (Loose company), published in 1970, allowed us to see the iconographic diversity and complexity of the sixteenth-century paintings and prints representing mercenary love. They had, theretofore, more often than not been lumped together as simply illustrations of the biblical parable of the Prodigal Son. However, if we acknowledge that the story of the Prodigal Son is but one of several sexual narratives developed in the sixteenth century, this group of images can be opened up to an entirely different kind of analysis: one that allows it to be seen as a broader, even endemic, culturally produced ideological paradigm.

It is of no small consequence that the narratives of these formative secular works are dedicated to the economic exchange of sexual relations. Michel Foucault's work on this period's legal and literary history recognized that "since the sixteenth century, the 'putting into discourse of sex,' far from undergoing a process of restriction (as moralist interpretations would have us believe), on the contrary, has been subjected to a mechanism of increasing incitement; that the techniques of power exercised over sex have not obeyed a principle of rigorous selection, but rather one of dissemination."[9] Indeed, Foucault, in speaking of this period, describes what is for him a "veritable discursive explosion."[10] Rather than seeing this explosion as merely about sex, Foucault goes on to ask the crucial questions, "What were the effects of power generated by what was said (represented)?" and "What are the links between these discourses, these effects of power, and the pleasures that were invested by them?"[11]

One of the most consistent criticisms of Foucault's work in this area points to his failure to consider feminist issues as fundamental to understanding the power equations created through the discourses of sexuality.[12] The compelling drive to develop visually the terms of gender difference, together with the persistent "upper hand" given to women in these images, prevents us from making Foucault's mistake.[13]

Despite the clichéd notion that prostitution as a social practice exploits women and that, by extension, a consideration of visual "images of women" as prostitutes would also yield an analysis of that exploitation, a close viewing of the visual language of these paintings produces a salutary caution against such easy "interpretations" of images. A careful scrutiny of these paintings reminds us that our categorized and delineated notions of historical realities are not the only ones possible and, perhaps even more significantly, that "realism" in art can never be a simple, passive "mirror of reality" but is always rather a dynamic, organic— that is, interactive—participant in the formation of realities. The realities shaped by visual culture are part of a discursive web, continually catching and disposing meaning on a myriad of social levels. John Tagg's discussion of nineteenth-century photographic realism is useful here. In articulating the characteristic components of realism as an artistic phenomenon he writes: "The dominant form of signification in bourgeois society is the realist mode. Realism is a social practice of representation, an overall form of discursive production, a normality which allows a strictly delimited range of variations. It works by the controlled and limited recall of a reservoir of similar 'texts,' by a constant repetition, a constant cross-echoing."[14] It is precisely the realist rhetoric of these images that historically enables them to perform so persuasively and productively in establishing the links Foucault saw with other formations of power hierarchies in early modern relationships. The apparent realism of the *bordeeltje* (the seventeenth-century Dutch name for bordello scenes) is achieved by combining early Netherlandish realistic formal advances, such as replicating the "look" of the material and tactile world through the nuanced modulation of light and shade made possible by oil paint, with anecdotal modern subjects presented in contemporary settings, costumes, and hairstyles. Modern form and subject were activated throughout by a lively sense of narrative. The sense is conveyed of a "caught moment" spontaneously enacted yet replete with consequences.

These pictures' "effect of reality," to creatively twist the term coined by Roland Barthes, is still successfully influencing current art-historical interpretations that treat the images positivistically, as descriptions of actual bordello conditions. In fact, unlike actual bordello conditions in the Netherlands—which, as the work of Lotte van de Pol has shown, occurred across a tremendously varied spectrum of social conditions and locations—the image of the bordello in Netherlandish art quickly adhered to a series of discernible visual conventions. The fact that the repertoire of social types as class of locale in sixteenth-century imagery is so unvarying should itself attest to its contrived nature.[15] The impulse to read the images realistically is often linked, quite illogically, with the desire to read them as moralizing texts warning their viewers against lust, greed, and various other canonical sins. Although this is not the place, much can and should be said about the way contemporary interpreters "naturalize" the coupling of these two incompatible ideas. And although these subjects do, in fact, bear some relation to Christian notions of female vice, the positive tone of most of these paintings and prints urges us to find more resonant ways of understanding them.[16]

It has long been observed that some of Vermeer's paintings had a certain relationship with this prestigious early Netherlandish genre tradition. The combined effect of the so-called *Procuress* in Dresden and the presence of Dirck van Baburen's earlier image, *The Procuress*, in the Boston Museum of Fine Arts, in no less than two of Vermeer's works—*The Concert*, in the Isabella Stewart Gardner Museum in Boston, and *The Girl Seated at the Virginal*, in the National Gallery in London—ensured the consideration of this subject on various levels. However, more often than not, contemporary discussions turn on Vermeer's keen interest in Utrecht Caravaggism as a formal rather than iconographic choice. I would like to redirect our attention by securing not just the Dresden painting but all of Vermeer's earliest genre paintings with men and women in them, within the various sexual narrative structures of the early Netherlandish genre tradition.

The first and most overt of these is, of course, the painting in Dresden dated 1656 (fig. 91). Often called *The Procuress* despite the minor role played by that figure, the painting has always been recognized as an image of mercenary love. The central couple engage in an exchange of money and physical favors within an ambience of bright colors and a rosy atmosphere. Unlike Van Baburen, for example, who gives the prominent foreground position to the old bawd in his Boston painting, Vermeer instead gives that position of prominence to a male figure often identified with the artist himself, an identification that rests on a comparison between this figure and the figure of the painter in Vermeer's later work *The Art of Painting*, in the Kunsthistorisches Museum in Vienna.

His prominence in the Dresden *Procuress*, as in the Vienna painting, warrants a serious reconsideration of the statement made by the group. The idea that this toasting man is the artist is not at all alien to Dutch culture; examples of artistic self-portraits in bordellos have a long-standing, one might say legendary, history in northern European paintings of the sixteenth and seventeenth centuries.[17] The often-cited examples in relationship to Vermeer's painting are Rembrandt's self-portrait with Saskia, of circa 1635, and Gabriel Metsu's self-portrait with his wife, of 1661, both considered self-portraits as the biblical Prodigal Son and all, remarkably, in the same museum in Dresden. There are, however, many other examples from the sixteenth and seventeenth centuries that show the Netherlandish artist as a rake. Among those from Vermeer's century may be counted Adriaen Brouwer's *Carousers*, in the Metropolitan Museum of Art in New York; Frans van

Mieris's *Bordello Scene*, in the Mauritshuis in The Hague; and innumerable paintings by Jan Steen. Whether we see Vermeer's figure as indeed a bona fide portrait or, as is more likely, a generalized representation of the artist, it certainly must be figured among the seventeenth century's most telling accounts of the northern artist's early identification with an illicit lifestyle and its representation.[18]

Vermeer's *A Maid Asleep*, in the Metropolitan Museum of Art in New York (fig. 92), is the painting whose relationship to the mercenary-love tradition is the least obvious and requires the most explanation. On all accounts it is a complex and experimental painting. It has been interpreted in a variety of ways. Most often, because of the sleeping condition of the woman, it is related to the sin of sloth. Its formative stages, revealed through X-rays (fig. 93) and more modern technologies, show a myriad of changes that range from superficial fine-tuning to fundamental alterations in the design and the concept of the subject. Among the latter the presence of a man either leaving or entering the room, seen through the *doorkijkje*, or view through the open doorway, and the dog in the interim space looking at him are the most consequential. By including them in the initial conception of this subject, Vermeer was participating in conventions well established within the bordello type. He draws on Netherlandish visual history, which developed the representation of contemporary interiors as meaningful and as having particularly sexual connotations for the women who inhabit them. I have already traced the early history wherein the pictorial space is structured as an enclosure that is, I propose, defined as both a woman's space and a woman's sexualized body. Thus, a figure represented in the open doorway of an interior space that houses a woman can be connected to the sixteenth-century visual convention wherein that space figures the woman's open, licentious body. The convention was often used in the sixteenth and seventeenth centuries, and it was eventually presented in an emblem of around 1630 (see fig. 71). In this context it becomes clear that Vermeer here turns to the subject as it was formulated in the sixteenth century and modernized in the seventeenth by another Utrecht painter, Jacob Duck, as in his *Bordello Scene*, in the Museum of Fine Arts in Dijon.[19]

Jacob Duck's painting *A Sleeping Courtesan* (fig. 94), present location unknown, at once recalls the older tradition and introduces certain changes that announce the type's future. The visual comparison between Duck's *Sleeping Courtesan* and the initial version of Vermeer's *A Maid Asleep* makes a strong argument for the iconographic connection between the two. The coin being tendered in Duck's painting relates this work on some level to the Dresden *Procuress* as well. This man's hat, his withdrawn position, and his diminished importance clearly compare to Vermeer's male figure. It is, however, Duck's focus on a sleeping maid at a table, itself a natural extension of his own developed specialty of portraying

sleep within the bordeeltje tradition, that connects the two paintings in a remarkably close way. The relationship between these two paintings clarifies the
position of Vermeer's early concept within the Netherlandish bordeeltje tradition
and links this work with its most immediate predecessor in his own oeuvre, the
Dresden *Procuress.*

Even before the more radical transformation that took place when he omitted the man altogether, Vermeer's formulation worked to move the subject away
from the realm of minne and toward that of liefde. The absence of a bed in Vermeer's work softened the licentious nature of the room and thus defined the room
in a more ambiguous way. Furthermore, Vermeer physically separated the sleeping woman and the man, for although he is seen through the doorway, the man
is in a distant secondary room, which, among other consequences, given her
sleeping state, functioned as a more naturalistic narrative. Vermeer's female figure is even more idealized than Duck's. She has white rather than black pearl ear-
rings and a youthful blush in her cheeks. All in all Vermeer's painting softened
the sexual narrative in its initial stage and moved the image along the spectrum
from denotative toward its ultimate state as connotative.

Finally, there is Vermeer's painting in the Frick collection in New York, *Officer and Laughing Girl* (fig. 95), which can also be located within the sexual project of early Dutch genre painting. Although it can be related to the guardroom
tradition popularized by the early seventeenth-century genre painters in Amsterdam, Pieter Codde and Willem Duyster, and the genre paintings of the Utrecht
Caravaggisti, its iconographic roots are more complex. The introduction of the
soldier into the female-dominated milieu of the bordello was a development that
once again can be attributed to Jacob Duck (fig. 96). The small painting on cop-
per of around 1630 in the museum in Cambridge is but one solution to the problem in Duck's work in this decade.[20] It is, in fact, Duck's only painting to develop
figures in a close-up, half-length view, connecting it closely with his compatriots,
the Utrecht Caravaggisti. Duck's *Soldier and Laughing Girl* brings together the
heterogeneous couple in a spirited way, reminiscent of the open expression of
happiness and well-being seen in other Utrecht *Procuress* paintings. Yet Duck's
couple is unencumbered by moralizing details. The picture, instead, develops a
broad treatment of the prurient relationship between the two. This is played out
in the contrast of masculine sexuality signaled by the pipe held by the soldier and
feminine sexuality figured by the glass of wine held by the maid.[21] In the cramped
space of the composition their arms cross.

Once again, the animation and caricatured quality of Duck's figures are characteristic for him at this early date. The broad, humorous treatment of heterosexual joie de vivre in the Cambridge painting links it to another tradition of

early Netherlandish secular images, one that stands somewhat to the side of mercenary love per se and is best represented by the art of Pieter Huys in his various versions of *The Bagpipe Player and His Wife*, which date between 1560 and 1570.[22] In this spirited half-length composition bagpipes rather than smoking pipes figure the masculine member, and open tankards, rather than a glass of wine, represent the woman's sex (fig. 97).[23] In a later version, signed and dated 1571, in the Staatliche Museum in Berlin, Huys included the indications of an interior space with a window behind the bagpipe player. The sexual innuendos are made all the more explicit by the inscription he inserted, which loosely translates:

> Ay, leave it alone
> it's a lost cause
> to grab my purse
> you have emptied it
> and my pipe is all piped out.[24]

Although similar, if somewhat more subdued, half-length depictions of soldiers and their mates were to have enormous popularity among artists working in the generation after Duck's (Ter Borch painted the subject a number of times), his painting informs Vermeer's in a particularly satisfying way. Duck's *Soldier and Laughing Girl* makes a good match with Vermeer's painting in the Frick Collection in New York.

Indeed, looking at the three paintings together—Huys's, Duck's, and Vermeer's—gives coherence and meaning to all three. And in doing so, one gains more than simply the revelation of a new subtradition in the tropes of venal love traced by early Netherlandish secular history. What is gained is access to the process of refinement and naturalization of the heterosexual subject as a favored narrative that occurred over the one hundred years or so from Huys, through Duck, to Vermeer. The process works through Huys's burlesque bawdiness, with its broad, vulgar expression of libidinous desire, to the still farcical, sexual innuendo in Duck's work, to the sanitized and romantic theater of Vermeer's painting. The normalization process takes place on the level of relationships, attributes, and space. The stage on which these scenes are played out goes far in establishing the mind-set necessary to understand them.

In the course of the next few years Vermeer's pictures of male-female relationships take on a specifically more ambiguous quality, one that allows them to be read less as salacious and more as civil—that is, within the terms of respectability and decorum.[25] Here civility becomes an alternative to sexuality as both the defining characteristic of the feminine and that which is figured by the feminine. *The Girl with the Wine Glass* (fig. 98), in Brunswick, offers the bridge. Its connection with the earlier paintings is partially established by the presence of a soldier, behind the table, who seems to be a bored participant of the event. It is also partially established by the strong effect of the "girl's" expression, smiling broadly and in her unmoderated exuberance, showing her teeth. Some have explained her clear breach of decorum by postulating that she is already drunk.[26] Let me suggest that this open sign of uncontrolled gaiety and emotion ties the painting, as a type, backward to the *Officer and Laughing Girl.* It is a sign best understood in the nexus of cultural, sociological, and anthropological concerns connected by the phrase "civilizing process," introduced by Norbert Elias and integral to the work of such English and Dutch scholars as Peter Burke, Keith Thomas, Jan Bremmer, and Herman Roodenberg, as well as the American art historian David Smith.

As Castiglione and Erasmus tell us, in the history of manners, as in the history of art, smiling women showing teeth generally signified lower-class status or the precivilized, childlike exuberance expressed, for example, on the occasion of having mastered a certain skill.[27] A good comparison can be made with Giovanni Francesco Caroto's, *Boy with Drawing,* in the Museo del Castelvecchio in Verona.[28] In all ways the "girl's" demeanor conflicts with the sophistication and status communicated by her dress and environment, which are further elevated by the still life, the respectable burgher portrait on the back wall, and the emblematic stained-glass window. She certainly is no courtesan, yet she is no lady; nor will tropes of vice and virtue help us here, even if the stained-glass image is usually identified as an emblem of moderation and control. Moderation is not the exclusive meaning of representations of alcoholic intake (see Chapter 2).

In the face of prevalent interpretations that see the man here as a suitor, I would see him, instead, as an instructor, allowing for the theatrical convention wherein instructors often turn into suitors. With this interpretation the work would then be also forward looking, participating in the same category of painting type as those Dutch genre paintings representing music, drawing, or writing lessons.[29] Vermeer's *Girl Interrupted at Her Music,* in the Frick Collection in New York, shares the same male model. What is being taught in the Brunswick painting could be precisely the kind of social graces—for example, the proper way to hold a glass, an item that Gerard de Lairesse would emphasize in his later treatise on art—that would bring the woman up to the level of her dress.[30] Vermeer's formulation of this man with his theatrical cape, mustache, and low-bowing gesture makes plausible his identification as a comic Monsieur, comparable to the comic doctors in Jan Steen's paintings. It is, however, not necessary for my argument, which rests, in any case, not on any particular narrative reading but in the shifting terms of that reading. In the paintings after 1660 the terms of the feminine have decidedly changed. The topic of woman as the representation of certain constructs of gender and class sidles from a world defined by the physical qua sexual to a world defined by the metaphysical qua civilized, from the world of minne to the world of liefde.

The practice of cultural analysis is like a game of volleyball, where information and knowledge move back and forth between the courts of "then" and "now." A well-hit ball strikes its mark and returns to the other court without touching the ground and ending the game. If the inquiry of sexuality and civility is in our court now, how does this reading of Vermeer fit our own structures for the constituencies of our social life? Why is Vermeer so compelling as an artist and idea? Surely his focus on women as a subject belongs in large measure to the answer to this question. We are delighted to speak about women in paintings and, especially in these two zones of discourse, as physical, material, and sensuous abandon and as metaphysical, abstract, and ordered control. As the heirs of early modern ideologies and their communicative structures, we welcome the opportunity to permit his paintings and their exhibition to channel communication between and among us. His works allow us to tell each other about ourselves by giving color and form, both literally and figuratively, to our values and feelings. Here, too, we can shift endlessly between the sensuousness of the paint and the women, their glistening eyes and moist lips, to the cool, controlled order of the rooms, the light and pictorial design that forever locks the figures in their environment. For us, in the "now" court, Vermeer allows us to find ourselves through his paintings as sexual and civilized beings. Who could ask for more from an artist?

Reference Matter

Notes

INTRODUCTION. Pro/visions, Re/visions, Tele/visions

1. This term was introduced in E. de Jongh's essay for the exhibition catalog *Rembrandt en zijn tijd*. See de Jongh 1971.

2. See, e.g., Bal 1999; and Pollock 1999.

3. Bal 1994, 1.

4. See the earliest and unintentionally self-revealing remarks by Peter Hecht in his review of the exhibition *Masters of Seventeenth-Century Dutch Genre Painting*. Hecht hysterically refers to the image of the woman in the painting: "so now the poor girl from Delft is traveling around the world as a potentially pregnant woman" (Hecht 1984, 651).

5. The "debate" continues; see the article by Marieke de Winkel in Washington 1998, 330–331.

6. See Montias 1989, 308–309; and Bal 1991, 2. Most recently the idea has been supported, if not completely properly acknowledged, by Cunnar 1990.

7. See de Jongh 1991, 123; see also the interesting remark by David Freedberg in the same publication (410), questioning why nobody seemed to be working on political representations in Dutch paintings!

8. Salomon 1998.

9. Washington 1995–1996.

10. Westermann 1997, 244n20.

11. See also the essays and general premise of the exhibition catalog of Grand Rapids, Michigan 1999.

12. Pollock 1988.

CHAPTER 1. Vermeer and the Balance of Destiny

1. Rudolph 1938, 405–433.

2. Ibid., 408–409. Rudolph points out that the technique of using an image within the image as a sign of the deeper meaning of the whole goes back to Jan van Eyck, where the Passion scenes around the mirror in the *Arnolfini Wedding Portrait* function to make clear the nature of the proceedings.

3. Ibid., 409.

4. Ibid. For the variety of meanings associated with these objects in the sixteenth and seventeenth centuries see Henkel and Schöne 1967. See also de Jongh 1975–1976; and Amsterdam 1976.

5. See Van Straaten 1977, 73; and Blankert et al. 1978, 44. Another popular interpretation of her relationship with the *Last Judgment* is that she becomes an honest woman as a result of the constant reminder of the last reckoning. See Swillens 1950, 105; Wheelock 1981, 106.

6. Carstensen and Putscher 1971, 1–6. This interpretation is accepted by Walsh 1973, 79.

7. *Catalogus van schilderyen, Verkogt den 16. May 1696*, in Amsterdam. Nummer 1, "Een Juffrouw die goud weegt, in een kasje van J. vander Meer van Delft, extaordinaer konstig en kragtig geschildert" (A young lady who weighs gold in a small box from J. vander Meer van Delft, extraordinarily artful and strongly painted). Taken from Blankert et al. 1978, 145.

8. Wheelock 1981, 106.

9. Grimme 1975, 54.

10. This idea was touched on in Slatkes 1981, 56.

11. See Meiss 1973, 43–68.

12. De Jongh 1973, 198–206.

13. Among others see Gowing 1952, 135; Wheelock 1981, 106.

14. For a general overview of the religious issues of the day and of the importance of this particular problem see Zilverberg 1971, esp. 22–25.

15. On Vermeer's Catholicism see Barnouw 1914, 50–54; Swillens 1950, 20–21; Van Peer 1959, 240–245; Van Peer 1968, 220–223; Montias 1977; and Montias 1980.

16. De Jongh 1975–1976, 69–75.

17. Montias 1980, esp. 49.

18. Harbison 1976, esp. 131–134.

19. Ibid., esp. 134n60.

20. De Jongh 1975–1976.

21. Ibid., 85.

22. Ibid.

23. Ripa 1644/1971, 590.

24. Visscher 1614/1949, xxx, 152 (page numbers refer to the reprint edition); "want in den Spieghel is niet dan een schijn, het dingh dat ghy daer in sien wilt, moet ghy selfs voor u brenghen: wat personagie ghy in de Wereldt spelen wilt, moet ghy in u selfs vormer."

25. Klibansky, Panofsky, Saxl 1964, esp. 159, 179, 254.

26. Welu 1975, 546n91.

27. Blankert et al. 1978, cat. no. 23, 165–166; see esp. the entries under cat. no. 24 for descriptions of this painting before 1778.

28. Ibid., 165.

29. The various other connections between the life of Moses and astrology are too complex to be discussed here and must be saved for a later time.

30. Welu 1975, 544–546; reproduced as fig. 21.

31. Seznec 1972, esp. 65.

32. Ibid., esp. 79–83.

33. Klibansky, Panofsky, and Saxl 1964, esp. 182. See also Wedel 1968, 60–89. For the idea in the literature of the time see Tillyard n.d., 52–60; and Seznec 1972, who discusses literature and art in Italy.

34. The importance of the Dutch home as the locus of the communication of the essential elements of the faith is an idea that pervades Dutch culture. It has been discussed in Sutton 1980, 46–51.

35. "The light so beloved by me, I pass to thee my precious child." This popular saying is found in Cats 1632, 132. It was also illustrated in the Jordaens drawing in the Hermitage in Leningrad. See d'Hulst 1974, cat. A210, 295.

36. See note 7 above.

37. Montias 1980, 49–52; and Kok 1981, 108–112.

38. De Jongh 1975–1976, 75n27.

39. "A young lady, who weighs gold in a small case . . ." The idea that this *kasje* referred to a perspective box of the sort made in Delft by Vermeer's contemporaries must surely be erroneous. See Van Gelder 1948, 34–36; the response by Boström 1949, 21–24; and Van Regteren Altena 1949, 24.

40. Blankert et al. 1978, 153, doc. 62 and cat. no. 15, 161–162.

41. Martin 1901, 77–78.

42. Harbison 1976, 131–132.

CHAPTER 2. Political Iconography in Jan Miense Molenaer

I would like to thank E. Haverkamp-Begemann, J. W. Smit, and Ethan M. Kavaler for reading this text and offering suggestions for its improvement.

1. The Dutch practice of making music at home for entertainment and as part of domestic plays called *tafelspelen* is discussed in Kren 1980, 76–77.

2. Several studies have examined the various associations and meanings of music in Dutch art. See, e.g., de Mirimonde 1962, 1964, 1966–1967; Fischer 1975.

3. These concepts are discussed in the introduction of Amsterdam 1976, 24–25.

4. Bandmann 1960 explores the traditional relationship between music and various states of mind. See also Philadelphia 1984, 313–314, 361–362.

5. London 1978, 16.

6. Würtenberger 1937, 53–54; and Haverkamp-Begemann 1959, 26–27.

7. The notion of the "clavis interpretandi" was formulated by Keyzelitz. The idea is there developed of a clue or signal within the painting that stimulates the spectator to think of a deeper meaning. See Keyszelitz 1956, esp. 15; "Das Bild im Bilde," 54–72, discusses the device seen in Molenaer's work.

8. The portrait was first seen as a member of the House of Orange by Bode and Bredius 1890, 73. They curiously believed it to be a portrait of Maurice, Frederick Henry's brother.

9. MacLaren 1960, 257–258 (who dated the picture in the early 1630s) proposed that it was taken from Mierevelt's painting of the stadholder. The identification and date were taken over in the catalog London 1978, 16.

10. For the standard account in English of the political situation in the Dutch Republic see Geyl 1961–1964. See also Price 1974, esp. 16–40.

11. Panofsky 1959, 108n5, was the earliest to isolate the long and prestigious history of the hat as a symbol of liberty and to express the need for it to be studied as such. I wish to thank Stephanie Dickey for pointing out this reference to me.

12. Appian 1913, 2.17.119.

13. Ibid. (both).

14. Ripa 1611/1976, 312–313 (page numbers refer to the reprint edition).

15. For numerous examples see Bizot 1688; and Van Loon 1732.

16. Ibid. (both).

17. Ripa 1644/1971, 573–574 (page numbers refer to the reprint edition). This is clear in the texts, as well as in the illustrations of the two editions. Where the 1611 edition speaks of a "capella" (312), the 1644 edition speaks of a "hoed" (573) rather than a "kap" or "muts."

18. Reproduced in Delft 1981, fig. 298. A similar image was printed to honor Maurice, William of Orange's eldest son and Frederick Henry's brother; see Peter-Raupp 1980, fig. 37.

19. Reproduced in Delft 1981, fig. 299.

20. The standard work on Hendrick de Keyser is Neurdenburg 1929. For an in-depth analysis of the iconography of William of Orange's tomb see Delft 1981, 214–226.

21. Delft 1981, 218.

22. Tengnagel's painting has been studied by Schneider (1921, 18–19). It is also discussed in Washington 1980–1981, 70.

23. See Peter-Raupp 1980, 84–90. The hat in this painting is not meant to be Ripa's "Governo della Republica" or "Regeering van de Gemeene beste," as suggested by Peter-Raupp 1980 (86), referring to Duverger 1972, 229, for this item in Ripa is clearly a helmet and not a hat. The idea of the "liberty hat" was much more common and more likely to be the intended meaning here, as Peter-Raupp (1980, 86) also says.

24. An exception to this rule is Cornelis Bisschop's *Allegory Honoring Cornelis de Witt*, in Briere-Misme 1950, 142.

25. The specific significance of the concept of "Liberty" as either a virtue or a political idea within the context of the Dutch nationalistic consciousness is examined in Delft 1981, 218–222, 225.

26. It may be said that this combination of genre and allegory is pervasive in northern European painting from the late medieval period through the seventeenth century. Its origins stem from the dual phenomenon of the interpretation of Scripture as exempla and the belief in the presence of God in all things, hence the "disguised symbolism" of early Netherlandish painting. Certainly the question warrants more investigation and thought. Recent views on the subject have often been too polarized to bring us closer to an understanding of this complex situation. See Alpers 1976, 1978–1979, 1983; and Miedema 1977.

27. Lyckle de Vries (1977, 66) has interpreted Steen's painting as expressing a negative attitude on Steen's part toward the stadholder and the young prince. I believe that the devices of the hat and portrait indicate that he was indeed sympathetic to the Orangist cause in this instance.

28. Ibid. De Vries has identified this portrait as similar in style to a portrait of William III painted by A. Raguineau around 1661.

29. Braun 1980, cat. no. 276, 124, dates the painting between 1666 and 1668 following de Vries 1977, 66. This is the so-called *stadhouderloze* period.

30. London 1978, 16.

31. See, e.g., the emblems in Henkel and Schöne 1967, cols. 1117–1119 and 1297–1301.

32. See note 2 above.

33. This painting has been studied in depth with special attention to this aspect of its iconography in Hinz 1973, 207–217. See also Amsterdam 1976, 183–185. The painting by Molenaer in the Virginia Museum of Fine Arts in Richmond has also been interpreted with this idea by Van Thiel 1967–1968, 91–99.

34. Political harmony is mentioned but not applied to this painting in London 1978, 16.

35. Henkel and Schöne 1967, col. 1297 (see also the discussion of this emblem on pp. 166–167).

36. Ibid., col. 1299.

37. Plato 1930, 4.414–416.

38. For the general popularity of Bodin in the sixteenth century see Sternfeld 1956, 324–326. For Bodin's influence on Dutch seventeenth-century political thought see Delft 1981, 225.

39. This idea was first expressed by Bodin in 1566 and later developed in the *Six livres de la Republic* in 1576. Sternfeld 1956, 325, 325n7.

40. Bodin 1583, 286–288.

41. Sternfeld interpreted this passage from the point of view of Bodin's influence on English political thought (Sternfeld 1956, 326). The passage by Shakespeare is also quoted in the notes of Paul Shorey, trans., Plato 1930, 414–415, note e.

42. Rosand 1977.

43. Ibid.

44. Ibid., 512.

45. Quoted from Nevo 1963, 25.

46. See the discussion on the personification of the Netherlands in Tengnagel's painting by B. Brenninkmeijer-de Rooij in Washington 1980–1981, 70.

47. Paris 1970–1971, 224; and Bol 1983, 282.

48. Bol 1983, 282.

49. Bizot 1688, 47: "De Koninginne van Engeland geeft aan twee personen, welke de Geunieerde Provincien verbeelden, een overvloed van bloemen en roosen; willende uitduyden, dat zy verbond met haar maakt."

50. Davis 1978, 150. See also Stone 1977, 152–154.

51. Davis 1978, 151.

52. Indeed, the entire genre of the domestic interior developed with full force only after midcentury. See Sutton 1980, 45–46.

53. It is at least worth noting that the phrase "La poule au pot" (a chicken in every pot) was first introduced at this time as a political slogan by Henry IV. See the popular print reproduced in Grand-Carteret 1928, 3:19.

54. I would like to thank Albert Blankert for suggesting this idea to me and for his help in clarifying some of the other ideas of this paper.

55. Van Loon 1732, 190.

56. The impresa of Charles V has been studied extensively both in terms of its conception and its influence on the emblems of other rulers in the sixteenth and seventeenth centuries. See Rosenthal 1971, 204–228; and Yates 1975, esp. 23–24. I would like to thank Virginia Anne Bonito for pointing out the significance of the columns of Hercules to me.

57. Rosenthal 1971, 217n54; Strong 1973, 115; and Yates 1975, 58, 103n1.

58. Rosenthal 1971, 214n44.

59. Ibid., 216–217; and Strong 1973, 115.

60. Rosenthal 1971.

61. Ibid., 218–220.

62. Bizot 1688, 172, 175.

63. Henkel and Schöne 1967, cols. 555–584, lists the various uses of dogs in emblems.

64. Philadelphia 1984, 261–262, examines the various interpretations of the foot warmer.

65. Ibid.

66. Peacham 1612/1973, 126 (page number refers to reprint edition).

CHAPTER 3. Pendants and Meaning Making in Gerard ter Borch

1. Ter Borch's place in the history of genre painting has been discussed in Gudlaugsson 1959–1960; and The Hague 1974, which together remain the standard accounts of the artist to date.

2. For Pieter Codde and Willem Duyster see Playter 1972. For the history of guardroom scenes in Dutch art see Borger 1996; and Salomon 1998.

3. Salomon 1998.

4. The later paintings have most recently been discussed as pendants in Helsinki 1995.

5. Gudlaugsson 1959–1960, 2:98, cat. no. 79; ibid., 158–161, cat. no. 146.

6. Salomon 1998, 76–78. This painting is also discussed in the final essay of this volume.

7. See Renger 1970.

8. Kraus and Kraus 1975, fig. 85.

9. Amman 1588/1880, 50 (page number refers to reprint edition).

10. This motif is in itself a very popular one in the genre paintings of the seventeenth century and is discussed later in the context of Jan Steen's art. For the literary history of this motif see Franits 1992, 123, 127, 128, 128n21.

11. While Mr. and Mrs. are full and blind
    With wine: see their best house member
    The dog / who wants his share too /
    Take hold of the roast for himself.
    Therefore let no one wonder /
    That great riches often go under:
    What the gentleman values as his right /
    The servant will also desire. (Amman 1588/1880, 50)

12. See Owst 1961.

13. The Hague 1974, 154, 172.

14. Klibansky, Panofsky, and Saxl 1964, fig. 89b.

15. Ibid., fig. 90d.

16. See Spamer 1970, pl. 1, fig. 2.

17. Ibid.

18. At times the same print would be used to illustrate different ideas even within the same text, as is the case, for example, in the illustrations Jost Amman made for Fronsperger 1573–1578.

19. The account of pendants in seventeenth-century Dutch paintings in Moiso-Diekamp 1987 (where these are rejected as pendants [484, D8]) has been considered by most to be far too restrictive in thinking. Among the criteria used to dismiss these as pendants includes the fact that they have no relevant connecting iconography. This misconception is the very aspect this essay corrects. All other considerations of these paintings treat them as pendants.

20. The notion of an "iconographic erosion" was first introduced by Snoep-Reitsma 1975; and later taken up by de Vries 1977; and Sutton 1980. See also Philadelphia 1984, lxii.

21. Gudlaugsson 1959–1960, 1:96–98, cat. no. 78.

22. Ibid.

23. This convention was first discussed in Van Thiel 1967–1968, 91–99.

24. Ibid., 93–94. The *kannekijker* as a motif was discussed by Van Thiel in his analysis of a painting by Jan Miense Molenaer.

25. See, e.g., Brouwer's *Merry Company* in the Rijksmuseum, Amsterdam, and Jan Miense Molenaer's *Musical Company* in the Museum of Fine Arts in Richmond, Virginia.

26. For a discussion of this painting and a summary of the recent interpretations see Washington 1997, 77–80.

27. This proverb is cited in Cats 1632, 87: "Gelyck by gelyck." It is also the subject of a drawing by Jacob Jordaens in Copenhagen (d'Hulst 1974, 293, cat. no. A207).

28. See Katzenellenbogen 1964, 55; and White 1969, 192.

29. White 1969, 192.

30. For a meal one cup is pleasant:
    To drink twice is necessary, thrice pleasurable:
    Four drinks is a detestable madness:
    Anything more is shame and grief. (Henkel and Schöne 1967, col. 272)

31. Ibid., col. 273.

32. Ibid.

33. This verse can be translated as follows:

Gratification, which (human) nature finds very pleasant

Harms when it becomes too excessive

But good wine that is drunk a little too richly does not hurt

Whenever riches, honor and happiness decline

So too declines physical strength, beauty and fresh appearance

You must just know, that that which helps can also hurt

That in good there is bad and in bad there is good. (Ibid., col. 275)

34. White 1969, 192.

35. Ibid., 192–202.

36. See Katzenellenbogen 1964. Although the literature on Lotto's painting has always placed it within the context of a moralizing framework, this specific association has not to my knowledge been made before. See note 24 above.

37. Discussed in Monroy 1964, 45–46, 91. Monroy relates this form of dialectic to the method and form of the Rederijkers. The text by Furmer was translated in van Coornhert 1585.

38. Lloyd 1966, 33, 37–42, 47.

39. See Salomon 1985, 72–74.

40. Salomon 1998, 57–66.

41. Ibid. I explain there how the role of the guardroom scene in the first half of the seventeenth century was intricately linked to the Dutch Republic's emerging sense of nationalism and was a useful cipher for a host of issues much larger than the military.

42. The phrase "civilizing process" was first discussed by Norbert Elias (1978; 1982).

43. Winkler 1921.

44. Ibid.; see also Brinkmann 1997, 67–74.

45. Its present location is unknown.

46. Although the main studies in this area leave off just at this point, all the evidence points in this direction. See Nierop 1984; and Marshall 1987. For a fuller discussion of these factors see Salomon 1998.

47. Gudlaugsson's general interpretation of this painting is somewhat skewed.

48. Gudlaugsson 1959–1960, 2:186–187, 1:284.

49. Once again the pairing of these two paintings has been unilaterally accepted from Gudlaugsson onward with the exception of Moiso-Diekamp (1987, 479, cat. D. no. 1). Philadelphia (1984, 148) suggests that the dates of the two paintings may, in fact, not be as different as Gudlaugsson suggested. It also seems to me that the style of these works is not that different.

50. Helsinki 1995.

51. De Jongh 1967, 50–52.

52. Amsterdam 1976; de Jongh 1971, 178–179; and Naumann 1981, 111–114.

53. The letter speaks.
    Love impatient of the way of long absence,
    Invents the means to join the spirit,
    Though physically absent, by a written paper,
    which paints the ache that lances her breast. (Van Veen 1608)

54. See Adams 1998.

<blockquote>
55. Cruel Venus, source of all pain
I chase and ban you totally from my heart
For you bring forth nothing but mournful pain
Away lewd love
I drive you from my senses
And stop it with the wine.
</blockquote>

This poem is on p. 83 of the album found in the Rijksprentkabinett, Amsterdam, inv. no. 1830.

CHAPTER 4. Jan Steen's Dissolute Household

1. The eighteenth- and nineteenth-century preference for this kind of interpretation of Steen's work is discussed in de Vries 1976.

2. Houbraken 1721, 3:15.

3. For the more interpretative approach see Gudlaugsson 1945; de Groot 1952; Martin 1954; Amsterdam 1976; de Vries 1976, 1977; and Philadelphia 1983, 1984.

4. Whereas this idea is commonly held today, it was first fully developed in de Groot 1952, esp. chap. 2, 56–68, 74–86.

5. The date was once legible on the left side of the wine keg. The last two digits are no longer discernable. See de Vries 1977, 62, no. 98x; and Braun 1980, cat. no. 179, 110.

6. This is true of many of Steen's subjects, including the "Fat Kitchen and Lean Kitchen" and the "Unequal Lovers"; see de Vries 1977, 155, nos. 17 and 18; 157, nos. 40 and 41; 168, no. 169; and 169, no. 177.

7. For various examples of this type of image and a discussion of the tradition in relationship to the work of Pieter Bruegel see Kunzle 1977, 1978a, and 1978b; and Bruyn 1978.

8. A collection of essays exploring this phenomenon in various cultures and at various times has been edited by Babcock (1978).

9. See the recent study of the Dutch paintings in the Linsky Collection of The Metropolitan Museum in New York by Liedtke (1984).

10. Schama (1979, 105) speaks of the inversion in Steen's work.

11. "Dat wij nu niet en doen, dat doen wij morghen." For a discussion of this print in the context of sixteenth-century *Merry Company* scenes see Renger 1970, 113.

12. Ibid.

13. Ibid., 24–25, 64.

14. For the formal implications of this problem in seventeenth-century Dutch genre painting see Sutton 1980, 19–21.

15. From the earliest, history prints have made use of the combined communicative powers of words and images. See Köln 1981, an exhibition organized around this idea.

16. Some other examples of words in paintings in the seventeenth century can be found in Alpers 1983, 169–221.

17. Bol 1982–1983, 56–57, 60. See also Philadelphia 1984, 333–334, no. 114.

18. Bol 1984, 69–77, treats Van de Venne as an illustrator.

19. In his article on Jan Steen, Schama writes, "Steen's array of action and gesture is pinned together by compositions that revolve on a central figure or group," yet further he says that "the bolt preventing the component parts from flying off into centrifugal chaos, or crumbling into debris, seems precariously secured" (Schama 1979, 105). I hope to show how firmly they were secured by their reference to well-known print structures.

20. Examples can be found in Van Marle 1931–1932, 2:155–165. For the oldest known example of this form see de Meyer 1970, 89–90.

21. De Vries 1976, 13; 1977, 58.

22. Pictures within pictures have been studied for their meaningful intentions by Keyszelitz 1956, 54–72.

23. Numerous emblems and prints make this meaning clear. See, e.g., Henkel and Schöne 1967, cols. 1398, 1399, 1664. For the meaning of the overturned pitcher see de Jongh 1968–1969, 47.

24. Schama 1979, 107; Philadelphia 1984, 322.

25. This motif has been isolated and studied by Steinberg (1970). He mentions Steen's Vienna painting on p. 275.

26. The iconographic relationship between lust and drunkenness has a long and interesting history in Netherlandish art of the sixteenth and seventeenth centuries. The range of its various manifestations includes purely mythological ones such as *Sine Cerere et Bacchus, Friget Venus* (see Renger 1976–1978); semimythological ones such as Jan Muller's drawing *Et Venus in Vinis*, in the Dartmouth College Museum and Galleries; and purely genrelike ones such as the Steen painting presently under discussion and the painting by Cornelis Bisschop in the Linsky Collection of The Metropolitan Museum in New York, (see Liedtke 1984, 96). The emblematic expression of this idea has been noted in Amsterdam 1976, 27–29; and Braunschweig 1978, 91, 145, 147.

27. This strange device recurs in several of Steen's paintings of dissolute households, including the painting in the Wellington Collection in London, *The Consequences of Intemperance* in the National Gallery in London, and *The Dissolute Household* in the Linsky Collection of The Metropolitan Museum in New York.

28. Reproduced and discussed in Renger 1970, 24–25, 46, 64–65.

29. *Spiritus erronei et fanatici*. See ibid., 64–65, for a consideration of the labels in this image.

30. Coornhert 1585, no. xiii.

31. Renger 1970, 54–56.

32. Van Veen 1607/1684, 32–33.

33. See Petterson 1987.

34. The standard work on Coornhert is Bonger 1978.

35. Temperance and diligence are well-known ideological constructions of the Dutch Republic in the seventeenth century. See White 1969 for an analysis of the various religious and economic motives behind them.

36. For the identification and examination of this motif, dubbed "the idle hand motif," see Koslow 1975.

37. Her folded hands can be seen as an expression of her idleness, as well as being a natural position in which to sleep; ibid., 120.

38. Maeterlinck 1910, 298.

39. Ibid., 130.

40. From Amman 1588/1880, 50.

41. Domestic negligence, or the lack of vigilance in the home, the subject of Maes's painting, Steen's painting, and numerous others, will be examined in a future study by the present author.

42. Self-reference is a complex issue. This is especially so because of the practice of seventeenth-century artists to use and reuse not only figures and motifs from painting to painting but also larger constellations of figures and motifs. Nevertheless, given Steen's propensity for quotation and reference to the work of others, it is an attractive notion to entertain. It would, however, imply that his own works to which he refers were on public view and thus would have been recognized in their new context. This might have

been possible if they hung in well-established middle-class Haarlem taverns, an idea I hope to pursue.

43. Van Veen 1608, 84–85; de Groot 1952, 65.

44. Mitelli 1678, reproduced in Bartsch 1981, 365, no. 90.

45. Coornhert 1585, no. v.

46. Panofsky 1931.

47. Ibid.

48. Stridbeck 1956, 120–122. See also the last chapter, "Der Schlaf im Wirtshaus," in Renger 1970, 129–142.

49. For the correct title and interpretation of this painting see de Vries 1977, 60, and 131n114.

CHAPTER 5. Jan Steen and Domestic Ideology

1. Jan Steen's art has been the subject of several important recent studies, including the exhibition and catalog of the National Gallery and the Rijksmuseum; see Washington 1996; Westermann 1997.

2. The idea of a civilizing process is by now well known, particularly within the study of early modern Dutch culture. The phrase was initially coined in Elias 1978; and Elias 1982.

3. Salomon 1985.

4. Enklaar 1937, 1940.

5. See, e.g., Pleij 1983.

6. See Chapter 7 in this volume.

7. The first half of this project was begun in a sense by the groundbreaking work of Konrad Renger, who studied Netherlandish genre painting of the sixteenth century; see Renger 1970. For a different view of the Dutch domestic interiors see Franits 1993.

8. See Chapter 4 in this volume.

9. Philadelphia 1984, 322.

10. *WNT* 1882–1926, vol. 2, cols. 1169–1173.

11. Steen's relationship with Pieter Bruegel the Elder is manifested on many levels. It is an obvious and well-researched one in all the Steen literature. For the most recent literature see Westermann 1997.

12. The literature on Marten van Cleve is very limited and mostly to be found in the literature on Pieter Bruegel the Elder and his followers. See Faggin 1965, 34–47; and, most recently, K. Ertz's entry, "Cleve, Marten van," in Saur 1998, 552–555.

13. Van Mander 1604/1980, fol. 230 (reprint edition).

14. Ertz, in Saur 1998, 552.

15. See Faggin 1965.

16. Freedberg 1989. Freedberg has not taken into account the history of this polemic, which may be seen to have been begun in the dialogue between Michelangelo and Francesca da Hollanda. Freedberg does not consider Marten van Cleve at all.

17. Faggin (1965, 35, 10–11) dates the work early, around 1560, and credits Frans Floris and Pieter Aertsen as the main stylistic influences on Van Cleve. In a footnote he notes that versions of the subject in the left side of the painting can also be found in the oeuvre of Jan Bruegel and that they are copies after a Pieter Bruegel the Elder lost original.

18. This subject was painted numerous times in the seventeenth century, most notably in the oeuvre of Pieter Brueghel the Younger. See Ertz 2000, 76–77.

19. See Salomon 1998, fig. 41.

20. Renger 1970, fig. 6, 28–29, 50, 53. For the history of the attribution see esp. 28n65.

21. Ertz, in Saur 1998, 552.

22. For an appreciation of Van Cleve's contribution in this area see Raupp 1986, 262.

23. "Ein Stuckh von Ohlfarb auff Holz, warin a Bauerngasterey, auf der rechten Seithen hangt ein geschlachter Ox, stehet ein Khinderwiegen, warin ein Katz und unden ahn ettliche Ruben.—In einer schwartzen Ramen, hoch 6 Span 2 Finger unndt 7 Span 7 Finger braidt.—Original von Martino von Cleef niederlandischen Mahler." (A piece of oil painting on wood, of a peasant hostel, on the right side a slaughtered ox hangs, a child's cradle stands with a cat and below a few root vegetables. In a black frame, height 6 span 2 finger and 7 span 7 fingers wide. Original by Marten van Cleve Netherlandish painter.) Quoted from Van Bastelaer and de Loo 1906, 376.

24. Hermesdorf 1977.

25. Marlier 1969, 351–352, fig. 217.

26. See ibid., where it is identified as "La Visite a la Nourrice." Marlier reviews the various versions, including the copies of Pieter Brueghel the Younger and Brueghel de Velours after a lost grisaille by Pieter Bruegel the Elder that was known under the title of "Visite a la Ferme." Marlier agrees with Faggin 1965 that Van Cleve's formulation of the subject is independent from Bruegel's and probably dates between 1555 and 1560, therefore predating it. All agree that Van Cleve's style here is more related to his mentor, Frans Floris, and to Pieter Aertsen.

27. Raupp 1986, 258, 260–261, and 261n3.

28. Marlier 1969, 352.

29. Interactions between the peasantry and other social orders have their own history in sixteenth-century Netherlandish art and literature. The subject known as the *Boerenverdriet* or Peasant Sorrow, which developed the legendary hostile relationship between peasants and roving soldiers, had articulated it most vividly. The Boerenverdriet was popular well into the seventeenth century, and Van Cleve depicted it himself in various pictures, at times outright and at times in a more nuanced way. More convivial interactions of the peasantry and the burgher class are represented by burgher visits to peasant festivities, for example in Bruegel's *Peasant Wedding*.

30. As I mentioned in note 42 of Chapter 3, Norbert Elias was the first to discuss the phrase "civilizing process."

31. Winkler 1921; Brinkmann 1997, 67–74.

32. Steen may even have been inspired to hang these objects above the head of his figures by the overhanging grill in the bordello interior of the right hand of the Prodigal Son painting.

33. Westermann (1997, 244n20) offers a contrasting opinion and believes these attitudes to be still current in Steen's time.

34. *WNT* 1882–1926, vol. 6, cols. 477–478.

35. Nora 1997, 2:ix.

36. De Jongh 1967 discusses the "virginally" framed Dutch mother.

37. See Chapter 4 for the iconographic precedents of the scene.

38. Ibid.

CHAPTER 6. Jan Steen and the Invention of the Modern Woman

1. Pollock 1993, 1998, 1999.

2. Washington 1996; and Westermann 1997.

3. "The *Woman at her Toilet* . . . is the most forthrightly seductive damsel in this series, issuing her invitation in full awareness of her abundantly displayed wares" (Westermann 1997, 236); and "a young woman sits provocatively at the edge of her bed while pulling on a stocking. She stares unabashedly at the viewer, implicitly a man, fully aware that her dress is pulled up over her knees and that her unlaced jacket reveals the fullness of her breast. Her inviting expression and suggestive demeanor offer the promise of uninhibited sensual pleasure" (Washington 1996, 160).

4. Westermann 1997, 252n133.

5. See my Introduction, and Mieke Bal's response to E. de Jongh, in Bal 1996, 12–13.

6. Amsterdam 1976, 64. This catalog entry is actually about the autograph variant in the Rijksmuseum in Amsterdam, but both versions are discussed.

7. Ibid.

8. Reproduced in Kraus and Kraus 1975, fig. 90.

9. The range of other seventeenth-century Dutch images of figures putting on or taking off a stocking is equally divided between male and female, paintings and printed emblems, lascivious and ethical morals. See Amsterdam (1976, 258–260) which illustrates but does not consider the differences in these images.

10. Cited in Kemp 1989, 152.

11. For this reason its effect can be compared to the look on Victorine Meurend's face in Eduoard Manet's 1863 painting of *Olympia*.

12. See Berdini 1998.

13. Cited in Kemp 1989, 147.

14. See Tickner 2000, 196–206, 306n67. Much of the literature on this topic concerns women as practitioners, although much, too, concerns "woman" as a sign of the modern, a concern that has been the life-long project of Griselda Pollock; see, e.g., Pollock 1993, 1998, and 1999; Pollock and Parker 1981.

15. Gent 1981, 7.

16. *WNT* 1882–1926, vol. 20, pt. 2, cols. 243–247; and de Pauw–de Veen 1969, 224, 244, 295–296.

17. Cropper 1986.

18. de Pauw–de Veen 1969, 59–60, 113, 173–174, 179. See also Salomon 1998, 31, 109.

19. See Blankert in Washington 1995–1996, 31–33.

20. Biesboer 1993, 88n1.

21. Ibid.

22. Ibid. See also Salomon 1998, 109.

23. Gudlaugsson 1959–1960, 2:15–16. Gudlaugsson reproduces the letter, dated July 3, 1635, from Gerard ter Borch senior to his son, Gerard ter Borch.

24. de Lairesse 1740, 114.

25. Ibid., 108–132. A summary of de Lairesse's various applications of the word can be found in de Pauw–de Veen 1969, 60–61.

26. de Lairesse, 1740, 113, 173–174.

27. Amman 1586/1872, xxxiv–xxxv.

28. This is one of the central theses of Salomon 1998.

29. This figure is also cited as a source of inspiration for Steen's contemporary Johannes Vermeer in his *Diana and Her Companions* of c. 1655–1656. See Washington 1995–1996, 98.

30. Salomon 1985, 150, 150n39.

31. de Brune 1624/1970, 101–108.

32. This would deny the more vacuous view of detail in what Roland Barthes (1982/

1991, 11–17) termed the "reality effect." For a discussion and critique of Barthes see Bal 1991, 217–218.

33. Van Veen 1607/1684, 46–47.

34. "Indien hy, voor den dagh, begint / In hooger beezigheit te werken" (Ibid., 47).

35. See Bal 1991, esp. chap. 6.

36. Hollstein 1968, 8:149.

37. "[W]ant de ledigheyd zonder leeringhen, als men zeght, is een dood, en begravinghe van een levendigh mensche" (de Brune 1624/1970, 107 [reprint edition]).

38. See Michalski 1932, figs. 12, 13, 16, 17, 20.

39. Ibid., 72.

40. Alciati 1626, emblem 10.

41. Situated somewhere between the distant past and Steen's immediate present is a series of remarkable engravings by Peter Flötner in which similarly ornate door frames mark off entrances to various rooms within a home, such as the sitting room and the kitchen. These are especially interesting, for, unlike the works of Dou or his fifteenth-century precedents, they clearly privilege the entrance over what is to be seen inside it. See Hollstein 1968, 8:146, 147.

CHAPTER 7. Early Bordeeltjes and Social "Realities"

I wish to thank Griselda Pollock, Lora Rempel, Barbara Bowen, Keith Moxey, and Adele Seeff for reading earlier drafts of this essay and offering their help. I am indebted to the Watson Library and the Education Department of The Metropolitan Museum of Art in New York and the Rijksbureau voor Kunsthistorisch Documentatie in The Hague for their continual support.

1. Itinerancy in the Netherlandish folk tradition has been studied by Enklaar (1937; 1940). Renger (1970), in his groundbreaking study of sixteenth-century secular imagery, discussed the development of prodigality as a subject in Netherlandish art.

2. *WNT* 1902, pt. 3, sec. 1, col. 527.

3. For a representative moralizing treatment see Amsterdam 1976. On the bordeeltjes as realist reflections on prostitution in the Netherlands see, e.g., how the illustrations are used in Van de Pol 1992, 179–218.

4. For a discussion of the "structural prefiguration" of the text and its function in predisposing interpretation see Iser 1978, esp. 107–134.

5. For an overview of these movements and their significance to art history see Bal and Bryson 1991; Moxey 1994. The art historian who has most brilliantly brought feminist theory and art-historical practice together is Griselda Pollock (1988; 1993; 1999).

6. Foucault 1980.

7. The first to draw attention to the weakened economic condition of women in the early modern period was Joan Kelly, when she asked the poignant question "Did Women Have a Renaissance?" in Kelly 1984, 19–50. The specific history of women's eroded participation in Netherlandish economic life has been studied by Howell (1986). See also Wiesner 1986 on women's loss of work in Germany for this same period. This point of view has been contested by Kloek (1990, 48–77).

8. This aspect has been explored for the seventeenth century by Franits 1993.

9. See Oestreich 1982.

10. See Schama 1987, 375–480.

11. For a history of the terms of early secular paintings see de Pauw–de Veen 1969,

167–179. For the most comprehensive study to date on this kind of early Netherlandish secular painting see Renger 1970.

12. A history of public inns and taverns in the Netherlands in the sixteenth century still remains to be written. The basic study is Hermesdorf 1977.

13. Although absolute information on the places bordeeltjes were exhibited is lacking, circumstantial evidence is strong. J. Michael Montias has been kind enough to share with me the fruits of his archival research in the inventories of seventeenth-century Amsterdam homes. He has, so far, found ten citations of a bordeeltje, found in variant spellings, in upper-middle-class Dutch homes. Unfortunately, such inventories were not made in the sixteenth century.

14. Indications of secular art in public spaces come from intimations in art and literature. See Moxey 1989, 93–95, for a discussion of a print of mercenary soldiers in a tavern scene by the Brunswick Monogrammist. See also Carroll 1987, 294, who cites Shakespeare, *Henry IV, Part Two*, 2.1.

15. Carroll 1987, 294 and note 40.

16. Brantôme 1666/1901, 1:365.

17. Pollock 1988, 50–90.

18. Foucault 1980, 12.

19. Ibid., 17.

20. Ibid., 10.

21. The term was first introduced by Barthes (1982/1991, 11–17). It has since been elaborated on in Bryson 1983, esp. 13–36.

22. The same confusion between literature and "real life" prostitution can be found in Böse 1985.

23. See Van de Pol 1990, 109–144, 192.

24. For Dolce, Paleotti, and Gilio see Barocchi 1960. For Molanus see Freedberg 1971, 229–45. See also Blunt 1940.

25. Comparisons between Venetian and Netherlandish histories are common and were made initially by the seventeenth-century Dutch themselves. See Burke 1974.

26. For a collection of essays that deal with sexual texts in the sixteenth century see Turner 1993.

27. For a recent review of the iconographic interpretations of Titian's *Venus of Urbino* as either celestial or terrestrial see Pardo 1993, esp. 59, 86–87n11. Her interpretation draws on both interpretive camps, the literalists and allegorists.

28. For a fuller analysis of the meaning and effect of the tipped-up body of Venus see Salomon 1985, 144–153.

29. See Pardo 1993, 60.

30. In this, Netherlandish painting participates in the theoretical assumptions inherited from ancient writers on rhetoric and the theater such as Aristotle, Cicero, and Terence. Ancient theory linked the "real" and the "low" as parts of the definition for comedy, essentially defined as the antipode of the ideal. See McFadden 1982; de Vries 1991, 209–244.

31. For the relevance of this story for contemporary religious debates see the publications by Barbara Haeger. The most recent is Haeger 1988, 127–140.

32. The function of the fool as a reference to the theater has been suggested by Silver 1974, 104–124; Moxey 1980, 125–148; and Moxey 1982, 86–102.

33. Schubert 1970.

34. For general Marian iconography in architectural terms see Kunstle 1926–1928; Kirschbaum 1968–1972, esp. cols. 190–193; and Timmers 1974, no. 328.

35. See Panofsky 1971, 132 and 132n2.

36. Ibid., 145.

37. For the "Garden Enclosed" see ibid., 132, 137, 145, and notes. Panofsky here documents the walled garden as a Christianized version of the "garden inclosed" [*sic*] of the Song of Songs, with Christ as the Bridegroom and the Virgin Mary as the Bride. For the "Locked Door" see Timmers 1974, 131, no. 138, who cites the source as the *Defensorium immaculatae virginitatis*. See also Babiæ 1968, 145–151; and Daniëls 1977–1978, 257–258.

38. See Van Rossen 1983, 41, 44.

39. The issue of the Immaculate Conception, whether Mary herself was conceived free from original sin—that is, without concupiscence—was hotly debated in the twelfth and thirteenth centuries but had been more or less accepted by the fourteenth. For a discussion of the various beliefs associated with the Virgin Mary see Warner 1976.

40. Joseph's presence in this panel is itself evidence of the increasing focus on his devotion in the early fifteenth century. For a history of the literature on this subject and a new interpretation see Hahn 1986, 54–65. She notes that both Meyer Shapiro and D. Arasse have viewed Joseph's activity as a symbolic displacement of thwarted sexuality; see ibid., 61 and 61n44.

41. Ibid., 56–57.

42. See, most recently, the exhibition catalog, New York 1994, 170–176, cat. no. 20.

43. See Ainsworth 1994 in ibid., esp. 43–51.

44. Indeed, rather than the oft-made claim that the seventeenth-century genre painters, such as Nicolaes Maes and Pieter de Hooch, were the first to introduce this kind of telescoped scene, this painting by Petrus Christus is the first that I know of. For a discussion of the formal implications of this layout see Sutton 1980, 20–23.

45. Leipzig 1973, inv. no. 509, cat. no. 5, 20–21, with illus.

46. Reproduced in Fuchs 1928/1973, fig. 6.

47. The fool in Quentin Massys's *Unequal Lovers*, in the National Gallery in Washington, functions similarly but not identically to the entering figure in these paintings and prints.

48. The print was designed by Romano and engraved by Marcantonio Raimondi. See the entry by Sylvia Ferino Pagden in Mantua 1989, 274–275; and also the entry by Bette Talvacchia in ibid., 279. See also Sylvia Ferino Pagden 1989, 227–236. Ferino Pagden (227) cites a smaller copy of this painting in Berlin in the eighteenth century and accepted as by Romano in the nineteenth.

49. Although the Hermitage painting has been attributed to Hendrik Goltzius, as a copy of a lost Romano original, Vasari's description of that original—"nel quale è un giovane ed una giovane abbracciati insieme sopra un letto in atto di farsi carezze, mentre una vecchia dietro a un uscio nascosamente gli guarda"—makes it clear that the compositional motif of the voyeur was part of Romano's original painting. See Ferino Pagden 1989, 227–228 and 235n17.

50. See Lawner 1988, 80; and Fernino Pagden 1989, 233. In fact, the earliest appearance of the entering-figure motif can be found in ancient Roman times in the Warren Cup, where the love-making couple are two men and the intruder is a young boy. Here, as in the cases cited above, the presence of the figure in the doorway brings with it the suggestion of a public space devoted to sex; see Clarke 1993, 275–294.

51. The phrase is from her important essay in Davis 1975, 124–151.

52. See Kunzle 1978a, 39–94; Dresen-Coenders 1988a, 73–84; 1988b, esp. 25–45.

53. Davis 1975, 130–134, 311n12.

54. These have been studied by Smith (1978).

55. Dresen-Coenders 1988b, 29.

56. De Meyer 1970; Dresen-Coenders 1977, 29–37, note 77; 1988b, 39–45.

57. Dresen-Coenders 1977, 34.

58. Ibid. Dresen-Coenders traces the changes in *de strijd om de broek* imagery from a relationship characterizing peasant life in its initial forms to the lower bourgeoisie in the early seventeenth century. Its final stages in the nineteenth century emphasize religious rather than class distinctions.

59. Reproduced in Dresen-Coenders 1988b, 40.

60. Van Deursen 1991, 81–95. See also Schama 1987, 402–403.

61. Quoted in Van Strien 1993, 215.

62. Van Deursen 1991, 341n16.

63. Ibid., 83. Kloek 1993, 55–57, stresses the amazement of foreigners at the bossiness of Dutch wives.

64. Cited by Kloek (1993, 55).

65. For a psychoanalytic interpretation of a Virgin Enclosed as the city see Vandenbroek 1991, esp. 82–84. For a thorough survey of this imagery in Netherlandish history see Van Winter 1957, 29–121.

66. This print has been discussed in Haverkamp-Begemann 1959, 14, 170, 171; and by Haverkamp-Begemann in the intro. to Rotterdam and Paris 1975, 95–96, cat. no. 119.

67. See intro. in Anderson 1991.

68. Schama 1987, 69–71. See also Johnson 1993, 159–218. Many of the other essays in this book shed light on this problem even though they deal with a later period.

69. Interestingly, Brandt in his *Historie der Reformatie . . .* , published in 1671, blamed sixteenth-century foreigners for spoiling native Dutch simplicity and modesty by bringing "fancy dress and manners" to the cities they visited. See Böse 1985, 31–39, esp. 31.

70. Culler 1988, 156. Culler mentions the fantasy of sexual freedom as a motive for tourism but does not develop the idea.

71. For a collection of interesting essays dealing with related material see Parker et al. 1992.

72. See Noordam 1987, 140.

73. See Van Strien 1993.

74. Van de Pol 1992, 191–192.

75. For an overview of this phenomenon see Lawner 1987, 1–60.

76. Cited in Girouard 1985, 135 and note 51.

77. See note 27 above for the views that Titian's *Venus of Urbino* is itself a portrait of a courtesan.

78. Held 1961, 201–218.

79. Quoted from Brantôme (Pierre de Bourdeille) 1666/1901, 223–224.

80. A copy of this book is in the Folger Shakespeare Library, Washington, D.C. Although this book has not, to my knowledge, been reprinted, it is often cited and parts reproduced. See Lawner 1987, 194, for examples from Brussels, Richmond, Florence, and Spain.

81. The connection between sixteenth-century printed fashion books and tourism is made by Van Ierlant 1988, 11–21; and du Mortier 1991, 401–413.

82. Culler (1988) discusses the difference between a traveler and a tourist.

83. Otis 1985, 23.

84. Quoted from Schama 1987, 467.

85. Homosocial bonding in English literature is investigated in Sedgwick 1985. See also Winnett 1990, 505–518.

CHAPTER 8. Gender, Class, and Age in Adriaen van Ostade

1. For the role of convention in prefiguring reception of Dutch marine paintings see Goedde 1987. For a discussion and critique of the way in which "images of women" in general have been analyzed see Pollock 1990, 202–218.

2. See Webster 1938.

3. Although Bruegel's formulation of the peasant in Netherlandish art is endemically cited as seminal, the specific conditions of his "influence" on the peasant genre have not, to my knowledge, been sufficiently articulated. For the most recent study of Bruegel's peasant imagery and its reception see Sullivan 1994.

4. See Carroll 1987, 289–314.

5. For the identification of landscape painting with northern European artistic production in general see Gombrich 1966.

6. See Thomas 1984, esp. 41–50.

7. The changing emphasis in peasant imagery from work to play is an intricate one with a long bibliography. This problem is most recently tackled by Sullivan 1994, 15–23. See also the essays by Wayne Franits and Lisa Rosenthal in Athens 1996. Inconsistencies within the possible receptions of peasants' festivity itself is argued by Carroll (1987).

8. Bode 1924 remains an essential study for Brouwer. See also Renger 1986; and the illuminating article by Renger 1972, 9–16.

9. For a group of extraordinary essays on the growing ideology of the city in the Netherlands see Van der Stock 1991.

10. This aspect of the kermis is emphasized in the inscriptions beneath prints that depict them. See Alpers 1975–1976, 115–144. A particularly characteristic example is the quote beneath the Kermis of Hoboken, after Pieter Bruegel.

11. The literature on Adriaen van Ostade is limited to specialized studies based on medium. See, e.g., Schnackenburg 1981; and, most recently, see Athens 1994 exhibition catalog with extensive bibliography. See also Schnackenburg 1984, 30–42.

12. For a recent analysis of the theory and practice of cultural politics see Moxey 1994.

13. For illustrations see Cazelles and Rathofer 1988, 18–21, 26–29.

14. McFadden 1982. See also de Vries 1991, 209–244.

15. De Vries 1991, 219; and Chapman 1993, 147.

16. Bellori quoted from Barasch 1985, 317.

17. See Franits and Rosenthal in Athens 1996 for a discussion of these issues and the bibliography pertinent to the debate.

18. Norbert Elias coined this useful concept in two volumes that appeared in 1939 collectively entitled *Über den Prozess der Zivilisation* and reprinted in translation in Elias 1978; and Elias 1982.

19. I have omitted Van Ostade's print of 1679 *The Doll* (*La Poupée Desirée*) (B.16), Athens 1994, 93–97, cat. nos. 39, 40, 41, although it might well belong to this discussion. The setting is not an interior but a porch. More significantly, the subject is so unusual that discussion of this print must be held over for another occasion, when justice can be done to its complexity.

20. There are several related subjects in the drawing oeuvres of Adriaen and his brother, Isack. Schnackenburg (1981) discusses them under the category of "Bauernfamilie bei der Mahlzeit." For Isack he lists cat. nos. 405, 413, 422, 509, 510, 531, and 549; for discussion see Schnackenburg 1981, 1:48. Adriaen's drawing, cat. nos. 91 and 92, in Amsterdam and the Ecole des Beaux-Arts, Paris, respectively, and cat. nos. 230 and 231 in London and Berlin, respectively, are also related to this subject. Another drawing by Adriaen,

cat. no. 236, *The Newspaper Reader*, of 1673, in the Lore and Rudolph Heinemann collection in New York, is a more common image of a present father in a domestic setting.

21. The literature on the ideology of the Dutch family in early modern times is extensive. See Franits 1993.

22. Van Ostade's etching *The Family* (B.46) is inscribed with the date 1647. See Athens 1994, 226–231, cat. nos. III and II2.

23. Schnackenburg 1981, 1:89–90, cat. no. 48, 174 x 154 mm (same size as the etching), ill. in 2:27, Pierpont Morgan Library in New York. The exhibition catalog by Stampfle (1979, 125, no. 89) details the minor changes Van Ostade made from the drawing to the print.

24. Klessman 1960, 92–115.

25. Van Ostade's *The Breakfast* (*Le Gourmet en Compagnie*) (B.50) has been dated between 1647 and 1652. See Athens 1994, 248–251, cat. nos. 118, 119, 120.

26. "Securae reddamus tempora mensa / venit post multos una serena dies. Tibull." The translation is taken from the entry by Leonard J. Slatkes [LJS] in Athens 1994, 251.

27. See Bastelaer 1992, 211–219.

28. For an explication of this parable see Chamberlin and Feldman 1965, 775–784. For the identification of the print see Slatkes [LJS] in Athens 1994, 251.

29. For a discussion of "structural prefiguration" within "texts" and its function in predisposing interpretation see Iser 1978, esp. chap. 5, "Grasping a Text," 107–134.

30. See Franits in Athens 1996.

31. See Slatkes [LJS] in Athens 1994, 230.

32. Slatkes has also remarked on the class difference between the figures in de Hooch and Van Ostade in ibid.

33. Ibid. For a psychoanalytic interpretation of the Virgin as an enclosed city see Vandenbroek 1991, esp. 82–84.

34. See Chapter 7 in this volume for the illustration and development of this idea.

35. Many of the sixteenth-century examples are illustrated in Renger 1970.

36. For *L'Heureuse Fécondité* and the related drawing of the same name see the exhibition catalog by Rosenberg 1988, 456–460, cat. nos. 222 and 223.

37. Reproduced in Fuchs 1928/1973, fig. 6.

38. The idea that a mother could still be a virgin is explained several times by the seventeenth-century Dutch moralist Jacob Cats in his book *Houwelick*. The popularity of this prescriptive book for the proper life of a Dutch woman cannot be overestimated. Cats says that a wife who "cohabits without lust" but only with procreation as a goal, remains a virgin. For a somewhat far-fetched application of this idea to marriage portraiture see de Jongh 1974, 166–192. For the references to Cats on married virginity see esp. 175.

39. See Moxey 1989, 47–50; Thomas 1984, 43; and Bakhtin 1984.

40. See Slatkes [LJS] in Athens 1994, 230.

41. Slatkes rejects an attribution to Van Ostade of the Budapest painting in ibid.

42. For a discussion of the Protestant heritage of respect for the poor and its influence on Rembrandt see Baldwin 1985, 122–135; and Stratton 1986, 77–81.

43. Thomas à Kempis, *In Imitatio Christi*. For a later, English, edition see Dibdin 1828. For a full discussion of this tradition see Baldwin 1985.

44. Quoted from Baldwin 1985, 125; for an extensive bibliography on Luther's religious interpretation of poverty see ibid., 133n41.

45. The print is by J. de Visscher after a peasant interior by Van Ostade; on this see Schnackenburg (1981, 58), whose modern German translation differs from mine. The seventeenth-century Dutch text reads,

Siet ons werck met soetheyt spillen.
In schijn van zulcke wonder grillen.
Doch houden echter met de sin
Ons kindje soet, en niet te min
Soo houden wij ons slechte kluys
voor 't prachte van een prachtich huys.

See also Slatkes [LJS] in Athens 1994, 177–178.

46. Schama 1987, 481–561, has an entire chapter on these discourses entitled "In the Republic of Children." The literature on the ideology of the family in the Dutch Republic is extensive; see Haks 1982; Groenendijk 1984; and Franits 1993.

47. Bedaux 1990, 109–160.

48. Unfortunately, these aspects of the relationship between parents and their children are discussed separately in the otherwise useful essay with bibliography by Noordman and Van Setten 1988, 141–162.

49. See note 19 above. See also the discussions of Elias in the essays by Franits and Rosenthal in Athens 1996.

50. Elias 1978, 53–54.

51. Ibid.

52. *Pater Familias* (B.33). See Athens 1994, 174–178, cat. nos. 84 and 85.

53. Schnackenburg 1981, vol. 1, p. 90, cat. nos. 49, 50, and ill. in vol. 2, p. 26; London, Brod Gallery, and London British Museum, Department of Prints and Drawings, respectively.

54. The Copenhagen drawing by Rembrandt tellingly known as *The Widower*, that is, a father raising a child without a mother, is cited by Slatkes [LJS] in Athens 1994, 177. A similar drawing of about 1643 in the Ashmolean Museum in Oxford, inv. no. P.172, by Isack van Ostade of a father feeding a child on his lap (Schnackenburg 1981, cat. no. 509, discussed in 1:177 and ill. in 2:214) is a more likely source for his brother's conception. See also note 21, above, for related images in the drawing oeuvres of Isack and Adriaen van Ostade.

55. For a number of essays on this important sociological phenomenon see Babcock 1978.

56. The phrase is from her important essay, "Women on Top: Symbolic Sexual Inversion and Political Disorder in Early Modern Europe," in Davis 1975, 124–151.

57. The full title of the latter is *Het leven en bedriff van Jan de Wasser en zijn wijf.* See de Meyer 1962, 428–431, 495–501; Dresen-Coenders 1988a, 73–84; 1988b, esp. pp. 25–45.

58. Schnackenburg 1981, cat. nos. 55 and 131, respectively. The earlier drawing is in Frankfurt am Main, Städelsches Kunstinstitut, inv. no. 901. It is the preparatory drawing for the painting listed as HdG 481a, which is known today only through the engraving by Jan de Visscher. For a discussion of this engraving see Stone-Ferrier in Lawrence 1983, 62–64, cat. no. 8. The later drawing is in Budapest, the Hungarian National Museum of Fine Arts, inv. no. 1555.

59. Franits 1993, 30, 71–76. There are some other examples of men spinning in a domestic setting by, for example, Jacob Ochtervelt and Brekelenkam, but they do not include children. For Ochtervelt see Kuretsky 1979, 59–60, cat. no. 17, and p. 192, fig. 142; and for Brekelenkam see Lasius 1992, 97–98, cat. nos. 59 and 61, ill. pl. 10, and color plate iv.

60. Yet even here I cannot agree with Stone-Ferrier (in Lawrence 1983, 64) that the wife and child in the etching after Van Ostade are mocking the husband in their laughter. The mother is also actively working, and their joint familial happiness seems to be the point of the inscription.

61. Although old age was the subject of a recent exhibition and catalog in Brunswick (1993), its ideological implications were not addressed.

62. De Brune 1624/1970, 318–322, emblem xliv.

63. The *Triumph of Death*, engraved by Galle after Wierix, shows the thread from a distaff being cut. This detail is discussed in Van Marle 1931–1932, 2:116. P. C. Hooft also uses the metaphor when he writes, "Gebrujkt uw leven ende spint den soeten draedt van een gelukkigh gelejde jeugd tot de grisheit toe" [Use life and spin the sweet thread from a happy youth to old age]. See "Spinnen" in *WNT* 1882–1926, vol. 14, col. 2833.

64. Quoted in the entry by S. William Pelletier [SWP] in Athens 1994, 229, cat. nos. 111 and 112.

65. For a history of St. Joseph's positive role in Northern art see Hahn 1986, 54–65. See also Schwartz 1975, 58–68.

66. See Schwartz 1975 for fifteenth-century examples in paintings and in mystery plays. Further examples are given in Foster 1978, 106.

67. See Schwartz 1975, 60. See also Baldwin 1985.

68. St. Bernard, quoted in Schwartz 1975, 62.

69. Quoted in ibid., 63.

70. I wish to thank Walter Liedtke for bringing this important seventeenth-century example to my attention.

71. *Saying Grace* (B.34). See Athens 1994, 179–183, cat. nos. 86 and 87.

72. The two primary articles are Franits 1986, 36–49; and Van Thiel 1987, 90–149.

73. Schnackenburg 1981, cat. no. 510, signed and dated 1644, Haarlem, Teyler Foundation, inv. no. P.82. See 1:177 and ill. in 2:215.

74. For Jan Steen and a discussion of this subject in Dutch art where other examples are cited see Philadelphia 1983, 29–31.

75. This phenomenon has been documented by de Vries, Montias, and others. For a discussion of the relationship between these images and the new prosperity achieved by some Dutch peasants see Stone-Ferrier in Lawrence 1983, 70.

76. Translation taken from Philadelphia 1983, 31n5.

Drie dingen wensch ick en niet meer
voor al te minnen Godt den heer
geen overvloed van Ryckdoms schat
maer wens om tgeen de wyste badt
Een eerlyck leven op dit dal
in dese drie bestaet het al.

77. See Duncan 1993, 2–26, 27–56.

CHAPTER 9. Vermeer's Women

1. A shorter version of this paper was initially given at the symposium "New Vermeer Studies," sponsored by the Center for Advanced Study of the Visual Arts, National Gallery and the University of Maryland at College Park.

2. This idea has most recently been discussed by Franits 1993. In his work he cites the relevant previous bibliography on domesticity and Dutch genre painting. For a more sophisticated discussion of the gendered and sexual implications in nineteenth-century images of domestic spaces see the classic chapter "Modernity and the Spaces of Femininity" in Pollock 1988, 50–90.

3. The art historian who is most fully responsible for this line of thinking is E. de Jongh. His articles and exhibition catalogs have spawned a whole generation of iconologists of female morality. His ideas have recently been restated in de Jongh 1995.

4. Philadelphia 1984.

5. Washington 1995–1996.

6. For the art historian as a special-case spectator see Holly 1990, esp. 385–388.

7. In Washington 1995–1996, 34.

8. Renger 1970.

9. Foucault 1980, 12.

10. Ibid., 17.

11. Ibid., 10.

12. See Diamond and Quinby 1988. For a feminist interpretation that brilliantly critiques the methods of Lacan and Foucault see Bal 1991.

13. These images are tangentially related to the discourse of the *omgekeerde wereld* (topsy-turvy world) often related to similar images of the period, sometimes grouped together under the name "power of women topos." See Davis 1975, 124–151; and Dresen-Coenders 1988a, 73–84.

14. Tagg 1988, 99.

15. Van de Pol 1990.

16. This seems more fruitful than postulating some form of collective hypocrisy on the part of the Dutch art consumer, a position first proposed and consistently held by Schama (1979; 1980; and 1987).

17. See Renger 1970, 132; Raupp 1984, 311–328; and Chapman 1990, 118.

18. The complex problem of self-image (as opposed to self-portrait) projected in this painting must be saved for another study. Briefly, these paintings have in common the presentation of a certain persona shared by some Northern Netherlandish artists, which is ultimately unclassical in its orientation and which projected the notion of the creative man as a knave or rogue and as a sexual male. He depicts himself as someone who lives on the periphery of ordered society and therefore can grab life with full gusto. I have elsewhere suggested the progressive identification of not only Northern artists but also Netherlandish culture in general with illicit sexuality as a component of their culturally constructed identification as presented to the "outside world." This was part of the articulation of what Benedict Anderson (1991) has called the "imagined community."

19. The description of Vermeer's painting in 1696, which Blankert in Washington 1995–1996, 35, calls its "title," are, for him, enough "proof that this beautiful dreamer is a direct descendent of the indecorously sleeping woman in a dingy inn in earlier paintings by Jacob Duck (c. 1600–1667)."

20. See Salomon 1998, 76–78, fig. 61.

21. For examples of the offer of wine as female sexuality in sixteenth-century Netherlandish love songs see Renger 1985, 40–41.

22. All five are reproduced and discussed in Mund 1980. See page 71 of that volume for the proposed dating.

23. For the open tankard as a reference to female sexuality in Netherlandish art and literature see Renger 1985, 40–41.

24. Ay laet staen, tis verloren
    mijn Borse ghegrepen
    Ghy hebtse gheleecht
    en mijn pijp al uuyt ghepepe.

The Dutch is quoted from Renger 1985, 39; the translation is mine and differs slightly from Renger's German translation.

25. I have made this point in my 1993 paper "Vanishing Acts; Male Narrativity and the Rhetoric of the Bordello," given at the conference "Questioning the Power of Netherlandish Painting," organized by the Historians of Netherlandish Art, Boston, Wellesley, Worcester.

26. Washington 1995–1996, 114–119.

27. For the tradition of low-class figures smiling broadly and showing their teeth in Lombard painting see Meijer 1971, esp. fig. 3. Lombard School (sixteenth century), *Four Figures and a Cat*, location unknown. For a general discussion see Thomas 1991. See also Hessel Miedema's various responses to Svetlana Alpers, where Miedema talks about laughter as a lower-class activity, in Miedema 1977, and, esp., 1981, 206–208.

28. Caroto's painting is illustrated in Lavin 1994, fig. 279.

29. Blankert notes that even Vermeer's *Music Lesson*, in the Frick Collection, New York, where the man was identified in the 1696 auction catalog as a "Monsieur," it is not clear whether he is meant to be understood as an instructor or as an older suitor. See Washington 1995–1996, 37.

30. See the illustration in de Lairesse 1740, 55.

Bibliography

Adams, Ann Jensen. 1998. *Rembrandt's "Bathsheba Reading King David's Letter."* Cambridge.

Ainsworth, Maryan. 1994. "The Art of Petrus Christus." In *Petrus Christus: Renaissance Master of Bruges.* Exh. cat., 43–51. Metropolitan Museum of Art. New York.

Alciati, Andrea. 1621 and 1626. *Emblemata.* Padua.

Alpers, Svetlana. 1975–1976. "Realism as a Comic Mode: Low-Life Painting Seen Through Bredero's Eyes." *Simiolus* 8:115–144.

———. 1976. "Describe or Narrate? A Problem in Realistic Representation." *New Literary History* 8:15–41.

———. 1978–1979. "Taking Pictures Seriously: A Reply to Hessel Miedema." *Simiolus* 10:46–50.

———. 1983. *The Art of Describing.* Chicago.

Amman, Jost. 1586/1872. *The Theatre of Women.* Designed by Jobst Ammon [*sic*], ed. Alfred Aspland. Repr. Manchester.

———. 1588/1880. *Kartenspielbuch.* Nuremberg. Repr. Munich.

Amsterdam. 1976. *Rijksmuseum. Tot Lering en Vermaak.* By E. de Jongh et al.

Anderson, Benedict. 1991. *Imagined Communities.* London.

Appian. 1913. *Roman History. The Civil Wars.* Trans. Horace White. London.

Athens. 1994. Georgia Museum of Art. *Adriaen van Ostade: Etchings of Peasant Life in Holland's Golden Age,* ed. Patricia Phagan.

———. 1996. Georgia Museum of Art. *Images of Women in Seventeenth-Century Dutch Art: Domesticity and the Representation of the Peasant,* ed. Patricia Phagan.

Babcock, Barbara A. 1978. *The Reversible World: Symbolic Inversion in Art and Society.* Ithaca.

Babiæ, G. 1968. "L'image symbolique de la 'porte fermée' à Saint-Clément d'Ohrid." In *Synthronon: Art et archéologie de la fin de l'Antiquité et du moyen âge, Recueil d'études,* ed. A. Grabar et al., 145–151. Paris.

Bakhtin, Mikhail. 1984. *Rabelais and His World.* Trans. Hélène Iswolsky. Bloomington.

Bal, Mieke. 1991. *Reading "Rembrandt": Beyond the Word and Image Opposition.* Cambridge and New York.

———. 1994. *On Meaning-Making: Essays in Semiotics.* Sonoma, Calif.

———. 1996. "Beeldangst. De intolerantie van de iconografie." *Filosofie Magazine* 5, no. 10:12–13.

———. 1999. *Quoting Caravaggio: Contemporary Art, Preposterous History.* Chicago.

Bal, Mieke, and Norman Bryson. 1991. "Semiotics and Art History." *Art Bulletin* 73, no. 2:74–108.

Baldwin, Robert W. 1985. "'On earth we are all beggars, as Christ himself was'; The Protestant Background of Rembrandt's Imagery of Poverty, Disability, and Begging." *Konsthistorisk Tidskrift* 54:122–135.

Bandmann, Günter. 1960. *Melancholie und Musik; Ikonographische Studien.* Cologne.

Barasch, Moshe. 1985. *Theories of Art: From Plato to Winckelmann.* New York.

Barnouw, J. J. 1914. "Vermeer's zoogenaamd 'Novum Testamentum.'" *Oud-Holland* 32:50–54.

Barocchi, Paola. 1960. *Trattati D'Arte Del Cinquecento, Fra Manierismo e Controriforma.* 3 vols. Bari.

Barthes, Roland. 1982/1991. "The Reality Effect." In *French Literary Theory Today: A Reader,* ed. Tzvetan Todorov, trans. R. Carter, 11–17. New York.

Bartsch. 1981. *The Illustrated Bartsch: Italian Masters of the Seventeenth Century,* ed. John T. Spike. New York.

Bastelaer, René van, and George H. de Loo. 1906. *Peter Bruegel L'Ancien; Son Oeuvre et Son Temps.* Brussels.

————. 1992. *The Prints of Pieter Bruegel the Elder; Catalogue Raisonné,* new ed., trans. and revised by Susan Fargo Gilchrist. San Francisco.

Bedaux, Jan. 1990. "Discipline for Innocence: Metaphors for Education in Seventeenth Century Dutch Painting." In *Reality of Symbols.* The Hague.

Berdini, Paolo. 1998. "Women Under the Gaze: A Renaissance Geneology." *Art History* 21, no. 4:565–590.

Biesboer, Pieter. 1993. "Judith Leyster: Painter of 'Modern Figures.'" In *Judith Leyster: A Dutch Master and Her World.* Exh. cat. by James A. Welu and Pieter Biesboer, 75–92. Worcester Art Museum. Worcester.

Bizot, Pierre. 1688. *Histoire Metallique de la Republic de Hollande.* Amsterdam.

Blankert, Albert, with Rob Ruurs and Willem L. van de Watering. 1978. *Vermeer of Delft.* Oxford.

Blunt, Anthony. 1940. *Artistic Theory in Italy, 1450–1600.* Oxford.

Bode, Wilhelm. 1924. *Adriaen Brouwer sein Leben und seine Werke.* Berlin.

Bode, W., and A. Bredius. 1890. "Der Haarlemer Maler Johannes Molenaer in Amsterdam." *Jahrbuch der Königlich Preussischen Kunstsammlungen* 2:65–78.

Bodin, Jean. 1583. *Method for the Easy Comprehension of History.* Trans. Beatrice Reynolds. New York.

Bol, Laurens J. 1982–1983. "Adriaen Pietersz. van de Venne, schilder en teyckenaar VIII. Grisaille schilderingen." *Tableau* 4:54–63.

————. 1983. "Adriaen Pietersz. van de Venne: Allegorisch-historische schilderijen." *Tableau* 5:276–283.

————. 1984 "Adriaen van de Venne als illustrator." *Tableau* 6:69–77.

Bonger, H. 1978. *Leven en Werk van Dirk Volckertsz. Coornhert.* Amsterdam.

Borger, Ellen. 1996. *Geschilderde wachtlokalen. De Hollandse kortegaard uit de Gouden Eeuw.* Zwolle.

Böse, J. H. 1985. "Had de mensch met één vrou niet connen leven . . . " *Prostitutie in de literatuur van de zeventiende eeuw.* Zutphen.

Boström, Kjell. 1949. "Peep-Show or Case?" *Kunsthistorische Mededeelingen van het Rijksbureau voor Kunsthistorische Documentatie* 4:21–24.

Brantôme, the Seigneur (Pierre de Bourdeille). 1666/1901. *Lives of the Fair and Gallant Ladies.* Vol. 1. Trans. A. B. Allinson. Repr. Leiden.

Braun, Karel. 1980. *Alle tot nu bekende schilderijen van Jan Steen.* Rotterdam.

Brière-Misme, Clotilde. 1950. "Un Petit Maître hollandais, Cornelis Bisschop (1630–1674)." *Oud-Holland* 65:139–151.

Brinkmann, Bodo. 1997. *Die Flämische Buchmalerie am ende des Burgunderreichs; Der Meister des Dresdener Gebetsbuch und die Miniaturisten seiner Zeit.* Brepols.

Brune, Johan de. 1624/1970. *Emblemata of zinne-werck*. Amsterdam. Repr. Soest.

Brunswick. 1978. Herzog Anton Ulrich-Museum. *Die Sprache der Bilder. Realität und Bedeutung in der niederländischen Malerei des 17.Jahrhunderts*. Exh. cat. by R. Klessman.

———. 1993. *Bilder von alten Menschen in der niederländischen und deutschen Kunst 1550 bis 1750*. Exh. cat. by Thomas Döring.

Bruyn, J. 1978. "Letters to the Editor." *Art Bulletin* 60:741–742.

Bryson, Norman. 1983. *Vision and Painting: The Logic of the Gaze*. New Haven.

Burke, Peter. 1974. *Venice and Amsterdam*. London.

Carroll, Margaret. 1987. "Peasant Festivity and Political Identity in the Sixteenth Century." *Art History* 10:294.

Carstensen, Richard, and Marielene Putscher. 1971. "Ein Bild von Vermeer in medizinhistorischer Sicht." *Deutsches Aerzteblatt-Aertzliche Mitteilungen* 68, no. 52: 16.

Cats, Jacob. 1632. *Spiegel van den Ouden ende Nieuwe Tijdt*. The Hague.

Cazelles, Raymond, and Johannes Rathofer. 1988. *Illuminations of Heaven and Earth: The Glories of the "Très Riches Heures du Duc de Berry."* Ithaca.

Chamberlin, Roy B., and Herman Feldman. 1965. *The Dartmouth Bible: An Abridgement of the King James Version, with Aids to Its Understanding as History and Literature, and as a Source of Religious Experience*. Boston.

Chapman, Perry. 1990. *Rembrandt's Self-Portraits: A Study in Seventeenth-Century Identity*. Princeton.

———. 1993. "Persona and Myth in Houbraken's Life of Jan Steen." *Art Bulletin* 75:147.

Clarke, John R. 1993. "The Warren Cup and the Contexts for Representations of Male-to-Male Lovemaking in Augustan and Early Julio-Claudian Art." *Art Bulletin* 75, no. 2:275–294.

Coornhert, Dirck V. 1585. *Recht ghebruyck ende misbruyck van tijdelijcke have*. Leiden.

Cropper, Elizabeth. 1986. "The Beauty of Woman: Problems in the Rhetoric of Renaissance Portraiture." In *Rewriting the Renaissance*, ed. Margaret W. Ferguson, Maureen Quilligan, and Nancy Vickers. Chicago.

Culler, Jonathan. 1988. "The Semiotics of Tourism." In *Framing the Sign: Criticism and Its Institutions*. Norman, OK.

Cunnar, Eugene R. 1990. "The Viewer's Share: Three Sectarian Readings of Vermeer's *Woman with a Balance*." *Exemplaria* 2, no. 2:501–536.

Daniëls, G. L. M. 1977–1978. "Maria felix coeli porta: Mariasymbolik." *Antiek* 12:257–258.

Davis, Natalie Zemon. 1975. *Society and Culture in Early Modern France: Eight Essays by Natalie Zemon Davis*. Stanford, CA.

———. 1978. "Women on Top: Symbolic Sexual Inversion and Political Disorder in Early Modern Europe." In *The Reversible World: Symbolic Inversion in Art and Society*, ed. Barbara A. Babcock, 147–192. Ithaca.

Delft. 1981. Stedelijk Museum het Prinsenhof. *De Stad Delft. Cultuur en maatschappij van 1572 tot 1667*.

Deursen, A. Th. Van. 1991. *Plain Lives in the Golden Age: Popular Culture, Religion, and Society in Seventeenth-Century Holland*. Trans. Maarten Ultee. New York.

Diamond, Irene, and Lee Quinby. 1988. "On Initiating Dialogue." In *Feminism and Foucault: Reflections of Resistance*, ed. Irene Diamond and Lee Quinby, 3–60. Boston.

Dibdin, Thomas Frognall, trans. 1828. *Of the Imitation of Christ.* London.

Dresen-Coenders, Lene. 1977. "De strijd om de broek; De verhouding man/vrouw in het begin van de moderne tijd (1450–1630)." *De Revisor* 4:29–37, 77nn.

———. 1988a. "De omgekeerde wereld; tot lering en vermaak." In *Helse en hemelse vrouwen: Shrikbeelden en voorbeelden van de vrouw in de christelijke cultuur (1400–1600)*, ed. Marlies Caron, 73–84. Utrecht.

———. 1988b. *Helse en hemelse, vrouwenmacht omstreeks 1500.* Nijmegen.

Duncan, Carol. 1993. *The Aesthetics of Power. Essays in Critical Art History.* Cambridge.

Duverger, Erik. 1972. "Abraham van Diepenbeeck en Gonzales Coques aan het werk voor de stadhouder Frederik Hendrik, prins van Oranje." *Jaarboek van het Koninklijk Museum voor Schone Kunsten*, 181–237. Antwerp.

Elias, Norbert. 1978. *The History of Manners.* Vol. 1 of *The Civilizing Process.* Trans. Edmund Jephcott. New York.

———. 1982. *Power and Civility.* Vol. 2 of *The Civilizing Process.* Trans. Edmund Jephcott. New York.

Enklaar, D. Th. 1937. *Varende luyden: Studiën over de middeleeuwsche groepen van onmaatschappelijken in de Nederlanden.* Assen.

———. 1940. *Uit Uilenspiegel's kring.* Assen.

Ertz, Klaus. 2000. *Pieter Brueghel der Jüngere (1564–1637/8); Die Gemälde mit Kritischen Oeuvrekatalog*, 1:76–77. Lingen.

Faggin, G. 1965. "The Genre Painter Marten van Cleef." *Oud-Holland* 1:34–47.

Ferino Pagden, Sylvia. 1989. "I Due Amanti di Leningrado." In Accademia Nazionale Virgiliana. *Giulio Romano. Atti del Convegno Internazionale di Studi su "Giulio Romano e l'espansione europea del Rinascimento,"* 227–236. Mantua.

Fischer, Pieter. 1975. *Music in Paintings of the Low Countries in the Sixteenth and Seventeenth Centuries.* Amsterdam.

Foster, Mary Bolger. 1978. "The Iconography of St. Joseph in Netherlandish Art, 1400–1550." PhD diss., University of Kansas, Lawrence.

Foucault, Michel. 1980. *The History of Sexuality. Volume I: An Introduction.* Trans. Robert Hurley. New York.

Franits, Wayne. 1986. "The Family at Grace: A Theme in Dutch Art of the Seventeenth Century." *Simiolus* 16:36–49.

———. 1992. "Housewives and Their Maids in Dutch Seventeenth-Century Art." In *Politics, Gender, and the Arts: Women, the Arts, and Society*, ed. Ronald Dotterer and Susan Bowers, 112–129. Selinsgrove, PA.

———. 1993. *Paragons of Virtue: Women and Domesticity in Seventeenth-Century Dutch Art.* New York.

Freedberg, David. 1971. "Johannes Molanus on Provocative Paintings." *Journal of the Warburg and Courtauld Institutes* 34:229–245.

———. 1989. *The Prints of Pieter Bruegel the Elder.* Tokyo

———. 1991. "Science, Commerce, and Art: Neglected Topics at the Juncture of History and Art History." In *Art in History / History in Art: Studies in Seventeenth-Century Dutch Culture*, ed. David Freedberg and Jan de Vries, 377–429. Santa Monica, CA.

Fronsperger, Leonhardt. 1573–1578. *Kriegsordnung und Regimentsampt.* Frankfurt.

Fuchs, Eduard. 1909. *Illustierte Sittengeschichte.* Vol. 1. Berlin.

———. 1928/1973. *Die Frau in der Karikatur. Sozialgeschichte der Frau.* Munich. Repr. Frankfurt.

Gelder, H. E. van. 1948. "Perspectieven bij Vermeer." *Kunsthistorische Mededeelingen van het Rijksbureau voor Kunsthistorische Documentatie* 3:34–36.

Gent, Lucy. 1981. *Picture and Poetry, 1560–1620.* Leamington Spa, Warwickshire.

Geyl, Peter. 1961–1964. *The Netherlands in the 17th Century.* 2 vols. London.

Girouard, Mark. 1985. *Cities and People: A Social and Architectural History.* New Haven.

Goedde, Lawrence. 1987. *Tempest and Shipwreck in Dutch and Flemish Art: Convention, Rhetoric, and Interpretation.* University Park, PA.

Gombrich, E. H. 1966. "The Renaissance Theory of Art and the Rise of Landscape." In *Norm and Form: Studies in the Art of the Renaissance.* Cambridge.

Gowing, Laurence. 1952. *Vermeer.* London.

Grand-Carteret, John. 1928. *L'Histoire, La Vie, Les Moeurs et la Curiosité par l'Image, le Pamphlet et le Document (1450–1900).* Paris.

Grand Rapids, Michigan. 1999. Grand Rapids Art Museum. *A Moral Compass: Seventeenth and Eighteenth Century Painting in the Netherlands.* Cat. with contributions by Arthur Wheelock Jr. et al.

Grimme, Ernst Gunther. 1975. *Johannes Vermeer.* Amerongen.

Groenendijk, L. F. 1984. *De nadere reformatie van het gezin; De visie van Petrus Wittewrongel op de christelijke huishouding.* Dordrecht.

Groot, Cornelis Wilhelmus de. 1952. *Jan Steen: Beeld en woord.* Utrecht.

Gudlaugsson, S. J. 1945. *De Komedianten bij Jan Steen en zijn tijdgenoten.* The Hague.

———. 1959–1960. *Gerard Ter Borch.* 2 vols. The Hague.

Haeger, Barbara. 1988. "Philip Galle's Engravings After Maarten van Heemskerk's *Parable of the Prodigal Son.*" *Oud-Holland* 102, no. 2:127–140.

The Hague. 1974. Mauritshuis. Koninklijk Kabinet van Schilderijen. *Gerard Ter Borch, Zwolle 1617–Deventer 1681.*

Hahn, Cynthia. 1986. "'Joseph Will Perfect, Mary Enlighten and Jesus Save Thee': The Holy Family as Marriage Model in the Mérode Triptych." *Art Bulletin* 58, no. 1:54–65.

Haks, Donald. 1982. *Huwelijk en gezin in Holland in de 17de en 18de eeuw.* Assen.

Harbison, Craig. 1976. *The Last Judgment in Sixteenth-Century Northern Europe: A Study in the Relation Between Art and the Reformation.* New York.

Haverkamp-Begemann, E. 1959. *Willem Buytewech.* Amsterdam.

Hecht, Peter. 1984. Review of London Royal Academy, "Masters of Seventeenth-Century Dutch Genre Painting." *Burlington Magazine,* October 1984, 648–651.

Held, Julius. 1961. "Flora, Goddess and Courtesan." In *De Artibus Opuscula XL. Essays in Honor of Erwin Panofsky,* ed. Millard Meiss, 201–218. New York.

Helsinki. 1995. The Museum of Foreign Art Sinebrychoff, Helsinki. *The Ter Borchs Meet Again.* Cat. by Marja Supinen.

Henkel, Arthur, and Albrecht Schöne. 1967. *Emblemata, Handbuch zur Sinnbildkunst des XVI. und XVII. Jahrhunderts.* Stuttgart.

Hermesdorf, B. H. D. 1977. *De herberg in de Nederlanden: Een blik in de beschavings-geschiedenis.* Arnheim.

Hinz, Berthold. 1973. "Das Familienbildnis des J. M. Molenaer in Haarlem: Aspekte zur Ambivalenz der Porträtfunktion," *Städel-Jahrbuch,* Neue Folge, 207–217.

Hollstein, F. W. H. 1968. *German Engravings, Etchings, and Woodcuts.* Ed. K. G. Boon and R. W. Scheller. 39 vols. Amsterdam.

Holly, Michael Ann. 1990. "Past Looking." *Critical Inquiry* 16, no. 2:371–396.

Houbraken, A. 1721. *De groote schouburgh der nederlantsche konstschilders en schilderessen.* 3 vols. Amsterdam.

Howell, Martha. 1986. *Women, Production, and Patriarchy in Late Medieval Cities.*
Chicago.

d'Hulst, R. A. 1974. *Jordaens Drawings I.* London.

Ierlant, M. A. Ghering van. 1988. *Mode in Prent, 1550–1914.* The Hague.

Iser, Wolfgang. 1978. *The Act of Reading: A Theory of Aesthetic Response.* Baltimore.

Johnson, Richard. 1993. "Towards a Cultural Theory of the Nation: A British-Dutch
Dialogue." In *Images of the Nation: Different Meanings of Dutchness, 1870–1940,*
ed. A. Galema, B. Henkes, and H. te Velde. Amsterdam.

de Jongh, E. 1967. *Sinne-en minnebeelden in de schilderkunst van de zeventiende eeuw.*
Utrecht.

————. 1968–1969. "Erotica in Vogelperspectief; Die Dubbelzinningheid van een
reeks 17de eeuwse genrevoorstellingen." *Simiolus* 3:22–74.

————. 1971. "Realisme en schijnrealisme in de Hollandse schilderkunst van de
zeventiende eeuw." Brussels, Paleis voor Schone Kunsten. *Rembrandt en zijn tijd,*
143–194. Brussels.

————. 1973. "Vermommingen van Vrouw Wereld in de 17de eeuw." *Album
Amicorum J. G. van Gelder,* 198–206. The Hague.

————. 1974. "Grape Symbolism in Paintings of the 16th and 17th centuries."
Simiolus 7:166–191.

————. 1975–1976. "Pearls of Virtue and Pearls of Vice." *Simiolus* 8:69–97.

————. 1991. "Some Notes on Interpretation." In *Art in History/History in Art: Studies
in Seventeenth-Century Dutch Culture,* ed. David Freedberg and Jan de Vries, 119–138.
Santa Monica, CA.

————. 1995. *Kwesties van betekenis: Thema en motief in de Nederlandse schilderkunst
van de zeventiende eeuw.* Leiden.

Katzenellenbogen, Adolf. 1964. *Allegories of the Virtues and Vices in Medieval Art from
Early Christian Times to the Thirteenth Century.* New York.

Kelly, Joan. 1984. "Did Women Have a Renaissance?" In *Women, History, and Theory:
The Essays of Joan Kelly,* 19–50. Chicago.

Kemp, Martin, ed. 1989. *Leonardo on Painting.* New Haven.

Keyszelitz, Robert. 1956. "Der 'Clavis interpretandi' in der holländischen Malerei des
17. Jahrhunderts." Unpub. diss. Munich.

Kirschbaum, Engelbert. 1968–1972. *Lexicon der christlichen Ikonographie.* Vol. 3. Rome.

Klessman, R. 1960. "Die Anfänge des Bauerninterieur bei den Brüdern Ostade."
Jahrbuch der Berliner Museen 2:92–115.

Klibansky, Raymond, Erwin Panofsky, and Fritz Saxl. 1964. *Saturn and Melancholy:
Studies in the History of Natural Philosophy, Religion, and Art.* New York.

Kloek, Els. 1990. *Wie hij zij, man of wijf; Vrouwengeschiedenis en de vroegmoderne tijd:
Drie Leidse studies.* Hilversum.

————. 1993. "The Case of Judith Leyster: Exception or Paradigm?" In *Judith Leyster:
A Dutch Master and Her World.* Exh. cat., ed. James A. Welu and Pieter Biesboer.
Worcester Art Museum. Worcester.

Kok, M. A. 1981. "Het Katholiek leven binnen de stad Delft in de jaren 1572–1650."
De Stad Delft; cultuur en maatschappij van 1572 tot 1667, 108–112. Delft.

Köln, Belgishes Haus. 1981. *Wort und Bild, Buchkunst und Druckgraphik in den
Niederlanden im 16. and 17. Jahrhundert.* Cologne.

Koslow, Susan. 1975. "Frans Hals's Fisherboys: Exemplars of Idleness." *Art Bulletin*
62:418–432.

Kraus, Dorothy, and Henry Kraus. 1975. *The Hidden World of the Misericords.* New York.

Kren, Thomas. 1980. "Chi non vuol Baccho: Roeland van Laer's Burlesque Painting About Dutch Artists in Rome." *Simiolus* 11:63–80.

Kunstle, Karl. 1926–1928. *Ikonographie der christlichen Kunst.* 2 vols. Freiberg.

Kunzle, David. 1977. "Bruegel's Proverb Painting and the World Upside Down." *Art Bulletin* 59:197–202.

———. 1978a. "The World Upside Down: Iconography of a European Broadsheet Type." In *The Reversible World: Symbolic Inversion in Art and Society,* ed. Barbara A. Babcock. Ithaca.

———. 1978b. "Letters to the Editor. Reply to J. Bruyn." *Art Bulletin* 60:742.

Kuretsky, Susan Donahue. 1979. *The Paintings of Jacob Ochtervelt (1634–1682).* Montclair.

Lairesse, Gerard de. 1740. *Groot schilderboek.* Haarlem.

Lasius, Angelika. 1992. *Quiringh van Brekelenkam,* Doornspijk.

Lavin, Irving. 1994. *Past and Present.* Princeton.

Lawner, Lynne. 1987. *Lives of the Courtesans: Portraits of the Renaissance.* New York.

———. 1988. *I Modi: The Sixteen Pleasures. An Erotic Album of the Italian Renaissance. Giulio Romano, Marcantonio Raimondi, Pietro Aretino, and Count Jean-Frederic-Maximilien de Waldeck,* ed. and trans. from the Italian. Evanston.

Lawrence. 1983. Spencer Museum of Art, University of Kansas. *Dutch Prints of Daily Life: Mirrors of Life or Masks of Morals?* Cat. by Cynthia Lawrence.

Leipzig. 1973. Museum der bildenden Künste. *Altdeutsche und altniederländische Meister des 15. und 16. Jahrhunderts.*

Liedtke, Walter. 1984. *The Metropolitan Museum of Art.* Jack and Belle Linsky Collection, Metropolitan Museum of Art. New York.

Lloyd, G. E. R. 1966. *Polarity and Analogy: Two Types of Argumentation in Early Greek Thought.* Cambridge.

London. 1960. The National Gallery. *National Gallery Catalogues. The Dutch School.* Cat. by Neil MacLaren.

———. 1978. The National Gallery of Art. *Dutch Genre Painting.* Cat. by Christopher Brown.

Loon, Gerard van. 1732. *Histoire métallique des XVII Provinces des Pays-Bas.* The Hague.

Maeterlinck, L. 1910. *Le genre satirique, fantastique et licencieux dans la sculpture flamande et wallone.* Paris.

Mander, Carel van. 1604/1980. *Het Schilder-Boeck.* Haarlem. Repr. New York.

Mantua. 1989. Palazzo Ducale. *Giulio Romano.*

Marle, Raimond van. 1931–1932. *Iconographie de l'art profane au Moyen-Age et à la Renaissance.* 2 vols. The Hague.

Marlier, Georges. 1969. *Pierre Brueghel le jeune.* Brussels.

Marshall, Sherrin. 1987. *The Dutch Gentry, 1500–1650: Family, Faith, and Fortune.* Westport.

Martin, W. 1901. *Gerard Dou.* Munich.

———. 1954. *Jan Steen.* Amsterdam.

McFadden, George. 1982. *Discovering the Comic.* Princeton.

Meijer, Bert W. 1971. "Esempi del comico figurative nel rinasciment lombardo." *Arte Lombarda* 16:259–266.

Meiss, Millard. 1973. "Light as Form and Symbol in Some Fifteenth-Century Paintings." Repr. in *Renaissance Art*, ed. Creighton Gilbert. New York.

Meyer, G. M. de. 1989. *Min en onmin: Mannen en vrouwen over hun omgang aan het einde van de vijftiende eeuw*. Hilversum, Verloren.

Meyer, Maurits de. 1962. *De volks-en kinderprent in de Nederlanden: van de 15e tot de 20e eeuw*. Antwerp.

————. 1970. *Volksprenten in de Nederlanden, 1400–1900*. Amsterdam.

Michalski, Ernst. 1932. *Die Bedeutung der ästhetischen Grenze für die Methode der Kunstgeschichte*. Berlin.

Michigan. 1975–1976. University of Michigan Museum of Art. *Images of Love and Death in Late Medieval and Renaissance Art*. Essays by Clifton C. Olds and Ralph G. Williams.

Miedema, Hessel. 1977. "Realism and Comic Mode: The Peasant." *Simiolus* 9:205–219.

————. 1981. "Feestende boeren-lachende dorpers. Bij twee recente aanwinsten van het Rijksprentenkabinet." *Bulletin van het Rijksmuseum* 29:191–213.

Mirimonde, A. P. de. 1962. "La Musique dans les oeuvres hollandaises du Louvre." Pts. 1 and 2. *La Revue du Louvre* 12:123–138, 175–184.

————. 1964. "Les Concerts des muses chez les maîtres du Nord." *Gazette des Beaux-Arts* 63:129–158.

————. 1966–1967. "La Musique dans les allégories de l'amour." Pts. 1 and 2. *Gazette des Beaux-Arts* 68:265–290; 69:319–346.

Mitelli, Giuseppe Maria. 1678. *Proverbi figurati consecrati al principe Francesco Maria di Toscana*. Bologna.

Moiso-Diekamp, Cornelia. 1987. *Das Pendant in der holländischen Malerei des 17. Jahrhunderts*. Frankfurt am Main.

Monroy, Ernst Friedrich von. 1964. *Embleme und Emblembucher in den Niederländen, 1560–1630*. Utrecht.

Montias, John Michael. 1977. "New Documents on Vermeer and His Family." *Oud-Holland* 91:267–287.

————. 1980. "Vermeer and His Milieu: Conclusion of an Archival Study." *Oud-Holland* 94:44–62.

————. 1989. *Vermeer and His Milieu: A Web of Social History*. Princeton.

Mortier, Bianca M. du. 1991. ". . . Hier sietman Vrouwen van alderley Natien . . . ; Kostuumboeken bron voor de schilderkunst?" *Bulletin van het Rijksmuseum* 39, no. 4:401–413.

Moxey, Keith P. F. 1980. "Master E. S. and the Folly of Love." *Simiolus* 11:125–148.

————. 1982. "The Ship of Fools and the Idea of Folly in Netherlandish Literature of the Sixteenth Century." In *The Early Illustrated Book: Essays in Honor of Lessing J. Rosenwald*, ed. Sandra Hindman, 86–102. Washington.

————. 1989. *Peasants, Warriors, and Wives: Popular Imagery in the Reformation*. Chicago.

————. 1994. *The Practice of Theory: Poststructuralism, Cultural Politics, and Art History*. Ithaca.

Mund, Hélène. 1980. "La peinture de moeurs chez Pieter Huys." *Revue des archéologues et historiens d'art de Louvain* 13:64–73.

Naumann, Otto. 1981. *Frans van Mieris the Elder (1635–1681)*. 2 vols. Doornspijk.

Neurdenburg, Elisabeth. 1929. *Hendrick de Keyser, Beeldhouwer en Bouwmeester van Amsterdam*. Amsterdam.

Nevo, Ruth. 1963. *The Dial of Virtue: A Study of Poems on Affairs of State in the Seventeenth Century.* Princeton.

New York. 1994. The Metropolitan Museum of Art. *Petrus Christus: Renaissance Master of Bruges.* Cat. by Maryan W. Ainsworth with contributions by Maximiliaan P. J. Martens.

Nierop, H. F. K. van. 1984. *Van ridders tot regenten; De Hollandse adel in de zestiende en de eerste helft van de zeventiende eeuw.* The Hague.

Noordam, D. J. 1987. "Lust, last en plezier: Vier eeuwen seksualiteit in Nederland." In *Een kind onder het hart: Verloskunde, volksgeloff, gezin, seksualiteit en moraal vroeger en nu.* Exh. cat. Amsterdam Historish Museum. Amsterdam.

Noordman, Jan, and Henk van Setten. 1988. "De ontwikkeling van de ouder/kind-verhouding in het gezin." In *Vijf eeuwen gezinsleven: liefde, huwelijk en opvoeding in Nederland,* 141–162. Nijmegen.

Nora, Pierre. 1997. *Realms of Memory: The Construction of the French Past.* Vol. 2. Trans. Arthur Goldhammer. New York.

Oestreich, Gerard. 1982. *Neostoicism and the Rise of the Modern State.* Cambridge.

Otis, Leah Lydia. 1985. *Prostitution in Medieval Society: The History of an Urban Institution in Languedoc.* Chicago.

Owst, G. R. 1961. *Literature and Pulpit in Medieval England: A Neglected Chapter in the History of English Letters and of the English People.* New York.

Panofsky, Erwin. 1931. "Zwei Dürerprobleme (Der Sogenannte 'Traum des Doktors' und die Sogenannten 'Vier Apostel')." *Münchner Jahrbuch der bildenden Kunst,* Neue Folge, 8:1–48.

———. 1959. Review of *Attributs et symbols dan l'art profane, 1450–1600; dictionnaire d'une langage perdu,* vol. 1, by Guy de Tervarent. *Art Bulletin* 41:107–108.

———. 1971. *Early Netherlandish Painting; Its Origins and Character.* New York.

Pardo, Mary. 1993. "Artifice as Seduction in Titian." In *Sexuality and Gender in Early Modern Europe: Institutions, Texts, Images,* ed. James Grantham Turner. New York.

Paris. 1970–1971. Musée du Petit Palais. *Le Siècle de Rembrandt: Tableaux hollandais de collections publiques françaises.*

Parker, Andrew, Mary Russo, Doris Sommer, and Patricia Yaeger, eds. 1992. *Nationalisms and Sexualities.* New York.

de Pauw–de Veen, Lydia. 1969. *De begrippen 'schilder,' 'schilderij,' en 'schilderen' in de zeventiende eeuw.* Brussels.

Peacham, Henry. 1612/1973. *Minerva Britanna,* ed. John Horden. Menston.

Peer, A. J. J. M. van. 1959. "Rondom Jan Vermeer van Delft." *Oud-Holland* 74:240–245.

———. 1968. "Jan Vermeer van Delft, drie archiefvondsten." *Oud-Holland* 91:267–287.

Peter-Raupp, Hanna. 1980. *Die Ikonographie des Oranjezaal.* Hildesheim.

Petterson, Inar. 1987. "Amans Amanti Medicus: Die Ikonologie des Motivs Der Ärztliche Besuch." In *Holländische Genremalerei im 17. Jahrhundert,* ed. Henning Bock and Thomas W. Gaehtgens, 193–224. Berlin.

Philadelphia. 1983. Philadelphia Museum of Art. *Jan Steen: Comedy and Admonition.* Cat. by Peter C. Sutton with appendix by Marigene H. Butler.

———. 1984. Philadelphia Museum of Art. *Masters of Seventeenth Century Dutch Genre Painting.* Cat. by Peter C. Sutton et al.

Plato. 1930. *The Republic.* Trans. Paul Shorey. London.

Playter, Caroline. 1972. "Willem Duyster and Pieter Codde: The 'Duystere Werelt' of Dutch Genre Painting, c. 1625–1635." PhD diss., Cambridge.

Pleij, Herman. 1983. *Het gilde van de Blauwe Schuit: Literatuur, volksfest en burger-moraal in de late middeleeuwen.* Amsterdam.

Pol, Lotte C. van de. 1990. "Beeld en werkelijkheid van de prostitutie in de zeventiende eeuw." In *Soete minne en helsche boosheit; seksuele voorstellingen in Nederland, 1300–1850*, ed. Gert Hekma and Herman Roodenburg. Nijmegen.

———. 1992. "Prostitutie en de Amsterdamse burgerij: Eerbegrippen in een vroeg-moderne stedelijk samenleving." In *Cultuur en maatschappij in Nederland, 1500–1850: Een historisch-antropologisch perspectief,* ed. Peter te Boekhorst, Peter Burke, and Willem Frijhoff, 179–218. Amsterdam.

Pollock, Griselda. 1988. *Vision and Difference: Femininity, Feminism, and the Histories of Art.* London.

———. 1990. "Missing Women: Rethinking Early Thoughts on Images of Women." In *The Critical Image,* ed. Carol Squiers, 202–219. Seattle.

———. 1993. *Avant-Garde Gambits, 1888–1893: Gender and the Color of Art History.* New York.

———. 1998. *Mary Cassatt: Painter of Modern Women.* New York.

———. 1999. *Differencing the Canon: Feminist Desire and the Writing of Art's Histories.* London.

Pollock, Griselda, and Rozsika Parker. 1981. *Old Mistresses: Women, Art, and Ideology.* New York.

Price, J. L. 1974. *Culture and Society in the Dutch Republic During the 17th Century.* New York.

Raupp, H. J. 1984. *Untersuchungen zu Künstlerbildnis und Künstlerdarstellung in den Niederlanden im 17. Jahrhundert.* Hildesheim.

———. 1986. *Bauernsatiren: Entstehung und Entwicklung des baüerlichen Genres in der deutschen und niederländischen Kunst, ca. 1470–1570.* Niederzier.

Regteren Altena, I. Q. van. 1949. "Hoge Kunst of Speilerei?" *Kunsthistorische Mededeelingen van het Rijksbureau voor Kunsthistorische Documentatie* 4:24.

Renger, Konrad. 1970. *Lockere Gesellschaft: Zur Ikonographie des Verlorenen Sohnes und von Wirtshausszenen in der niederländischen Malerei.* Berlin.

———. 1972. "Bettler und Bauern bei Pieter Bruegel d.Ä." *Sitzungberichte der kunstgeschichtliche Gesellschaft zu Berlin* 20:9–16.

———. 1976–1978. "Sine Cerere et Baccho Friget Venus." *Gentse Bijdragen tot de Kunstgeschiednenis* 24:190–203.

———. 1985. "Alte Liebe, gleich und ungleich: Zu einem satirischen Bildthema bei Jan Massys." In *Netherlandish Mannerism: Papers Given at a Symposium in National-museum Stockholm, September 21–22, 1984,* ed. Görel Cavalli-Björkman, 35–46. Stockholm.

———. 1986. *Adriaen Brouwer und das niederländische Bauerngenre, 1600–1660.* Munich.

Ripa, Cesare. 1611/1976. *Iconologia.* Padua. Repr. New York.

———. 1644/1971. *Iconologia of Uytbeeldinghe des Verstands.* Trans. D. P. Pers. Amsterdam. Repr. Soest.

Rosand, Ellen. 1977. "Music in the Myth of Venice." *Renaissance Quarterly* 30:511–537.

Rosenberg, Pierre. 1988. *Fragonard.* Exh. cat., Metropolitan Museum of Art. New York.

Rosenthal, Earl. 1971. "'Plus Ultra, Non Plus Ultra.' and the Columnar Device of Emperor Charles V." *Journal of the Warburg and Courtauld Institutes* 34:204–228.

Rossen, Maaaike van. 1983. "De poort in de muur: Vrouwenkloosters onder regel van Caesarius." *Vrouwen in de geschiedenis van het Christendom. Jaarboek voor vrouwengeschiedenis*, ed. Els Kloek, Tineke van Loosbroek, Jeske Reis, and Yvonne Scherf, no. 4:40–45. Nijmegen.

Rotterdam and Paris. 1975. Museum Boymansvan Beuningen and Institut Néerlandais. *Willem Buytewech, 1591–1624*. Intro. E. Haverkamp-Begemann.

Rudolph, Herbert. 1938. "'Vanitas': Die Bedeutung mittelalterlicher und humanistischer Bildinhalte in der niederländischen Malerei des 17. Jahrhunderst." In *Festschrift Wilhelm Pinder zum 60. Geburstag*, 405–433. Leipzig.

Salomon, Nanette. 1985. "A Woman's Place: The Queen in *Las Meninas*." *Notes in the History of Art* 4 (winter/spring): 72–74.

——. 1998. *Jacob Duck and the Gentrification of Dutch Genre Painting*. Doornspijk.

Saur, K. G. 1998. *Allgemeines Künstler-Lexicon*. Vol. 19. Munich-Leipzig.

Schama, Simon. 1979. "The Unruly Realm: Appetite and Restraint in Seventeenth-Century Holland." *Daedalus* 108:103–123.

——. 1980. "Wives and Wantons: Versions of Womanhood in 17th-Century Dutch Art." *Oxford Art Journal* 3:5–13.

——. 1987. *The Embarrassment of Riches: An Interpretation of Dutch Culture in the Golden Age*. New York.

Schnackenburg, Bernhard. 1981. *Adriaen van Ostade, Isack van Ostade: Zeichnungen und Aquarelle*. 2 vols. Hamburg.

——. 1984. "Das Bild des bäuerlichen Lebens bei Adriaen van Ostade." In *Wort und Bild in der niederländischen Kunst und Literatur des 16. und 17. Jahrhunderts*, 30–42. Erftstadt.

Schneider, Hans. 1921. "Der Maler Jan Tengnagel." *Oud-Holland* 39:13–27.

Schubert, Dietrick. 1970. *Die Gemälde des Braunschweiger Monogrammisten; ein Beitrag zur Geschichte der niederländischen Malerei des 16. Jahrhunderts*. Cologne.

Schwartz, Sheila. 1975. "The Iconography of the Rest on the Flight into Egypt." PhD diss., New York University.

Sedgwick, Eve Kosofsky. 1985. *Between Men: English Literature and Male Homosocial Desire*. New York.

Seznec, J. 1972. *The Survival of the Pagan Gods: The Mythological Tradition and Its Place in Renaissance Humanism and Art*. Princeton.

Silver, Lawrence A. 1974. "The 'Ill-Matched Pair' by Quinten Massys." *Studies in the History of Art* 6:104–124.

Slatkes, Leonard J. 1981. *Vermeer and His Contemporaries*. New York.

Smith, Susan Louise. 1978. "'To Women's wiles I fell': The Power of Women 'topos' and the Development of Medieval Secular Art." PhD diss., University of Pennsylvania.

Snoep-Reitsma, Adrienne Elizabeth. 1975. *Verschuivende betekenissen van zeventiende eeuwse nederlandse genrevoorstellingen*. Utrecht.

Spamer, Adolf. 1970. *Der Bildbogen von der "geistlichen Hausmagd."* Göttingen.

Stampfle, Felice. 1979. *Le siècle de Rubens et de Rembrandt: Dessins Flamands et Hollandais du XVIIe siècle de la Pierpont Morgan Library de New York*. Exh. cat. New York.

Steinberg, Leo. 1970. "The Metaphors of Love and Birth in Michelangelo's *Pietas*." In *Studies in Erotic Art*, ed. Theodore Bowie and Cornelia V. Christenson, 231–285. New York.

Sternfeld, Frederick W. 1956. "Le Symbolisme Musical Dans Quelques Pièces de Shakespeare Presentées à la Cour D'Angleterre." In *Fêtes de la Renaissance*, ed. Jean Jacquot, 318–333. Paris.

Stock, Jan van der, ed. 1991. *La Ville en Flandre: Culture et Société, 1477–1787*. Brussels.

Stone, Lawrence. 1977. *The Family, Sex, and Marriage in England, 1500–1800*. London.

Straaten, Evert van. 1977. *Johannes Vermeer, 1632–1675: Een Delfts Schilder en de cultuur van zijn tijd*. The Hague.

Stratton, Suzanne. 1986. "Rembrandt's Beggars: Satire and Sympathy." *Print Collector's Newsletter* 17:77–81.

Stridbeck, Carl Gustaf. 1956. *Bruegelstudien*. Stockholm.

Strien, Cornelis Daniël van. 1993. *British Travelers in Holland During the Stuart Period. Edward Browne and John Locke as Tourists in the United Provinces*. Leiden.

Strong, Roy. 1973. *Splendor at Court: Renaissance Spectacle and the Theater of Power*. Boston.

Sullivan, Margaret A. 1994. *Bruegel's Peasants: Art and Audience in the Northern Renaissance*. New York.

Sutton, Peter C. 1980. *Pieter de Hooch*. Ithaca.

———. 1983. *Jan Steen: Comedy and Admonition, Philadelphia Museum of Art Bulletin* 78, nos. 337–338:29–31.

Swillens, P. T. A. 1950. *Johannes Vermeer, Painter of Delft, 1632–1675*. Utrecht.

Tagg, John. 1988. *The Burden of Representation: Essays on Photographs and Histories*. Amherst.

Thiel, P. J. J. van. 1967–1968. "Marriage Symbolism in a Musical Party by Jan Miense Molenaer." *Simiolus* 2:91–99.

———. 1987. "Poor Parents, Rich Children, and Family Saying Grace: Two Related Aspects of the Iconography of Late Sixteenth- and Seventeenth-Century Dutch Domestic Morality." *Simiolus* 17:90–149.

Thomas, Keith. 1984. *Man and the Natural World: Changing Attitudes in England, 1500–1800*. London.

———. 1991. Introduction to *A Cultural History of Gesture*, ed. Jan Bremmer and Herman Roodenburg. Ithaca.

Tickner, Lisa. 2000. *Modern Life and Modern Subjects: British Art in the Early Twentieth Century*. New Haven.

Tillyard, E. M. W. n.d. *The Elizabethan World Picture*. New York.

Timmers, J. M. 1974. *Christelijke Symbolik en Iconografie*. Bussum.

Turner, James Grantham, ed. 1993. *Sexuality and Gender in Early Modern Europe: Institutions, Texts, Images*. New York.

Vandenbroek, Paul. 1991. "Culture Urbaine: Unité Apparente, Discorde Sous-Jacente." In *La Ville en Flandre: Culture et Société, 1477–1787*, ed. Jan van der Stock. Brussels.

Veen, Otto van. 1607/1684. *Emblemata Horatiana*. Amsterdam.

———. 1608. *Amorum Emblemata*. Antwerp.

Visscher, Roemer. 1614/1949. *Sinnepoppen*. The Hague.

de Vries, Lyckle. 1976. *Jan Steen de schilderende Uilenspiegel*. Amsterdam.

———. 1977. "Jan Steen 'de Kluchtschilder.'" PhD diss., Groningen.

———. 1991. "The Changing Face of Realism." In *Art in History/History in Art: Studies in Seventeenth-Century Dutch Culture*, ed. David Freedberg and Jan de Vries, 209–248. Santa Monica, CA.

Walsh, John, Jr. 1973. "Vermeer." *Metropolitan Museum of Art Bulletin* 26, no. 4: unpaginated.

Warner, Marina. 1976. *Alone of All Her Sex: The Myth and Cult of the Virgin Mary*. New York.

Washington, DC. 1980–1981. The National Gallery of Art. *Gods, Saints, and Heroes: Dutch Painting in the Age of Rembrandt.* Cat. by A. Blankert et al.

———. 1995–1996. The National Gallery of Art. *Johannes Vermeer.*

———. 1996. The National Gallery of Art. *Jan Steen: Painter and Storyteller.* Cat. by H. Perry Chapman et al.

———. 1997. The National Gallery of Art. *Lorenzo Lotto: Rediscovered Master of the Renaissance.* Cat. by David Alan Brown, Peter Humfrey, and Mauro Lucco.

———. 1998. The National Gallery of Art. *Vermeer Studies.* Cat. by Ivan Gaskell and Michiel Jonker.

Webster, J. C. 1938. *The Labors of the Months in Antique and Mediaeval Art to the End of the Twelfth Century.* Princeton.

Wedel, Theodore Otto. 1968. *The Medieval Attitude Toward Astrology, Particularly in England.* New Haven.

Welu, James A. 1975. "Vermeer: His Cartographic Sources." *Art Bulletin* 57, no. 4:544–546.

Westermann, Mariët. 1996. *A Worldly Art: The Dutch Republic, 1585–1718.* New York.

———. 1997. *The Amusements of Jan Steen: Comic Painter in the Seventeenth Century.* Zwolle.

Wheelock, Arthur K., Jr. 1981. *Jan Vermeer.* New York.

White, Lynn. 1969. "The Iconography of 'Temperantia' and Virtuousness of Technology." In *Action and Conviction in Early Modern Europe: Essays in Memory of E. H. Harbison,* ed. Theodore K. Rabb and Jerrold E. Siegel, 197–219. Princeton.

Wiesner, Merry E. 1986. *Working Women in Renaissance Germany.* New Brunswick.

Winkler, Friedrich. 1921. *Der Leipziger Valerius Maximus; mit einer Einleitung über die Anfänge des Sittenbildes in der Niederländen.* Leipzig.

Winnett, Susan. 1990. "Coming Unstrung: Women, Men, Narrative, and the Principles of Pleasure." *PMLA* 105, no. 3:505–518.

Winter, Jhr. P. V. van. 1957. "De Hollandse Tuin." *Nederlands Kunsthistorisch Jaarboek* 8:29–121.

WNT. 1882–1926. *Woordenboek der Nederlandsche Taal.* The Hague.

Würtenberger, Franze. 1937. *Das holländische Gesellschaftsbild.* Schramberg.

Yates, Frances A. 1975. *Astraea: The Imperial Theme in the Sixteenth Century.* London.

Zilverberg, S. B. J. 1971. *Geloof en Geweten in de Zeventiende Eeuw.* Bussum.

Index

Orcagna, Andrea, 33
Ortelius, Abraham, 55

painting-within-a-painting: *Astrologer*, 16;
  Choice Between Wealth and Youth, 45–46;
  The Family, 97; *In Weelde Siet Toe*, 49;
  The Musical Duet, 20; van Eyck's use of,
  119n2; *Woman Holding a Balance*, 13–14
Paleotti, Gabriele, 81
Panofsky, Erwin, 2, 30, 49, 84
Pater Familias (Van Ostade), 101–3, *fig. 76*
Peacham, Henry, 26
pearls, as symbol, 15, 17
The Peasant Family (Van Ostade), 99, *fig. 84*
Peasant-Husband Holding a Cross-Reel (Van
  Ostade) (Budapest), 101–2, *fig. 88*
Peasant-Husband Holding a Cross-Reel (Van
  Ostade) (Frankfurt), 101–2, *fig. 87*
Peasant Interior (Van Cleve), 54–59, *fig. 50*
peasants, in Netherlandish art, 93–96
pendants: Steen and, 6; Ter Borch and, 5,
  27–39, 58, 124n19, 125n49
Philip II, 25
Phyllis Riding Aristotle (Housebook Master),
  87, *fig. 73*
Pillars of Hercules, 25–26
Plato, 23
Pleij, Herman, 53
politics, in *The Musical Duet*, 20–26
Pollock, Griselda, 3, 9, 63
popular imagery, 29–30, 43–50, 73–74; of
  Van Ostade, 93–105
porta clausa (locked door), 84, 97–98
Portrait of a Young Boy (de Jongh), 100
poverty, 99, 103
power, sexuality and, 80–81, 86–87, 109
"power of women" imagery, 87
Prayer Before the Meal (Steen), 104–5, *fig. 89*
predestination, 15
pregnancy, in *Woman Holding a Balance*,
  13–18
Prinsjesdag (Prince's Day: Celebrating the
  Birth of Prince William III) (Steen), 22,
  fig. 9
prints. *See* popular imagery
private life. *See* domesticity
private ownership of art, 81–82
The Procuress (Van Baburen), 111
The Procuress (Vermeer), 61–62, 108, 111, 113,
  fig. 91
"The Prodigals" (Wierix), 47, *fig. 41*
The Prodigal Son (Van Hemessen), 77, 83,
  fig. 67

The Prodigal Son (Beuckelaer), 77, 83, *fig. 64*
The Prodigal Son in a Tavern (Anthonisz.),
  47, *fig. 40*
Prodigal Son in a Whorehouse (Master of the
  Prodigal Son), 56–57, 59, *fig. 51*
Prodigal Son parable, 83
prostitution: in early modern period, 88–91;
  interpretation of, 110; Netherlandish,
  88–89, 91. See also *boordeeltje*
Protestant Reformation, 81
proverbs, as subjects of paintings, 56, 59
public life, *boordeeltje* (bordello scenes), 77,
  80
Putscher, Marielene, 13

quotation in painting. *See* self-reflexivity

realism: apparent realism, 2; *boordeeltje*
  (bordello scenes), 77–78, 80–81, 83; and
  construction of realities, 110; definition
  of, 1; idealism versus, 95; interpretation
  of, 1–2; literary versus visual, 51; moralism
  and, 110–11; narrative and, 83; peasant
  representations and, 95; as social practice,
  110
reality effect, 81, 110
reception history of author's essays, 4–5
reception theory, 78
religion. *See* Catholicism; Christianity;
  family; Protestant Reformation
Rembrandt van Rijn: *The Adoration of the
  Shepherds*, 99, *fig. 83*; *Self-Portrait with
  Saskia in the Tavern*, 62, 111
Renaissance, Netherlandish, 18
Renger, Konrad, 44, 109
Republic (Bodin), 23
Republic (Plato), 23
Reresby, Sir John, 88
right/left differentiation, 34
Ripa, Cesare, 16, 21
Roman History (Appian), 21
Romanism, 6
Romano, Giulio, 86
Rome, 89
Roodenberg, Herman, 115
Rubens, Peter Paul, 55
Rudolph, Herbert, 13, 119n2

Samson Shorn by Delilah (Van Leyden), 87,
  fig. 74
Saying Grace (Van Ostade), 103–5, *fig. 77*
scales, as symbol, 16–17
Schama, Simon, 100

The authorized representative in the EU for product safety and compliance is:
Mare Nostrum Group
B.V Doelen 72
4831 GR Breda
The Netherlands

www.ingramcontent.com/pod-product-compliance
Lightning Source LLC
Chambersburg PA
CBHW080955170526
45158CB00010B/2809